Not Ours Alone

Not Ours Alone

Patrimony, Value, and Collectivity in Contemporary Mexico

Elizabeth Emma Ferry

COLUMBIA UNIVERSITY PRESS   NEW YORK

COLUMBIA UNIVERSITY PRESS
Publishers Since 1893
NEW YORK, CHICHESTER, WEST SUSSEX

Copyright © 2005 Columbia University Press

Library of Congress Cataloging-in-Publication Data
Ferry, Elizabeth Emma.
 Not ours alone : patrimony, value, and collectivity in contemporary Mexico / Elizabeth
Emma Ferry.
  p. cm.
 Includes bibliographical references and index.
 ISBN 0-231-13238-7 (cloth : alk. paper) — ISBN 0-231-13239-5 (pbk. : alk. paper)
  1. Miners—Mexico—Guanajuato (State) 2. Guanajuato (Mexico : State)—Social
conditions. 3. Cooperative societies—Mexico—Guanajuato (State)—History. 4. Cooperativa
Minera Santa Fe de Guanajuato—History. 5. Mineral industries—Mexico—Guanajuato
(State)—History. 6. Silver mines and mining—Mexico—Guanajuato (State)—History. 7.
Globalization. I. Title.

HD9506.M63G8327 2005
334'.68232423'097241—dc22

                                                          2005045453

Casebound editions of Columbia University Press books are printed on permanent and durable
acid-free paper.
Printed in the United States of America

c 10 9 8 7 6 5 4 3 2 1
p 10 9 8 7 6 5 4 3 2 1

To my parents, Anne and David Ferry

June Nash

In her book Elizabeth Emma Ferry presents an impressive argument that residents in the historic mining community of Guanajuato, Mexico, are committed to a collective identity related to the mining wealth still active in that industry's declining economy. The residents' assertion of the enduring value of place and religion is another instance of the persistence of local identity with place, despite the assumptions of disjuncture in a globalizing economy. With the decline in the mining economy, the tourist industry replacing it attracts visitors as much with the area's history of mining as with the religious architecture that survives from the colonial period.

Ferry's exploration of the nature of this patrimonial relation echoes with that of other mining communities where mine workers consider that their offspring have a right to a job by virtue of the sacrifices they themselves endured working in the mines. This is believed to be as sacred a right among the miners of Bolivia with whom I worked in the 1970s as it is for the miners of Guanajuato. It defines their sense of the relationship between the community and the state, as well as their collective relations with family and community. The fertility of the Guanajuato mines, ranked as the richest in the world in the eighteenth century, extends to its citizenry and particularly those who work the "mother lode." Paradoxically the very concentration of power and wealth in the mining economy conducive to a "pyramid" of power at the same time has resulted in a coalescence of collective challenges to that power.

Recent critiques of the "peoples and places" paradigm have made us more cautious of correlating the identities of people with geography. Yet the replication of similar gender characteristics and cosmologies related to powerful figures above and below the earth in mining centers around the world captures similar metaphors of the relation between natural and supernatural entities through which this identity is reproduced. With her comprehensive ethnographic summary of the lives of the workers and their families both underground and in their community celebrations, and as projected in cosmological understandings, Ferry brings to life this relationship between people and places. She makes understandable the astounding reality that men are willing to enter daily into a devil's contract to work underground in the most inhumane environment. Not only do they accept this destiny, but in the name of patrimony they actively attempt to reproduce it for their children in the interest of reproducing their society. Not all workers feel this way, but those who identify with the generations of relatives and ancestors who have preceded them into the mines are deeply committed to patrimony and not just to exploiting the minerals. Ferry's exploration of the relation between different kinds of property and ways of behaving is enriched by linguistic methodology as well as by participant observation. In her analysis of the discourse by which people position themselves as "old-fashioned," linked to the "preservation of patrimony," and hence "more moral," she shows how new collectivities become legitimized in these local movements that reflect global trends.

Certainly the concept of inalienability helps to explain the special quality of lineal ties engendered in mining. That the resources beneath the ground are, in Mexican law, the inalienable property of the state lays the basis for collective claims to mineral, and increasingly petroleum, resources. It lies at the crux of the increasing conflict between indigenous people and the state when they assert their rights to a share in these resources, as the Zapatistas are now doing. The concessions politicians are currently making to international trade partners in yielding this patrimony set the state on a collision course with this sector of the citizenry.

The debates themselves reveal the contours of emergent political forces in response to demographic, ecological, and labor factors. The critique of essentializing categories based on labor, gender, and ethnicity opens the way for developing a coherent ethnographic practice for analyzing processes of change in particular settings. Ferry provides the outline for such a practice in chapter 3 that is played out in subsequent chapters dealing with the debates and power plays within the Santa Fe Silver Mining Cooperative.

As has become painfully clear in studies of cooperatives, the cooperative form of organization provides a shaky bridge between the interests of producer and consumer, capital and labor, and even state and community. In 1973 Nicholas Hopkins and I compared the many forms that cooperatives, collectives, and co-participation in management assumed worldwide in a session we organized with Jorge Dandler for the Ninth International Congress of Anthropological and Ethnographic Sciences (Nash and Hopkins 1976). Particularly noteworthy in our attempt to assess these alternative modes of organizing production and consumption practices taken by cooperatives worldwide was that they contained the same contradictions from which they were attempting to escape. This was true at the very inception of utopian forms of organization at the end of the nineteenth century, when cooperatives were seen as the future for social action. At the end of the nineteenth century Marcel Mauss (1899) could speak lyrically about "the union and the cooperative society" as the "foundations of the future generated within the capitalist structure." Calling them the "preserving forces, the guarantees against reaction," he saw them as "the legitimate heirs of capitalism" that will "guarantee the perpetuation of the future society." A little over a decade later, on the basis of her analysis of the exploitation of labor as a condition for capitalist survival, Rosa Luxemburg (1970, 13:69) pointed out that the cooperative "either becomes pure capitalist or, if workers' interests continue to predominant, ends by dissolving." Mauss's student, Charles Gide (1930,7), pointed to this same paradox that "the more successful the cooperative is economically, the more likely it is to fail socially" (Nash and Hopkins 1976, 17 et seq.).

Cooperatives in both capitalist and socialist countries in the interim between world wars, the emergence of Soviet forms of collectivism, and capitalist developmental schemes have been plagued by centralized planning or by archaic paternalistic control perpetuating authoritarianism encroaching on participatory organizations. Thus the Mexican experience with cooperatives following the 1910–17 Revolution reveals an innovative form of cooperativism that sustains the resistance to the alienation plaguing these historic antecedents.

Elizabeth Ferry points out that this has at its heart the inalienability of the patrimonial resource base that it sustains. The instrumental means of retaining democracy is the vote enjoyed by every member of the general assembly which gives them a role in major decisions regarding administration and organization. By sharing in the profits of the cooperative, they retain an interest and motivation to produce. The cooperative differs from private mines in that the goal of the cooperative is to preserve the source of jobs rather than to maximize extraction of commercial minerals in the minimal amount of time. In fact, the major inheritance a miner passes on to his sons is a job in the mines. This prevalent goal also has the effect of minimizing the technological innovations in production in cooperatives, in contrast to neoliberal principles of capitalism directed toward minimizing the labor component of production costs. The "inheritance" of jobs also contributes to the familistic quality shared by miners.

All this seems very familiar to me from my experience in the Oruro mining community of Bolivia. Bolivia failed to maintain the integrity of this "moral economy" not because the miners' union yielded but rather because of the direct intervention of the International Monetary Fund (IMF) in 1985. Bolivia was the first Latin American country in which the IMF imposed conditions for debt recovery that year and the closing of the mines required of the Bolivian president, Paz Estenssoro.

The striking difference in the experience of Bolivia and Mexico with regard to the perpetuation of the Mexican patrimonial hold in mining communities, and, by extension, rural semi-subsistence agricultural communities, raises certain questions: How has this come about, and how long can it survive?

First, we can point to the strong sense of community, reinforced by church rituals and neighborhood exchange systems, that provides the context for the expression of a moral economy as an important basis for survival. The town itself offers an impressive setting for the processions in which miners exhibit their faith in Santa Fe, the patron saint of the city. But this is also present in other communities, whether of miners or agriculturalists. With the insights Ferry provides from her historical research and fieldwork we can summarize some of the contextual issues reinforcing patrimony.

From the time of the discovery of the mines starting in the mid-sixteenth to the end of the twentieth century, Guanajuato has been a major producer of gold and silver for the world mining system. Like other mineral-producing mines generating the currency to drive the European-centered world mining system, this status gave Guanajuato's mines a special role in that emerging system. When the attention of foreign interests became focused on the industry, with the United States and other advanced industrial countries investing in Mexican mines, the miners' confrontations with these foreigners made the miners heroic figures in local history.

The deep sense of community among the miners also derives from the their strong feelings of shared history. As Ferry states, "[The miners of] Guanajuato typified the oppressed and exploited position of Mexican workers in industries dominated by foreign (and especially U.S.) capital." Thus, in effect, they were not only producing the currency in the emerging world system, but they were also producing its history. Furthermore, in a series of strikes, Guanajuato miners stood out in their union struggles as courageous national heroes. As they took their struggles to Mexico City, they began to typify not only the oppressed workers of a particular locale, but also, by drawing on the powerful language of nationalism, they became emblematic of all Mexicans exploited by the United States.

The miners' success in the strikes of the 1930s in many cases resulted in the sale of their patrimony. But for some it provided the basis for the formation of utopian cooperatives that proliferated in this era of postrevolutionary nationalism. The goal of the cooperatives was to reduce the dependency of the Mexican economy on foreign capital. The heroic dimension of that role gradually dissipated as part-time workers diluted the sense of unity in the mining family.

The cooperative mining company avoided these contracts and was lauded for its ability to minimize the forced migration of youths, which was considered a corrupting force on both the youth and the nation. Thus the cooperatives' role in minimizing such forced migration added to their luster.

Ferry's balanced view of the mines, both cooperative and private, does not allow her to remain fixed in any one position. Political corruption, associated with the declining economic returns of the mine workers, is also part of the record. Characteristics identifying the cooperative as familial, paternalistic, Mexican, rooted in place, and committed to the prosperity of Guanajuato are linked to the oppositve view that they are corrupt, clientelistic, lazy, backward, and wasteful. Debates over the proper role of the cooperative evoke the entire gamut of citizens' and workers' obligations. In the process, we gain a glimpse of Mexican reflexivity that far exceeds that of U.S. workers. The cooperative is actively disposed to promoting such allegiances, more so, Ferry tells us, than other class-based politics. Given the historical roots of the mining cooperative, these projections command the country's attention.

Third, we can locate these two prior conditions in the centrality of the region's economic role in the colonial period. This historical rootedness was enhanced in the Bajio, an area that was central to the acculturation and progress taking place at this time. Primary production was further enhanced by the country's complex economy, with its textile manufacturing and commercial agriculture, as well as the mining activities that had developed in the eighteenth century. The Bajio became the center for the independence movement, and hence the cradle of the Mexican nation looming over Mexico City, with miners playing an essential role. This sense that the mining economy was the root of the Mexican nation served to enhance the status of the area.

The strong sense of place cultivated in this historic and geographic epicenter of the emergent nation continued to foster an aura of importance that underpins the role of citizens to this day. Members of the cooperative sacrificed wages, working overtime without compensation in the 1930s when profits declined and workers acquired the mine properties from private companies. National pride in the government-subsidized enterprise diminished in subsequent decades, reaching a crisis in 1994 when the neoliberal policies of President Carlos Salinas de Gortari restricted support. The question is, given the diminishing economic importance of metal, combined with the depletion of the mines, can the cooperative survive? Clearly the more the directors respond with efforts to rescue the remaining private companies, such as hiring temporary workers and denying supernumary employment to lineal descendents of mine workers, the less motivated mine workers will be to support themselves as cooperative members.

One of the remaining alternatives for the miners is to turn to tourism. Guided tours of the mine shafts, the selling of stone samples by miners, and effigies of the miners and the culture they cultivated now provide a Walt Disney world in which foreign and national visitors can experience mining. Like the balancing of strategies to maintain the mining economy, the management of these cultural offshoots requires a strategically grounded theory of national patrimony, which Ferry proposes in historic and cultural terms. The United Nations Economic, Social, and Cultural Organization (UNESCO) has developed a world catalogue of patrimonial cities that confirms the value of the regionally acclaimed sites that might stabilize opportunities for enhancing income.

Paradoxically, the most remarkable achievement of the cooperative mine is that it can continue to survive even though it does not produce a profit. This is also the virtue of the subsistence rural agricultural system that enables indigenous communities to preserve distinctive cultures. Ferry guides us into the life that sustains the mining culture in the daily schedule of work, showing how the idiom of patrimony provides women with the terms they need to call their husbands to account. Thus familial responsibilities are an extension, through the paycheck, of the patrimony of the mines that puts it to proper use. The highly sexualized metaphors of mining and insemination, production and reproduction, daily reinforce the idea of what Ferry rightly calls the "circular nature of production and reproduction within the realms of patrimony." So intense is this experience that men fear the presence of sexual partners in the interior of the mines for fear that the vein will become jealous and escape them.

Thus mining families have effectively preserved the moral economy within commercialized mining through the cooperative and its material as well as metaphoric functions enabling reproduction of family and community. While all this sounds a familiar note with Bolivian mining communities, a major difference is in the asymmetrical gender power of the Mexican communities: Mexican expressions of machismo do not recognize the complementary female sexual power that I witnessed in Bolivia. Ferry points to exceptions in this asymmetry, particularly in the case of a woman who worked along with men and was accepted on a par with them, but the tendency to exclude women's direct entry into the patrimonial conspiracy of masculinity is rooted in men's direct access to the riches of the mine through gendered roles in production, and to political power vested in the state. In contrast, women in the Oruro mining community do not need to take on a male role to enjoy the power and respect of men. Men defer to their opinions not only in the home but also in union meetings which wives may attend, even when they are not working in the mines. They are fully integrated into the "mining family," and most men will attest that it is the women who decide when they should go on strike because the women know best when the paycheck no longer covers basic needs. In the days prior to the technological inventions that obviated the need to work the mines largely by hand, women, called "pallires," often lead the protest marches. Maria Barzola is the most renowned martyr of the 1942 march for higher wages that ended in a massacre, and Domitila Barrios de Chungara alerted the nation to the power of grass-roots organization in the hunger strike that brought down the military government of Hugo Banzer.

This contrast between Bolivian and Mexican gender relations highlights the importance of gender relations in reinforcing patrimony in Guanajuato. The miners' appeal to "let's save the patrimony of the mines for our sons" is not contested, and the bias toward male power related to their masculinity is underlined by the treatment of homosexuals as marginal in authority. Ferry sums this up in her linguistic analysis of the terms "land," "subsoil," and "culture" in relation to "value" and "collectivity" at the national level in Mexico, showing how patrimony, which encompassed the inalienability of the subsoil, workers' rights, and communal land, was central to the legitimization of the nation.

So essential were these values that when they were denied by the neoliberal governments of Salinas and Ernesto Zedillo at the end of the twentieth century, the Institutional Revolutionary Party (PRI), which claimed the sanctity of these laws, was doomed. The first move against these fundamental rights came with the reform of Article 27 guaranteeing land to those who till the soil in 1992, followed in two years by the betrayal of patrimonial obligations in the signing of the North American Free Trade Agreement (NAFTA). By putting international pacts ahead of responsibilities to citizens vested in the 1917 Constitution, NAFTA betrayed a host of patrimonial obligations, particularly to campesinos, miners, oil workers, fisherfolk, and others who relied on their right to extract national resources for their daily livelihood. Each year since its passage in 1994 Mexicans have become increasingly aware of the consequences of this agreement.

By extending the implications of patrimony to the entire gamut of property relations, Ferry provides a compendium of interest to national as well as international readers. Emblematic of a growing privatization of patrimony is the Guadalupe mine that has been purchased from the cooperative and converted into a luxury hotel. While miners have adjusted to the necessity to yield their absolutist premises in order to survive in the current era of rampant globalization, still they continue to resist changing the basic values that sustain their way of life. Elizabeth Ferry provides a valuable resource to help us rethink these changes in this current time of transition.

REFERENCES

Gide, Charles. 1930. *Communist and Cooperative Colonies*. Translated by Ernest F. Dow. London: Harrupt.

Luxemberg, Rosa. 1970. *Rosa Luxemburg Speaks*. Edited and with an introduction by Mary Alice Waters. New York: Pathfinder.

Mauss, Marcel. 1899. "L'action socialiste." *Le mouvement socialiste* (Paris) (October 15): 449–462.

Nash, June, and Nicholas Hopkins. 1976. "Anthropological Approaches to the Study of Cooperatives, Collectives, and Self-Management." In *Popular Participation in Social Change: Cooperatives, Collectives and Nationalized Industry,* ed. June Nash, Jorge Dandler, and Nicholas Hopkins, 3–12. The Hague: Mouton.

I am indebted to several funding sources for supporting the research and writing of this book: the Institute for Global Studies in Culture, Power, and History of The Johns Hopkins University; the Latin American Studies Program of The Johns Hopkins University; the University of Michigan Department of Anthropology and International Institute; the Center for U.S.-Mexican Studies of the University of California at San Diego; and the Brandeis University Latin American Studies Program. I am also grateful to the Centro de Investigaciones en Ciencias Sociales de la Universidad de Guanajuato (CICSUG) for granting me affiliation during my stay in Guanajuato.

In acknowledging the many people, both in Mexico and the United States, who helped me, let me begin at the source. I wish to thank everyone at the Sociedad Cooperativa Minero-Metalúrgica Santa Fe de Guanajuato, S.C.L., #1, for giving support, information, and, most important, friendship. I especially thank the following people: Engineer Jesús Baltierra, the *gerente* of the cooperative; Juan Cabrera; Zulema Cuevas; Alejandra González; Jorge Martínez; Mauricio Martínez; José Augusto Montoya; Sergio Montoya; Cirilo Palacios (and his family); Ricardo Padrón; Agustín Parra; Carlos Ruiz; José Salas; Emiliano Torres; and Cándido Tovar. Thanks most of all to Agustín López.

In Santa Rosa de Lima I could not have done without the help of Agripina Paz, Pancho Granados, Don Roberto Quezada and Doña Goya Gutierrez, Don Tomás Ulloa, and the girls in my English class, especially Dany, Paty, Chuya, and Diana.

In Guanajuato the following people associated with the university helped me tremendously: Laura González, Luis Miguel Rionda, Ana María and María Elena Ruíz, and Jorge Uzeta of the CICSUG; Luis Rionda Arreguín, Armando Sandoval, and Ada Marina Lara of the Centro de Investigaciones Humanísticas afforded me much information, advice, and companionship; Licenciado Isauro Rionda Arreguín, the *cronista* of Guanajuato and director of the State Archive

(AGEG), graciously allowed me to interview him several times. Margarita Villalba and I visited the cooperative mines on several occasions and had a number of useful discussions about the Valenciana. In addition, her thesis helped me to provide historical context. Other friends in Guanajuato were extremely important to me, especially Luis Gerardo González, Oscar Pastor Ojeda, Eloïsa Pérez Bolde, Tim Richardson, and Cecilia Romo.

A number of people from The Johns Hopkins University have been and continue to be important influences. Jason Antrosio, Elizabeth Dunn, Sarah Hill, Roger Magazine, Carlota McAllister, Christopher McIntyre, Erik Mueggler, Eric Rice, and, especially, Paul Nadasdy deserve much of the credit for this book and none of the blame. I am also greatly indebted to my professors at Johns Hopkins for my development as an anthropologist and for their support in this specific project, especially Donald Carter, Gillian Feeley-Harnik, and Sidney Mintz. I wish to thank Michel-Rolph Trouillot and Katherine Verdery for pushing me to refine my ideas and language, directing my reading, and encouraging me along the way. Thanks especially to Katherine for a great year at the University of Michigan and for all the attention and support she has given me.

At the University of Michigan I found a congenial and stimulating group of scholars who helped me to sharpen my descriptions and my arguments, including Jasmine Alinder, Marty Baker, Fernando Coronil, Paul Eiss, Gabrielle Hecht, Webb Keane, Mani Limbert, Setrag Manoukian, Aims McGuiness, David Pedersen, Julie Skurski, and Genese Sodikoff. These people made me feel welcome both intellectually and otherwise.

I wish to thank a number of people who were Research Fellows with me at the Center for U.S.-Mexican Studies at the University of California, San Diego, in 1999–2000. These people helped to create a rich atmosphere of intellectual exchange in which to write and revise my thesis. My thanks especially to Alejandra Castañeda, Cynthia Cranford, María Luz Cruz Torres, Emily Edmonds, Emiko Saldívar, Paola Sesia, Gabriela Soto Laveaga, Casey Walsh, Carlos Vélez-Ibáñez, and Andrés Villarreal. Dr. Eric Van Young also provided excellent comments and guidance.

So far in my career I have been blessed with welcoming and intellectually stimulating colleagues. I am particularly grateful to the following people for their intellectual support and companionship: at Mary Washington College, Alejandro Cervantes-Carson, Tracy Citeroni, Eric Gable, Rachel Gelder, Steven Hanna, Margaret and Peter Huber, Allyson Poska, Curt Ryan, and Sara Zuk; at Queens College of the City University of New York Kevin Birth, Murphy Halliburton, Miki Makihara and Donald Scott; at Brandeis University, Mark Auslander, Andrew Cohen, Robert Hunt, David Jacobson, Sarah Lamb, Janet McIntosh, Richard Parmentier, Ellen Schattschneider, Sara Withers, and Javier Urcid.

Many thanks to William Fisher for, in the first place, instilling in me a love of anthropology, and, in the second place, putting me in contact with Columbia University Press. I thank my editors at the Press, Wendy Lochner, Anne Routon and, most especially, Suzanne Ryan.

Bunny Davidson provided me with encouragement and a wonderful example; I wish she could have been here to see what came of it. Anne Ferry and David Ferry gave me superb advice and comments and edited every chapter extensively. Stephen Ferry encouraged me to purge my language of jargon and to exercise my imagination; he also gave me valuable comparative data on Potosí, Bolivia, and supplied photographs of the interior of the Valenciana mine. Aime Ballard-Wood, Robert, Dorothy, and Charlie Wood, and, of course, Emmett Victor Wood have been a constant source of humor and comfort. Thanks to Beverly Castaldo-Brown, Nina Davidovich, and Howard Rabinowitz for showing me the richness of life outside the academy.

Finally, thanks to David Carrico Wood, my best reader and best friend, and to Sebastian Carrico Wood and Isaiah Davidson Wood, my two wonderful (and exceptionally well-timed) sons.

Sections of the following chapters have appeared as parts of published articles:

Chapter 1: "Inalienable Commodities: The Production and Circulation of Silver and Patrimony in a Mexican Mining Cooperative," *Cultural Anthropology* 17, no. 3 (2001): 331–358.

Chapter 4: "*Nuestro Patrimonio:* Controlling the Commodification of Silver and Cultural Properties in Guanajuato, Mexico," in *Social Relations of Mexican Commodities*, ed. Casey Walsh, Elizabeth Emma Ferry, Gabriela Soto Laveaga, Paola Sesia, and Sarah Hill (La Jolla: Center for U.S.-Mexican Studies Press, 2003).

Chapter 8: "Envisioning Power in Mexico: Legitimacy, Crisis, and the Practice of Patrimony," *Journal of Historical Sociology* 16, no. 1 (2003): 22–53.

Not Ours Alone

CHAPTER I

Introduction

Inalienability, Value, and Collectivity

The idea seems to have spontaneously suggested itself to a great number of early so-cieties, to classify property into kinds. One kind or sort of property is placed on a lower footing of dignity than the others, but is at the same time relieved of the fetters which antiquity has imposed on them. . . . The lawyers of all systems have spared no pains in striving to refer these classifications to some intelligible principle; but the reasons of the severance must ever be vainly sought for in the philosophy of law; they belong not to its philosophy but to its history.
—Sir Henry Sumner Maine, *Ancient Law*

I have ideas, old-fashioned ideas on the matter. . . . The disposition of a family prop-erty, even though it be one so small as mine, is, to my thinking, a matter which a man should not make in accordance with his own caprices—or even his own affections. He owes a duty to those who live on his land, and he owes a duty to his country. And though it may seem fantastic to say so, I think he owes a duty to those who have been before him, and who have manifestly wished that the property should be continued in the hands of their descendants.
—Anthony Trollope, *The Way We Live Now*

Wealth in Guanajuato, Mexico

In 1936 a series of articles came out in the Guanajuato paper *El Noticioso* con-cerning the destruction of a chapel on the grounds of the Rayas mine dedicated to the mine's patron saint, San Juan de Rayas. The articles deplored the fact that the Guanajuato Reduction and Mines Company had virtually destroyed this chapel several years earlier. They had removed the floor pavings and interior walls to use in making a bridge at the nearby processing plant and, shamefully, had melted down the chapel bell to sell as raw silver. Worse still, the local authorities had allowed these acts to go unpunished, demonstrating the "official indifference towards artistic patrimony [*patrimonio artístico*]" ("Honda Indignación por el Descuido de Monumentos Artísticos," *El Noticioso*, August 23, 1936). A related article on the same day became eloquent in its outrage, saying that the acts were "against tradition and culture. The nation was the victim. What does it matter to the greedy Yankees that with the complicit negligence of the authorities that metal is today circulating as coins?" ("Avorazamiento Horrendo," *El Noticioso*, August 23, 1936).

Here the implied opposition between the "tradition" and "culture" of the Mexicans and the capitalist greed of the North American mine owners is embodied in the fact that the church bell is now circulating as coins. The article indicts Yankee capitalism based on the commutability of currency and opposes it to the locally distinctive value of place and religion. The bell of the eighteenth-century church, as a unique specimen of European culture and Catholicism, also reminds us of how different the practices of Spanish mine owners were from those of the North Americans. Where the Spanish left beautiful and gracious traces of their presence and of the richness of the mines it is implied, the *estadounidenses* took everything away with them.

Written at the time of a series of labor strikes within Guanajuato mines, most of which were owned by U.S. companies, these articles play on a tension between those forms of value that remain in Guanajuato and enrich it as a place and those that leave Guanajuato in the form of money. The articles establish a moral universe that privileges distinctive and rooted wealth over currency.

More than fifty years later, in 1988, UNESCO included the city of Guanajuato and its surrounding mines in the prestigious and influential list of World Heritage Cities (*Ciudades de Patrimonio Mundial*). In 1991 Guanajuato celebrated the 250th anniversary of having received the title of "city." In the printed program for this event the official chronicler (*cronista*)[1] for the city, Isauro Rionda Arreguín, gave an introductory statement that included a reference to the honor conferred by UNESCO:

> In the extensive Mexican territory a small number of federal states can be proud of the caliber [*estampa:* mark, brand], gallantry, and personality of the city of Guanajuato, in the state of Guanajuato. This has been for all time a cause of satisfaction and contentment for the great majority of inhabitants and for the nationals who visit it. And Guanajuato has never failed to surprise us with new motives for honoring her, as has now happened with the designation by UNESCO of [the title] of City of World Patrimony and its inscription, by virtue of this, in the selective list of world monu-

ments with this characteristic. . . . The city of Guanajuato offers to humanity its architectonic richness and its notably sublime and beautiful singularity; but not as a complex of walls, ramparts, arches, doors, and buildings [that are] well constructed and surprising but empty and static, but rather as a propitious and optimal environment for the development of aspirations and creative and artistic qualities of its inhabitants, above all those who were born here and who have left their bones here. . . . We Guanajuatenses, men and women who are well born and better raised, feel honorably committed in the presence of humanity to preserve, augment, and enrich this patrimony, which is not ours alone [*que no es solo nuestro*].

> Archivo General del Estado de Guanajuato,
> program for the festivities of the 250th anniversary of
> Guanajuato's foundation as a city, 1991

In its own way this statement draws on a similar interplay between rooted, intrinsic wealth, on the one hand, and universally recognized, mobile wealth, on the other. Rionda tacitly proclaims that native Guanajuatenses have a particular pride in the city and owe their fine qualities to its "propitious and optimal environment." In this sense, Guanajuato's "patrimony" seems to belong only to its native citizens. But recognition from outside (in the form of UNESCO) expands the collectivity that can lay claim to Guanajuato's patrimony, as Rionda points out at the end, saying, "this patrimony, which is not ours alone."[2] Through his use of this slippage, Rionda acknowledges the distinctive value of the city to its own inhabitants while remaining open to—and actively courting—resources from outside. Along with the rise of tourism and the recent emphasis on cultural property and patrimony, Guanajuato's "walls, ramparts, arches, doors, and buildings" appear to have both intrinsic value and an increasing commercial value. At the same time the expression "not ours alone," while appearing to be inclusive, even universalistic, smuggles in an ambiguous "we"—*whose* patrimony, after all, is "not ours alone."

These two events, separated by decades of authoritarian rule, political democratization, and massive reconfigurations of economy and trade, encapsulate the predicament of those living in Guanajuato, and, in particular, members of the Santa Fe Mining Cooperative and their families. In its most simple form, the predicament can be stated as a question: *How do you use forms of inalienable wealth to maintain and reproduce the collectivity and at the same time make a living from that wealth?* The multilayered solutions to this problem on the part of Santa Fe, and the theoretical questions entailed in such solutions, comprise the substance and argument of this book.

> *The Cooperative is not only for us, but for future generations.*
> —Apprentice in the Department of Industrial Safety, September 1997

This book examines the ways in which members of the Sociedad Cooperativa Minero-Metalúrgica Santa Fe de Guanajuato (Santa Fe Cooperative, as I mostly call it here) and their families, as well as citizens of the city of Guanajuato and Mexico, address the question stated just above, especially through their uses of an idiom of *patrimonio*—patrimony—to lay claim to resources and gain access to loci of power. They do this by classifying certain kinds of resources as patrimonial; that is, those that are passed down from prior generations and, in turn, intended to be passed on to future generations.

Let me give a few brief examples. When I asked one man, celebrating his retirement from the Cooperative at the age of sixty-five, if he had sons in the Cooperative, he help up three fingers, and said: "That's the inheritance I've given them (*les saqué;* lit., I took out or extracted for them)."

In the fall of 1997 I attended a secret meeting of one engineer who hoped to be elected president of the administrative council. In describing his commitment to the Cooperative, he said: "This is a business to leave to your children. It's not just for two or five years, but for many years."

On a ride in the dump truck that transports ore from the Valenciana to the central plant, the driver said to me: "We [the Cooperative members] are concerned with keeping this place of work for our children and even our grandchildren. If it's not mining, we have to find other ways so that the Cooperative survives."

The book explores how members and their families use these claims to constitute and contest the boundaries of competing collectivities. When we examine this idiom in an ethnographic context and discern its power, far-reaching implications become apparent not only for Guanajuato and Mexico but also for the study of value and inalienability in anthropology and the analysis of comparable idioms in other places.

The Santa Fe is now the only remaining mining cooperative in Mexico of approximately eighty mining cooperatives formed in the 1930s and 1940s. In the Santa Fe, workers are part owners; they receive shares in the enterprise's profits in addition to their wages (technically defined as advances on these profits); they also have rights to subsidized groceries, water, land, and other goods; they elect their leaders and vote on how to distribute resources and invest capital. The mines controlled by this cooperative are sites of former glory—they lie on Guanajuato's *Veta Madre,* or Mother Lode, and were exceedingly rich centers of silver production in the colonial period. The Valenciana mine, the focus of my study, was the most productive silver mine in the world in the latter half of the eighteenth century. During the time of my fieldwork from 1996 to 1998 the Santa Fe Cooperative controlled seven mines in and near Guanajuato; a central processing plant; silver and ceramics workshops; and multiple support departments such as materiel management, carpentry, a motor pool, a supermarket, a health clinic, and sundry offices. At this time the Cooperative had approximately nine hundred members. Over 90 percent of these members were men, and all or nearly all would identify themselves as *mestizo* (of mixed indigenous and European ancestry, an unmarked Mexican ethnoracial category that is constructed as the majority and contrasted to the category "indigenous").

After a series of strikes in the 1930s the North American company in possession of the mines now held by the Cooperative ceded them to the workers. With the help of the federal government under President Lázaro Cárdenas, the workers formed the Santa Fe Cooperative in 1939. This act, which took place immediately following the expropriation of the petroleum companies, has stood in the minds of many Mexicans and Guanajuatenses as emblematic of the Cardenista period of postrevolutionary nationalism. This history makes the Santa Fe Cooperative an ideal site for studying local negotiations of national political and economic change.

While focused on languages and practices of patrimony in the Santa Fe Cooperative, this book also has significance for the historical and anthropological literature on mining and for the study of Mexico more generally.

MINING AS ECONOMIC, POLITICAL, AND SOCIAL PRACTICE

In a review article on the anthropology of mining written twenty years ago, Ricardo Godoy writes, "The physical and social isolation of mining communities, coupled with the harsh working conditions and the labor requirements of the mining industry, give rise to recurrent patterns of population dynamics, labor recruitment practices, and political organization" (1985: 205). The Santa Fe Cooperative and the mines and neighborhoods associated with it, exhibit many of the features common to mining enterprises and complexes. These features include highly centralized sunk capital costs; harsh and dangerous working conditions (for those working underground); relative immobility of production sites since, obviously, the mines must be located where the mineral deposits are; extreme dependence on global markets; regional development of ancillary products and services; and active state intervention in the areas of taxation, inspection, and leasing of concessions. The existence of common features in mining enterprises means that insights emerging from the extensive anthropological literature on mining have proven very useful for this investigation. In paying attention to them, however, we must beware of naturalizing the processes of labor, political, and domestic organization that often occur in mining contexts and in the Santa Fe. The characteristics of mining listed here encourage processes and formations of a certain kind, but they do not determine them. With this in mind, we can say that these common characteristics have made certain historical and theoretical themes central to mining studies.

The interrelated themes of political organization and concentration of power, processes of identity formation, and cosmology and ideology relate intimately to my own study of the economic and social relations of mining in the Santa Fe Cooperative. First, the high concentration of capital and labor, territorial isolation, and heavy state intervention make the organization of power and authority, and resistance to it, appear in particularly stark terms in mining contexts. Although the mines of Guanajuato, nestled on the outskirts of the state capital of one of Mexico's most populous and centrally located states, are not "isolated" in comparison with many mining enterprises, the Guanajuato case does share other features with mining districts in general. Not surprisingly, then, many scholars of mining focus on the political organization and the concentration of power in the hands of institutions, especially corporations, state forces, and unions (among others, Brading 1971, Bakewell 1984, Burawoy 1972, Greaves and Culver 1985, Klubock 1998, Hardesty 1998, Heyman 1995, Sariego Rodríguez 1994, Nash 1979, and Van Onselen 1976) and organized or unorganized resistance to these powerful institutions (among others, Chávez Orozco 1960, Kingsolver 1989, *Salt of the Earth* 1954).

In a second review article, also published in the *Annual Review of Anthropology*, Chris Ballard and Glenn Banks (2003: 287) write that "during the two decades since this journal published a seminal review of anthropological perspectives on mining (Godoy 1985), the field has been transformed by dramatic developments in the mining industry and corresponding shifts in the nature and emphasis of related research and theory."

These shifts follow trends both in the mining enterprise and the struggles surrounding it, and in anthropological theory and methodology, by including a much broader range of actors, raising issues of state-corporate-community stake holding, environmental degradation, indigenous rights, globalization, and so on (Howard 1991, Kirsch 2002, MacMillan 1995, Robinson 1986, Welker 2004), and using multi-sited, advocacy-based, and other nontraditional research designs (Finn 1998, Kirsch 2002). This research, much of which is centered on Asia and the Pacific (where much of the large scale mining exploitation has taken place in the last twenty years) casts questions of labor, capital, and power on a much broader scale than did many earlier anthropological and historical studies of mining.

Arrangements of power and resources, as well as challenges to existing power relations, are fundamental issues in the Santa Fe Cooperative. The formal cooperative organization, in which power and resources are supposed to be shared among a group of claimants and passed down along generational lines, often conflicts with the centralization of capital that allows small groups within the Cooperative to control access to resources with relative ease. This tendency is reinforced by a "pyramid" model in Mexican politics based on patron-client relations and on the traditional connections between cooperative leaders and the leading political party, the Institutional Revolutionary Party (PRI).[3]

At the same time the council system and the vitality of patrimony as a basis for claims sometimes allow for successful challenges to existing arrangements of power. This study thus adds a new element to analyses of political organization and power in mining enterprises, focusing on a particular form of property relations and its associated claims. How do languages of patrimony both provide legitimacy to those who hold power in the Santa Fe and frame protests or critiques of current relations of power?

Processes of identity formation have also received a great deal of attention from mining scholars. These processes include the construction of identities based on class, race, ethnicity, locality, and gender. Such concerns were evident even in relatively early anthropological work on mining. For instance, anthropologists working in Zambia's Copper Belt in the 1940s and 1950s addressed demographic changes, migration, and urbanization in mining contexts (among others, Epstein 1958, 1981, Mayer 1962, Wilson 1941–42, and Wilson and Wilson 1965). Here mining was treated as a mechanism and marker for cultural change, dependency (Nash 1979), teleological transitions to "modernity" (Ferguson 1997, 1999), and class formation (Moodie and Ndatshe 1994, Sheridan 1998, Van Onselen 1976, Wilson 1941–42). This literature explores the effects of locality on identity, class formation, and domestic organization. In these cases migration to urban areas to work in the mines fundamentally affected workers' understandings of their place and provenance in the country. Constructions of gender and sexuality also change fundamentally; for instance, gold miners in Botswana recreate male-female "country" sexual and familial relationships with younger male mine workers in the "town" (Moodie and Ndatshe 1994). As in these studies, the rootedness of the cooperative mines, communities, and families, the inalienable character of the subsoil, and the association with earth, veins, and rocks express the importance of place and locality in the idiom of patrimony.

Scholarship on the division of labor in African mining enterprises often focuses on the association of racial or ethnic groups with different jobs (Burawoy 1972, Guy and Thabane 1988, Moodie and Ndatshe 1994). In addition, some scholars of mining in Latin America and the United States have noticed the

identification of some miners with a Hispanic (nonindigenous) and white eth-
nic and racial identity or both (Alonso 1995, Kingsolver 1989, Finn 1998,
Klubock 1998). This is certainly the case in the mines of Guanajuato. In other
Latin American contexts (for example, in the Andes) mining has employed ex-
clusively Indian labor and is specifically associated with indigenous identity
(Bakewell 1984, Harris 1988, Nash 1979).

A number of recent studies have looked at the construction of masculinity
and femininity in mining communities among miners, their wives, and other
women who live and work in mining communities (Finn 1998, Johnson 2000,
Kingsolver 1989, Klubock 1998, Lawrence 1998, Nash 1979, Simmons 1998). The
attention to mining and the construction of gender has flourished relatively recently, in keeping with recent investigations into constructions of masculinity.

Constructions of place and gender are fundamental to the configuration of
power and value in the Santa Fe Cooperative. The gendered division of labor in
mining and the language of patrimony as a mode of classifying patrilineally
transmitted possessions contribute to a notion of mining as a male activity and
one constitutive of particular versions of honorable masculinity. The production
of silver from the mines and the reproduction of sons in the houses of Cooperative members together generate and transmit possessions to which all members
have a legitimate claim. This book explores how gender and place are continually reproduced and debated in the cooperative, and how these understandings
vary under changing circumstances.

The literature on mining and metallurgy has also addressed questions of cosmologies and ideology. Eugenia Herbert, in introducing her discussion of metallurgy and gender in African societies, states that "because [this book] is about
cosmologies, it is about power: where it resides; who may invoke it, by what
means and for what ends; and how to protect against it since power is always
double-edged" (1993: 1). Indeed, processes of mediation between relations of
power at the group level and identity formation at the individual level might usefully be described as the production and transmission of cosmologies and ideologies; it therefore comes as no surprise that cosmologies and ideologies have
been central themes in the anthropology of mining. Cosmological and ideological systems in mining communities have often entailed symbolism of gender,
sexual reproduction, life and death, and the supernatural in various forms.

A fascinating although rather static example is Mircea Eliade's analysis of
mining, metallurgy, and their symbolic connections to obstetrics in *The Forge
and the Crucible* (1962). Herbert's book, *Iron, Gender, and Power* (1993), makes a
similar argument in a more historically grounded and theoretically sophisticated
manner, and convincingly establishes the links between metallurgy, sex, gender,
and power in Sub-Saharan Africa. She foregrounds technologies and rituals of

transformation to explain these links. The notion of transformation as a central feature of gender, reproduction, and birth can help us understand why mining and metallurgy are so often seen as gendered and reproductive activities.

June Nash (1979), in her ethnographic study of tin miners in Oruro, Bolivia, traces the gendered symbolism of surface and underground, death and life, male and female, the saints of Spanish Catholicism, and the deities of Andean religion as a set of complementary oppositions. In her analysis, El Tío (*the uncle*), a priapic icon resembling the Spanish *conquistadores,* who dwells in the mine and who must be propitiated with alcohol, cigarettes, coca, and other male comestibles, provides a charged locus for the complexities of gender and mundane and supernatural power in Bolivian mining. (see also S. Ferry 1999).

Michael Taussig reinterprets Nash's ethnography in *The Devil and Commodity Fetishism in South America* (1980) to fashion an argument on the resistance of indigenous miners (whom he sees as recent participants in capitalist production) to the fetishism involved in mineral extraction and sale on the world market. For Taussig, El Tío is the physical manifestation of miners' critique of exchange value and the exploitation of the mine and of their own labor. While his analysis suggests important questions of power, the supernatural, and value, he tends to reify use and exchange value in such a way as to flatten the complex social relations of mining as described by Nash.[4]

This book examines the production and transmission of cosmologies of gender, reproduction, and place as primary modes of linkage between systems of power at the group level and formations of individual and relational identity. By looking at power and identity through these cosmologies, I analyze the relationship between organized economic activity and political, social, and cultural forms.

While drawing on themes central to the scholarship on mining, this book also addresses a significant gap in this scholarship. Within this literature we find surprisingly sparse discussion of value, exchange, and property relations, especially from a theoretical perspective. Some work has been done on property relations, especially forms of land tenure in more or less rigorously controlled mining sites and communities (Wilson 1941–42, Brading 1971, Deutsch 1987, Villalba 1999). But with the exception of Taussig's study and a few others (Harris 1988, Manning 2002), the theme of value and its production and circulation in mining has been discussed little and theorized even less.

Property relations and the production of value are fundamental processes in mining enterprises (especially in the extraction of precious metals). The substance of the ore and its provenance in the earth, its daily price set on the world market, and its historical association with specie and currency mean that silver and gold participate simultaneously in a number of regimes of value (Appadurai 1986). Furthermore, the juridical category of national patrimony in Mexico and the cooperative organization of the Santa Fe silver mine make questions of property claims and relations ever present. For these reasons, the Santa Fe Cooperative provides an ideal case for studying such questions. In this book I show how patrimony brings together material and cosmological relations of power, identity formation, and understandings of how value is and should be made and transferred.

RESOURCES, POWER, AND COSMOLOGY IN CONTEMPORARY MEXICO

With respect to the study of power and resources in Mexico, this book takes the Santa Fe as a local terminus (Wolf 1956) of national processes and, in particular, the ways in which Mexicans classify certain resources as inalienable possessions of the nation or of a given local collective. I argue that this has been a highly charged "root metaphor" in Mexico since the colonial period, and has become more intense and vital in the twentieth century. Chapter 8 lays out the importance that this mode of classifying resources has had in organizing debates over who are legitimate members of the nation or other collectivity and who have rights to use and obligations to transmit these patrimonial possessions.

The book thus draws attention to a vital feature of Mexican social, political, and economic life, which has been noted in particular cases but never explored as a national idiom. By focusing on the ways in which Mexicans assign qualities of value to resources, and use these assignments to debate the nature of competing and overlapping collectivities, it also provides tools for reexamining the workings of power in contemporary Mexico.

In analyzing how power is organized and legitimated in the Santa Fe Cooperative, and in Mexico more generally, I use Eric Wolf's discussions of the interaction of ideology and power (1990, 1998). Wolf posits a four-part scheme of "modes" of power—individual, interpersonal, tactical or organizational, and structural—but he focuses on the last two of the four aspects of power that he outlines. He defines "tactical" power as "the power that controls the settings in which people may show forth their potentialities and act interpersonally." [5] "Structural" power, on the other hand, "orchestrates the settings themselves" (1992: 587). In this formulation, power is best thought of as an arrangement or field made up of different elements. At the same time, unlike some Foucauldian conceptualizations of power, it does not render human intention and agency completely beside the point. Within this field, people and groups can be more or less advantageously situated and can make better or worse use of their opportunities. We will see multiple examples of this in our examination of the uses of patrimony in the Santa Fe Cooperative.

Wolf also links power to signification and the organized, interested forms of signification that we might call ideology. As an ideology, patrimony condenses and re-presents understandings of how existing arrangements of power came to be, and how and why they should be maintained. It helps to convince even those disadvantageously situated within these arrangements that maintaining them is natural, moral, and in their own interest. However, in order to see how this works, we need to know more about the historical and juridical underpinnings of Mexican patrimony.

The Mexican practice of classifying property as patrimony has its roots in medieval and early modern European forms of kinship and inheritance; the particular form of inheritance varied from region to region depending on whether property was transmitted according to unigeniture or as partible inheritance. With the rise of state power in Europe, this classification of familial property also came to designate the properties of monarchs as the heads of state. Under this system, state property passed down through the royal lineage as royal patrimony. Patrimony thus came to refer both to familial property passed down through particular lineages and to a more generalized category of state property held in the name of the monarch/nation (Clavero 1974, Goody, Thirsk, and Thompson 1976, Sabean 1988, Stone 1977).

This European model of patrimony, elaborated in a number of different regional forms, was enacted in New Spain through entailed estates (*mayorazgos*) in the hands of both Spanish and indigenous nobility (Clavero 1974, Cooper 1976, MacLachlan and Rodríguez 1990, Taylor 1972), and in the Spanish colonial designation of New World property as royal patrimony. This category of "royal patrimony" eventually became that of "national patrimony." As the late-nineteenth-century jurist and proto-anthropologist Andrés Molina Enríquez (1909: 147) put it: when Mexico declared independence in 1810, and the "juridical personality of the king died," the patrimony of the Spanish king automatically became Mexican national patrimony (see also M. de la Peña 1924). One of the central domains of national patrimony is that of subsoil resources.

Like all Mexican enterprises engaged in subsoil resource extraction, a cooperative does not own the mineral deposits it exploits but leases them by concession from the federal government, as per Article 27 of the 1917 Constitution (which is in turn a legacy of Roman and later Spanish colonial law). Article 27 of the 1917 Constitution provides the foundational text of Mexican nationalism with regard to property relations and helps to establish the centrality of the notion of national patrimony in postrevolutionary state formation. In drafting the article, the constitutional delegates of the newly established revolutionary government explicitly attempted to remake property relations in order to remake the nation. Article 27 posits national patrimony as the basis of all private property in Mexico; in doing so it established a mandate for the postrevolutionary state, acting in the name of the nation, to intervene in all property relations.

In the words of Adolfo Gilly (1994: 181; translation mine): "[Article 27 had] two basic dispositions: land to the peasants, and the subsoil to the nation. This pair of principles, which locates public domain over private interests, is what makes the article the masterpiece of the constitutional edifice." This privileging of public domain over private interests created the conditions by which languages of patrimony were reinvigorated as ways to mobilize labor and lay claim to resources. As I describe in chapter 8, this feature of Mexican property law, which pertains not only to subsoil resources but also to collectively held land under the *ejido* agrarian reform program and, in a somewhat different way, to cultural properties, came to play a central role in the politics of the postrevolutionary state.

By establishing the subsoil as national patrimony but leasing concessions for its exploitation, Article 27 separates use rights from rights of alienation. Those possessions that are supposed to be used but not used up they describe as patrimony. Even as they treat the silver from the mines and other products (such as mineral samples) as commodities to be exchanged on the global market, and fully realizing that they are exploiting a nonrenewable resource, members continue to insist upon silver's inalienability. On investigation, this seeming contradiction reveals itself as a system of competing and coexisting forms of value.

At the same time that an idiom of patrimony emerges out of national juridical structures and the rhetoric of nationalism, local notions of gender, generativity, and kinship also inflect its uses. Cooperative members assert that they have received patrimonial possessions from past generations and that they have an obligation to pass them down to their *hijos y nietos* (children and grandchildren, in this case usually referring to sons and grandsons). (This preference for patrilineal transmission with respect to some things [such as Cooperative membership and its benefits, houses, and silver] occurs in a context in which kinship is seen as bilineal and many objects are transmitted through both male and female lines).

The familial organization of a cooperative (most cooperative members are related to other cooperative members through ties of biological and ritual kinship [*compadrazgo*; ritual co-parenthood]) enhances these uses of patrimony. Furthermore, local notions of honor and masculinity among miners and analogies of mining as sexual reproduction animate the products of the mines. Patrimonial possessions are thus seen to result from a process of androcentric reproduction and patrilineal transmission.

Patrimony, Inalienability, and Collectivity

How can we define and describe an idiom or langue of "*patrimonio?*" *Patrimonio* (or, hereafter, patrimony) derives from the Latin *patrimonium,* meaning "paternal estate." The term can refer literally to property handed down from father to children or from ancestor to descendants, or to the ancestral property of a corporate group or class. It is used much more commonly in Romance languages than in English, and is often translated into English as "heritage." In this book I preserve the cognate term "patrimony," since it contains strongly gendered and kin-inflected associations that are diluted in the word "heritage."

In current usage patrimony denotes collective, exclusive ownership by a social group, often organized or conceptualized as a patrilineal kin group. To describe something as patrimony places limits on its exchange by classifying it as ideally *inalienable*; such patrimonial possessions are meant to remain within the control of the social group that lays claim to them and usually to be passed down intact from generation to generation. These "objects" often include landed property, so-called cultural properties, and, in the case of Mexico, subsoil resources. Such objects need not be tangible; they may fall into the category described as "incorporeal property" by Lowie (1928), including myths, rituals, forms of knowledge, and so on.[6] I understand "patrimony" in the Santa Fe and in Mexico more generally as the ethnographic instantiation of the analytical concept of inalienability.

By using an idiom of patrimony to describe a given class of objects, actors are making claims about the ability of such objects to constitute a collectivity and to establish rights to use the objects and simultaneous obligations to maintain and transmit them to future generations. The idiom of patrimony thus frames the collectivity (or multiple collectivities) as a diachronic kin group constituted through its claim over inalienable possessions (Weiner 1992).

In the case of the Santa Fe Cooperative leaders, members, and members' families understand certain products and possessions (especially those that come from the mines) as subject to limits and constraints on their exchange. Such objects are supposed to be handed down more or less intact to the Cooperative's future generations, that is, the descendants of current members. For instance, in March 1998 I had a conversation with Manuel Torres, a worker in the automotive department whose father and grandfather had been miners and whose grandfather had been one of the Cooperative's founding members. We spoke about his wish to have his son also work in the Cooperative, perhaps as an engineer or chemist. He said:

But, you know, there are some who don't think this way, who don't want
their sons [or "children"] to go into the Cooperative. The people who
have relatives and ancestors [*generaciones*] here, come in with a love [*cariño*]
for the work, to take care of the Cooperative and leave it to their sons [or
"children"] as an inheritance, if possible. And the others, who don't have
family here, devalue it [*la desvalen*].

The notion of the Cooperative as a kind of inheritance and the accompanying
obligation to take care of it for future generations, as well as the distinction
drawn between those who properly value the Cooperative and those who do
not, are typical expressions of what I am calling a patrimonial idiom in the
Cooperative.

Cooperative actors often call on this notion of patrimony as ideally inalienable property to make claims over power and resources, even as they treat the
silver from the mines and other products as commodities to be exchanged on
the global market. This book examines the tensions arising out of this situation,
versions of which we saw in the two examples quoted above, and their attempted resolution by actors in Guanajuato. Upon investigation, this seeming
contradiction reveals itself as a system of competing and coexisting forms of
value. This perspective allows us to rethink the category of inalienability as it has
been treated within social theory. In order to put this reformulation in context,
I will lay out several issues that have been central to the anthropology of property and value.

Since its earliest investigations in the nineteenth century, anthropologists
(and proto-anthropologists) of property relations have focused on the ways that
people categorized types of property in different cultural contexts. This concern
arises in part from anthropology's imbrication with colonialism, which brought
Europeans into close contact with other forms of property relations. This contact sparked both comparative interest and administrative problems that called
for swift solutions. The colonial confrontation with other systems of property relations brought attention to the nature of property as a social institution. It also
made social theorists recognize that European notions of ownership and other
rights were not necessarily compatible with other ways of understanding the relations between people and things, or among people with respect to things.

At the same time, in keeping with their own preoccupation with the relationship between property and sociality, these social theorists looked to catego-
rize differences between types of societies through an investigation of property
relations. The work of the early anthropologist Sir Henry Maine (1963 [1861])
provides a clear example of this tendency. Maine identified a distinction between forms of property that has great contemporary relevance for our discus-

sion of patrimony. In the quotation that begins this chapter, Maine refers to the "fetters" that bind certain forms of property to their owners. By "fetters" he means the complex rituals necessary to alienate these kinds of property, which were not required for property of the other kind. The two categories are defined in Roman law as *res mancipi* and *res nec mancipi* (or "chained" and "unchained" property). Like many early property theorists, Maine posited an evolutionary passage from societies dominated by chained property to those dominated by unchained property.

In *The Gift* Marcel Mauss points out the same dichotomy as does Maine, saying:

> Among the Kwakiutl and Tsimshian, the same distinction is made between the various kinds of property as made by the Romans, the Trobriand peoples, and the Samoans. For these there exist, on the one hand, the objects of consumption and for common sharing. . . . [7] And on the other hand, there are the precious things belonging to the family. . . . This latter type of object is passed on as solemnly as women hand over at marriage the "privileges" to their son-in-law, and names and ranks to children and sons-in-law. It is incorrect to speak in their case of transfer. They are loans rather than sales or true abandonments of possession. (1990 [1950]: 43)

While the concepts and questions laid out by Mauss in *The Gift* have never left the domain of anthropological interest, for some time inalienability as such was passed over in favor of other, related formulations (such as gifts and commodities or spheres of exchange).

Annette Weiner was probably the person most directly responsible for bringing inalienability back into anthropological discussions. In the beginning of her 1992 book, *Inalienable Possessions*, she notes that Malinowski cannot account for reciprocity among the Trobrianders and is forced to use "custom" as a deus ex machina to resolve the problem (1992: 32). She goes on to say, "Expunged from [Malinowski's] consideration was what Maine called the most ancient and important obstacle to the free circulation of objects: the classification of all property into immovables and movables" (32). Reciprocity, then, becomes a way to exchange immovable (inalienable) possessions so as to guarantee their return, what Weiner calls the "paradox of keeping-while-giving."[8]

Weiner's notion of inalienable possessions has been critiqued from a number of perspectives. For instance, Nicholas Thomas notes (in his commentary on Weiner's 1985 article in *American Ethnologist*) that, by establishing a typology of alienability and inalienability, Weiner tends to gloss over historical particularities and to privilege her theoretical model over concrete forms (1991: 22–24). Godelier, in his re-analysis of Mauss's work in the light of Lévi-Strauss, Weiner, and others, emphasizes that it is the dynamic, dialectical interplay between alienable and inalienable forms of property that defines social life, thus drawing attention away from Weiner's more static typologizing (1999: 36–37). In spite of these critiques—to which I will add my own based on an examination of patrimony in the Santa Fe—Weiner made an appreciable contribution in reestablishing the importance of inalienability in discussions of value.

One of Weiner's contributions to the discussion of inalienability within social theory was her explicit assertion of the connection between inalienable value and the collectivities defined through its use and possession. As she states, "What makes an object inalienable is its exclusive and cumulative identity with a particular series of owners through time" (1992: 33).

In a parallel vein, Jeannette Edwards and Marilyn Strathern have recently interrogated English concepts of property and collectivity, arguing that, "there is a moral propriety to the indigenous English conception of 'ownership' which suggests that it is as natural to (want to) possess things, as part of one's own self-definition, as it is to be a part of a community or family" (2000: 149). Given the importance and the taken-for-grantedness of this connection, it should come as no surprise that the relation between wealth and one's relation to it, collectivities and one's relation to them, and between value and sociality more generally have been central questions within European social theory since at least the eighteenth century.

While it is probably true that patrimony as a powerful Mexican idiom for organizing property relations and collectivities owes something to pre-Columbian understandings of property, I am primarily interested in patrimony as a Mexican language of inalienability with roots in European concepts of ownership and belonging. This interest derives in part from the fact that the region of Mexico I focus on was not an area of dense pre-Columbian settlement and it is thus a more than usually difficult matter to trace indigenous influences. In chapter 8 I lay out the circumstances within which a language of patrimony was transmitted from Spain and France during the colonial period and the nineteenth century and consolidated as a peculiarly Mexican instantiation in the postrevolutionary period. It is worth noting that the ways people in this book use patrimony to propose, lay claim to, and police the boundaries of legitimate collectivities bears much resemblance to the perspectives of European anthropologists of property relations and to the intersecting concepts of owning and belonging described by Edwards and Strathern.

From the perspective of both earlier and more recent work on forms of value, especially inalienable value, I wish to propose some new directions in our

analysis of the articulation of value and collectivity and the ways they are conceptualized in diverse contexts. My research into the ways that patrimony is
used as a language for classifying resources as inalienable in the Santa Fe Cooperative and in Mexico more generally provides us with a rich opportunity for
examining these questions in the context of commodity production and in light
of heated debates over state formation and economic activity.

LANGUAGES OF VALUE

I suggest that we focus on how people characterize objects rather than on the
characterizations themselves—what we might call value as a category. Of
course, the question arises: what is the advantage of focusing on how people assign value rather than on the assignments themselves? I situate this question
within a long-standing debate in the anthropology of exchange over how objects in circulation should be studied.

Earlier analyses of exchange and value in social life have tended to treat gift
and commodity exchange as holistic and bounded systems distinct from and
often opposed to each other. These systems were then used to characterize and
distinguish "Western" and "non-Western" societies (cf. Gregory 1982). These
dichotomous and diacritical tendencies have been roundly criticized over the
past two decades on the grounds that they reify differences between "West" and
"non-West" and consign the latter to a timeless, unreflective domain: the "people without history" (among others, Piot 1991, Ferguson 1985, Ferry 2002,
Godelier 1999, and Graeber 2001).

One approach scholars have taken is, in the words of Arjun Appadurai, that
of "focusing on the things that are exchanged, rather than simply on the form
and functions of exchange" (1986: 3) Rather than talking about commodity or
gift economies, these scholars look at phases or situations of exchange through
which things may pass. Focusing attention of the social life of things and speaking of "phases" or "situations," does indeed avoid the tendency to draw rigid dichotomies that often accompanied earlier discussions of exchange. It also has
significant methodological advantages, and it is not surprising that Appadurai's
book presaged a boom in commodity studies in anthropology. However, such
formulations continue to analyze exchange primarily by positing the existence
of categories of exchange (albeit temporary or situational) and then attempting
to see what kinds of things belong in each category at particular moments.

To focus on categories of value, however culturally variable, assumes that
value is a settled question in the minds of our informants and that our job as
anthropologists is to discover and describe the nature of these settlements. But

as the data from the Santa Fe Cooperative demonstrate with particular force and clarity, the social power of value comes from its unsettled nature. The anthropologist's job, then, is to observe and document people's attempts to use these unsettled aspects of value and the consequences of their attempts.

My argument here parallels that of David Graeber in his recent discussion of the anthropology of value (2001). Graeber highlights the work of Nancy Munn (1986) in going beyond fundamentally static notions of value as meaningful difference to consider actions themselves as value–producing. Munn's famous analysis of the production and exchange of Gawan canoes (1977) is a prime example of this perspective. But where Graeber focuses on how ethnographically observable actions can be seen to produce value, I look at how debates over the ways that objects—and also actions—should be valued (which process I describe as "languages of value") are *themselves* a series of material and discursive actions.

In other words, people have at any given moment a number of "languages" available to them for characterizing objects in circulation as commodified, gift–like, inalienable, and so on. These languages are often in tension; actors also have differential access to them. And they use these languages within a context that may constrain the use of some idioms and support the use of others. This perspective avoids reifying the categories of "gift," "commodity," and so on, and helps us understand how multiple or hybrid forms of value occur simultaneously, something which is not explained by phases or situations of exchange. It also emphasizes acts of assigning value as political and social as well as economic acts, inflected by the relations of power within which they occur and thus yields an analysis that is richer and more politically informed (in the broadest sense).

Second, in Guanajuato, and in other contexts where languages of inalienability play a central role, actors depict these languages as arising outside of or prior to capitalism. These depictions resonate with earlier anthropological discussions that focused on inalienability as a salient feature of non–Western, non–capitalist exchange.[9] In contrast, this book analyzes the uses of inalienability in the context of commodity production for global markets. In doing so, it shows that, as Maurice Godelier (1999: 36) has pointed out: "Nor is the social merely the juxtaposition or even the addition of the alienable and the inalienable, for society is brought into existence and sustained only by their union, by the interdependence of these two spheres and by their difference, their relative autonomy."

However, even as we acknowledge this at the analytical level, we must recognize the ways that our informants make use of a rigid separation, both temporal and spatial, between these forms of value. The excerpt from Anthony Trollope quoted at the beginning of this chapter provides a good example. In it, Roger Carbury, an impoverished squire and holder of the Carbury family estate, explains to his cousin Isabel Carbury that he intends to leave his property to her brother, Felix, a dissipated fool who also happens to be the nearest male heir. His assertions underscore the role of inalienable forms of property, in this case the patrilineal entailed estates of nineteenth-century Britain, as constitutive elements of kinship, nationalism, and other forms of collectivity. But, significantly, Roger Carbury identifies his own perspective as "old-fashioned" and perhaps difficult to understand.

Like Roger Carbury, and also like many anthropologists, cooperative members and other Guanajuatenses interpret geohistorical categories (Coronil 1996) in terms of alternating paradigms of civilization and backwardness and original purity or later decline or both. These interpretations can be extremely effective in actions manipulations of languages of inalienability. For instance, when they assert their allegiance to the preservation of patrimony, they position themselves as "old-fashioned" and others as more modern but less moral. The trick is to recognize the culturally determined nature of these distinctions and their force for ourselves as well as our informants while also examining the role these distinctions play in the political struggles over value and collectivity that we observe in the field.

Examining value as a set of languages with intimate connections to the negotiation and maintenance of collectivities has implications not only for Guanajuato or Mexico more generally but also for many other parts of the world. An attention to these issues could provide a fresh perspective to a broad range of contemporary issues, including debates over property, "identity," "rights," and so on. Based on in-depth ethnographic research on the decisions and negotiations through which people assign value to resources and in doing so debate the legitimate boundaries of collectivities, this book contributes to the study of local responses to large-scale change in Mexico and to the anthropology of value more generally. It also provides a blueprint for other ethnographic analyses of value in contemporary contexts.

SUMMARY OF CHAPTERS

Chapter 2 describes the development of the Santa Fe Cooperative in the twentieth century and something of the everyday life of Cooperative members through a description of places, people, and events that played a significant part in my fieldwork and subsequent analysis. This discussion provides a backdrop to the chapters that follow.

Chapter 3 describes the origins of the mines and mining economy in Guanajuato and examines how the interplay among demographic, ecological, and labor factors helped produce a social and economic system unique in Mexico. These social and economic factors, and local historical consciousness concerning the origins and development of the city, came to have powerful effects on the organization and deployment of languages of value in the region, the city and the Cooperative.

In chapter 4 I discuss recent challenges faced by the members of the Santa Fe Cooperative and some of the ways they have sought to overcome these challenges. The chapter provides further temporal depth by including information from the early 2000s and gives a sense of how the debates described in this book have continued to play themselves out.

Chapter 5 explores the material realms within which actors use languages of patrimony to describe wealth and resources. It focuses especially on the simultaneously analogous and opposed realms of mine and house, where gendered and generational notions of value, productivity, and sociality help to organize expectations of the proper behavior of men and women and the right use of patrimonial wealth.

Chapter 6 examines the organization of authority and obligation in the Santa Fe Cooperative, focusing especially on several cases: the general topic of loans, wages, and provisioning; an attempted coup by miners in the fall of 1997; and efforts by the founding members (*socios fundadores*) and their children to control a greater share of Cooperative resources. All these areas concern the ways in which actors use languages of patrimony to invoke notions of proper affective and economic obligation and to translate these into authority and power over resources.

Chapter 7 turns to the material substances of patrimony and compares two material commodities that are extracted from the mines and sold on the world market. Silver, the quintessential patrimonial substance, is produced alongside mineral specimens but is distributed, consumed, and valued in markedly different ways. Through an analysis of these substances, the chapter proposes new perspectives of inalienability as well as the nature of mining as a socioeconomic activity.

Chapter 8 broadens the focus of this book by examining the potency of languages of patrimony in Mexico more generally. It traces the genealogy of these languages in the colonial and republican periods, and the consolidation of the state after the Mexican Revolution. Focusing on three domains—land tenure, subsoil resources, and cultural properties—the chapter discusses shifts in the ways these languages have been used over the course of the twentieth century. In the process, I propose a new perspective for understanding the composition and negotiation of power in Mexico.

Finally, the conclusion reflects on the possible fate of the Santa Fe Cooperative and discusses how languages of inalienability can be seen operating in other contemporary contexts. It suggests ways in which these languages of inalienability might be profitably examined in light of the conclusions of this book.

Locating this study within the anthropological literature on inalienability has allowed me to bring insights about the relation between value and collectivity gained through the study of other places, especially Melanesia, to Mexico and Latin America. At the same time I also bring a fresh perspective to the anthropology of inalienability and inalienable possessions. Most of the scholars working within this tradition have looked at these concepts as aspects of noncapitalist exchange, at times operating alongside or in articulation with capitalism but at the same time analytically and/or ethnographically distinct. My examination of patrimony in the Santa Fe Cooperative demonstrates the power of inalienability at the very heart of a long-standing capitalist economic formation.

By studying how ideas of inalienability are negotiated within the contemporary context of commodity production for a global market, this book provides a new perspective on the process and consequences of classifying objects as inalienable. In doing so, it brings an original and illuminating perspective to a number of central ethnographic questions regarding Mexican social and political life. These include the future of Mexican nationalism, the proper obligations of workers, citizens, corporations, and the state, and the production of legitimate collectivities in the face of rapid political and economic change.

The Santa Fe Cooperative in Guanajuato, Mexico

From father to son, so goes the chain.
—Cooperative member, February 1997

In order to examine the workings of patrimony in the Santa Fe Cooperative we need a vivid sense of the Cooperative as a set of places, inhabited by people, and punctuated by events that organize time in meaningful ways. After describing the Santa Fe Cooperative and its mines, I turn my attention to these aspects of Cooperative life, describing three *places* where I concentrated my study, five *people* with whom I worked closely and who represent different sectors of the membership, and four *events* that encapsulate aspects of the religious and civic life of the Cooperative and the city, the rhythm of the working week, and the organization and life cycle of Cooperative families. Through this tripartite structure I hope to give the reader an understanding of the Cooperative's makeup, its relation to the city of Guanajuato, and something of the everyday lives of those Guanajuatenses (many of them part of Cooperative families) with whom I lived and worked from 1996 to 1998 and whom I visited on many subsequent trips to the field. Along the way I give some details concerning my field methodology and describe the unfolding of my fieldwork experience.

THE SANTA FE COOPERATIVE AND ITS MINES

The Santa Fe Cooperative holds the mining concessions to the oldest and most important mines of the *Veta Madre* system; it is one of the two largest mining enterprises in the area, with approximately nine hundred members as of the late 1990s. Members come from the city of Guanajuato and nearby towns and villages. Many of them come from long-term "Cooperative families" that include several generations of workers. In this respect the Cooperative is like many min-

FIGURE 2.1 View from the panoramic highway of the central plant of the Santa Fe Cooperative, with the church of Cata on the right

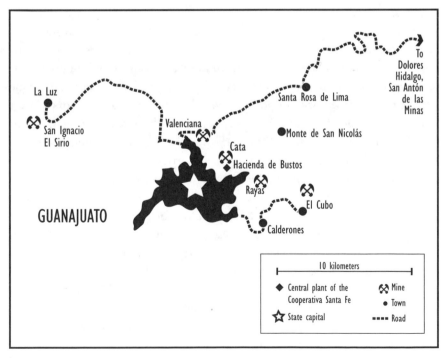

MAP 2.1

ing concerns of long standing in which labor and familial traditions tend to accrue over time (cf. Godoy 1985).

The Cooperative holds the concessions to seven mines in and around the city of Guanajuato and also runs a mineral concentration plant, a series of workshops for support services, two tourist sites, a construction company, a silversmith, and a ceramics workshop. In 1997 the Cooperative produced 28,146.4 kilograms of silver and 238.2 kilograms of gold, which were sold to the Grupo México foundry in the city of San Luis Potosí at an average price of $4.88 and $331.02 per oz. Troy, respectively.[1] Mineral grades in the Cooperative are approximately one gram of gold and 100–125 grams of silver per metric ton (Annual Reports 1977–97, Sociedad Cooperativa Minero-Metalúrgica Santa Fe de Guanajuato).

Cooperative workers are eligible for membership after a trial period of six months of work. Cooperative members make up about 90 percent of the workforce.[2] In former years the president of the administrative council functioned mostly as a figurehead, and the true wielder of power held the post of director (*gerente*) (interview with Engineer Estanislao Zarate, August 18, 1999). Since 1992 the president of the administrative council has been the most powerful figure. The council system also intersects with the organization of labor and expertise so that the president of the administrative council has at least nominal power over production, investment, accounting, and other technical and financial affairs.[3]

The Cooperative differs from private mining enterprises in that members have a vote in the general assembly and thus a role in major decisions concerning financial administration, labor organization, and so on. Consistent with international and national guidelines for cooperatives, each member has only one vote, regardless of seniority or position. Members thus wield some control over Cooperative policies and practices, at least potentially. Instead of wages, Cooperative members receive advances (*anticipos*) of future profits (although they are still paid different rates depending on their particular job). During profitable times members also receive another share of these profits several times a year.[4] Finally, the Cooperative functions as a consumers' as well as a producers' cooperative, so that members have rights to consume goods bought by the Cooperative at lower prices; in some cases these goods are further subsidized out of Cooperative profits. They include food, medicine, construction materials, educational loans, textbooks, and other occasional benefits.

Cooperative *jefes* (leaders or chiefs; see chapter 6), members, and outsiders very often said to me that the Cooperative differs from other mining companies in Guanajuato (and other enterprises in general) in that it has a "social goal" (*fin social*): to preserve the source of jobs (*guardar la fuente de trabajo*). Many workers consider their jobs in the Cooperative as patrimonial possessions that can or should be handed down to their sons and grandsons, and feel that the Cooperative has a unique responsibility to hold onto those jobs. From this basic difference in objective follows a whole series of consequences: undercapitalization, a large and disproportionately old workforce, subsidies and other benefits, strong social ties within the Cooperative, the ability to continue with very little margin of profit, and so on.

Cooperative leaders, members, families, and outsiders also point to the familial character of the Cooperative. At different moments they say that it is like a family, peopled by families, and organizes labor, production, and consumption in terms of the family rather than the individual worker. In this way it stands in marked contrast to the other mining companies that are increasingly relying on short-term contract work. By providing food, building materials, educational subsidies, and jobs, the Cooperative emphasizes a notion of itself as "*familiar*" (familial). An employee of the municipal government, who worked in the Cooperative for six years, told me:

> A cooperative member is a very special kind of worker; he feels like an owner and therefore he has a strong feeling [*celós*; literally, jealousy] for his work, he feels very strongly, he has a lot of affection [*cariño*] and emotion [*afecto*] for the work. Another thing is that it [the Cooperative] is very familial, cooperative members come in families [*vienen todo en familia*].

One student at the University of Guanajuato School of Mines described the Santa Fe Cooperative to me as "*la más casera*" (the most homemade; domestic) of the three mining companies in Guanajuato. He used this term to describe the more rudimentary conditions in Cooperative mines when compared to the mines of Peñoles and El Cubo (see chapter 3). The designation "*casera*" thus suggests a familial organization and stance that extends itself into areas of production, industrial safety, and so forth.

The Santa Fe's familial organization, low wages, lack of capital, benefits, and subsidies, and emphasis on long-term guarantees of labor all derive from its cooperative organization. Because it is cooperatively organized, it must respond to workers' demands for labor guarantees and benefits. In addition, the Cooperative's organization and accompanying emphasis on maintaining jobs have made it resistant to the "flexible" strategies taken by other mining companies such as downsizing, outsourcing, and contract labor.

Many of these organizational characteristics can be described in Polanyian terms as "embeddedness" (Polanyi 1944). The Cooperative as enterprise is more

deeply embedded in structures of kinship and locality than other mining companies. At the same time, while engaging in production for exchange in a quintessentially price-setting market, it also operates in many instances along principles of reciprocity and redistribution among the membership. These qualities
contribute to a feeling, among members and observers, that the Cooperative is
an example of an obsolete economic form in Mexico. And from the perspective of ascendant neoliberalism, they are right.

But as Polanyi knew well, while the notion of differently embedded institutions with dominant forms of integration (reciprocity, redistribution, and market
exchange) might usefully describe economies as a whole (if such things can be
said to exist), at a lower level such institutions can easily coexist and even support
one another. For instance, it is the entirely external character of the silver market
and the arrangement of prices on a global level that helps the Cooperative survive with little capital investment and extremely flexible production goals.

The Santa Fe Cooperative holds the concessions to the oldest mines along
the Veta Madre. These include four mines in the city of Guanajuato (Valenciana,
Cata, Rayas, San Vicente); two in the nearby town of La Luz (San Ignacio and El
Sirio); and one mining exploration project in San Antón de las Minas in the
nearby *municipio* (township) of Dolores Hidalgo.[5] Rayas is the largest mine, with
a workforce of approximately one hundred men working in three shifts, including twelve drillers (*perforistas*). The next largest mine is Cata, which employs approximately sixty men in three shifts; followed by San Vicente, with a workforce
of forty-seven men who work only a day shift. San Vicente has the most machinery inside the mine; the introduction of this machinery is the result of San
Vicente's newer and therefore wider tunnels and the fact that its main entrance
is an adit (*bocamina*) rather than a mineshaft (*tiro*). At the end of 1998 the Cooperative was building a metal *horca* (scaffold) at the old *tiro de Garrapata* in order to
take out (*mantear*) the ore more efficiently and to continue extracting reserves in
the southeast portion of the Rayas and San Vicente mines. In the spring of 1999
the Cooperative began hauling the extracted ore from San Vicente by way of
Garrapata.

In the nearby La Luz system, approximately 20 kilometers from the city of
Guanajuato, the Cooperative operates the mines of San Ignacio and El Sirio
("the Candle"). These mines are smaller, with thirty-two and twenty-four men,
respectively. They are also more dangerous than the other mines, because the
rock in the northeastern part of the district is softer and thus more prone to
cave-ins. San Ignacio, in particular, is known as "*la mina más pinche*" ("the most
fucked-up of the mines"). Two of the three fatalities which occurred in the Cooperative during my fieldwork happened in this mine.[6] Workers who caused

trouble with the members of the administrative council or other engineers were sometimes sent to San Ignacio as a punishment or a tactic to force them to leave the Cooperative.

The smallest Cooperative mine is San Antón, located in the small town of San Antón de las Minas in the *municipio* of Dolores Hidalgo, about 40 kilometers from Guanajuato. The Cooperative is carrying out exploratory studies (diamond drilling) to determine the cost-effectiveness of exploiting San Antón's reserves. At the moment it still produces only minimal amounts of ore. But many people have great hopes for San Antón, since it contains gold rather than silver and has never been fully exploited. It was first worked by the La Providencia Mining Company from 1897 to the outbreak of the Mexican Revolution in 1910, and few records exist on the work that was done during that time. The information that does exist is quite favorable, however, and many call San Antón "*la futura de la Cooperativa*" ("the future of the Cooperative") (La Providencia Annual Report 1897). Exploitation and exploration are proceeding very slowly, as the Cooperative lacks complete records of previous underground workings; the mine has also been flooded out on several occasions. In 1999 Luismín, a company from San Luis Potosí with some Canadian capital, offered to take over exploitation in exchange for a large share of the profits. But the Cooperative general assembly voted against the deal. The concession was finally sold to Luismín in 2003.

Places

During my fieldwork I focused on three sites within the cooperative: the central processing plant (*Hacienda de Bustos*); the Valenciana mine; and the community of Santa Rosa de Lima, approximately 10 kilometers outside the city of Guanajuato, where many Cooperative members live and where I lived from 1996 to 1998.

CENTRAL PLANT (HACIENDA DE BUSTOS)

Until 1948 the Cooperative beneficiation plant (hacienda de beneficio) was located on the Avenida Juárez in what was called the Hacienda de Flores.[7] Until this time the Cooperative had been using cyanide processing since the first years of the twentieth century.[8] The Cooperative offices and workshops moved to the Hacienda de Bustos in the neighborhood of Cata on the panoramic highway that encircles the city. The Hacienda de Bustos (known colloquially as "la hacienda," "la planta," "la Coope," or "Bustos," is located next to one of Guanajuato's most charming churches, the temple of Señor Villaseca de Cata, which was built by the eighteenth-century owners of the Cata mine. The Cooperative has periodically donated labor for restoration of the church, and one of its chapels is entirely lined with minerals given by miners. The temple of Cata is fronted by a quiet plaza with the offices of the Guanajuato State Institute of Culture off to the side.

The Hacienda de Bustos consists of a series of whitewashed buildings surrounding an enormous steel structure covered with a corrugated tin roof. The buildings are built on the slope of the canyon; at the very top is the Cata mine. These buildings are stacked on top of one another and, extending up the hill, give the impression that the Cooperative dominates this entire swath of the city (which was certainly true in the past). Painted on the roof is the name of the Cooperative: Sociedad Cooperativa Minero-Metalúrgica Santa Fe de Guanajuato (see Figure 2.1); one can see it on the descent of the panoramic highway from Mellado and Cerro del Cuarto. In this complex of buildings are the beneficiation mills and the sampling and assay laboratories. In addition, the Hacienda de Bustos houses the social work, provisions, engineering, topography, exploration, health, and safety, and personnel departments; the Cooperative supermarket, administrative council, and legal offices; and a small chapel at the entrance where periodic masses are held. Finally, the motor pool, welding, electricity, and carpentry workshops, and the supply and maintenance departments for the mines, are also located at the central plant. As of April 1998 approximately 380 people worked in this plant.[9] The Cooperative clinic, silversmith workshop, and ceramics workshop are all within several hundred yards of this complex, on separate properties nearby.

Two roads lead to the Hacienda de Bustos. The official entrance faces the panoramic highway with an iron gate that is kept shut unless trucks or cars are entering or leaving. There are always two men guarding this entrance. Visitors to the Cooperative offices must ascend a small flight of steps to the left of the main gates and speak to Gaby, the receptionist. She receives official papers and announces the arrival of visitors to Cooperative officials. To the right of the main gates a paved road begins to climb the canyon slope, going past the Cooperative supermarket, the health and safety department, the automotive shop, and then the dispatch point for the trucks and transport train bearing ore from the different mines. This is a great dusty plain inhabited by a family of dogs who live to bark at passing cars and trucks. It stands at the top of the beneficiation mills; the ore is dumped into chutes that feed the grinding and crushing cones (quebradoras).

The road, now unpaved, continues past the Cooperative baseball and soccer fields and exits onto the highway that goes up to the Valenciana, in what seems at first to be an entirely different part of the city. This is the Cooperative's private road. Navigating it assumes a level of familiarity with both the Cooperative and the topography of the city (as well as a vehicle suited to a dusty rutted road). These two roads exemplify the way in which the Cooperative's history and geography are intimately tied to the history and geography of the city of Guanajuato. The roads also embody the layers of official and unofficial access with which anyone with extended dealings with the Cooperative must become familiar.

The main working hours of the Hacienda de Bustos are from 6:00 A.M. to 4:00 P.M. (although the beneficiation mills continue throughout the night to take advantage of cheaper electricity rates). During this time there is constant movement in and out of the plant. Workers check in and out at shift changes; buses transport workers; trucks carry ore; pickups take engineers and supplies to the different mines; clerks deliver reports, receipts, and other papers to the mines and workshops off-site, or deposit money in the banks in the city center; leaders issue communications. During these hours the Hacienda de Bustos works as a tremendous nerve center for the Cooperative. This movement among dispersed sites means that much of the communication within the Cooperative happens by radio or messages sent with drivers, rather than by telephone.

As one drives the roads of Guanajuato, especially the panoramic highway and the road to the Valenciana (which continues on to Santa Rosa, Dolores Hidalgo, and the San Antón mine), one sees a truck or bus bearing the orange Cooperative logo every few minutes for most of the day. The drivers and passengers of these vehicles salute one another as they pass, usually raising one arm or honking the horn. When drivers recognize pedestrians from the Cooperative (including the anthropologist), they give them a ride to the plant or to one of the mines, if they happen to be going that way.

Having focused on the Hacienda de Bustos as one site for analysis, I began by investigating labor and production practices. I traced the work process from mineral extraction, assay, and concentration through its transport to and smelting at the foundry in San Luis Potosí.[10] Understanding this process gave me a clear sense of how the Cooperative negotiates production and labor to conform to the world silver market, infrastructure limitations, and type and distribution of mineral resources. I also conducted formal interviews and informal conversations within a context of participant observation. I interviewed plant workers, engineers, department heads, and council members. I accompanied the members of the industrial safety department in all aspects of their jobs, including mine visits, allocation of safety equipment, and preparation of paperwork for the Secretaries of Health and Labor. Through them I made contacts in nearly all the mines and workshops of the Cooperative. Participant observation in the plant and mines established through these contacts formed the basis of my research. In these investigations I learned about official and unofficial Cooperative production and labor policies, conflicts over the imbalance between miners and surface workers, and struggles over distribution of resources and authority.

VALENCIANA

The Valenciana, Guanajuato's most famous mine, is situated to the northwest of the city of Guanajuato, at the first crest of the road to Dolores Hidalgo that snakes through the Sierra de Santa Rosa. On the way up this road one passes several dejected-looking hotels whose names invoke the mining past of Guanajuato (Hotel Socavón [Adit], Hotel Valenciana, and Hotel Ruta de Plata [Silver Route]), some gracious homes, and the municipal water authority (SIMAPAG). The last climb before the Valenciana is the steepest, and, on the right, one can see a huge gray extension about fifty meters below the highway. This plain is the first tailings dump (*presa de jales*) of the Cooperative; it is no longer in use. It extends approximately two hundred meters by seventy meters and has a few trees growing on it, some houses of Cooperative workers, and a soccer field. The *presa de jales* embodies the Cooperative's dominance of Guanajuato in previous decades as well as its continued control of much of the land in the north of the city.

Just after the *presa de jales*, on the other side of the road, is an immense fortification made of the agglomeration of gray granite and green and pink porphyry (*cantera verde y rosa*) characteristic of eighteenth-century Guanajuatense architecture. This is the mine of Tepeyac, owned but no longer worked by the Cooperative. The head of production for the Cooperative, Esteban Sandoval, lives in the former offices of the mine. The shaft is still open and cool moist air from underground seeps mistily into the air. Passing this mine, the road takes a sharp left and leads into the Valenciana plaza, where one sees one of the "jewels of Guanajuato": the Church of San Cayetano, a magnificent example of Churrigueresque architecture.

The working entrance to the Valenciana mine (*Tiro de San José* or *Tiro General*) is located about 150 meters away from the plaza and church, down a recently paved road. Its architecture demonstrates much more than industrial utility. Built in the 1770s, it shows the social and cultural importance of mining in Guanajuato during that period, at least in the minds of its owners. A granite wall with an entrance of two massive wooden doors surrounds the mine. The doors lead to an entry hall supported by columns on the inside, with the ticket takers and a store for Cooperative silver and ceramic products on the left and the chapel to Santo Cristo de los Mineros on the right. The walls of this chapel are freshly whitewashed, and cut flowers are placed on the altar weekly. Swallows swoop and roost among the beams.

The Valenciana is the most famous of the Cooperative mines. It was mined extensively from its first bonanza in 1768 to the beginning of the War of Independence in 1810. In 1804 Alexander von Humboldt reported that "in 1771 they [the owners of the mine, António Obregón y Alcocer and Pedro Feliciano Otero] drew enormous masses of silver and from that period until 1804, when I quitted New Spain, the mine of Valenciana has continually yielded an annual produce of more than 14 millions of *livres Tournois* (L583,380)" (Humboldt 1811: 153). Monroy reports that from 1788 to 1810 the Valenciana made a net profit of 12,167,585 pesos (quoted in Brading 1971: 285). In order to get some sense of how much money this was at the time, we can compare it to the wage of an unskilled worker in the Valenciana mine during the same period: 4 *reales* per day, or 150 pesos per year (Brading 1971: 290–291). In its heyday the Valenciana employed more than thirty-three hundred men, one-quarter of whom worked directly on the veins removing ore (Brading 1971: 291, Villalba 1999).

Today, however, the Valenciana is the smallest of the Cooperative-controlled mines in Guanajuato City. From December 1996 to June 1998 the numbers of workers ranged from thirty-seven to forty-four workers (including underground and surface workers), presided over by a shift head (*cabo*), foreman or captain (*capitán*), and engineer. It has three drillers (*perforistas*) with one assistant each; the rest of the underground workforce are car-men (*carreros*) and general laborers (*peones*). Work activities, structures of authority, and patterns of production at the Valenciana are comparable to the other Cooperative mines in most respects, although work in the Valenciana is more difficult than in the other mines. This is because of the age and narrowness of the tunnels and the lack of machinery such as *scooptrams* (small bulldozers that can be driven right into the mine). Valenciana is also smaller and often less productive than the three other Cooperative mines in Guanajuato City (Cata, Rayas, and San Vicente). The mine produces approximately 100 metric tons of ore-bearing rock each day (at about 100 grams of silver and .85 grams of gold per metric ton). From June 1997 to May 1998 the Valenciana produced 3,020.05 kilograms of silver and 26.44 kilograms of gold. Like San Vicente and San Antón, it has only one shift, whereas Rayas and Cata and the two La Luz mines have three shifts.

From July 1997 to June 1998 I developed an extended case study of the Valenciana mine. In addition to visiting the interior of the mine, I spent multiple days on the surface collecting data and interviewing workers after they emerged from the mines. I interviewed twenty of the forty Valenciana workers, focusing on their experiences in the mines and their work histories. I obtained wage and production data (see Appendix II) and examined how the Cooperative negotiates the shift from mining to tourism in Guanajuato by opening to visitors the grounds of the mine and an old mine entrance.[11] Finally, I studied exchange networks of mineral specimens extracted from the mines to supplement the relatively low pay of the Cooperative (see chapter 7).

SANTA ROSA DE LIMA

From the city of Guanajuato, the road to Dolores Hidalgo climbs several hundred more meters through the Sierra de Santa Rosa. Alexander von Humboldt described this area in the following way:

> In the centre of the intendancy of Guanajuato on a ridge of the cordillera de Anahuac, rise a group of porphyritic summits known as the Sierra de Santa Rosa. This group of mountains, partly arid and partly covered with strawberry trees and evergreen oaks, is surrounded by fertile and well-cultivated fields. (1811: 169)

That Humboldt introduces his extended description of Guanajuato and its mines with this paragraph testifies to the striking aspect of Sierra de Santa Rosa.

The highway, built in 1920 (Espinosa 1920: vol. 3), follows one of the roads by which mules brought silver to Mexico City and eventually to Veracruz for transport to the Old World. The narrow highway passes a state park and several private ranches, and then enters a relatively flat straightaway. From the bus or car one can see the houses of Santa Rosa de Lima strung like beads along the town's only paved road, the Camino Real (*Royal Road*, named in honor of the old route from Zacatecas and the king's silver that was transported along it). This road crosses the highway at the town's first entrance at the *Cruz Grande* (Big Cross). A small chapel marks the entrance to the town; inside the chapel a large cross over the altar gives the place its name. A few hundred meters farther is the bus stop and the main entrance to Santa Rosa, with the Restaurante de la Sierra (a popular weekend destination for Guanajuatense families) and the Hotel El Crag. The hotel's name is an acronym: "**C**ómo **R**ecuerdo de **A**lfredo **G**uzmán" ("In Memory of Alfredo Guzmán," the patriarch of the town's leading family). It is almost always empty, except when travelers to Dolores are stuck on the road too late at night, groups of bicyclists or motorcyclists decide to break their journey in the country, and during the Lenten season when Catholic evangelists visit from the nearby city of Irapuato.

Most of Santa Rosa's houses line the Camino Real to the south of the highway, but the parish church (which serves some forty tiny communities in the surrounding areas) stands in "*la plaza*," a hundred meters below the rest of the town on the other side of the highway. Around the church are grouped about twenty dwellings that can be reached by a steep staircase of about a hundred steps or a roundabout dirt road that leads from the *Cruz Grande*.

The town of Santa Rosa was sparsely inhabited in the seventeenth and eighteenth centuries, when it served as a way station for muleteers on the way back from the northern mines. Don Tomás Ullóa, one of the town's oldest citizens (he was eighty-eight years old in 1997) and semi-official historian, told me that the Guzmán family became rich by robbing the mule trains of the king's silver as it passed through Santa Rosa. Several local festivals feature a ritualized game in which children chase down a *burro* laden with the "king's silver" (*la plata del rey*—actually cookies wrapped in silver foil).

Don Tomás described the difference between Santa Rosa and other mining towns in the area: "this mining town (*mineral*) distinguishes itself very profoundly in that it never became a ghost town." For instance, after the War of Independence, when the Spanish mercury for processing ore was no longer available and the mining economy went bust, in Santa Rosa "nature gave itself in a reduced but continuous form." He described at length the squirrels, rabbits, fishes, and little potatoes and wild beans that the townspeople ate during this period—"very tasty, and very rich in vitamins."

The town began to draw a larger population in the nineteenth century, when miners and prospectors came to exploit the area's silver and gold deposits (interview with Tomás Ulloa, April 1997; AMG *libros de registro*, 1880–1920). The mines of Monte de San Nicolás, some 5 kilometers away, provided a livelihood for many men in the early part of the century, until the mine was closed in the 1960s. One Rosense recalled for me:

I remember when the Monte [de San Nicolás] was very pretty, with lots of houses, because it was a town very rich in mining. But there was a strike about forty years ago, and the mine closed and a lot of people left. There's still a lot of gold in that mine, but it's costly to get it out, on account of the gases that are in there.

Many of the men from the Monte then went to work in the Cooperative mines. There are still some small working mines in Santa Rosa that employ a few men, and others enter old mine entrances as independent prospectors (*gambusinos*). The town is known for its Cooperative connections, the plentiful fruit crops in the summertime (many households have plum, pear, and quince trees), the local production of *mezcal* and fruit jellies, and its healthy climate. People often remark on the "*aire sano*" (healthy air) of Santa Rosa, and the town used to house a sanatorium for sufferers of silicosis and other mining-related lung diseases. It is also the only place near Guanajuato where snow falls (every several years). Some people (both outsiders and residents) praise the "nobility" (*nobleza*) of the inhabitants, while others (both outsiders and residents) describe a propensity to drinking and violent behavior among Santa Rosa's men.

Approximately forty-five Cooperative members (mostly male) live in Santa Rosa. In addition, many households have members who used to work in the Cooperative but left during the crisis of 1991–92. Some of those who do not work in the Cooperative work in government or at the University of Guanajuato. Others work in construction around Guanajuato or in the high-end ceramics workshop Cerámica de Santa Rosa. Still others travel to mines in the north of Mexico on contract. Older men and young boys work as *leñeros* (woodcutters) or *carboneros* (charcoal makers) in the live oak woods surrounding Santa Rosa. These men must sell their wood and charcoal to the powerful Guzmán family that controls the concession to the forest and runs the town's only restaurant and hotel. Finally, an increasing number migrate seasonally to the United States to work in agriculture, construction, janitorial work, and other pursuits.

Because of the prosperity enjoyed by the Cooperative in the 1980s, when the price of silver was high and the mines were producing the richest ore in decades, Cooperative members living in Santa Rosa are by no means the town's poorest inhabitants. Rather, many live in fine brick houses with cement (rather than tin) roofs and cisterns so that they do not have to carry water from the town spring.[12]

I first went to Santa Rosa because people always mentioned it as a place where lots of Cooperative members lived. When I asked people in Santa Rosa about the economic activities of the town, they almost invariably responded that "the majority" or "almost everybody" worked for the Cooperative. According to the National Institute of Statistics, Geography, and Information (INEGI) housing census of 1996, there are 181 individual dwellings (*viviendas*) in Santa Rosa de Lima with a total population of 925 people.[13] Of these, 429 of the inhabitants (46.4 percent) are men and 563 (60.9 percent) are over the age of fifteen.[14]

This means that, according to the INEGI census and the records of the Cooperative, it is not true that the majority of men in Santa Rosa work for the Cooperative. In fact, only 10.5 percent of the male population and 8 percent of the population over fifteen work there. Even so, it is significant that both outsiders and inhabitants consider Santa Rosa to be a bastion of Cooperative members. Furthermore, it may make more sense to think in terms of "Cooperative households" rather than individual workers. Most productive, reproductive, and consumption activities are carried out at the level of the household, and the household is the smallest social unit that lays claim to Cooperative patrimony.

From this perspective, up to 25 percent of Santa Rosa households are "Cooperative households."[15]

Santa Rosa is a Cooperative town in another sense as well. The relatively high number of Cooperative families exerts pressure on the Cooperative to ask for services and other benefits for the whole town. During the time I was in Santa Rosa, the Cooperative supplied water for the town's secondary school, donated buses and the use of a driver (who lives in the town) for school trips and local festivals, and lent a bulldozer to carve a baseball field out of one of Santa Rosa's steep hills. Leaders of the Cooperative told me that these donations of water, transport, and labor are an integral part of the Cooperative's "social goal," to help the families and communities of Cooperative members. Furthermore, these actions demonstrate an acknowledgment of Santa Rosa as a place closely tied to the Cooperative.

By living in Santa Rosa I achieved several things. First, I integrated myself much more fully into the life of the Cooperative by getting to know the families of workers as neighbors. A few mothers asked me to teach English to their children on Sundays, so I began a free class in my home. Many of my pupils came from Cooperative families;[16] over time I established strong connections with several of these families. I attended weekly masses, birthday parties, and baptisms, and visited mothers in their homes to cook Mexican specialties or just to chat. I also carried out thirty formal interviews with workers and their wives in Santa Rosa.[17] These interviews focused on household organization, work histories of all members of the household, and comparisons between the Cooperative and other mining companies. I sought out families in which some members worked in the Cooperative and others in El Cubo, Peñoles, or on contract in mines in Coahuila and other parts of northern Mexico. Finally, I gathered several genealogies from Cooperative families living in Santa Rosa. In the course of recording these genealogies, I learned how sons are steered toward certain jobs and residences, and how daughters marry into different communities and labor traditions.

People

A marked feature of long-term ethnographic fieldwork is the tendency of the anthropologist to form close relationships with one or more "key informants," who provide an insider's perspective on the life of the place under study. These perspectives, necessarily partial (Rabinow 1977), help to form the anthropologist's point of view and arguments. Here I describe five friends who, in their roles as informants, showed me their views of the Cooperative and of Guanajuato. They also give a sense of some of the viewpoints of different sectors of the Cooperative (miners and plant workers; older and younger workers; Guanajuatenses and Rosenses; members of long-standing Cooperative families and newcomers; men and women).

MARTÍN GARCÍA MONTERO

Martín García could best be described as my "key informant" in this study. During my fieldwork he was the second in command in the industrial safety department in the Cooperative. An almost absurdly slight man, his nickname in the Cooperative is "Rambo." He is a fast-talking, sociable, sometimes irascible person and an accomplished *alburero*—one who excels at the typically Mexican sexually charged argot known as *albures.* Martín is married to Isidra, whose brother and nephew also work in the Cooperative (and through whom he got the job). They have two young children, five and nine years old. They are both in their early thirties and have been married for about ten years.

In addition to working at the Cooperative, Martín works several evenings a week as a tour guide in the center of town and one other twenty-four-hour shift as a volunteer fireman. He makes five hundred pesos a week (about fifty dollars in November 1998) at the Cooperative and approximately the same amount as a guide (although his income as a guide varies dramatically depending on the season). Isidra is a primary school teacher. They live in a working-class neighborhood in the city of Guanajuato and are slowly adding a second story to their house. Because of Martín's extra work, Isidra's profession, and the fact that they have only two children, they have more disposable income than many Cooperative members, and this is observable, for instance, in their compact disc player, VCR, and occasional subscription to Direct TV.

One of the main duties of the industrial safety department was to go down in the mines every week to check on safety conditions. This makes Martín one of the relatively few people in the Cooperative who frequently crosses the social and political boundary between surface workers and miners. Because of my connection with Martín, I was able to go down in the mines multiple times, thus achieving greater access to the world underground than would otherwise have been possible. In addition, the fact that many Cooperative members thought that Martín and I were having an affair meant that other men in the Cooperative considered me "off-limits," even when my husband was not in Guanajuato. For his part, Martín made sure to tell David that he would take care of me and protect me during those times when David was not around.

Martín is generally skeptical of the Cooperative leadership, believing that it generally does not make good on the promises held out by the ideology of patrimony. Although critical of the PAN party, he voted for them in the local and governmental elections as a kind of protest against the PRI and, by extension, the Cooperative leadership. At the same time, when asked about the difference between people in the other mining companies and in the Cooperative, he says, "in the other companies they get along fine, but here the people are more noble."

Martín has always been interested in emergency medical services and has pursued training as a volunteer fireman. Since my fieldwork, he has left the Cooperative and now works as an emergency medical technician (EMT) for the state government of Guanajuato. Like many Cooperative members, the flexible nature of Cooperative work and the opportunity to take off work (without pay) allowed him to acquire skills that ultimately helped him to leave.

ALVARO GRANADOS AGUILAR

Alvaro Granados works as the captain in the Valenciana mine and lives in Santa Rosa on the main road. One of eight children, he was raised by his mother from the age of three after his father died. He went to work when he was twelve, transporting gravel from the hills around Santa Rosa to Guanajuato. At seventeen he entered the Cooperative. All four of Alvaro's brothers worked in the Cooperative at one time, although three of them left in the crisis of 1991–92. Alvaro is married to Gregoria, with whom he has three daughters and a son; the two youngest were frequent members of my Sunday English class in Santa Rosa. Gregoria's sister, Juana, is married to Alvaro's nephew, Jaime (who is close to him in age and more like a younger brother than a nephew).[18] Both Gregoria and Juana work in the home taking care of the house and raising their children.

Alvaro and his immediate family live in a house made up of several small whitewashed cement rooms arranged around a central patio with a separate bathroom and kitchen. The house is always spotlessly clean, in spite of the pigs and chickens that occasionally wander through. This house belongs to his wife and is adjacent to his in-laws. During my time in Santa Rosa Alvaro was building another house next to his brother's further up the Camino Real. Fifty percent of the materials for this house came from the Cooperative. When I asked why he was building the house since he already had plenty of space for his family, he said, "This house isn't mine—it belongs to my wife. I could be lazy (echar hueva), but I want one that is mine." Building a house for his wife and children is an integral part of what he sees as the proper responsibility of a husband and father.

Alvaro always expresses great affection and loyalty toward the Cooperative. During my first extended conversation with him, he said:

The Cooperative concerns itself with the whole family, not only with the workers. For example, they gave a truckload (*pipa*) of water to the secondary school, since the majority of the students are the children of [Cooperative] workers. They care about the workers and their children, who are the future of the Cooperative. They are building a basketball court here, so the kids don't fall into delinquency.

On another occasion he said to me:

> With all the help the Cooperative has given us, we still don't love her—it's a shame. Here in Guanajuato, if you haven't been to school (*si no tienes estudios*), there's nothing but mining.

That Alvaro worked in the Valenciana, the mine where I spent the most time, and also lived in Santa Rosa just a few doors away from me, helped me to see the Cooperative, its mines, and towns like Santa Rosa as overlapping worlds, peopled by brothers, *compadres*, fathers and sons, neighborhood rivals, fellow members of baseball teams, *rondallas* (singing groups), congregations, classrooms, and so on. I believe that this sense is ever present for many members and their families, integral to how they experience the Cooperative.

CHANO VÁSQUEZ SAENZ

During my time in Guanajuato, Chano Vásquez worked as the *lampistero* in the Valenciana mine, taking care of the lanterns and also the dynamite, detonators, and other explosives equipment for the miners. A rail-thin man in his early fifties, he had worked for twenty-three years in the mine before being "*echado pa'fuera*" (thrown out of the mine) because of lung damage. He lives in a village outside Guanajuato called Calderones, which lies near the mines controlled by Peñoles and supplies many workers to those mines. Calderones is also known as the town where the famous "*cantera verde*" stone comes from that adorns all the important public buildings in Guanajuato. Chano walks every morning from this town to the plaza de Embajadoras where he catches the bus to Valenciana. His wife, Lupe, son, daughter-in-law, and two grandchildren live with him. His brother and nephew work in the Cooperative; nearly all his other male relatives, as well as 95 percent of the men in his town, work at Las Torres. When we visited him in Calderones, he showed us the house where his wife had lived as a girl, right next to his own. I asked him how long they had courted:

> In those days it wasn't like that, everything was secret (*puros escondidos*). You never would ask for permission to get married, you just take her to your

house and then tell them [the woman's family]. Otherwise they'd get really mad.

Although Chano has not had much formal education, he is a highly intelligent and intellectually curious person, and I spent many hours with him discussing all kinds of subjects.[19] He has traveled only to Mexico City (he once thought of going to the United States as a temporary migrant worker under the U.S.-sponsored *bracero* program, but when he arrived at the office to sign up, the line was too long and he left); however, he spends a lot of time watching television programs and reading about other places. In some ways he was a terrific informant, being so intelligent and thoughtful. But in keeping with his consciously idiosyncratic character, he refused to answer any generalizing questions about his opinions, always saying, "Who knows what other people say about that." Talking with him helped me to counteract the generalizing tendency that often plagues the ethnographer.

Manuel Torres Colmenero

Manuel Torres works in the automotive workshop of the Cooperative. His father was a founding member and his brothers and some other relatives work in the Cooperative. He also has training as a *yesero* (plasterer) and gets jobs outside the cooperative working on the interiors of houses and churches. He is in his mid-thirties, married, and lives, with his wife and three children, in the Barrio El Carrizo, where a number of Cooperative members live. We became acquainted because he is Martín's *compadre*.

Manuel is a strong supporter of the Cooperative, which he sees as a noble institution, although fallible and fraught with difficulties. During my time in Guanajuato he was a member of the administrative council in charge of sports and other leisure activities (baseball and soccer tournaments, festival preparations, raffles, etc.). In 2001, when the Cooperative found itself submerged in debt, he spoke with me about what he thought should be done:

> MT: We could extract from (*jalar*, lit., "pull from") San Antón on the weekend, the trucks are parked at the plant, only Clotildo [the geologist in charge of the Valenciana Mine] says we'd have to mix it with the tailings that are above the cerámica.
>
> EF: But that wouldn't be too hard, would it?
>
> MT: No, not at all. But the trick is to decide and to be united. . . . You know, like in Cruz Azul [the largest producers' cooperative in Mexico, which produces cement (and which also sponsors a popular national

soccer team)], everyone who enters the Cooperative should take a course in what cooperativism is about.

Like many of the younger men who work in the workshops (*talleres*) at the central plant, Manuel is from a venerable Cooperative family and strongly espouses a cooperativist viewpoint. He began by working in the mines as a sampler but was later transferred to the plant: "at that time there was the idea that if the father gave his life in the mines [that is, died as a result of silicosis or an accident], then the son should work in the plant, and I was one of those cases." The cooperative helped him get his training in automotive work, both on-site and by sending him to courses in León.

After the miners' pilgrimage in May 1998 (see below), we watched Manuel's and Martín's young sons, Manuelito and Omar, playing together while wearing miners' helmets.

> Martin said, "They look like thumbtacks."
> Manuel replied, "Now they can go into the mine when they're big."
> "Let's hope not. Let's hope they can do better," countered Martín.

This exchange exemplifies two viewpoints among the generation of Cooperative members in their thirties and forties, and it is not surprising that Martín is the only member of his family to be in the Cooperative (although his wife belongs to a Cooperative family) whereas Manuel has many generations in Cooperative mines and is the son of a founding member.

However, when I returned in 2003, I found that Manuel had left the Cooperative and was working in the motor pool for the municipal government. Although he seemed happy in his new job, he spoke sadly about the Cooperative's future. I cannot help but feel that his leaving the Cooperative foreshadows its demise (see chapter 9).

Doña Nacha López Guzmán

Ignacia López (Doña Nacha) is a stately woman in her sixties who lives along an unpaved extension to the Camino Real near the cemetery. She married Alfredo Salazar at the age of sixteen. He has worked in the Cooperative his entire working life. She has six living children of nine pregnancies. Of her two sons, both worked in the Cooperative, but one has left. The other, Arturo, is unmarried and the only child still living with Nacha and Alfredo. Three of her daughters are married to men who were in the Cooperative, but one of them left in the crisis and moved to León. The pair have a certain stature in Santa Rosa; Don

Alfredo was the *delegado* (representative to the municipal government) while I was in Santa Rosa, and Doña Nacha is related on her mother's side to Santa Rosa's richest family, the Guzmáns.

Their house, a series of adobe buildings arranged around an open area, although spacious and commodious in area, is modest in materials by Santa Rosa's standards. This may reflect an older generation's taste for adobe over brick and concrete. Like many houses in Mexico, there is no separate "living room" but rather two rooms with beds, one of which is also used as a sitting room during the day. All the rooms have blue linoleum floors; the walls are painted aqua and white. There is a large formal photograph of Nacha and Alfredo on their wedding day hanging above the beds in the central room.

Like nearly all the older wives in Santa Rosa, Doña Nacha "dedicates herself to the home," that is, she does not have a job. She described a typical day to me:

> I wake up at 5:30 A.M. to make lunch for Alfredo and Arturo and wash and clean till about 9:00, then go to the tortillería,[20] then afterwards wash the dishes, wash the floors, make the rice. Later Alfredo and Arturo come home at four, and they are hungry, so the meal is ready for them when they get here. At night we have just a little milk.

Doña Nacha has a lot of experience with the Cooperative through her husband, sons, and sons-in-law, as well as a lifetime of experience in Santa Rosa. When I asked her how Santa Rosa had changed over the years, she said:

> Now people eat better, because I remember that my mother-in-law said that they used to have nothing but tortillas and beans. Before they only worked as charcoal makers and woodcutters, and the salary from that is very small. When the Cooperative came around, they paid a bit better, though still not much. But people began to eat better.

Nevertheless, she often criticized the Cooperative leadership for not living up to its promise to take care of the workers and their families.

Through Doña Nacha I learned the perspective that women tied to Cooperative members have on the Cooperative, its ideology, and its practice. I also saw firsthand the tremendous amount of continuous work that goes into maintaining a household of miners, their children, and eventually their grandchildren. One morning, when I went to Doña Nacha's house to learn to make gorditas, her grandson, Paquito, announced chirpily:

One day I am going to be tall like my papa and I am going to drive the truck [his father's job in the Cooperative] and my mama is going to do the washing, Gaby [his sister] is going to cook, and Paty [his other sister] is going to iron for me and my papa and we are going to work and take vacations at school [*en la primaria*]!

This manner of foretelling the future aptly captures the gendered work Paquito has seen done by Doña Nacha, Don Alfredo, and his own parents to ensure the reproduction of the family.

Events

Finally, I describe here four periodic events (weekly, yearly, and occasional) that punctuated my time in Guanajuato and that serve as arenas for social relations and practices significant to the Cooperative and its members. These events include a variety of activities that take place on Saturdays, the day Cooperative members are paid; a *quince años* party given for Alvaro's daughter; the *Viernes de Dolores* (Dolores Friday), which takes place on the Friday before Good Friday; and the annual miners' pilgrimage that occurs at the end of May.

SATURDAYS

This first "event" is actually a whole category of events that take place on Saturday afternoons. Saturday is the day that Cooperative members are paid, for which they must come to the central plant to receive the "envelope" (*sobre*) containing their week's wages in cash along with a pay stub recording the gross pay and various deductions for the week. The practice of going to the plant to be paid is called "*venir a cobrar.*"

Like many Mexicans, Cooperative members work half a day on Saturday, leaving the mines or workshops at around noon to go to the cashier's window that is located on one side of the central plant. Sometimes the worker himself goes to the window; at other times his wife will go for him, often bringing one or more children in tow. Policemen hover in the small plaza next to the Cooperative (since so much cash is being dispersed on this day). Trucks from various mines periodically come by and drop off workers, and the city bus discharges more workers and their families every time it comes by. The Cooperative supermarket is full of people (especially women) doing grocery shopping while they are there. Sometimes vendors of clothes, jewelry, cosmetics, and other goods pass through to tempt workers or their wives. The president of the administrative council and the director are also kept busy listening to various requests for loans and other considerations.

All these comings and goings help to create a festive and convivial atmosphere at the central plant on Saturdays. There are several small stores, taco stands, and ice cream vendors in the plaza, and many people are hanging around having lunch, snacks, and beer. People often feel generous, since they have finished the work week, have Sundays off, and have just been paid. This is the time they can spend a little, often inviting one another to a beer or plate of food. I quickly learned to eat lightly on Fridays so I would be able to do justice to the Saturday gifts of food and drink. These gifts were an important part of my relationship with friends; since I often paid for them during the week, Saturday became a day on which they could return the gesture.

I also found that Saturdays, as the cusp between work and home time, were a crucial part of *my* work. On Saturdays I was able to meet new people, hear the week's gossip, learn more about how people were related to one another, and so on. Because Saturday is the day that everyone sits down for a moment and reflects on the week, often accompanied by a beer, they were in a mood for the kind of conversations that perhaps taught me the most about their lives.

After people do their business at the plant and perhaps sit for a time with their friends, many go home or to a variety of other activities, such as baseball or soccer games, house building, community work on roads, water systems or chapels, and so on. Occasionally a *comida* will be taking place somewhere else that people will go to, with others from the Cooperative or elsewhere. These *comidas* can vary from being a barbecue of meat roasted on a grill made from a barrel with the top sheared off and a hole in the side (see Limón 1994) to a more luxurious and carefully planned event such as a *quince años* or wedding. In many cases, especially the more spontaneous events and those that do not celebrate a birthday or wedding, men do not attend with their families, but with other men or with their girlfriends (*novias*)—and sometimes with a "semi-neuter" anthropologist such as myself.

Whatever men do on Saturday, it tends to be seen as time they spend away from their families engaging in specifically masculine activities. These activities often entail spending money received from the Cooperative and are coded as particular forms of spending patrimony well or ill. Drinking, spending time with girls, roasting meat, hanging around doing nothing (*echar hueva),* attending or playing in sports events, performing community work, building one's own house or that of one's brother, *compadre,* or brother–in–law are all considered typically male activities, but not all are approved of by everyone. Many women and some men (such as Don Alfredo) heartily disapprove of men who drink on Saturdays, saying that often they arrive at home on Sundays without a penny (*sin un cinco*). The social worker of the Cooperative told me that women show up to collect the *sobre* on Saturdays to make sure their husbands do not spend it all, and this may have some truth to it.

On the other hand, many men with whom I spoke considered it their right as men to "*echar hueva y tomar unas chelas*" (hang out and drink some brews) as long as they also met their familial obligations financially (by providing for their wives and children) and socially (by devoting much or all of Sunday to the family and the house). For instance, one member of the cooperative told about a fight he had with his wife. One Saturday he had been paid five hundred pesos for helping with security for the Televisa crew when they were shooting a soap opera at Rayas. After partying with the crew, he came home and gave her a wad of cash, saying, "We'll spend this tomorrow." According to my friend, she accused him of going to a prostitute, and said, "You're a worthless man" (*no vales como hombre*). To us, he complained,

> It's true that she has a job and I'm grateful to her for that. But I give her eight hundred pesos a week, so she doesn't have anything to complain about. I deserve a little *desmadre*" (cutting loose, partying; lit., "motherlessness").

The gendered terms in which this argument over how money and time should be spent is typical.

Since Saturday afternoon is the threshold between the work week and the day of rest (*séptimo día; día de descanso*), as well as payday, it marks the moment when Cooperative patrimony, now in the form of money, is given over to the individual worker. Will he convert it into another patrimonial substance, such as a house (see chapter 5), or will he spend it foolishly on drinking and women? Or if he does some of both, spending some time and money on these unproductive male activities and some on the productive ones of community work and house building, what is the appropriate balance?

These questions are hotly debated both within households and among husbands and wives, fathers and children, and also neighbors and coworkers. For example, one Saturday my husband sat down to talk and drink beer with some Cooperative members and acquaintances on a bench across from our house in Santa Rosa. The next day I was visiting Don Alfredo and Doña Nacha at the other end of the road. Don Alfredo told me gently, "Your husband should be careful of those *señores* [gentlemen]. They're not good people, and some say it doesn't look well to drink in the street."[21]

By no means are such conflicts particular to the Cooperative; indeed, they are common throughout Guanajuato and Mexico. The notion of patrimony as a Cooperative resource that should be properly converted into family patrimony provides a local idiom for voicing these broader themes.

QUINCE AÑOS

Another category of periodic event is the various familial festivals that commemorate baptisms, third birthday parties (*tres años*) for boys and girls, first communion, fifteenth birthday parties (*quince años*) for girls,[22] weddings, and so on. In my time in Guanajuato and Santa Rosa, I attended dozens of these fiestas, in some cases contributing as *madrina de flores* or *madrina de recuerdos* (lit., "godmother of flowers" or "godmother of souvenirs") or in other small roles. Here I describe one of these, the *quince años* celebration for Alvaro's oldest daughter, Gloria.

Gloria's *quince años* began with a mass, at 3:00 P.M., with Gloria wearing a white dress much like a wedding gown, and the church adorned with flowers. As the mass was taking place, trucks carrying Cooperative members were climbing the Camino Real to Jaime's house, which has a bigger space for parties than Alvaro. Earlier in the day the Cooperative had sent a tent to set up for shade. Tables and chairs were delivered along with cases of beer and soda.

By about 4:00 people began arriving; they were immediately given a beer or soda (most men drank beer, and most women drank soda). A *mariachi* group began to play as plates of chicken with mole sauce, rice, and beans were served. Later, when it grew dark, cake was served and a band playing Mexican dance music (*conjunto*) replaced the mariachis, while tequila and locally brewed mezcal made their appearance along with the beer and soda.

FIGURE 2.2 *Quince Años,* evening

In addition to Alvaro's large family, many of whom are Cooperative members, about eight workers came from the Valenciana and most of the jefes (leadership of the cooperative, mostly engineers) attended with their *novias*. The Cooperative had loaned Alvaro some of the money for this celebration, but Alvaro was also pleased that the jefes, especially the president of the administrative council, Jesus Castillo, had decided to come. After I had a *comida* at my house which Castillo attended, he said to me: "You and I are the only ones in Santa Rosa whom he's [Castillo] visited. Everyone invites him, but he doesn't come. It makes one feel good."

After attending the mass I strolled over to Alvaro's house, where I flitted about taking photographs for much of the meal, then sat down with the Valenciana people and listened to the mariachis. Alvaro joined us for a time, and we talked about his daughters and son. The band began to play a pretty *ranchera* air, one I didn't recognize, and Alvaro told me, "this one always reminds me of my mom (*mi jefa*); she loved this song." Later in the evening I danced a bit, including with Kike, Alvaro's six-year-old son, and slipped out with many of the other women as the party became a bit wilder.

From Alvaro's perspective, this was an intensely familial event. A celebration for his daughter, it was held at his nephew/brother-in-law's house. His brother and sister-in-law were the godparents, and he told me beforehand that his brothers and cousins had helped to pay for it, saying, "It cost eighteen thousand pesos [about two thousand dollars] and I paid for ten thousand. Imagine if I didn't get along with them [the other members of his family], I would have had to pay for the whole thing."

But from the perspective of others who came from Guanajuato, this fiesta was a Saturday event attended by men without their wives. The jefes came, with their girlfriends, leaving their wives at home. In fact, the only time Jesús Castillo acknowledged to me any illicit or secretive quality to his relationship with his *novia*, Patricia, was after this *quince años*. I had been taking pictures throughout the afternoon, and later I showed him some with him and Patricia among the crowd. He admired the pictures in a courteous manner and then said, lightly but without joking, "I'm going to need the negatives for those pictures." The intersection of family relations and "Saturday" relations in this fiesta comes up often at events tied to the Cooperative, where there is not a rigid separation between work and family, and where competing notions of masculinity and femininity overlap with debates over the right and wrong use of Cooperative resources.

VIERNES DE DOLORES

On the Friday before Good Friday, Guanajuatenses celebrate the Viernes de Dolores, a festival in honor of the Virgin of the Sorrows (Dolores). This is an aspect of the Virgin Mary who mourns for her dead son. As the *cronista* told me, "she is the patroness of the miners, because many mothers have to suffer for their sons who died in the mine, the way that Mary had to suffer for Jesus." This festival captures a general tendency to link the risk and potential tragedy of mine work to the network of saints and virgins who help to mitigate sorrow and uncertainty for many Guanajuatenses. In the words of Luis Miguel Rionda:

> The terrible pain . . . of seeing her son torn apart and victimized in a supreme sacrifice inspired an analogy for the miner with the final and inevitable destination that they had to risk daily in the bowels of the earth. (1994: 2)

This festival is but the most public and most festive example of a whole series of human-divine interactions on the surface and underground. By consigning themselves to the deities when they go down in the mine and by honoring them in loving ways both underground and on the surface, miners and their families hope to find refuge from the mine's threatening forces.[23]

In spite of these grim associations, the Viernes de Dolores is a particularly festive and convivial event. As one miner told me, "The pilgrimage [see below] is more solemn [*solemne*], the Viernes de Dolores is more joyful [*alegre*]." Festivities begin for many in Guanajuato itself on the night before, where people go out to bars and nightclubs or to drink with their friends. Many people stay up all night and then have breakfast in the central square of Guanajuato (the Jardín de la Unión). They then spend the day (it is a holiday for nearly everyone in the city) visiting the various altars to the Virgin constructed in peoples' homes and businesses, especially in the city's mines, where the miners dole out *caldo de camarón* (shrimp broth), *agua fresca de betabel* (beetroot punch), and ice cream.

The altars have a number of requisite components, including a picture or statue of the Virgin, garlands made of colored paper (especially purple, yellow, and white) with punched-out designs, garlands of oranges and bananas (often gilded), bunches of baby's breath, fennel, chamomile and applemint (*mastranto*), branches of poplar or oak, small jars of wheatgrass, and sometimes *petates* (straw pallets) with designs of seeds on top, offerings of loaves and fishes, candles, and so on. Some of these elements have distinct biblical references, such as the loaves and fishes, while others appear to be more general marks of fertility and natural abundance (the various fruits and flowers). Like many contemporary "Catholic" rituals, this one also seems to have some indigenous influence, and the manifestation of the Virgin of the Sorrows may be connected to the Aztec goddess Coatlicue, the mother of the sun and moon, or to her Otomí or Tarascan counterparts (L. M. Rionda 1994: 7).

On March 21, 1997, the first time I attended the festival, I arrived at the Jardín at 8:30 A.M., having stayed up all night in keeping with tradition. The tony Posada Santa Fe on the Jardín was hosting a breakfast for important civic figures, including the governor, mayor, and city council, the city's *cronista*, the rector of the university, and so on. I then moved on to a ceremony honoring the abbot of Guanajuato as the "Distinguished Guanajuatense of 1997." He received a plaque and a silver tray made by the Platería Santa Fe (the Cooperative's silver workshop).

Afterward I wandered—if "wander" can be used to describe inching forward through the packed streets—about the city looking at the multiple altars to the Virgin in the municipal government offices, storefronts, churches, and private homes. A group from the municipality also passed through, judging altars for the annual competition. Everywhere hundreds of people were coming from mass, strolling with their families, buying and selling flowers, balloons, souvenirs, and snacks from ambulant vendors.

On my way to the Cooperative's central plant I passed the Alhóndiga, on whose broad plaza about fifteen devoted PRIistas were limply celebrating Benito Júarez's birthday. In the preceding weeks there has been some disgruntlement among Cooperative members, who usually have both Júarez's birthday (a national, state-sponsored holiday) and the Viernes de Dolores (a local holiday) as paid holidays but who will only get one day this year, since both fall on March 21.

At 11:30 A.M. I showed up at the plant for mass. In his homily the priest exhorted, "your hearts should be as shining, clean, and pure as gold and silver. . . . We give thanks to the Virgin of Dolores for saving the Cooperative from bankruptcy [in 1991–92] . . . in this festival of Guanajuatense, of miners." Afterward, along with throngs of Cooperative members and other Guanajuatenses, I participated in the main event of the celebration: visiting the different departments at the central plant and the Valenciana mine to see the altars, and to eat and drink. There was a happy, welcoming atmosphere and it was a pleasure to be part of it, in spite of—and maybe partly because of—my pounding head.

The cost of the altars and food had been discounted from workers' paychecks—70 pesos each spread out over six weeks. This happens every year; in the words of Yolia Tortolero Cervantes:

> Paying the cost of the festival allows the miner to appropriate it, to make it his own, even though it must be coordinated with the chief of personnel and permission to use the installations . . . depends on the bosses (*patrones*—a word used more frequently in the private mining companies than in the Cooperative). (1992: 55)

FIGURE 2.3 Altar to the Virgen de Dolores, chapel at the central plant, Santa Fe Cooperative

As soon as Martín saw me at the automotive workshop, he said, "Are you hung over, girl? (*¿andas cruda, hija?*). We retreated to his office with Manuel and several others and drank beer while I elaborately translated and explained the expression "the hair of the dog that bit you," and we gossiped about the Cooperative. Months later Martín, Manuel, and I recalled that this was the moment when we became friends. It was also the day that my fieldwork began in earnest.

Later I went to the Valenciana, where there were still about seventy-five people, although things were winding down. I said hello to Alvaro and his family; the boys were playing soccer on the lawn, and the girls were wandering about eating ice cream. Everyone was dressed in their Sunday best. I asked Clotildo (the Valenciana's engineer) about the significance of the different objects on the altar, and he responded, "Everything has a meaning, I just don't remember what it is at the moment." After eating still more dried shrimps in broth and ice cream, I left feeling nauseated, tired, and happy. By 6:00 the streets of Guanajuato were nearly deserted.

The next day the front page of the paper showed a picture of the Guadalupe Mine thronged with visitors, with the words:

> Although the miners in this time of crisis had wanted to work this day so they could be paid double [for Júarez's birthday and for the Viernes de Dolores], they still contributed to the festival as God commands [*como Dios manda*].

This excerpt, while tinged with barbed journalistic rhetoric, also captures a sense of the exchange system that operates between miners and deities. By contributing their labor, money, and affection "as God commands," miners strive to create the conditions under which saints and virgins reciprocate by protecting the safety, health, and prosperity of those underground.

Peregrinación de Mineros

The miners' pilgrimage (*peregrinación de mineros*) takes place on the last weekend in May, the culmination of a month of celebrations honoring Guanajuato's patron saint, Our Lady of Santa Fe. The saint's image resides in the Basilica, an enormous church made of Guanajuatense pink marble (*cantera rosa*) and stone that stands at the crest of the Plaza de la Paz. Every evening in May members of a different occupation march in procession to the Basilica to pay their respects, carrying images of the Virgin of Santa Fe, brightly embroidered banners, and marks of their trade. The taxi drivers arrive in their gaily decorated taxis, the market

¡Nuestra Señora de Gto.! - ¡Rogad por Nosotros!

FIGURE 2.4 Souvenir of the Miners' Pilgrimage, produced by the Santa Fe Cooperative 1941 (*front*)

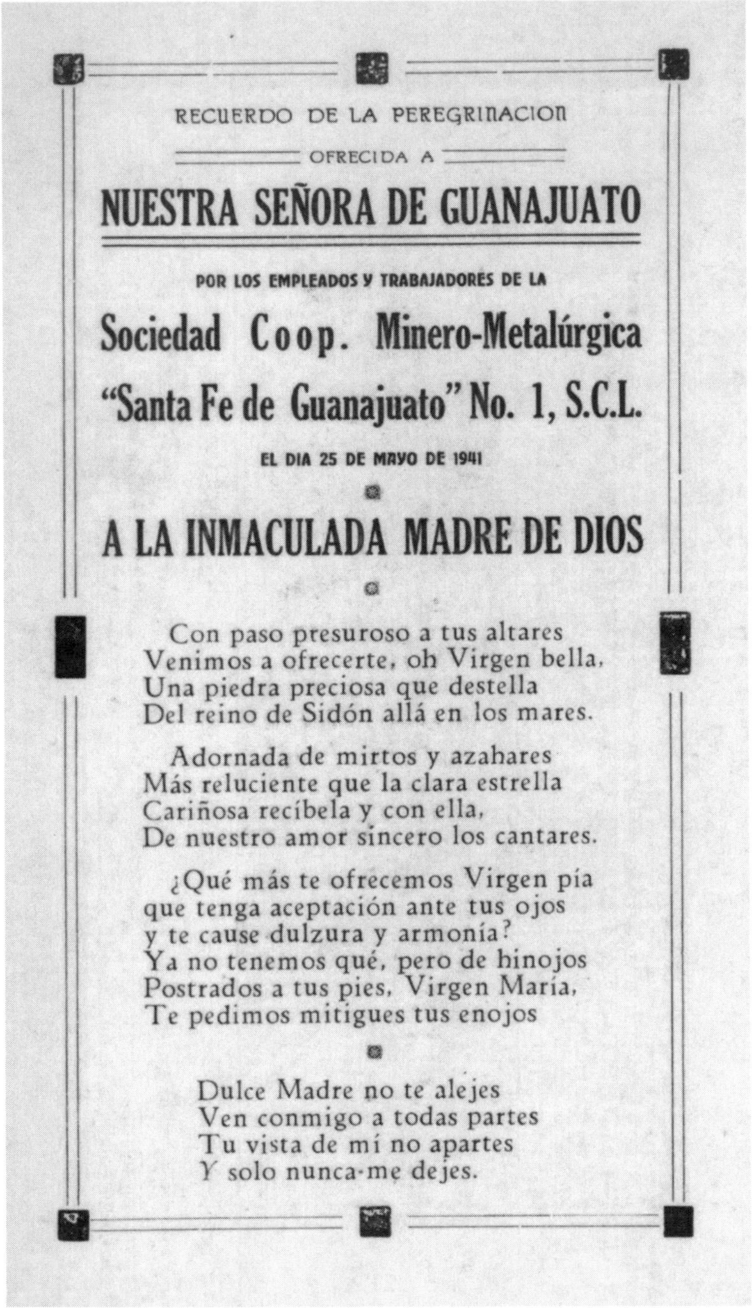

RECUERDO DE LA PEREGRINACION

OFRECIDA A

NUESTRA SEÑORA DE GUANAJUATO

POR LOS EMPLEADOS Y TRABAJADORES DE LA

Sociedad Coop. Minero-Metalúrgica

"Santa Fe de Guanajuato" No. 1, S.C.L.

EL DIA 25 DE MAYO DE 1941

A LA INMACULADA MADRE DE DIOS

Con paso presuroso a tus altares
Venimos a ofrecerte, oh Virgen bella,
Una piedra preciosa que destella
Del reino de Sidón allá en los mares.

Adornada de mirtos y azahares
Más reluciente que la clara estrella
Cariñosa recíbela y con ella,
De nuestro amor sincero los cantares.

¿Qué más te ofrecemos Virgen pía
que tenga aceptación ante tus ojos
y te cause dulzura y armonía?
Ya no tenemos qué, pero de hinojos
Postrados a tus pies, Virgen María,
Te pedimos mitigues tus enojos

Dulce Madre no te alejes
Ven conmigo a todas partes
Tu vista de mí no apartes
Y solo nunca me dejes.

FIGURE 2.5 Souvenir of the Miners' Pilgrimage, 1941 (*back*)

vendors carry the image that normally resides in the Hidalgo market at the bottom of the Avenida Juárez, and the university professors wear academic robes.

For me, this procession was particularly significant as it took place one week before I was scheduled to leave Guanajuato, having completed nearly two years of fieldwork among Cooperative members and their families. I had had a seemingly prototypical fieldwork experience, falling in love with the place and the people, radically changing my own understanding of how place, occupation, family, and livelihood might be experienced, and, in the process, becoming an anthropologist—with all the joys and difficulties that entails. I was marching as part of the Cooperative's security squad in this year's celebration, wearing a uniform and helmet lent to me by Martín. Several kids from Santa Rosa, children of Cooperative members and students in my Sunday English classes, flocked around me and posed for pictures.

Leaders of the Cooperative headed the procession, arm in arm with the mayor and followed by the two other main mining companies in Guanajuato: El Cubo and Peñoles Grupo Guanajuato (often known locally as "Las Torres" for the mine where the offices and processing plant are located). We wind our way through the Plaza de la Paz, carrying banners for particular mines and workshops, and wearing helmets with miners' lanterns. At the head of the Co-

FIGURE 2.6 Miners' Pilgrimage, 1998

operative group a car bears a miniature wooden replica of the Basilica made by the Cooperative's master carpenter. Every year he makes a different replica of Cooperative mines or Guanajuato churches and public buildings.

As we entered the Plaza de la Paz, at the top of which stands the Basilica, those ahead signaled us to turn on our lamps, and the crowd cheered as fireworks went off above our heads and the band played a triumphal march. When we reached the Basilica, fathers gathered up their children and took their wives by the hand. Martín said almost tenderly to Manuel, "Here we go, *comadre*" [although Manuel is his *compadre*, he always calls him, affectionately, by the feminine term]. We filed into the church, holding our helmets in our hands. Each pilgrim crossed him- or herself in front of the image of Santa Fe and the Baby Jesus (both with silver crowns donated by the Cooperative) and received a postcard of the golden altarpiece as a souvenir of the occasion. The director of the Cooperative stood near the exit of the church and shook each of our hands, saying: "Thanks for accompanying us today."

For much of the month people pay little attention to the pilgrimages, unless they happen to belong to or have relatives in the trade celebrating its pilgrimage on that evening. But the whole city turns out for the miners' pilgrimage. The streets are packed all the way up the Avenida Juárez, every available lamppost and tree is laden with children and teenagers, and the windows above the street are all full. The miners' pilgrimage, the crowd that turns out to watch it, and the place of the Santa Fe Cooperative at its head encapsulate much of Guanajuato's sense of itself in the latter years of the twentieth century and exemplify the role that the Santa Fe Cooperative has played and continues to play in the city. My participation in this pilgrimage crowned a sad and lovely time that I spent getting to know the *gente cooperativista* and seeing their courage and imagination in facing the decline of their livelihood and their way of living.

CHAPTER 3

Labor, History, and Historical Consciousness

The mines that the Cooperative works are legendary mines, mines of distinguished ancestry.
—Jesús Baltierra, Director, Santa Fe Cooperative, December 1996

The Cooperative is something representative of Guanajuato . . . if something comes from the Cooperative, it comes from Guanajuato.
—Director, Cerámica Santa Fe, a satellite industry of the Santa Fe Cooperative, March 1997

The negotiations with respect to resource allocation and relations of power that exist in the Santa Fe Cooperative do not arise in a vacuum; they are born of long-standing economic arrangements, labor traditions, and legal and political institutions operating in Mexico since the beginning of the colonial period (and in some cases before then). This chapter traces some of these patterns and institutions, focusing on two key aspects of the context within which Cooperative uses of patrimony take place.

First, I look at how patrimony is construed by those who make use of it as integral to the history of labor in Mexico and Guanajuato, and especially to the Santa Fe's organization as a producers' cooperative. Producers' cooperatives in Mexico have generated forms of labor organization that have tended, in turn, to foster notions of ownership and obligation central to the language of patrimony.

Second, I describe the context for the development of a particular historical consciousness among Cooperative members, their families, and other Guanajuatenses in order to see how local constructions of this place and its role in the formation of Mexico feed into understandings of patrimony. As we will see in the following chapter, this sense of history, embodied in the built environment of the city, feeds into more recent uses of patrimony as "*patrimonio*

MAP 3.1

histórico" in the wake of a world silver crisis and the rise of tourism to Mexico and Guanajuato.

THE HISTORY OF LABOR

The city of Guanajuato is the capital of Guanajuato State, located in the center-west region of Mexico (see map 3.1).The city is the *cabecera* (municipal seat) of the *municipio* of Guanajuato, which has approximately 140,000 people. Of these, 75,000 reside in the city itself (INEGI XII Censo de Población y Vivienda 2000). Guanajuato is one of the few state capitals in Mexico that is not also the largest and most influential city in the state. Nearby León, with a population of 4 million, is the fifth largest city in Mexico and the seat of economic power (as well as the home of President Vicente Fox and a stronghold of the ruling PAN party). Guanajuato's status as political capital dates from its earlier fame and influence as a center of silver mining.

The Guanajuato mining district is located in the central part of Guanajuato State. It has three systems of mineral deposits: the Veta Madre ("Mother Lode"),

La Luz, and Villapando systems, where the silver, gold, and copper are distributed in veins in a matrix primarily composed of quartz, calcite, and pyrite (Monroy 1888). The ratio of gold to silver in the district is approximately 1:100, although in some mines (such as those of the El Cubo) it reaches 1:10. The Mexican Council on Mineral Resources estimates that from the 1550s to 1990 the district has produced 660 metric tons of gold and 33,469 metric tons of silver (*Consejo de Recursos Minerales* 1992). Six of the seven mines controlled by the Cooperative—El Sirio, San Ignacio, Valenciana, Rayas, Cata, and San Vicente—are located within the Guanajuato mining district on the Veta Madre.[1]

Silver was discovered in Guanajuato in 1548; local legend has it that it was discovered by muleteers on their way back from Zacatecas (Marmolejo 1988 [1886]). However, the scale of exploitation was relatively small until the mid-eighteenth century, when the great bonanza was struck at the Valenciana mine in 1768. This strike transformed the history of the city. The historian David Brading (1971: 261) reports that "at the close of the eighteenth century Guanajuato was the leading producer of silver in the world. Its annual output of over 5 million pesos amounted to one-sixth of all American bullion, gold and silver combined, and equaled the entire production of either viceroyalty of Buenos Aires or Peru."

In the second half of the eighteenth century, then, Guanajuato was the leading silver mining center in Latin America, a position it inherited from the mines of Potosí in colonial Peru (in what is now Bolivia) in the sixteenth and Zacatecas in the sixteenth and early seventeenth centuries (Bakewell 1971, 1984, Brading 1971). A substantial historical literature on gold and silver mining in Latin America during the colonial period has stimulated discussion on a number of topics that shed light on the conditions that produced the mines of the Santa Fe. These topics include the influence of mining on the economic development of regions (Brading 1971, Fisher 1975, Russell-Wood 1984), the comparative uses of forced and free labor in different mining centers (Bakewell 1984, Cole 1985, Tandeter 1993); the part played by ore-shares (*partidos*) as a part of mine workers' wages (Brading 1971, Chávez Orozco 1960, Ladd 1988, Zulawski 1987, Villalba 1999); the role of entrepreneurs and merchants in the development of the silver economies (Hoberman 1991, Brading 1971, Garner 1980); and the effects of state fiscal reforms on the industry (Brading 1971, Tandeter 1993).

These studies provide valuable information on the forces that shaped Guanajuato as a mining center, including the high proportion of free wage workers, the ethnic and cultural mixture among the workforce, the development of a highly complex and interdependent economic system in the surrounding region, and the cultivation of the mining industry by the Spanish state under the period of the Bourbon reforms. As I describe in more detail below [see below,

"The Labor of History"], these influences helped Guanajuato become a highly *mestizo* city, almost completely dependent on mining and related activities.

However, the industry was severely damaged in the War of Independence that began in 1810; the mines were abandoned and allowed to flood (Rankine 1992, Ward 1828: 441). In 1825 the Valenciana mine was purchased by the Anglo-Mexican mining company, who drained the mine and instituted steam power. However, as elsewhere in Mexico, British management proved unequal to the task of raising silver mining to its former glory (Randall 1972). In the case of the Valenciana, the costs of drainage and the absence of new methods for processing ore inhibited production, and the company quietly shut down operations in 1848 (Rankine 1992: 31). The district revived with the bonanza of the mines of nearby La Luz in the 1840s (Blanco, Parra, and Ruiz Medrano 2000: 124, Rankine 1992, Jáuregui 1996, Krantz 1978), and again with the arrival of electric power and cyanide processing to Guanajuato in the first years of the twentieth century (Blanco, Parra, and Ruiz Medrano 2000, Meyer Cosío 1999, Martin 1905).

During the height of the Mexican Revolution the situation of the miners of Guanajuato typified the oppressed and exploited position of Mexican workers in industries dominated by foreign, and especially U.S., capital. During the debates over the drafting of the 1917 Constitution Nicolás Cano, a miner from Guanajuato and delegate to the Constitutional Congress, sketched the plight of the city's miners (Niemeyer 1974: 103, Diario de los Debates, 1:876–878). The "grave decline" in the mining industry, especially in the years 1914–16 at the height of the revolution, further exacerbated miners' desperation (Blanco, Parra, and Ruiz Medrano 2000: 180).

In spite of the example the revolutionaries made of Guanajuato's miners, however, for the most part Guanajuato's mines continued in foreign hands until the mid-1930s. The U.S. mining companies had begun to arrive in the last several years of the nineteenth century, and their presence increased dramatically after the arrival of electricity to Guanajuato in 1904. Between 1897 and 1913 about seventy mining companies operated in Guanajuato, the vast majority U.S.-owned (Meyer Cosío 1999: 101). One of the largest of these companies was the Guanajuato Reduction and Mines Company, founded in Denver, Colorado, in 1904. In the same year "la Reduction Company," as it came to be (and is still) called in Guanajuato, bought the holdings of the Casa Rul, the family that owned Valenciana, Cata, Mellado, and Rayas, as well as a processing plant and numerous buildings and surface holdings (Martin 1905, Meyer Cosío 1999: 150–151). Percy Martin, an observer from the United States who in 1905 wrote *Mexico's Treasure-House*, a book intended to publicize the potential of the mines of Guanajuato, remarked:

Those who trouble to read the following pages will realize why it is that these mines are passing into the hands of Anglo-Saxon capitalists one by one, and how the opportunities that exist today for participating in this attractive enterprise may soon fade away. (1905: 10)

The government of Guanajuato State went out of its way to make these Anglo-Saxon capitalists welcome. In 1905 the Guanajuato Reduction and Mines Company signed an agreement with the state government of Guanajuato allowing it to construct and use railroads, dams, and pipes; to freely use the public lands of the municipality; and to dump residue from the mines and processing plant into the Guanajuato River (Concession from State of Guanajuato to the Guanajuato Reduction and Mines Company; printed in Jáuregui 1985: 149–157). During its tenure from 1905 to 1938, the Reduction Company became one of the most powerful of Guanajuato's mining companies.

The agreement between Guanajuato State and the Reduction Company aptly demonstrates the extent to which the Porfirian government favored foreign investors in mining as in other industries. In the years during and following the Mexican Revolution, state ideology and economic policy moved toward a nationalist stance (Aguilar Camín and Meyer 1993, Carr and Ellner 1993, Knight 1990, R. Bartra 1989). Within this tendency the nationalization and collectivization of resources was a central technique and the domain of subsoil resources a major focus. The expropriation of foreign petroleum companies and the nationalization of the oil industry in 1938 provide the most famous examples of this trend (Brown and Knight 1992, Meyer 1990, Silva Herzog 1963).

At around the same time, in the mid-1930s, serious labor problems began to occur in Guanajuato. This labor unrest formed part of a national trend. Marvin Bernstein writes:

The keynote of [mining] labor relations in the 1930s was the growing belligerency of the Sindicato Industrial de Trabajadores Mineros, Metalúrgicos, y Similares de la República Mexicana. . . . Organized in 1934, it expanded with the Cardenás administration's tacit approval to . . . unite the mine labor movement. The union's attitude kept alive the fear of expropriation in the mineowners' minds. In 1935 and 1936 a wave of strikes hit the mining industry as the union determined to make up the Depression wage losses. (1965: 192)

These strikes formed part of the "syndical explosion" of the 1930s, affecting "railroads, mines and smelters, oil camps and textile factories" (Knight 1990: 13, Hernández Chávez 1979: 140). In the mining industry the economic crisis caused by the Great Depression and the drop in world silver prices encouraged the development of "active embryonic local union organizations in various regions throughout the country" (Aguila 1997: 222). The crisis following 1929 also made mining companies lower or freeze wages and lay off massive numbers of miners, promoting further upheaval. In Guanajuato a series of mining and other strikes exploded after the formation of the national syndicate. A citywide electricity strike caused further crises in the mining industry, and the mine owners petitioned the federal government to order an end to the strike so as to keep the mines working.

On November 17, 1935, the workers of the North American Guanajuato Reduction and Mines Company went on strike. They demanded that the company pay higher wages, resume exploitation at the Valenciana mine, and sign a collective bargaining agreement (Rivera Rodríguez 1992: 42). On February 17 approximately six hundred miners marched in a "Hunger Caravan" (*Caravana de Hambre*) from Guanajuato to the National Palace in Mexico City to appeal for aid from the federal government in resolving the conflict. A letter to President Cárdenas from Section 4 of the Miners' Union states that

[the protestors hoped] in this way to resolve as quickly as possible this conflict . . . and to prevent this company from making a mockery of our legendary hospitality and of our laws. So that they will see that we are not those "peones" that they were used to dealing with thirty years ago [before the Revolution of 1910, that is]. (AGN fondo Lázaro Cárdenas 523.6/15)

The national office of the PNR (what is now the PRI) and the Miners' Syndicate paid for the support of these miners during the month they stayed in the capital (Letter from Sindicato de Trabajadores Mineros, Metalúrgicos y Similares de la República Mexicana April 11, 1936, AGN fondo Lázaro Cárdenas 434.1/211)). One founding member recounted:

In that time, the union was very strong—not any more, now they're a bunch of drunks. When we went to Mexico [City], it took us thirteen days to walk there. Lots of people asked us who we were and we said, "Well, we're miners." Lots didn't know what mining was. They gave us food along the way, and the union gave us a peso a day while we were on strike.

Another told me, on a lighter note:

They gave us a dinner one night while we were in Mexico to honor us for the Caravan. We all ate a lot because we had been walking so far—and that night, wow! We were up all night, grabbing our stomachs and taking turns at the toilet.

The Caravana de Hambre received national attention, and letters poured in to the Office of the Presidency from union locals from all over the country, calling the Reduction Company and its director Augustus McDonald, "hypocrite YANKEE [capitals in the original]," "raptor," "giant octopus," "butcher's dog," and other uncomplimentary names. These letters seem to draw on a powerful language of nationalism to portray the Reduction workers as emblematic of all Mexicans exploited by the United States.

The strike lasted until April 1936, when the company finally gave in to many of the miners' demands (although they did not resume work at the Valenciana but continued only to work over the already extracted ore). But another strike broke out in 1938; this time the Reduction Company preferred to abandon its place in Guanajuato, leaving the mines and other holdings—and a debt of twenty-five thousand pesos—with the workers of section 4 of the syndicate (Jáuregui 1985, Sariego et al. 1988). In the words of one founding Cooperative member, "We are the owners now. McDonald said to us, 'Boys, since we can't make a living [indemnizar], we're going to leave you the mines.'" Another, the son of a founding member, told me: "The Reduction company left all its mines and lands as an inheritance [to the workers]—almost the whole of Guanajuato. There were the absolute owners. But they were ignorant miners and they kept selling everything off."

In June 1939 this section reorganized as a producers' cooperative. In doing so they joined a national cooperative movement that took off in the late 1930s.

Mexican Producers' Cooperatives

The producers' cooperative movement in Mexico formed part of an international movement originally founded on the principles of utopian socialists such as Charles Fourier and Robert Owen. Although cooperative societies in some form were founded in Europe as early as the 1790s (Hacker 1989: 77), the originary point for modern cooperatives is often taken to be the Rochdale, England, weavers' cooperative in 1844 (Fox 1920, Thornley 1981, Birchall 1994). The Rochdale cooperative was primarily a consumers' cooperative, but its principles, including democratic organization and the division of profits among the workforce, were taken as the basis of producers' *and* consumers' cooperative charters in many countries, including England, France, the United States, and Mexico (Birchall 1994, Cano Jáuregui 1986, Shaffer 1999).

Cooperatives were intended to mitigate the worst effects of capitalism by ensuring that workers received the full value of their labor. As June Nash and Nicholas Hopkins have argued, "Accepting the free market as a base for economic organization, [cooperatives] worked toward limiting the control of capitalist institutions by providing islands of autonomous production and distribution" (1976: 16). In many contexts cooperatives have been seen as a "third way" between state-sponsored socialism and capitalism (Hacker 1989: 87). As Gabriela Vargas points out, from their formation in Europe at the end of the eighteenth and beginning of the nineteenth centuries they functioned as a way to preserve older forms of guild membership and labor systems under another name (Vargas 2000: 148). Rosendo Rojas Coria, the author of a comprehensive history of cooperatives in Mexico published in 1952, places twentieth-century Mexican cooperatives within a venerable history that included Aztec communal lands (*calpulli*), guilds, charities, and mutual aid societies (Rojas Coria 1952: 32–41, 75–93). While this is perhaps an exaggeration (with a dose of romanticism), certainly many founders and supporters of Mexican cooperatives represented their organizations as part of an indigenous tradition of communal property.

The cooperative movement, as interpreted in Mexico in the 1920s and 1930s, drew on socialist theories of alienation for its justification. Within this conceptualization, producers' cooperatives were supposed to unite the capitalist and the worker in one person, so that the entire value of members' labor would be returned to them. At the same time, since the aim of the cooperative was not to produce more and more capital but to meet the individual and social needs of its members, cooperatives would help to keep the price of commodities low. Consumers would also be organized into cooperatives to keep prices lower still.

Cárdenas's agenda included the formation of both producers' and consumers' cooperatives in the Six-Year Plan presented when he came to power in 1936 (Cárdenas 1986 [1934], *Cooperativismo Integral,* no. 1 [February 15, 1936]). Within the plan, producers' cooperatives formed part of a general Cardenista attempt to reduce Mexican dependence on foreign investment.[2] However, the expansion of the cooperative movement did not gather speed till the latter half of his administration, following the passage of the new Law of Cooperatives in 1938. According to the records of the now defunct Dirección General de Fomento Cooperativo, in 1938, 34 producers' cooperatives and 9 consumers' cooperatives were established. In the following two years the last two of Cárdenas' *sexenio* (six-year term), 492 and 460 producers' cooperatives and 330 and 202 consumers' cooperatives were formed. By 1941 the number had dropped to 230 producers' cooperatives and 69 consumers' cooperatives (printed in Jaramillo Machinandiarena 1982: 150).

The rise in cooperatives, particularly producers' cooperatives, was connected to the rise in strikes and labor unrest. In many cases producers' cooperatives (especially those engaged in industrial production) consisted of the former workers and holdings of companies against whom the Cardenista government had ruled in labor disputes. Unable to meet the demands of the government, these companies chose to leave their capital and infrastructure as indemnification of their debts. Such was the case regarding the Santa Fe Cooperative.

Although they had the official support of the government and ruling party, producers' cooperatives came in for a fair amount of criticism. Unions in particular tended to be suspicious of industrial producers' cooperatives (Rojas Coria 1952: 374). Writing in 1936, Joaquín Ramírez Cabañez criticized unions that "rudely combat or turn their back on cooperatives with indifference" (97). In part this distrust of producers' cooperatives came from the fact that, as worker/owners, Cooperative members straddled the divide between worker and capitalist. Some union members tended to think of these Cooperative members as incipient capitalists rather as workers and to resent them as traitors to the class struggle. They pointed to instances when cooperatives functioned almost entirely as capitalist enterprises and characterized them as *sindicatos blancos* ("sweetheart unions").

Reservations such as these did not prevent new cooperatives from forming each year. By 1975, 2,786 producers' cooperatives were in existence, with a total of 142,600 members (Jaramillo Machinandiarena 1982: 148). Some of this tension persists today between the miners' union and the Santa Fe Cooperative. Members of the union described the Cooperative to me as having betrayed the workers' movement or as being "in league with the state" (*ellos son más del estado*), while Cooperative members made more ad hominem remarks about the union officials.[3]

This tension between producers' cooperatives and other segments of the industrial working class, especially unions, is consistent with at least some cooperatives in other nations. Sharryn Kasmir, who has studied the much-vaunted Mondragón cooperatives in the Basque country, concludes her book by saying, "a central finding . . . has been that cooperatives can divide working classes" (Kasmir 1996: 198). She relates this conclusion to the experience of early cooperatives, such as those founded by Robert Owen in northern England (23). Nash and Hopkins point out that, even when cooperatives grow out of existing communitarian systems, "the traditional social structures are often authoritarian, particularly within the family. . . . Under such conditions, the community will either reject a cooperative because it threatens its own kind of egalitarianism, or the cooperative will simply reinforce and accentuate the inequalities (between old and young, between men and women, etc.) already present in that community" (1976: 13). This latter possibility captures at least part of the experience of the Santa Fe Cooperative.

Mining cooperatives were not the most common type of producers' cooperatives (these were forestry, manufacturing, and fishing cooperatives, respectively), although a sizable number of mining cooperatives were formed. Of the 4,928 producers' cooperatives established between 1938 and 1976, 222 were occupied in the extractive industry sector, many of which were probably engaged in some kind of mining.[4] Many of these mining cooperatives were, like the Santa Fe, located in the center of Mexico (rather than in the north) on the sites of former colonial mines that continued to employ large numbers of people while producing less than the more recently founded northern mines (Aguila 1997: 135–136). Since they were less economically viable, these mines were more likely to be turned over to the workers in the event of labor conflict (Sariego et al. 1988: 154–155, Rojas Coria 1952: 410).

The producers' cooperative movement and the mining cooperatives in particular represent one attempted solution to worker exploitation and Mexico's dependence on foreign capital. Founded on socialist principles by way of nineteenth-century English utopianism, the movement's objectives were at least somewhat consistent with those of the postrevolutionary state. For this reason it is not surprising that the years when more cooperatives were formed coincided with the two high points of Mexican postrevolutionary nationalism: the Cardenista period and the years immediately following it; and the administration of Luis Echeverría (1970–76), when the federal government tried to use nationalist ideology and policy to reconsolidate state power and legitimacy after the 1968 student movement and massacre at Tlatelolco (Jaramillo Machinandiarena 1982: 150).

OTHER MINING COMPANIES IN THE GUANAJUATO MINING DISTRICT
A comparative look at the Cooperative and the other mining companies in Guanajuato gives us a sense of how organization as a producers' cooperative works out in practice. The Santa Fe is one of three major mining enterprises in Guanajuato.[5] The other two are la Compañia Minera del El Cubo and Peñoles Grupo Guanajuato. The El Cubo company was founded in 1921 as a foreign-owned enterprise; it came under Mexican control in 1973. It exploits the El Cubo mine, which was discovered in 1700 and which is located some 30 kilo-

meters to the northeast of the city of Guanajuato. In 1997 El Cubo reported that it produces approximately 650 metric tons of ore-producing rock per day from its mine (brochure, La Compañia Minera El Cubo). It produces the largest quantity of gold in the Guanajuato district with a grade of 8–14 grams of gold per metric ton and approximately 200 grams of silver per metric ton (Arvizu Flores 1997: 83–84).

When I went down in the El Cubo mine, the engineer showed me many new projects that were being carried out, including cement floors at every second level under exploitation. According to the union local president, "There used to be a lot of deaths in El Cubo, but now the only accidents are on account of stupidity. The rock there is very hard, so there are no cave-ins, nothing like that, the mine now is really nice [bonita; see chapter 5]. The veins are old, but they're good."

Profits from the high price of gold at that time allowed El Cubo to carry out these projects. At that time the company employed approximately 150 workers who are members of Section 142 of the national miners' syndicate. The union local reported that El Cubo is gradually phasing in temporary contract workers as union members retire, and this was confirmed by Engineer Eduardo García during my trip to the mine. At the same time, according to the union's local president,

> [El Cubo's superintendent Rodríguez] is very concerned about the ghost towns [in the area] like Rosa de Castillo and Monte de San Nicolás. . . . He doesn't want them to lose their population, so he gives jobs to the older people doing other things, for instance he has planted thousands and thousands of trees—if you go see the trees growing, it's very pretty.

These actions are consistent with a certain community spirit that seems to prevail in El Cubo, making it in some respects similar to the Santa Fe Cooperative. In other ways, especially union-management relations and attention to health and safety equipment and regulations, it has more in common with Peñoles. In 2003, during my most recent visit to Guanajuato, I heard that El Cubo had almost closed operations but had committed to continuing for another year.

Peñoles Grupo Guanajuato is the local branch of Peñoles, Mexico's second largest mining corporation; it began its work in the southernmost part of the Veta Madre in 1968 and soon found rich deposits in the mine of Cedros. Currently the company exploits three mines on the Veta Madre—Las Torres/Cedros, Cebada, and Peregrina. In addition, Peñoles sends teams of contracted labor (contratistas) into smaller mines in the southern area of the Veta Madre and in the La Luz system (Bolañitos, Golondrinas, Santa Rosa [not the same as the town of Santa Rosa de Lima]). In 1997 the company reported mineral grades of 1.98–2.20 grams of gold and approximately 200 grams of silver per metric ton.[6] It produced approximately 2,100 metric tons per day (Arvizu Flores 1997: 88).

Peñoles employs approximately six hundred workers of whom about half have permanent positions and union representation. The rest work on temporary work contracts, although they receive social security benefits for the duration of their contract, and if they work more than a few months during the year they are entitled to a share in the yearly profits under Mexican law. Peñoles has been aggressively pursuing a labor-management policy of "*Calidad Integral*" (Total Quality Management) to improve productivity and competitiveness in the uncertain silver market. *Calidad Integral* is an intiative Peñoles is promoting in all its Mexican holdings; in 1993 Grupo Guanajuato was awarded the Second *Premio de Calidad Integral Peñoles* (Peñoles Total Quality Prize) (*Peñoles* 5, no. 5 [June 1993]). The Peñoles beneficiation plant at Las Torres outside Guanajuato is adorned with posters and signs proclaiming *Calidad Integral* and even some Japanese words painted on the walls for the edification of the workforce. As in other places, *Calidad Integral* in Peñoles Grupo Guanajuato goes hand in hand with the increasing use of temporary workers, outsourcing, and the declining strength of the union. The Cooperative functions according to markedly different policies than those that operate in these mining companies (especially in Peñoles). Cooperative leaders, members, and outsiders are keenly aware of these differences and have sharply different opinions about them. As I was told by one Cooperative member, who lives in the town of Santana that supplies members to the Cooperative and is also a worker in the mines of Peñoles:

> Las Torres [the local name for Peñoles] pays better than the Cooperative, but the work is very hard, they have another manner of working there, to take out the mineral as quickly as possible. In the Cooperative the goal is to maintain the source of jobs.

A miner in the Cooperative mine of San Ignacio told me that:

> Some of the guys around here work for Las Torres, in one way it's better, because they make more money, but they work twelve hours a day. They go in at seven and come out at seven, the whole week they never see the sun.

Miners in Guanajuato often move between these mining companies, according to their particular tastes and life situations. Younger men with fewer responsibilities may welcome contract work at either El Cubo or Las Torres, where they can make more money but are not given health benefits or other forms of security. Men also sometimes choose to go to the north of Mexico (Coahuila, Durango, or Chihuahua) to work on three-month contracts. The recruiting office for these mines is on the outskirts of Guanajuato near the bus station. A number of men who have had problems with the Cooperative leadership or who lost their jobs at Las Torres or El Cubo have taken this option.

In September 2003 Peñoles closed down in Guanajuato mines, citing low productivity. In early 2004 the Canadian company Mexgold acquired the holdings of the El Cubo Company for U.S.$13.5 million and the assumption of U.S.$7 million in long-term debt. In October 2004, as this book was going to press, Mexgold also bought the Peñoles holdings. Meanwhile, the Cooperative continues to operate, having sold the rights to exploit the mine of San Anton to the Mexican company Luismín for U.S.$900,000, and having discovered a new vein of gold ("Las Dudas Mineras" A.M. Guanajuato, June 27, 2004).

Views of the Cooperative

Unlike Peñoles and El Cubo which have shareholders from Mexico, Canada, and South Africa, the Cooperative has no outside investment whatsoever. This means, some Cooperative members observe, that the money made in the Cooperative stays in Guanajuato. The engineer in charge of the Valenciana once said to me: "If I want to eat in a restaurant, I eat in Guanajuato. If I get my shoes shined, I do it in the Jardín de la Unión. It is the same with the Cooperative. The money we make stays in Guanajuato." By emphasizing how the Cooperative's profits remain at home, this engineer draws on an understanding of Cooperative patrimony as rooted in place. Within this formulation, silver leaves Guanajuato for sale on the world market but returns to Guanajuato in the form of money that can later rematerialize as houses, churches, and other patrimonial substances (see chapter 7).

Members of the Cooperative also point out that working in the Cooperative keeps men from migrating. In a speech in San Antón de la Minas, Martín exhorted his audience:

> Mexico has a young labor force [*pura mano de obra joven*], they shouldn't go to the other side [the United States], we just need to work with a bit of quality [*calidad*]. . . . What does it mean to be in a Cooperative? It means to be owners, to be bosses. If something is yours you have to take care of it, work well, with quality [*con calidad*] and lower costs. That way you can

leave it to your sons, your grandsons, so that they don't have to go to the other side [the United States], they can stay here in Mexico.

This speech proffers a vision of the Cooperative as the last stand against the corrupting forces of migration, suggesting once again that the Cooperative promotes being rooted in place even as it produces for global circulation.

From this perspective the Cooperative stands in contrast to the other mining companies that hire short-term contract workers and thus do not provide a stable alternative to migration, and, in any case, often hire workers from outside Guanajuato. One worker in the San Ignacio mine near the town of La Luz said of the other, non-Cooperative mines nearby, "They're just kids [*pura muchachada*] that work there, and from outside, from Jalisco and Michoacán. Everybody here is from here in Guanajuato." Statements like these depict the Cooperative as a bastion of Guanajuatanness and Mexicanness in a landscape of national and regional betrayal and degeneration.

So far, these images of the Cooperative are proud and positive but by no means are they the only ones presented. Clearly negative characterizations of the Cooperative are at least partly tied to its fortunes. In 1984 the governor of Guanajuato State formally recognized the Cooperative's success at contributing to the "elevation of [the] standard of living of its members," through profit shares equivalent to nine and a half months of salary, and offering support for health, education, and housing. The newspaper article reporting this acknowledgment included a photo of the Cooperative supermarket's shelves fully stocked with food (Contacto, February 18, 1984). Now the Cooperative only gives approximately one to two months salary as profit shares. Alicia, who works at the Bocamina, once said to me, "Ten years ago, when someone asked where you worked, you said 'In the Cooperative!' with pride. Now people just say 'I work in a mining company.'"

Some characterize the Cooperative as generally corrupt and riven with economic and political inequalities. Many Cooperative workers (especially but not exclusively miners) say that the Cooperative leaders are stealing Cooperative patrimony for their own personal use. Others point the finger at the accounting department or cliques of surface workers (often from long-standing Cooperative families). Outside observers of the Cooperative also often depict it as politically corrupt. The Cooperative has an abiding connection to local structures of the PRI; the former director was municipal president on two different occasions in the 1980s (1980–82 and 1986–88); and Jesús Castillo, the president of the administrative council during the time of my fieldwork, is a PRI regidor (city councilor). Many people refer to the Cooperative as a political trampoline for the PRI. As part of this characterization, the Cooperative is seen to suffer from the same ills as Mexico's ruling political party, such as anachronism, corruption, loss of legitimacy, and so on. This happens within as well as outside the Cooperative. For instance, miners sometimes call surface workers "*dinosaurios*" (to emphasize their lumbering anachronism), borrowing the word from internal and external critics of the PRI. However, the PRI itself has lost power and legitimacy in Guanajuato, as in other places. The Cooperative continues, no doubt, to extract some benefits from its municipal ties to the PRI, but these have greatly diminished in recent years.[7]

Finally, Cooperative insiders and outsiders describe the Cooperative as promoting inefficiency, waste, and complacency among workers. These people compare the Cooperative unfavorably with other mining companies which they describe as more "*norteamericano*" (North American, that is, more like the United States) and thus supposedly both more efficient and possessing a greater work ethic. Within the Cooperative the criticism of laziness is sometimes aimed at specific groups of workers, such as surface workers, miners, hospital personnel, or office people (accountants, secretaries, administrators, and so forth). Miners, for example, often say of surface workers, "They're a bunch of lazy bums [*son unos huevones*]." Chano (see Chapter 2) characterized these disputes well, saying:

> It's true that it's very different working in the mine than working outside and working in the mine is very risky in many ways. And it's true that they should earn more than those who [come] from outside, they earn very little. But it's not true what they say in the mine, that all the ones from above are *huevones* and don't do anything, it's not true. Everybody has his place, there is work below and work above.

Those who criticize the Cooperative, its membership, or particular groups of members sometimes associate these with negative aspects of Mexico as a whole. One Cooperative engineer told me, "It is very good that you are studying the Cooperative. Because everything you find that is wrong with the Cooperative, that's what's wrong with Mexico." This is the flip side of the positive associations of the Cooperative as *muy mexicano*. Instead of the Cooperative appearing as a noble holdout in the face of degenerate forces, it appears as an emblem of Mexican primitivism surrounded by modern, rational enterprises.

To sum up, these characterizations of the Cooperative portray it as familial, paternalist, quintessentially Mexican, rooted in place, and committed to the prosperity of Guanajuato and its citizenry, but also as corrupt, clientelistic, lazy, backward, and wasteful. These opinions vary dramatically, but they all address two basic questions: What are the proper obligations of the Cooperative toward its members, and vice versa? And what are the proper ways in which Cooperative, national, or global patrimony can turn into family patrimony? Furthermore, these questions are precisely those that suffuse debates over political and economic change in Mexico. Thus, by arguing over the proper distribution and consumption of resources, Cooperative leaders (jefes), members, and their families also argue over what Mexico has and should become. In these debates people hold sharply differing opinions, but they are all likely to express them in terms of family, gender, generativity, labor and place, concepts that are condensed into the idiom of patrimony.

The Santa Fe's status as a producers' cooperative, its differences from the other mining companies in the district, and its image in the eyes of members and observers have informed local uses of languages of patrimony in vital ways. The Cooperative's formative principles, based on the juridical category of national patrimony and divorced from other forms of class-based politics (such as those operative in labor unions), have helped to condition among Cooperative members a powerful sense of belonging premised on mutual claims to inalienable resources and drawing on a notion of the collectivity as a patrilineally organized kin group. The status of the subsoil resources as patrimonio nacional encourages an analogy between the Cooperative and the national collective, whose members also define themselves in terms of their mutual claims to inalienable resources. Finally, the ever-present examples of El Cubo and Peñoles with their fundamentally different objectives and organizing principles serve to underscore the Cooperative's distinctiveness.

In addition to these aspects of the Cooperative's organization, that the Cooperative controls some of Mexico's most famous mines and that it draws on labor traditions deemed central to Guanajuatense and abajeño historical consciousness also inform local uses of patrimony. The next section examines the conditions under which these forms of historical consciousness have developed.

THE LABOR OF HISTORY

Unlike many of the cities in that region classically defined by archaeologists and ethnologists as Mesoamerica, Guanajuato (located slightly north of the boundaries of Mesoamerica, at least as traditionally defined [Kirchhoff 1966]) was not a pre-Columbian settlement. It exists because of the discovery of silver in the sixteenth century, and the bonanzas along the *Veta Madre* and in the La Luz mining district in the eighteenth and nineteenth centuries, respectively. While not all Guanajuato's fame and prosperity came directly from mining, the mines formed a nerve center of an economic system that was nearly unique in Spanish America and that laid the foundation for its importance in the colonies and for the distinctive historical consciousness still evident among its citizens. By tracing histories of Guanajuato as a city and the Bajío as a region whose economy has been driven by silver mining, I hope to give a sense of the underpinnings of this historical consciousness.

The city of Guanajuato is located in the southern region of the large territory formerly (before the arrival of the Spanish) covered by a number of nomadic and seminomadic groups including Pame, Guachichile, and Guamare, disparagingly called "Chichimec" (roughly translated as "uncivilized dog") by groups to the south (Jiménez Moreno 1988: 35–43, Powell 1952: 33). The Spanish adopted this term, and the area north of the Lerma River Valley came to be known in the colonial period as *el gran Chichimeca.*

This region proved to be one of the most difficult parts of Spanish America to conquer because of the sparseness and mobility of its populations. The so-called Chichimec War lasted from approximately 1550 to 1600, and strongly influenced settlement and labor patterns in the northern part of New Spain. The area was dotted with Spanish garrison towns (*presidios*), mostly to insure the safe transport of silver from the mines of Zacatecas, where silver was discovered in the 1550s, (and to a lesser extent, Guanajuato) and missions until the later seventeenth century (Bakewell 1971, Jiménez Moreno 1988, Powell 1952). The Mexico-Zacatecas highway (also called the Camino Real or King's road), which passed near Guanajuato, was the major thoroughfare during this time.[8]

Until the mid-seventeenth century indigenous laborers were brought to the mines by means of the *repartimiento* (a system of forced labor recruitment) (Blanco, Parra, and Ruiz Medrano 2000, 65). However, as time went on, an increasingly high proportion of laborers worked for wages (and for a share of ore known as the *partido*) rather than as enslaved or indentured servants. Wages and, in particular, the *partido* were comparatively high for New Spain.[9]

Those indigenous people who migrated to Guanajuato tended to lose their connections to their natal communities, and to learn Spanish and adopt other practices associated with mestizo culture relatively rapidly. For this reason most Guanajuatenses, including Cooperative members, identify themselves as mestizo rather than indigenous. The city and region became one of the first centers of the process of ethnic and cultural mixture, leading to a separate ethnocultural category, "mestizo," and several commentators have linked this to its role in the War of Independence and the foundation of Mexico as a sovereign nation. Eric Wolf, for instance, writes:

> The Bajío and its rim were . . . not only the scene of relatively intense capitalist development, but also a hearth of cultural change leading to the formation of new sociocultural groups. . . . Mine, hacienda and industry served to divorce people from their corporatively organized villages and integrated them instead into groups of economic specialists. (1955: 190)

These changes, Wolf points out, were largely brought about by the necessity of workers to consume products such as food and clothing purchased at the company store (*tienda de raya*) rather than produced within the household or village. As I show in chapter 6, consumption practices among today's Cooperative members have a similar effect.

The city and its mines were served by an extensive complex of haciendas and farms just to the south in the Bajío region. These producers supplied foodstuffs and leather for the mines and surrounding populations (Brading 1971, Guevara 2001, Wolf 1955). David Brading states that,

> By the eighteenth century . . . the Bajío had come to form a prosperous intermediary zone quite distinct from either the vacant ranges and scattered mine camps of the north or the central valleys with their blend of Indian communities and latifundia. In the first place, its population was both heavily and mainly mestizo. Moreover its towns were industrial: Querétaro and San Miguel el Grande [today San Miguel de Allende] were New Spain's leading centers for the manufacture of woollen textiles; Celaya and Salamanca wove cotton; León made leather goods; and Guanajuato had become the chief silver producer in all Mexico. Then again, with such an extensive town market to supply, the region's agriculture greatly prospered. It was precisely this combination of urbanisation, textiles, mining, and agriculture which made the Bajío an area exceptional not merely in Mexico but in all Spanish America. (1971: 224)

Ángel Palerm (1980) called this complex and prosperous system that grew up around the mines of Guanajuato in the eighteenth century "the first world economic system."

Many of the mine workers in Guanajuato city were indigenous people displaced from lands further to the south, especially Purepecha, Tarascan, and Otomí, along with some of African, European, and mixed African-European ancestry (Brading 1971). This produced, in the words of María Guevara,

> in the degree to which the indigenous people were seminomadic or immigrants from below the Lerma or Anáhuac rivers, dislocated from their

communities; to which the Spaniards tried to avoid the pressure of the centralized imperial State; to which, although dispersed and not very numerous, Africans participated centrally in production and culture, it was a society constructed as something new. (2001: 170)

In addition, settlement patterns in Guanajuato city in the eighteenth century did not conform to the segregationist policies of the colonial government. For this reason, indigenous, African, and European people were brought into proximity in neighborhoods as well as in their places of work (Guevara 2001). In the words of Eric Wolf, the "cultural integration" brought about as a result of the particular form of economic development in the region led to new forms of political consciousness that culminated in the movement for independence from Spain in 1810 (Wolf 1955). This analysis, still convincing to most observers, also plays into the intense regionalism in the Bajío.

Luis González (1988, 89), one of the most important historians of the region, states that, "from the tenderest infancy, we Mexicans are told and told again of the deeds of the conspirators for independence in Guadalajara, Valladolid and Querétaro. Father Hidalgo's *grito* in the town of Dolores is a commonplace in national history [literally, 'history of bronze,' in reference to the mestizo as national protagonist]."

The Bajío's place in national history and its moniker, "cradle of the Mexican nation," derives from the fact that the movement for independence from Spain, led by a group of *criollos,* began in the towns of the Bajío. The *grito* (the cry for independence that signaled the beginning of the insurrection) was sounded by Father Miguel Hidalgo in the town of Dolores (now Dolores Hidalgo) on September 15, 1810. The Spaniards' first major defeat was in Guanajuato city on September 28, when the revolutionaries stormed the public granary (*alhóndiga*) where the Spaniards had garrisoned themselves. The miners played an important role in this battle; a mine worker from the Valenciana known as "El Pípila" is said to have been the first to break through the Alhóndiga's massive doors.[10] The link between mining and the cultural formations that led to the War of Independence was aptly described by one Cooperative member, an accountant: "Guanajuato exists because of mining. Wealth was discovered here in this region, and because of this there came to be cultured people here who read about the beliefs of others [*otras doctrinas*], and from that came independence."

The unique form of economic development in the Bajío, with the mines of Guanajuato as the center and driving force, as well as the pivotal role played by the region and the city in the War of Independence, have given a particular flavor to Mexican Bajío regionalism and to Mexican nationalism in the Bajío. This narrative, which traces the birthplace of the nation to the War of Independence and locates it in the Bajío, stands in contrast to and tension with narratives that trace the birth of the postrevolutionary state to the Mexican Revolution and locate its power in the capital, Mexico City. These tensions sharpened in the 1920s, when the emerging national state came into conflict with landed elites and popular classes in the Bajío over land reform and anti-clericalism. The Bajío's intense Catholic devotionalism gave form to these conflicts, which came to be known as the Cristero War after the *cristeros*, those counterrevolutionaries opposed to the antagonism of President Calles's government toward religion (J. Meyer 1976, Blanco, Parra, and Ruiz Medrano 2000).

Integral to a sense of Guanajuato as a city whose exceptional qualities helped to form the Mexican nation is the idea that the city owes its existence to mining. A quotation from the German mining expert and naturalist Alexander von Humboldt (1811: 171), who visited Guanajuato in 1803 and spent a month in its mines, epitomizes this sense: "One is astonished to see in this wild spot large and beautiful edifices in the midst of miserable Indian huts. The house of Colonel Don Diego Rul who is one of the proprietors of the mine of Valenciana, would be an ornament on the finest streets of Paris or Naples."

This feeling of the grace and civility infused in the built environment of the city by means of the riches emerging from the mines continues to inform the sense Guanajuatenses have of their city today, as an elegant enclave of world-class baroque architecture that nonetheless owes its beauty and distinctiveness to the extraction of silver from the local mines. Inhabitants describe Guanajuato as a city "born of silver," a phrase that emphasizes both the causal connection between the mines and the city and the generative quality of the mines and the earthy, muddy ore that is taken from them. They also often describe the physical structures of the city as being made of silver, emphasizing that the roads and walls of churches, plazas, and houses have a high silver content since they were mined in the area. As one Guanajuatense said to me, "When you walk on the roads, you are walking on silver."[11]

Guanajuato's citizens demonstrate a strong sense of place based on the practices associated with mining, the local landscape, and the built environment. In recent years the walls, churches, plazas, and mines, built as a result of mineral extraction, have themselves become a source of wealth, as Guanajuato moves from a city dominated by the mining industry to one oriented toward tourism. This shift gives rise to new implications of a language of patrimony, now expanded to include "patrimonio histórico" as embodied in the city's industrial, religious, and civic architecture.

CHAPTER 4

Recent Challenges and Responses

[Guanajuato's] historical patrimony is a vein for tourism.
—Headline in *El Nacional,* November 1996

In this book I argue that members of the Santa Fe Cooperative produce and negotiate a language of patrimony that helps them to confront the political and economic challenges they face. This language, a local version of a powerful national idiom (see chapter 8), posits patrimony as a category that includes the products of the mines, the mines themselves, and Cooperative jobs. Current Cooperative members have received these possessions from past generations and have a responsibility to pass them on to their children and grandchildren.

However, the value of all these ideally inalienable possessions depends on the actual alienability of one of them: silver. If silver cannot be exchanged, the mines lose their value and the jobs disappear. But the more that silver is exchanged, the more the mines are exhausted and the jobs become superfluous and ineffective. As one engineer put it: "It's not like a seed you put in the ground that grows many times, when it runs out there's no more—and we know that it will run out one day, we have to recognize that."

This book examines the conceptual and practical strategies Cooperative members and their families use to negotiate this predicament. In this chapter I focus on the increasing challenges posed by the fall of the price of silver, the decreasing outputs of the mines and economic and political restructuring in Mexico, and on the ways Cooperative members attempt to meet these challenges. These efforts are framed by debates over the responsibility of the enterprise to its members and vice versa, the legitimate boundaries of the Cooperative as collectivity, and the proper mode of valuing resources. As a background to this discussion, I briefly trace the fortunes of the Cooperative since its formation in 1939 to the mid-1990s.

Some founding members of the Cooperative recall the spirit of cooperation of the enterprise's first years. One told me, "We called it a cooperative, because everybody cooperated." Another said:

> The company did not want problems with the workers, so they said, here are the properties. The directors at that time [when the Cooperative was starting out] were young men. We began to work right away as a Cooperative, without pay, to build up capital. But in approximately a month already we were getting the same wages that the company had been paying.

However, at times in these early years the Cooperative administration was reduced to paying wages in *bonos* (or IOUs for future cash payment); former workers tell how a local merchant known as El Caporal (the Chief) became rich redeeming these certificates at half their face value. Cooperative workers also faced competition from *buscones* (underground prospectors) who entered the mines without permission and sold the ore to clandestine buyers. On August 26, 1939, the Cooperative appealed to the federal government for help in this conflict (letter from Catarino Castillo, director of the Cooperative, to President Lázaro Cárdenas, AGN fondo Lázaro Cárdenas 432.1/93).

By the mid-1940s the Cooperative administration had run the business into the ground and was again forced to ask for help from the Ministry for Nonrenewable Resources. In 1947 the federal government authorized a loan of five hundred thousand pesos to help build a flotation processing plant at the Hacienda de Bustos, nearer to the most productive mines, and appointed an engineer from Non-Renewable Resources to administer the Cooperative (Buchanan 1964, Jáuregui 1985: 89–90). This engineer, Alfred Terrazas Vega, ran the Cooperative until his retirement in 1972, when he was succeeded by Engineer Edgardo Meave Torrescano.

The 1970s and 1980s were good years for the Santa Fe. In the mid-1970s ore exploitation in Rayas reached an extraordinarily rich section of the Veta Madre called the Clavo de Rayas; this bed yielded exceptionally rich ore for more than ten years. Some of the ore extracted from the Clavo de Rayas was of such high grade that the Cooperative sent it directly to the foundry in San Luis Potosí (normally ore needs to be concentrated first in order to make transporting it cost-efficient) (interview with Meave Pérez [the son of Meave Torrescano], August 9, 1999). Furthermore, the years of the Clavo de Rayas coincided with the greatest event in the world silver market of the last hundred years: the attempt by the Hunt brothers of Texas to corner the market, which drove the price of silver as high as fifty dollars in 1980 (J. Williams 1985).

One former Cooperative member described this period to me:

> Before the crisis in mining, in 1991–92, when the price of silver fell, the Cooperative gave really good profits to its members, at Holy Week, in May, on the Día del Minero [July 11], el grito [September 15], and the Christmas bonus—almost the whole year there were payments from the profits, but suddenly [in 1991] they said there was no more money, so lots of people left the Cooperative. In that time the people suffered greatly.

In the early 1990s the price of silver fell precipitously, to a yearly average of $4.82 in 1990, $4.04 in 1991, and $3.93 in 1992 (Silver Institute 1998). Furthermore, the Clavo de Rayas was exhausted. Meave Torrescano was able to arrange for considerable support and protection for the Cooperative from his civic connections (he was mayor of Guanajuato for the PRI in 1980–82 and in 1986–88). But eventually debts with the electric company (CFE) and other creditors caught up with the Cooperative, and an intense financial and political crisis broke out at the end of 1991. The Cooperative suspended wages (anticípos) during Christmas week, and the newspapers predicted its imminent bankruptcy. Workers marched to the State Auditorium on the outskirts of the city for a public meeting with the governor (Carlos Medina Placencia), who, according to rumor, hoped to privatize the Cooperative for his own benefit. Somewhat miraculously, the Cooperative kept going.

In the summer of 1992 the administrative council, led by Meave Torrescano, was voted out and Meave Torrescano, his son Meave Pérez, and his supporters left the Cooperative.[1] A new administrative council, led by Engineer Jesús Castillo, took control, and the state government of Guanajuato arranged a loan for the Cooperative that helped it to avoid bankruptcy. The Cooperative was aided by a moderate rise in silver prices in the mid-1990s as well as the devaluation of the peso in 1994, which helped those industries, such as mining, that paid costs in pesos but sold their product in dollars.

By the 1990s, however, the conditions under which the Cooperative was founded at the height of the 1930s had changed radically. One feature of this change has been the reduction in the authority of central state agencies over the economy, and (for our purposes) particularly over cooperatives. As one engineer put it, "the government no longer hangs out with cooperatives [ya no anda con cooperativas]." In 1994 the new Cooperative law in Mexico abolished all governmental agencies specifically related to cooperatives and turned over their supervision to the Secretary for Economic, Commercial, and Industrial Development (SECOFI). According to the lawyer for the Santa Fe Cooperative, the tax breaks, training and educational opportunities, and generous loans available for cooperatives in years past have been reduced to a slight advantage in social security payments. The withdrawal of state support has not been total: the state government of Guanajuato brokered a loan for the Cooperative in 1992, which allowed it to overcome a severe financial and political crisis. But, generally speaking, the Cooperative finds itself orphaned by state agencies that used to offer it credit on generous terms, technical and administrative support, and a sense of political and economic legitimacy.

Changes in labor organization and production in Mexican industry have also seriously affected the Cooperative. Mining companies in Mexico, like industrial and manufacturing enterprises worldwide, are increasingly using "new" production and labor strategies, such as laying off workers, outsourcing, and moving invested capital from place to place relatively rapidly.[2] Mining companies, in particular, are increasingly hiring temporary workers to avoid union interference, as well as the costs of pensions, disabilities, family social security, and so on. As the secretary for Fomento Minero of Guanajuato State told me, "Contract work is the tonic that Mexican mining companies are drinking these days" (cf. Arvizu Flores 1997).

In addition, the mines of the Cooperative, which have been worked extensively since the mid-eighteenth century, are approaching exhaustion. The life expectancy of the mines has been extended several times through the development of more cost-efficient technology for processing ore. For instance, the Valenciana mine was declared to be mined out at the end of the nineteenth century and remained closed for many years but was then reopened in 1966 (interview with Engineer José Echegoyén, August 7, 1999). From 1977 to 1997 the Valenciana produced 144,229.8 kilograms of silver, which accounted for 23.47 percent of the total silver production of the Cooperative during those years.[3] But the fact remains that silver and gold are nonrenewable resources.

To add to this decline, the bottom has fallen out of the world silver market. The price of silver is set daily in London and in New York; the Cooperative silver is sold at the New York price to a foundry owned by Grupo México in San Luis Potosí (one of only two foundries of this type in Mexico).[4] The price for silver ranged from around $4.00/oz to $7.00 between November 1996 and June 1998 (the period of my fieldwork in Guanajuato), down from approximately $48.00 in January 1980 (partly owing to the machinations of the Hunt brothers, who attempted to corner the world silver market). Appendix I shows yearly average prices for silver from 1976 to 2002. The drop in price was largely caused by the conviction of the Hunt brothers, which discouraged silver speculation, and by the increasing use of video and digital technologies that have drastically reduced the demand for silver-based film.

It is clear, then, that the Cooperative finds itself at the mercy of many forces. The fact remains, however, that it is still here, when all its counterpart mining cooperatives have been closed or privatized. How has it managed to survive this long? Reasons for its survival include the presence of a large working-class population in Guanajuato with few viable alternatives and the fact that the Cooperative does not have any outside investors it must answer to. These conditions mean that the Cooperative can pay very low wages relative to other mining enterprises in the area and can stay in business for a relatively long time while merely covering its costs.[5]

Two linked strategies for survival have characterized recent efforts of the Cooperative to weather its crises: self-sufficiency at the central plant, and Cooperative-wide diversification of activities. For instance, many activities at the central plant form part of a Cooperative objective of economic self-sufficiency. In one interview the engineer in charge of the Cooperative's ore-processing (beneficiation) mills stated self-sufficiency (*auto-suficiencia*) as an objective of the refining process. When I asked him why, he said, "What's happening is that the Cooperative mines are *very very* 'worked' [*trabajadas*], and we don't have the grades of gold and silver that they have in El Cubo or Las Torres [Peñoles]. If you don't have good grades of ore, you don't make good profits, and if you have low profits you have to lower your costs. That's why we have foundry A, for example, so we don't have to buy milling balls from outside."[6] I then asked him whether these strategies also worked to preserve jobs, and he responded, "That's right, because preserving jobs is the most important goal of the Cooperative."

This solution to low ore grades and low profits makes some sense in the Cooperative's case, since the Cooperative does not have to answer to outside stockholders but only to its own workforce, and since it sells to a market in which supply and demand is not the central governing force at the local level. In other words, global and even national supplies of silver and gold may affect world prices, but the Cooperative and the other mining companies in Guanajuato neither affect prices nor enter into direct competition with one another.

But this strategy also has severe consequences. First, the jobs in the Cooperative are more stable than in the other mining companies, but the wages are considerably lower, owing both to the low profits of the mines and to the size of the workforce. The stability of Cooperative jobs, and the family benefits and subsidies, partly make up for the low wages, especially in the climate of "flexibility" encouraged by the conservative (PAN) government of Guanajuato state, within which young men find few long-term economic opportunities. Because of this, young men often choose to join the Cooperative when they marry or enter into domestic and familial obligations.

Second, the undercapitalization of the Cooperative mines that both prompts and results from a strategy of economic self-sufficiency means that they produce less efficiently and that the health and safety conditions are considerably worse than in the other two mining companies in Guanajuato (El Cubo and Peñoles Grupo Guanajuato). I became extremely aware of this difference when I visited the mines of these companies. These mines had lighted tunnels underground, new ladders and safety equipment, and rigorous safety regulations. Peregrina (the Peñoles mine) also had fire doors installed at regular intervals and an underground tram for carrying the engineers from place to place. El Cubo was constructing a reinforced concrete floor at each level to prevent cave-ins. The Cooperative ends up paying a great deal of money for accidents and illnesses caused by the poor conditions of its mines. The 1997 report from the Cooperative Department of Industrial Safety calculated that the Cooperative paid 112,783.35 pesos in worker's compensation in 1997. This sum does not include the large amounts paid to social security for work-related accidents and illnesses.

Another strategy for economic survival and for maintenance of a large workforce is the diversification of activities in order to "preserve the source of jobs." As stated above, the Cooperative currently holds the concessions to exploit four mines in the city of Guanajuato, two mines in the nearby town of La Luz, and one in San Anton de las Minas, in the neighboring *municipio* of Dolores Hidalgo. In addition, it runs silversmith and ceramics workshops, a construction company, a tourist site in the Bocamina San Cayetano, a processing plant, a laboratory for testing ore concentrations, a series of workshops to provide support services (carpentry, welding, automotive shops, etc.), and offices. The silversmith, ceramics, and tourist jobs were created explicitly to give jobs to older miners and children of miners, and to diversify the Cooperative in the face of falling silver prices.

These policies are based on the Cooperative's stated purpose and reason for being: it is argued that the Cooperative does these things because it has a "social goal," that of preserving jobs. At the same time this goal precludes a solution adopted by many industries: what is called, in English, "downsizing," or letting workers go and pressuring the remaining workforce to do more work, either for incentive pay or under threat of also being laid off. Many say that, as a result, the Cooperative finds itself in the position of having more workers than it needs, especially on the surface. The tension between these two perspectives reveals itself in production policies, labor organization, and profit sharing.

The Cooperative regulates production to take advantage of variations in the price of silver, following standard practice for mining. However, its leaders also state as a primary aim the slowing down of production to preserve the veins and the source of jobs for future generations. This practice is explicitly in contrast with other mining companies, whose goal is to produce as efficiently and quickly as possible so as to provide a good return for investors and to render up capital for other projects elsewhere. In 1991 the former director of the Cooperative was reported as saying, "It would be very easy to conduct intense exploration, but the modernization would not allow the source of jobs to last for long" (*El Nacional*, December 18, 1991). The Cooperative has no outside investors and no plans to acquire further mining concessions.

Cooperative members and their families have individual tactics for facing the current hard times. They search for extra income through a variety of channels. Often it is the Cooperative member himself (90 percent of Cooperative members are men) who brings in extra money, since it is a point of pride for many Cooperative members that their wives "*se dedican al hogar*" (dedicate themselves to the home).[7] Workers in the carpentry, metalwork, and mechanics departments at the central plant take in extra jobs, working on their own time but enjoying members' rights to the Cooperative tools and workspace. Cooperative members and their families set up stands in prime spots around the mines to sell trinkets to tourists. And the Cooperative, unlike the other mining companies, allows its workers to take out stone samples from the mines (the silver veins in the district of Guanajuato lie in a matrix primarily made up of white quartz, amethyst, pyrite, calcite, and silver minerals). These stones circulate through extended markets in Guanajuato, finally being sold to collectors, rock shops, and museums.

But none of these tactics and strategies can entirely extricate the Cooperative from the bind it is in. In 1998 approximately 615 of the Cooperative's 800 person workforce were engaged in ore extraction activities either directly or through providing support services. Table 4.1 shows rough figures for the numbers of workers involved in each stage of the process. Table 4.2 gives the approximate breakdown for the rest of the workforce.

Ore extraction, processing, transport, and sale comprise the backbone of the Cooperative in terms of both the profits generated and the number of workers involved.[8] Furthermore, the new administrative council, elected in December

TABLE 4.1 COOPERATIVE WORKERS IN ORE EXTRACTION, BENEFICIATION, TRANSPORT, AND SUPPORT SERVICES IN 1998

Mines	Beneficiation	Sampling/Assay	Ore Transport	Support Services	Total
320	50	15	20	210	615

TABLE 4.2 COOPERATIVE WORKERS IN OTHER ACTIVITIES IN 1998

Offices	Ceramics	Silver-smithy	Con-struction	Tourism	Hospital	Super-market	Provisions	Total
50	25	20	30	15	15	25	10	190

1999, promises to put more of the labor force and capital investment in the mines. This means that in spite of the Cooperative's efforts at self-sufficiency, regulation of production, and diversification of activities, it is still caught fast in a basic paradox. In order to keep patrimonial possessions and pass them on, the Cooperative must continue to extract and sell the exhaustible resources of the mines.

To survive, the Cooperative depends on the daily, monthly, and yearly yields of its mines. Like all mining companies, it plans not only in terms of these yields but also in terms of the reserves it keeps in store for future exploitation. The volatility of the silver market in comparison with other metals means that silver mining companies must balance yields and reserves as part of their everyday tactics to maximize profit and minimize risk.[9] This tension between yields and reserves, which prevails in mining everywhere, is even more pronounced in this case. The Cooperative and its members employ a social logic that runs alongside and sometimes conflicts with the economic logic of production and the market. This social logic draws on what I have been calling an idiom of patrimony, framed in terms of perceived obligations to pass down the resources of the mines, and the jobs mining these resources, to future generations. The importance of preserving jobs and slowing down production as far as possible draws on this social logic.

THE CITY AND MINES OF GUANAJUATO: WHOSE PATRIMONY?

I now turn to a description of significant shifts in the ways *patrimonio* has been used in Guanajuato over the past twenty years. In order to understand these shifts locally we need to know something about the international deployments of "patrimony" as a name for cultural and other kinds of "properties." In recent years a number of scholars have studied the ethics and politics of cultural property (García Canclini 1995, Greenberg 1989, Handler 1991, Messenger 1989, B. Williams 1991). In particular, debates over the display of Native American and other indigenous groups' bones and sacred objects in museums, the "repatriation" of cultural property removed from nations of origin under colonialism, and the return of objects taken from Jewish families during the Holocaust have come in for a great deal of often very charged discussion. The best of these discussions focus on the historical context of these conflicts and explore the questions of power that organize their management and diffusion. Other scholars, without neglecting these questions, also address the theoretical issues raised by the definition of objects (and practices) as cultural property.[10] I focus here on two of the best known and most successful of these efforts.

In his 1988 book, *Nationalism and the Politics of Culture in Quebec*, Richard Handler describes Quebecois understandings of *patrimoine* as an outgrowth of Western understandings of property and polity, saying:

> To speak of the *patrimoine* is to envision national culture as property and the nation as a property-owning "collective individual." Thus the concept typifies what I have called an objectifying logic. It allows any aspect of human life to be imagined as an object, that is, bounded in time and space, or (amounting to the same thing) associated as property with a particular group, which is imagined as territorially and historically bounded. Moreover, possession of a heritage, of culture, is considered a crucial proof of national existence. . . . "We are a nation because we have a culture." (141–142)

Here Handler draws on Louis Dumont's (1970: 33) definition of the nation as "in principle two things at once, a collection of individuals and a collective individual" (quoted in Handler 1988: 32). He sees *patrimoine* as a constitutive feature of Quebecois nationalism precisely because it assumes that the nation possesses patrimonial objects as an individual would.[11] In a later article (1991), Handler connects this notion to Lockean notions of property and the origins of society, and to C.B. Macpherson's (1962) concept of "possessive individualism." Categories of cultural property (and patrimony), he argues, grow out of the notion that "a group's existence as a unique individual is believed to rest upon its undisputed possession of property, and that property often comes in the form of historically significant objects." (67). This notion of "cultural property" wields a great deal of power in the contemporary world, so much so that "those who would assert what they see as their rights against the powers-that-be must articulate their claims—in the case discussed here, claims concerning a more equitable division of cultural property—in a language that power understands" (70–71), that is, the language of individual possession.

Nestor García Canclini (1995: chap. 4) also analyzes patrimony in terms of nationalism and cultural property. He poses the question of the "social uses of the patrimony" within the larger problematic of projects of modernity in Latin America, arguing that modernizing projects must take into account and in many cases make alliances (however uneasy) with traditionalist perspectives that emphasize the preservation or renewing of the past. García Canclini focuses on "cultural patrimony" as a central site for the legitimation of power through its performance or staging. He focuses on this process in Mexico, stating:

> It is logical that, among Latin American countries, Mexico, because of the nationalist orientation of its postrevolutionary policy, should be the one that is most concerned with . . . preserving its patrimony and integrating it into a system of museums and historical and archaeological centers. (117)

García Canclini emphasizes how power works in the management and diffusion of cultural patrimony, pointing out that while the rhetoric of patrimony claims that it belongs to everyone, in fact patrimonial performances and their transmission in schools, museums, and television reproduce social inequality and consolidate "modern hegemonic sectors" (135). He thus advocates that patrimony be "studied as a space of material and symbolic struggle between classes, ethnic groups, and other groups" (136). I adopt this perspective in my analysis of cultural properties and patrimony.

An interest in pre-Columbian "antiquities" (*antigüedades*) began to take hold in Mexico in the seventeenth century, but it was not until 1808 that the first official institution dedicated to the preservation and study of antiquities was founded (the Junta de Antigüedades) (Tovar y de Teresa 1997: 89). During much of the nineteenth century there was not much institutional or public interest in the preservation of what are now referred to as "cultural properties." At the end of that century the first laws were passed that made an explicit juridical connection between archaeological sites and artifacts and the Mexican nation, establishing the Mexican government as the custodian of these objects in the name of the nation.

From that time, according to Rafael Tovar y de Teresa (1997: 92), there has been a "sustained process of broadening the concept [of cultural patrimony]" to include an increasing number of objects, including incorporeal things such as languages, cultural practices, and "traditional knowledge" (Hayden 2003, Jardel and Benz 1997, Nadasdy 1999). This process has intensified over the past several decades, during which time the term "patrimony" (and, even more, its French and Spanish cousins *patrimoine* and *patrimonio*) has expanded exponentially to include both biological and metaphorical or "imagined" kinship. It can now designate both material and economic and more figurative forms of property, such as the genetic code, cultural practices and traditions, nature preserves, as well as the idea of the past and memory as the property of the nation (Andrieux 1998, Florescano 1997, Jeudy 1990).

In Mexico, where *patrimonio nacional* has been important since the colonial period and central since the Constitution of 1917, the expansion to refer to the resources of other imagined communities began to occur in the late 1980s and has picked up speed ever since. Strategic use of this slippage in patrimony's referents has allowed local actors in Guanajuato to move between the notion of the subsoil as national patrimony and that of the mines as "*patrimonio histórico.*" These uses are made possible and necessary by the decline of the mining industry and the rise of tourism in Guanajuato.

Indeed, the expansion of the category of patrimony directly follows the rise of tourism to the city. Tourism to Mexico and Guanajuato began to rise in the 1940s. This increase came partly in response to World War II, which drastically reduced European travel for North Americans, and partly from the concerted efforts of the Mexican government. Miguel Alemán Valdés, who served as head of the Ministry of Governance (which housed tourism promotion) from 1940 to 1946 and then as president from 1946 to 1952, focused efforts on promoting foreign tourism (Saragoza 2001: 92). Local newspapers report hotel construction and urban improvements for visitors in the 1940s.[12] In 1953 the state government of Guanajuato declared Guanajuato City a "typical [in the sense of "traditional"] city" (*población típica*) and established a "pro-Guanajuato Committee" to "protect and conserve the architectonic style of the buildings and streets of [the city]" (*Periódico Oficial de Guanajuato*, December 22, 1953). The committee included the governor, mayor, director of public works, director of tourism, a representative from the University of Guanajuato, and three other members, who had to have resided in Guanajuato for more than five years and who were to be chosen by the governor. The establishment of this committee by the state government seems to have been in response to an increase in tourism. Since Guanajuato had become one of the places associated with "old" Mexico, maintaining the style and character of the city with its winding *callejones* (alleys) and quaint plazas became quite important (Saragoza 2001: 100).

Tourism in Guanajuato continued at a steady but slow pace until the late 1970s, when it began to increase dramatically. New mining discoveries and the arrival of the mining company Peñoles, as well as high silver prices in the late 1970s and early 1980s, aided tourism by providing capital for infrastructure, urban improvements, and state-sponsored publicity. The opening of the School of Restoration at the University of Guanajuato Faculty of Architecture in 1972 further helped to promote local expertise in the maintenance of Guanajuato's architectural patrimony.

In 1982 the Instituto Nacional de Antropología e Historia.(INAH) declared Guanajuato a "zone of monuments of historic patrimony" and established new sets of norms for construction within the city limits. Tourism continued to rise in the 1980s and 1990s. In 1988 the municipality of Guanajuato petitioned for and gained inclusion in the UNESCO's list of World Heritage Cities. This was a pivotal moment for the expansion of languages of patrimony in Guanajuato, linking it to continental and global trends in the uses of the term.

In making use of the expanding applications of patrimony, Mexicans are following an internationalist trend emerging from Europe in the period between the wars and intensifying after World War II. This growth of patrimony as an important language for classifying collective resources is marked by a series of international conventions and treaties: the Athens Conference of 1931, the International Charter on Restoration in Venice (1964), and the UNESCO treaties of 1954 and 1972.

Following its formation and intensifying after 1972, UNESCO has increasingly become the established authority for the designation and management of cultural properties. Its definition of "cultural heritage" was established in its 1972 Convention concerning the Protection of the World Cultural and Natural Heritage, which has become the standard for internationalist definitions of "cultural heritage."[13] In this convention UNESCO defined cultural heritage as:

> monuments: architectural works, works of monumental sculpture and painting, elements or structures of an archaeological nature, inscriptions, cave dwellings and combinations of features, which are of outstanding universal value from the point of view of history, art or science;
>
> groups of buildings: groups of separate or connected buildings which, because of their architecture, their homogeneity or their place in the landscape, are of outstanding universal value from the point of view of history, art or science;
>
> sites: works of man or the combined works of nature and man, and areas including archaeological sites which are of outstanding universal value from the historical, aesthetic, ethnological or anthropological point of view. (UNESCO World Heritage Convention 1972)

UNESCO here establishes a globalist definition of "cultural heritage" and cultivates the idea of its "outstanding universal value," to which the world as a whole has a claim. Along with this idea comes an emphasis on the physical context of sites, their interaction with their environment, and the social history that accrues around them. For this reason, UNESCO's criteria for a site's inclusion

on the World Heritage List insists upon an attention to ecological and historical context, and the norms and practices of managing World Heritage Sites are
oriented toward these questions. Groups and actors involved with cultural patrimony in Guanajuato have increasingly accepted this definition and the norms
that go along with it, and have consistently attempted to valorize local sites in
terms of their "universal value." In effect, this expansion of the idea of patrimony works to loosen the control over who can lay claim to, exploit, and benefit from patrimonial resources.

Interestingly UNESCO's valorization of context and place articulates neatly
with local perceptions of the value of the past and its material traces. Guanajuato, like many other places, has long cultivated a local pride of place based on
the assumed value of its history and the reproduction of that history in buildings, churches, plazas, mines, and so on. The intrinsic value of Guanajuato's place
and history as patrimony has become increasingly important in Guanajuato in
the past two decades, coinciding with the decline of mining, the rise of tourism,
and transnational movements of labor and capital. To a large extent, it supplants
nationalist understandings of *"patrimonio nacional"* that have prevailed in previous decades. In part, the rise of what I am calling "globalism" succeeds because
it fits in so well with long-standing localist tendencies in Guanajuato that see
the mines and the past they represent as significant for their local rather than
national importance. At the same time the UNESCO version of *patrimonio
mundial* provides opportunities for negotiating the economic crisis caused by
the decline of the mining industry by emphasizing that tourists from far and
wide should visit Guanajuato because it has "universal value."

From the 1970s to the present, tourism to Guanajuato has continued to increase as part of an explosive nationwide trend. From 1970 to 1994 the number
of tourists visiting Mexico grew from 2 million to 17 million, and income from
foreign tourism increased from U.S.$415 million to U.S.$6.4 billion (Clancy
2001). Along with this increase, "patrimony" has become an extremely common
language in the city, and many individuals and organizations make use of the
concept. Furthermore, the UNESCO list often figures prominently in discussions of cultural patrimony and in the history of Guanajuato in general. As always, a characterization of resources as patrimony implies without necessarily
clearly defining the collectivity defined in relation to this patrimony and its
right use and disposition, thus opening the way for heated debates over whose
patrimony is really being talked about.

These new uses of history and the traces of the past accompany the creation
of new types of cultural and historic patrimony, especially mining patrimony.
The Santa Fe Cooperative has joined these attempts to use the material remains

of the past to attract resources, in part through a definition of these remains as patrimony. Even so, some observers within the Cooperative (and others) view with suspicion the efforts of Guanajuatan groups to take advantage of these new uses of patrimony. For instance, the president of the administrative council of the Cooperative once remarked to me, referring to the president of a local group dedicated to *patrimonio histórico*, "Basically, he's turning 'patrimonio histórico' into the patrimony of himself and his family [*el patrimonio propio de él y su familia*]." This statement plays on the multiple referents of the word "patrimony" to criticize local attempts to appropriate control over how patrimony is used to attract resources for individual gain.

In using a language of patrimony in these new ways, local and other actors seek to shift its referential domain from a purely economic understanding to what might be called a "mnemonic" notion, where memory and the traces of the past are the patrimonial possessions (Ferry n.d.).[14] However, the same debate persists in these newer uses of patrimony and raises important questions: Can and should patrimony be exchanged as a commodity? Who can legitimately participate in the use and exchange of patrimonial resources?

For the purposes of understanding the dynamics and conflicts surrounding cultural patrimony in Guanajuato, here I describe several projects planned and developed over the past two decades. The Santa Fe Cooperative began to develop its mining tourism after the political and economic crisis of 1991–92, when the director and head of the administrative council (who were father and son) were ousted, and when the state government of Guanajuato intervened to bail out the Cooperative. The new administrative council sought ways to promote new economic opportunities to provide a margin in times of low silver prices, and to continue to offer jobs to Cooperative members and their sons.

As part of these efforts, the Cooperative refurbished the grounds of an old entrance into the Valenciana mine known as the Bocamina San Cayetano (an adit that one can walk down into by means of narrow steps rather than a vertical mine shaft). They blocked off the steps about 50 meters down and developed a short tour for those who wish to "know the interior of the mine" (see figures 4.1, 4.2, 4.3). They left the surface ruins basically untouched and did not restore the partially fallen walls; through the holes in these walls one can see the majestic Valenciana church framed against the blue sky. They trained climbing geraniums over the walls, planted grass, installed bathrooms, and set up a display of dioramas of the different Cooperative mines (these models are made each year by the master carpenter for the procession in honor of the Virgin of Guanajuato), ceramics and silversmith exhibits, and old photos of the mines from the turn of the century. The effect is tranquil and appealing. The Cooperative charges eight pesos (around eighty cents) for adults and four pesos (forty cents) for children to visit the Bocamina. It is most often visited by Mexican tourists, often with their families, and occasionally by school groups. From January 1997 to April 1998, 78,626 people visited the Bocamina.[15]

The Cooperative did not begin charging a fee to enter the main area of the Valenciana mine (three pesos per person) until the late 1980s (Engineer Cándido Tovar, personal communication). Before then, the mine grounds were open to all, and visiting dignitaries or other honored guests were taken to see them. For instance, William Jennings Bryan was given a private tour of the grounds and was reported to have described the Tiro Central as "a hole big enough and deep enough to bury the gold standard" (quoted in Rickard 1907: 182).

In past years some visitors to the Valenciana mine's main entrance (Tiro de San José) recognized the potential for tourism. For instance, in 1949 a North American doctor and his wife (Dr. and Mrs. Holbrook) living in nearby Irapuato visited the mines and were struck both by the mine itself and by its lack of safety precautions. Mrs. Anna Jane Holbrook even wrote to President Miguel Alemán, saying:

Recently I visited an abandoned gold mine [sic] near the city of Guanajuato (I believe it is called the Valenciana mine) and found it one of the most interesting spots I have seen in Mexico; however, I should like to call your attention to the need for a secure wall around the large hole in the ground there, some 700 meters deep, and for signs to show that one is approaching the hole. Presently there is nothing to keep a person from walking right into the hole without warning. Too, I believe that this mine should be better advertised to tourists visiting Mexico, as it is indeed an unusual and thrilling spectacle.[16]

On the grounds of the mine, tourists and school groups can see the magnificent ramparts of the mine, the air compressor, and the old steam chimneys from the British period (the second quarter of the nineteenth century). They can also watch mining cars travel up from the depths and empty into a waiting dump truck; they can peer down the working mine shaft; they can buy quartzes and trinkets from vendors on the grounds. More people, and more tour buses, visit the Valenciana than the Bocamina, especially since the road to the mine was paved in the fall of 1997. From December 1996 to April 1998 as many as 75,514 people visited the Valenciana mine. More foreigners, and especially North Americans, come to the Valenciana than the Bocamina, but Mexican visitors form a large proportion of tourism to both sites.

FIGURE 4.1 Brochure for the Bocamina de Valenciana (Bocamina San Cayetano)

Mina de Valenciana. Bocamina de "San Cayetano".

FIGURE 4.2 Visit to the Bocamina San Cayetano, early twentieth century. *Antuñez Echegaray 1964: 288*

In spite of these efforts, tourism does not yet provide a significant source of income for the Cooperative. The engineer in charge of the Valenciana once estimated that the Valenciana might make three hundred pesos in tickets on a good day; he then showed me one wheel of a mining car and said that three hundred pesos would just barely pay for the ball bearings for that one wheel. Nevertheless, in spite of these meager returns, the Cooperative continues to promote its tourist enterprises, partly to give work to Cooperative families, and partly in the hopes of developing more lucrative projects.[17] However, some members are skeptical of these efforts both within and outside the Cooperative. When I showed Alvaro an article published in the paper El Nacional on how tourism was replacing the mining sector in Guanajuato, he responded in angry agitation, "You think we'd be able to feed our families working as tourist guides?"

In the summer of 1999, the state departments of Tourism and Economic Development, through a contact with the director of tourism from Oaxaca, invited a representative of Industrial Heritage Consultancy (IHC) in Cornwall, England, to visit Guanajuato and discuss the possibility of developing "Guanajuato's mining heritage" for tourists (Luis Antonio Marín, personal communi-

FIGURE 4.3 View of the Valenciana Church from the patio of the Bocamina San Cayetano

cation). IHC is developing a similar project in Real del Monte, Hidalgo, a mining center that operated, albeit shakily, in the nineteenth century with mostly British capital, Cornish managers, and Mexican workers (Randall 1972). In July 1999 a consultant from IHC visited Guanajuato and conducted an analysis of the possibilities for developing the region's mining heritage. The IHC report includes as strengths the fact that Guanajuato is already a World Heritage Site, and is "without doubt one of the world's most historically important silver mining districts with a history of production dating from the 1540s and the discovery of the Veta Madre in 1558. This importance is recognized by the World Heritage citation" (IHC 1999). The colonial period workings of the Veta Madre (the vast majority of which are owned by the Cooperative) the report describes as "without doubt 'the jewel in the crown' of Guanajuato's mining heritage." Furthermore, the report cites the support of the state government and "the recognition of the need to develop the mining heritage" by the state, the Cooperative, the School of Mines, and local tourism industry as a major advantage (IHC 1999). Finally, the IHC consultant emphasizes that since the Cooperative owns most of the best sites, it would be hard to launch a successful project without its collaboration, and suggests that the grounds of the Valenciana could be a central point for a "main heritage discovery centre."

The IHC report also points to some weaknesses or potential obstacles to a mining heritage project in Guanajuato. It focuses particularly on the lack of coordination between different sites, the presence of "untidy areas" outside the city center, and the fact that the presentations of information connected to different sites "are not of a standard which reflect well for a World Heritage site nor do they do more than hint at the important part Guanajuato has played both in Mexican and international history." Finally, the report suggests that negotiating with the Cooperative where "850 opinions" have to be taken into account "could result in problems in making decisions."

IHC's proposal clearly demonstrates some of the features of recent internationalist perspectives on patrimony. We can see the effects of UNESCO's policy toward patrimony in the emphasis on industrial heritage, social history, and the coordination and coherence of several dispersed sites. The many references to UNESCO and the World Heritage List, including the judgment of the presentations as "not of a standard" befitting a World Heritage Site, demonstrate how deeply UNESCO has penetrated into the norms and language of international patrimony specialists, and the degree to which UNESCO can determine international "standards" to be followed in local patrimony projects. These many references also suggest how specialists attempt to use UNESCO's prestige to influence understandings of cultural patrimony in places like Guanajuato.

The visit from IHC and subsequent attempts to follow up on a *proyecto de patrimonio minero* have involved much greater coordination between different actors involved with patrimony than any previous effort I am aware of. In August 1999 I accompanied a group of people on a trial tour of several mining sites, including the site where silver was first discovered in the Guanajuato district in 1548 (San Bernabé, now a deserted mine overgrown with ferns and frequented by lizards).

This trial tour included most of the partners in the project with the objective of deciding on an appropriate route, identifying logistical problems, and getting a rough idea of how much the tour should cost. We circled the city of Guanajuato in a minibus and a pickup truck passing by the town of La Luz, the mines of San Juan and San Bernabé, the mine of Guadalupe, the Valenciana mine, and finally the Bocamina San Ramón, a privately owned museum and restaurant located at another old entrance to the mine. The project is aimed at tourists with enough time in Guanajuato to spend an entire day away from the main attractions of the city, and those with a serious interest in mining or history or both.

As we proceeded on the tour, the planners discussed the fact that they wished to reach a new type of tourist than had been targeted in previous projects. They also stressed the points that IHC had emphasized in its assessment of Guanajuato's potential: the importance of a coherent presentation of different sites and the relationship between them; and the need for better presentation of the information, more social history, coordination of different actors, and so on.

By the time of my next visit to Guanajuato in the summer of 2001, IHC had disappeared from the scene and the ruta de la plata project had been modified into a "centro de patrimonio minero" focused on the Rayas mine.[18] This project, which includes the same partners as the previous project with the exception of IHC, was intended to "provide alternatives to reactivate, by means of tourism, the mining enterprises that have confronted serious financial obstacles to maintaining their operations." The project was officially inaugurated in April 2002 ("Buscan explotar potencial turístico de las viejas minas guanajuatenses," *Chopper,* April 20, 2002, 18). Like the ruta de la plata project, the Rayas project integrates a number of complementary sites into the same complex, thus continuing the emphasis on context and interaction of sites proposed by IHC and consistent with the principles of UNESCO.

I returned again to Guanajuato in the summer of 2003. At this point the Rayas project, like the ruta de la plata project before it, seemed to have stalled. The general assembly of the Cooperative had not approved renting the Rayas surface structures to the state government. According to an official in the State Ministry of Tourism, the ministry planned to propose to the municipal presi-

dent that an offer be made to the Cooperative to purchase these holdings out-
right, without interfering with the extraction activities of the mine. Although
the Cooperative had renovated a new Bocamina in the old mine of Sechó, by
the summer of 2003 it was still attracting few visitors, although the Bocamina
San Cayetano continued to be a popular destination. However, the president of
the administrative council talked to me at length about his idea to establish a
dual structure of the Cooperative that would depend on mining for 30–40 percent of its income and on tourism for 60–70 percent (see figure 4.4). He out-
lined his plan to establish an underground tour in the mine of San Vicente,
where visitors rode in wagons pulled by a tractor. Warming to the idea, he said:

> We could say "if you'd like to know the entrails of the mine, come with
> us!" We could have people next to the cars drilling and doing other stuff,
> it could be really cool [*padrísimo*]! And it wouldn't take a lot of dough [*lana*]
> . . . if we got a flat tire, we could fix it right there and go on. It wouldn't
> matter if there was some water in there, it would add to the ambience.

At the same time, in the midst of his excitement, he expressed great resentment
that the general assembly of members did not trust him and would not allow
him to make such changes.

It seems that, as mining declines in Guanajuato and tourism and international investment become increasingly important, new understandings of patrimony come to the fore. Cultural patrimony becomes much more essential (and
at least potentially more lucrative) and international languages of patrimony
gain more and more power to define what "cultural patrimony" should include

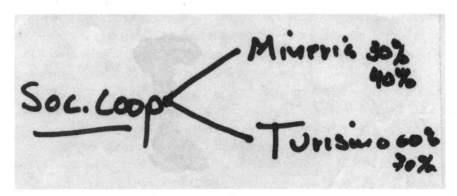

FIGURE 4.4 Sketch of Plans for Mining Tourism. *Drawn by the president of the administrative council, Santa Fe Cooperative, summer 2003*

and how it should be managed. At the same time we find a proliferation of local and international state and nongovernmental actors entering an arena that used to be dominated by the INAH. Along with these trends come new uses of patrimony to open up both subsoil resources and cultural properties to non-Cooperative members, non-Guanajuatenses, and non-Mexicans. The notion of *patrimonio mundial* provides a case in point.

THE SANTA FE COOPERATIVE AT THE TURN OF THE MILLENNIUM

In the fall of 1996, when I arrived in Mexico, the PRI was reaching the limits of its legitimacy in many areas and was soon to lose its majority in the Congress. The nation's economy was fighting its way back from the financial crash of 1994 and the absconding of President Carlos Salinas, who only five years before had been touted by many observers as the triumphal leader of neoliberalism and technocratic governance. In Guanajuato State, the governor, Vicente Fox (who is now the first opposition-party president of Mexico since 1929), was busily attracting foreign investment and transnational corporations; in 1994 the biggest General Motors factory in the hemisphere opened in Silao, the township adjacent to Guanajuato City. Permanent jobs were being steadily replaced by short-term contract work, especially in mining but also in construction, schools, health care, and so on. In this context the Cooperative seemed to some like a last bastion of fair labor practice and civic and national dignity, and to others like a remnant of an obsolete political and economic system.

Since I left Guanajuato in 1998 a number of changes have occurred. The governor of the state has become the first non-PRI president since 1929; the trends of migration, short-term contract work, and privatization of state enterprises and services have increased; and the Cooperative has entered a new and deeper crisis. These difficulties have become particularly intense since a new administrative council was elected in January 2000. The new administration, without the strong ties to the local PRI or the ability to mobilize both miners and surface workers of the former elected leaders, quickly encountered problems. By the spring of 2001 the Cooperative's external debt had grown exponentially, and the miners were increasingly discontent. The Cooperative was forced to suspend payment of workers for one week, and on a number of occasions miners in Rayas refused to go down in the mine. The Cooperative appealed to the state and federal governments for help, requesting a loan of three million dollars from the federal agency Consejo de Recursos Minerales. However, as the director of the Cooperative put it:

The change in the municipal administration [in the 2000 elections the PRI lost the mayoral election for the very first time, ceding its place to an independent candidate with support from both the PRD and the PAN], the change in the state administration, and the change in the federal administration, all this came to influence everything. [Because of this] the Cooperative is out of step with the times.

Engineer Jesus Franco, the director of Fomento Minero of Guanajuato State expanded on this point:

The problems of the Cooperative come from the imbalance in the workforce, from the fall of the price of silver, and from the lack of new machinery. But if the government were supportive, all these problems could be resolved. But the new government in Mexico is not interested in supporting cooperatives.

As part of the negotiations over a possible loan, the Consejo de Recursos Mineros in Mexico City arranged for a new superintendent of mines to work in the Cooperative. This engineer, whom I will call Engineer Colunga, had extensive experience working in Peñoles, one of the two largest mining companies in Mexico. He began to address what he saw as the most serious problems facing the Cooperative: low production, an older workforce *"sin conciencia"* (without consciousness; thoughtless), and obsolete machinery. He instituted weekly meetings for each mine and department, posted principles of *calidad* (quality management) in the different mines, and suggested ways to *liquidar* (pay out the shares in the Cooperative) to older members so that the Cooperative would no longer have to pay their wages and social security.

As might be expected, the response to his proposals was mixed. Some workers, including those from long-standing Cooperative families who considered themselves staunch Cooperativistas, applauded his efforts, often using the current language of praise (*trabaja con calidad; es gente de calidad* [he works with quality; he is a person of quality]).[19] Others, especially those who work in the Rayas mine, one of the biggest of the Cooperative mines, were vehemently opposed to Colunga and the changes he was trying to make. In the summer of 2001 these workers refused several times to go down in the mine, arguing that Colunga did not respect them and their work.[20] That he was from outside the Cooperative added to their resentments.

The government did end up lending the Cooperative two million pesos (instead of three million dollars), but this was not enough to help them over the financial crisis. One critic of the president of the administrative council later asserted that "he [Colunga] turned it [the money] into dust." Colunga left the Cooperative shortly thereafter, in the fall of 2001. One engineer opined that "he talked a lot and was very convincing, but things didn't turn out the way he said." The new superintendent of mines came from a long-standing Cooperative family and was uninterested in the model of labor management proposed by Colunga and others in 2001.

In the spring of 2002, under the direction of a new administrative council, the Cooperative sold off several of its properties to a private developer, including the sports fields and the abandoned mine of Guadalupe, purportedly for two hundred thousand pesos or about twenty thousand dollars. By doing so, it was able to pay off about two-thirds of the external debt (around twenty thousand pesos) with the proceeds.[21] However, these sales also occasioned a considerable amount of resentment on the part of some members, who felt that the proceeds from these sales were diverted into the pockets of Cooperative *jefes*. This rancor can be understood as one expression of a general anxiety over the liquidation of Cooperative patrimony and the future of the enterprise under conditions of economic crisis.

By the time I returned in the summer of 2003, the mood in the Cooperative and in Santa Rosa was somber. The rest of the external debt remained, and the members had still not been paid for a period of ten weeks in 2000–2001. Many members had retired or left the Cooperative during this time—in fact, the membership was now down to barely three hundred from between eight hundred and nine hundred during 1996–98. Several members, including the current president of the administrative council, told me that they expected that the enterprise would not survive another year. One female member recounted her desire to have another child, "but with the situation here in the Cooperative, it's not possible [*no se puede*]."

CONCLUSION: THE PARADOX OF THE COOPERATIVE'S SURVIVAL

Throughout my fieldwork in the Santa Fe Cooperative both insiders and observers occasionally talked to me about the failures of the Cooperative to live up to its promises and its general lack of success as an economic institution. Some complained that it was not a "real" Cooperative, whereas others blamed its problems on its very cooperative structure and its corresponding lack of economic efficiency. Finally, many people, both insiders and outsiders, described the Cooperative as a corrupt institution where the engineers and members of the government councils robbed the membership with impunity.

Others, and sometimes the very same people who complained about the Cooperative, also praised it for its economic and social commitment to the city and nation as well as its "social goal" of maintaining an important source of jobs for Guanajuato. Some pointed to the benefits given to members and their families at different points in the life cycle: scholarships for children and young adults, jobs for members' sons, and pensions and other benefits for retired members.

It is not my purpose in this book to make a final decision about the validity of these varied arguments. However, the closer the Cooperative seems to move toward its final act, the more apparent becomes the paradox of its survival until now, at least to this observer. On the one hand, it is undeniable that, under current circumstances and at many (though not all) periods of the Cooperative's history, its members have earned less than miners in private mining companies in the area, and that the Cooperative has struggled since its inception with administrative problems, accusations of corruption from all sides, and periodic outbreaks of rancor and unrest, especially when the price of silver is low. All these features are typical of producers' cooperatives in twentieth-century Mexico. It is also true that these aspects of Cooperative structure and history are major threats to its survival in the early 2000s.

At the same time, not only is the Santa Fe the only remaining mining cooperative in Mexico but it has been so for more than a decade. Since the stated goal of the Cooperative is the maintenance of jobs for workers, by this standard it seems that the Cooperative has been more successful than any of its cousins and that every day it continues to survive is a further success. Moreover, its organization as a cooperative has helped its survival until now. A private company with outside investors and commitments to high productivity would never have lasted this long.

In an interview with two Cooperative engineers in early 1997, I asked them what the advantages and drawbacks were of working as a member of the Cooperative. One replied: "The obstacles we face are the price of silver and a lack of resources. The advantage is that we have very low production costs." The other engineer added, "and we have the advantage that we can continue to work with zero profits, just enough to eat. If Las Torres [the local term for the mining company Peñoles in Guanajuato] were to arrive at this point, it would close." Indeed, as reported above, Peñoles closed its Guanajuato operations in September 2003.[22] Thus the very aspects of cooperativism that are killing the Santa Fe are also what have enabled it to survive until now.

CHAPTER 5

Realms of Patrimony: Mine and House

I have memories [or "souvenirs"] of the Valenciana on my body.
—Founding member of the Santa Fe Cooperative, August 1997

How do Cooperative members and their families deploy and order patrimony in the domains of mineral production and social and sexual reproduction, particularly in the mine and the house? Productive and reproductive practices in these spaces organize patrimonial possessions and ascribe difference in locally specific ways (especially between underground and surface, male and female, and Cooperative and newcomer/outsider).

Production and reproduction express the "conceptual schemes immanent in practice" that order power and difference in the Cooperative (Bourdieu 1977: 118).[1] I focus especially on two spaces of production and reproduction, the mine and the house. Within these spaces, local difference and differential claims on Cooperative patrimony (such as those between male Cooperative members and their wives) come to seem both natural and proper. In this context, even long-standing disagreements and periodic searing conflict are expressed in terms of widely held understandings of underground and surface, male and female, and "Cooperative families" and newcomers/outsiders.

To emphasize the way these practices configure power and difference in the Cooperative, I trace two main conduits within the Cooperative: the extraction of silver from the mines and the investment of silver in the form of money into the houses of Cooperative families. These processes work in tandem (and in tension) to produce the two most important realms of patrimony: mine and house.[2] I then examine how the domains of mine and house are constructed as parallel though distinct. Members and their families organize these spaces conceptually, according to oppositions (such as those between male and female, underground and surface, and Cooperative and newcomers/outsiders) and, by analogy, as "analogic practice" (such as that between production and reproduction). I borrow the phrase "analogic practice" from Bourdieu's distinction between "the *fait accompli* and dead letter of the already effected analogy" and "analogic practice" wherein actors produce and negotiate different conceptualizations within the terms available to them (Bourdieu 1977: 119). Analogic practice thus implies a process of analogy making by actors who are continually debating and renegotiating available symbolic forms and arrangements. Through analogic practice connecting production and reproduction, Cooperative members and their families make sense of, negotiate, and imagine alternatives to the current political and economic crisis. They also contest both prevailing local understandings of patrimony and its legitimate claimants. In doing so they try to reorder patrimony within the Cooperative.

House and mine provide metaphors and models of sociality for Cooperative members and their families. Patrimony and its just and proper disposition suffuse these models of sociality. Vernacular categories of difference, localized in the houses and mines of the Cooperative, also entail ideas of the proper behavior of those belonging to different categories, and their differential claims on the patrimonial possessions of the group. Thus the physical ordering of distinct spaces and the traversals of their boundaries relate intimately to the ordering of power and legitimacy.

In this chapter I describe the two realms within which patrimony holds most sway as an idiom for classifying objects and prescribing behavior. Central to this idea is the notion that patrimonial possessions, as the name suggests, are meant to be transferred from father to son. This is not to say that Cooperative families are entirely organized according to patrilineal principles. Indeed, in many contexts, Cooperative members, like other Mexicans, reckon kinship bilineally. Only certain kinds of property (those seen as patrimony) are supposed to be passed along the male line. These special cases underscore patrimony's gendered character.

The Extraction of Silver and the Mine as Lived Space

Of the seven mines in operation under the control of the Santa Fe Cooperative, I focus particularly on the extraction process in the Valenciana mine. In the Valenciana, as in the other mines, workers extract the ore from the mine and bring it to the surface, where it begins the process of merging with ore from other mines and starts its journey of separation from the Cooperative. That process continually recreates the mine as a gendered and morally and politically inflected space and orders difference within that space.

The Valenciana mine employs approximately thirty-five (35) underground workers and ten surface workers, presided over by a shift head (*cabo*), foreman

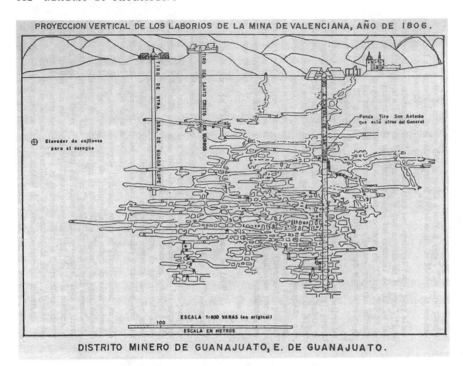

FIGURE 5.1 Cross-section of the Valenciana mine, 1806. *Antuñez Echegaray 1964:287*

or captain (*capitán*), and engineer.[3] It has four drillers (*perforistas*) with one as-sistant each; the rest of the underground workforce includes car-men (*carreros*) and general laborers (*peones*). Unlike most of the other Cooperative mines, which have three shifts, the Valenciana only has one shift per day; it produces approximately 100 metric tons of ore-bearing rock daily (at about 100 grams of silver and .85 grams of gold per metric ton). From June 1997 to May 1998 the Valenciana produced 3,020.05 kilograms of silver and 26.44 kilograms of gold.

The day shift at the Valenciana begins at 7:00 A.M. in the *horario de verano* (summer schedule) and 6:00 A.M. in the *horario normal* (normal schedule).[4] Workers leave their homes while it is still dark, eating a small breakfast that their wives, who rise at the same hour or somewhat earlier, prepare for them. In Santa Rosa de Lima, workers destined for any of the four mines in Guanajuato City wait at one of two places: the Restaurant de la Sierra, at the main exit from the highway into the village, and at the Cruz Grande (Great Cross), a small church at another entrance to the Camino Real (the town's only road).[5] Workers from the nearby pueblos of Monte de San Nicolás and Puerto de Santa Rosa, and from the lower part of Santa Rosa (*la plaza*) walk to meet the bus at 5:30 A.M.

from October to April and 6:30 A.M. from April to October. It is dark, often chilly, and the workers, still drowsy, hardly speak.

The bus lets Valenciana workers off at the Plaza de Valenciana. The mine's entrance is located about 150 meters away from the plaza and church, down a recently paved road. Its architecture demonstrates much more than industrial utility. Built in the 1770s it shows the social and cultural importance of mining in Guanajuato during that period, at least in the minds of its owners. A granite wall with an entrance of two massive wooden doors surrounds the mine. The doors lead to an entry hall supported by columns on the inside, with ticket-takers and a store for Cooperative silver and ceramic products on the left and the chapel to Santo Cristo de los Mineros on the right. The walls of this chapel are freshly whitewashed, and cut flowers are placed on the altar weekly. Swallows swoop and roost among the beams.

Passing through the portals, most of the workers cross themselves in front of the image of Cristo de los Mineros in the chapel to the right of the main portal and walk down a flagstone path through the middle of grassy lawns. The walls surrounding the grounds, covered with climbing geraniums, have seven triangular points. The tourist guides are fond of saying that these points were meant to represent the Spanish crown;[6] in fact, they were the supports for pulleys in the mule-driven system for raising and lowering mineral and workers (*malacate de sangre*). The mineshaft is topped by a metal headframe erected in the 1960s when the mine was reopened.

To the left is a shed with the air compressor (built in New York by Ingersoll-Rand in 1906) that powers the pneumatic drills used in the mine. To the right are two obelisk-shaped towers 20 meters tall and made of orange brick (an unusual construction material for Guanajuato). These are the steam chimneys built by the British Anglo-Mexican Mining Company in the nineteenth century, when the *malacate de sangre* was replaced by steam power. To one side there is an old mining car that has been planted with flowers and quartzes, and crowned by an image of the Virgin of Guadalupe, the patron saint of Mexico. Several former mine workers who now work on the surface keep the grounds in impeccable condition. They water the flowers and lawns, keep the walkways clean and scrubbed, and wash the trucks of *jefes* (Cooperative leaders; see chapter 6) when they bring them by. The clean, pretty and parklike setting of the mine projects a sense of palpable pride. A sign on one of the mine's ramparts proclaims "Take care of the flowers; they are nature's best offerings."

The men go to the locker rooms and change into their work clothes, including rubber boots, helmet, and leather belt. They are also supposed to have respirators that filter out dust and silica particles, leather gloves, and plastic earplugs. However, miners and plant workers often complained that the boots and gloves wore out before they became eligible for a discount for new ones, and that when they asked for replacements these were unavailable. Similarly, hardly anyone has a respirator in working order; men sometimes cover their mouths with a bandanna when they work in very dusty or smoky areas of the mine.

After changing, the workers go to a window in the mine offices, where each receives a lamp that is recharged every night. Most workers carry a bag for lunch, a bottle of water or fruit drink (*agua de sabor*), and a small serrated knife tucked into the clip for their lantern or held by a rubber band on the helmet. This blade is called a *charrasca* and is used by the drillers (*perforistas*) to cut fuses or for other tasks. It can also be used in the event of an accident to free a worker from clothes or boots trapped under fallen rock. Surface workers also carry *charrascas*; it is a badge of Cooperative membership.[7]

As the miners are getting their lanterns, the engineer and captain discuss the day's work, any problems, or specific tasks. Usually they talk about the difficulties caused by equipment failure. The captain then tells the miners what areas to go to for that day's work. In the Valenciana, this is relatively stable; the *perforistas*, in particular, work in the same area every day for months at a time. The captain gives the *carreros* and *peones* specific tasks each day, and doles out new drills *(bro-*

FIGURE 5.2 *Pueble,* Valenciana mine. *Photo by Stephen Ferry*

cas) to the *perforistas*. Sometimes a worker who has been scarce on the job recently pokes his head in the door, and asks the captain "*¿Deme chance?*" (Give me a chance [to return to work]?) The captain responds gruffly, usually with a slight affirmative nod.[8] This part of the morning, when the captain and engineer plan the day and give directions, is called *pueble* from the verb *poblar* (to people or populate). The word gives a sense of the mine as an empty city or terrain waiting to be peopled by miners. In the following pages I describe the mine's interior and details of the work underground. This description comes from some two dozen trips I took into the Valenciana and other mines of the Cooperative, and from interviews with miners at the Valenciana.

The workers descend into the mine in two groups at around 7:30 A.M. (6:30 from October to April). In the Valenciana they descend by means of the *caleza,* the metal car that transports workers and mineral up and down the mineshaft (Tiro de San José), as this is the only way to enter the mine.[9] As the *caleza* descends the Tiro de San José, one can see the elegance of the mine's architecture. The shaft is octagonal and striped with green porphyry (*cantera verde*) of Guanajuato. The car descends quickly, reaching the first level under exploitation (360 meters below) in about a minute. It leaves behind the sunny, well-kept park on the surface and carries the miners into the dark and dusty mine. The men disembark at several levels; at each level there is an enlarged cavern with wooden benches and an altar with candles. Except immediately at the dispatch point, there are no lights installed in the mine, only the beams cast from the miners' helmets. The lights rake across shadowy spaces and glint off the dust in the air. The areas near the mineshaft are always chilly from the column of cold air that gets trapped in the shaft. The wind roars dimly even when the air above is completely still.

A tunnel leads off from each dispatch point, soon engulfing the workers in darkness except for the circle of light cast by the lantern. The tunnels are about 3 meters high, roughly rounded, with numbers painted on the rock in places, old drill holes and chisel marks, and hollows filled with glinting amethyst or white quartz. In many tunnels iron rails for the mining cars run underfoot. The walls sweat water, and workers often walk in puddles up to their shins. The air smells musty, occasionally smoky or filled with fumes if one is close to where the *perforistas* are working. These tunnels intersect constantly at odd angles and open up suddenly into huge caverns. There are points where miners scrabble over piles of blasted rock or inch down a gravelly slope. As they move away from the shaft, the air becomes hotter and thicker. There is one place in the Valenciana on level 430 called "*El Infierno*" (Hell), where the temperature reaches 95 degrees Fahrenheit. In these pockets of heat, workers strip off their jackets and shirts.[10]

Workers take their places at three levels in the mine: at 365, 390, and 430 meters below the surface. The *perforistas* work at designated points, known as *rebajes*

FIGURE 5.3   Inside the Valenciana. *Photo by Stephen Ferry*

or *huecos* (hollows) where they drill a series of holes in the rock, preparing to place explosives there that they will detonate at the end of the shift. The drill is about 1 meter long, with a metal strut for support and a hand-operated trigger. Powered by the air compressor on the surface, it releases water into the hole as it drills, so that the silica dust will not become airborne. This innovation has significantly reduced, but has not eradicated, the incidence of silicosis (a disease caused by the piercing of the lungs with silica dust—effectively ground glass). The drill makes a loud jackhammer noise, and shakes your arm and leg bones while you are using it.[11]

The rock knocked down by the blasts remains until the next shift, when other workers load it with shovels, picks, and crowbars into mining cars. These workers work in pairs or threes. The mining cars (about three feet in length, and holding approximately a metric ton of rock) are pushed along iron rails to the chute, or on level 360, to the dispatch point (*despacho*). One worker at the dispatch guides the cars on to the *caleza* and keeps track on small slips of paper of how many he has loaded. Since the rails and the cars are fairly old and the metal has worn down, the cars go off the rails from time to time. If the car is full, it often takes six or seven people to put it back on the rails.

The shift head (*cabo*) generally accompanies the car-men, while the engineer and captain make a tour beginning at approximately eight in the morning to each of the work areas in the mines, checking up on the work and looking

FIGURE 5.4 Pushing the mining car back on the track. *Photo by Stephen Ferry*

for any problems. Clotildo, the engineer of the Valenciana, told me that they also make sure to check up on any people who are slacking off, suspected of stealing (*lupios*) or leaving their work area to collect mineral specimens (*achichicles; see* chapter 7). The engineer accompanies visitors from other departments within the Cooperative, such as the topographers from the Department of Engineering, the superintendent of mines, or the head of production.[12]

After approximately three hours of work, workers in the different areas of the mine take a break for lunch. Each worker has brought a lunch in most cases made by his wife or mother.[13] This meal can consist of beans, sausage with eggs, pork rind (*chicharrón*), along with avocado, and perhaps rice cooked with tomato, peas, and carrots (*sopa de arroz*). Miners eat either at one side of the work area or in one of the lunch areas (*comedores*) at different levels. Someone has brought corn tortillas and they share their lunches, making tacos and heating them up over small stoves in the *comedores*. The smell of hot tortillas, meat, and chiles mixes with the smoke and dust. Several workers told me that food eaten down in the mine tasted better than it did anywhere else.

After they finish lunch at about 11:30, workers return to their work for another hour and a half to two hours. In order to return to the surface by 1:30, some workers leave their work areas half an hour early, because it takes that long to walk back to the dispatch. In some of the larger mines, workers must walk for as long as an hour to reach their work site. Workers move from place to place in the mines through the tunnels and up and down ladders made of iron cable with wooden rungs. These ladders are twisted and crusty with mineralization; sometimes they are missing rungs. In other mines, such as those owned by El Cubo and Peñoles, the ladders are made of thicker wood and have rungs measured to be uniformly spaced. Not so in the Cooperative.[14]

Generally work is fairly silent except at lunch, especially in the stopes (*rebajes*) where the noise of the drill (*perforador*) makes it almost impossible to hear. Also, the darkness outside the circle of lantern light (as mentioned above, there are no lights installed in Cooperative mines) cuts down interaction between workers except when they pass one another in the tunnels or work together. People often communicate with one another in short bursts of jokes or quick messages, or by whistling, rather than longer conversations. During my visits in the mines I noticed the whistling particularly. When I asked about it, people told me that they whistled to locate one another in the darkness of the mine. It seems that this practice has carried over from the mine to other areas of the Cooperative, for workers in the plant also often communicate by whistles.[15] As with the use of the *charrasca*, whistling is a practice adapted to the space of the mine that comes to stand for the community of miners. Other workers then extrapolate and imitate the practice to indicate Cooperative membership.

Workers ascend the shaft at around 1:30 (2:30 in the summertime). A number of workers descend back into the mine shortly thereafter to work an overtime shift. Others go off to other jobs or tasks, such as helping a brother, brother-in-law, or *compadre* to build a house. The *perforistas* and their helpers wait for everyone else to leave the mine and then set their charges and leave themselves. They shower and change into street clothes and wait for the Cooperative buses to arrive. The transformation from being "dirty" (*sucio, mugroso*) to "clean" (*limpio*) marks their emergence from the world of the mine. The state of being "dirty" when connected to the mine is a source of pride, as is the state of cleanliness when connected to the surface. Workers bathe as soon as possible when they return to the surface, comb their hair, and change back into clean clothes (usually jeans and long or short sleeved button-down shirts or T-shirts); all this is part of their translation back into the world of the surface. I sometimes brought a camera to the mine, and workers often asked me to take their pictures. Some preferred to have their picture taken once they had returned to the state of "cleanliness," and others asked me to photograph them when they emerged from the mine "all dirty so that my kids can see the work their father does." Being dirty from the mine signifies the honor of mine work. Furthermore, workers' movements up and down the mine shaft, changes of clothing, the transformation between being "clean" and "dirty," and modifications of behavior all mark the passage between the distinct domains of mine and surface.

Workers who are headed to the central plant or who live in Guanajuato city leave first on a bus headed to Dos Rios, down the hill toward the center from the Valenciana. Those who are headed to Santa Rosa de Lima (about five workers) walk to the Valenciana plaza and wait for approximately half an hour to catch the Cooperative bus that leaves from the plant. The mood on the bus is subdued, except on Saturdays. In Santa Rosa, unless they are planning to have some beers or mezcal together, workers usually head to their respective homes with hardly a word, where they will eat the midday meal (*comida*) served to them by their wife or mother. There they reenter the familial space of the house and their roles as stewards of family patrimony instead of producers of Cooperative patrimony. At the same time, in their movements between mine and house they link the two.

What kind of space is produced through the practices of extraction described above, and how is that space perceived by workers and others? First and foremost, the mine is produced as a space that is *distinct* from the world of the surface in very specific ways. The transformations of workers' appearance and behavior as they cross the threshold between mine and surface underscore this distinction. In contrast to the surface, the mine (*la mina*) or underground (*bajo tierra*) is a different world.[16] It is dark, dirty, dangerous, full of loud noise but little human speech, and populated by men who are temporarily estranged from their familial ties and bound to a community of mining companions (*compañeros*).

To navigate the mine and work within it require specialized knowledge, tools, forms of communications, and attitudes. Many workers employed a metaphor of the mine as underground city to express these qualities (see Figure 5.1). Those who work *bajo tierra* are citizens of this underground city by virtue of their local knowledge of its paths and byways and of their participation in a different kind of sociality that operates underground. Life underground is also said to be more egalitarian, for the hierarchies of the *superficie* are suspended in the darkness of the mines. In addition, the ever present danger of the mine intensifies the solidarity of the miners. This city belongs to the miners and not the *jefes* of the Cooperative; *bajo tierra* becomes a space for political mobilization in times of crisis.

The common conceptualization of the mine as city has three main features. First, it is a province of specialized knowledge, only open to those who work there daily. This experiential knowledge brings with it a manly honor and authority. Second, it is a place of enveloping and sheltering darkness. Octavio, one of my neighbors in Santa Rosa de Lima and a *perforista* in Rayas, told me that his brothers and mother did not like his working in the mine, especially because his father had died of silicosis (*cascado*). He told me, "I left for awhile and worked outside [of the mine and the Cooperative] as a bricklayer but I didn't like it. One gets attached to the mine. The sun bothers me now."

Other workers talked about how much they missed the protective darkness of the mine once they no longer worked there. Third, it is a place of solidarity, an underground realm of *communitas,* in Victor Turner's (1969) sense. As one miner put it, "With the miners, what one has he brings to share, they are very generous, and because of the work we all have to be united below ground."

The metaphor of an underground city occurs in other contexts in Guanajuato. For instance, a popular local legend, now mostly for tourist consumption, relates that near the Bufa, a mountainous cliff outside Guanajuato, there is an enchanted city (*una ciudad encantada*) made of silver that is only visible on Holy Thursday. One Holy Thursday our friend Chano, the *lampistero* at Valenciana, took us to see the enchanted city and the princess who waits for a young man who must, like Orpheus, carry her to the Basilica without looking behind him. He brought us to the Bufa telling my husband, David, to prepare himself for some lifting, and teased him mightily when the princess (and the city) failed to appear.

Guanajuatenses also describe the famous tunnels that run underneath the city (many of them built by the Cooperative during the mayoral administration of the former Cooperative director Edgardo Meave Torrescano) as an underground city. And recent archaeological excavations next to the Church of San Diego in the center of town have resurrected popular interest in the idea of an "old Guanajuato" buried underneath the current city streets. As one shopkeeper told me, "Beneath Guanajuato lie many Guanajuatos." I suspect that the metaphor of the mine as underground city gives rise to images of subterranean and esoteric silver cities in other contexts in Guanajuato.

Miners themselves distinguish between mine and surface in conceptual terms, portraying the mine as an esoteric, other-worldly, and perilous place. A common image of *bajo tierra* is that the mine is a domain consecrated to particular saints and virgins. Each mine has one or several patron saints: Valenciana is consecrated to San Cayetano and Cristo de los Mineros; Rayas to San Juan, San Miguel, and Santa Fe de Guanajuato; Cata to the Señor de Villaseca and the Virgin of the Sorrows [*Virgen de Dolores*]; San Ignacio, San Vicente, and San Anton to the saints whose names they bear.[17] These saints were originally designated by the Spanish owners of the mines, who often pledged to use some profits for a chapel or temple to their own patron saint. Thus we find an eighteenth-century church next to and associated with almost all the mines in Guanajuato.

Each entrance to a mine also has its own saint, and thus its own saint's day. On August 8, the day of San Cayetano, I attended a mass and small party at the Bocamina San Cayetano. Don Pancho, one of the workers at the Bocamina, sketched a map with his finger for me that showed how spatial and temporal landscapes can overlap through the consecration of mines to different saints. "Right here," he said, pointing to one spot "is the Bocamina, San Cayetano, August 8, up here is San Ramón, the Cooperative doesn't own that any more, August 31, and down the road here [tracing the path to the Tiro de San José] is San José, that's March 19, but there they never get the money together to give the poor little saint a little party [*darle al pobre santito una fiestecita*]." Each place that he denoted with his finger corresponded simultaneously to an entrance to *bajo tierra* and to a calendar date consecrated to a particular saint. Many places underground also bear sacred names, such as La Merced, Todos Santos, or the names of particular saints such as Santa Isabel or Santo Tomas. These are not necessarily marked by shrines but simply refer to caverns, walls, tunnels, or geographic features of *bajo tierra*.[18]

All the mines, near their entrance, have a shrine to the patron saint or virgin of the mine. One worker described the act of making the sign of the cross at the entrance as "consigning ourselves to God so that he will let us come out again alive and healthy." A card commemorating the 1992 festival for the Santa Cristo de los Mineros, the patron of the Valenciana mine, expresses this sentiment well:

> Santo Cristo de los Mineros
> Care for us and protect us
> In our work,
> Dangerous and treacherous
> Light us in the darkness
> In the Entrails of the Earth
> Where we work, Your Servants
> The Miners
> Santo Cristo de los Mineros
> I promise that I and all
> My companions the miners
> Will always adore you. (Mineral de Valenciana, January 1992)

By crossing themselves, workers also mark a threshold between one domain (*superficie*) and another (*bajo tierra*). Inside the mine there are smaller altars to popular saints and virgins, including but not limited to the patron saint or virgin of the mine. Many of the consecrated images underground are to local and regional favorites. Each level has an altar to the Virgin of Guadalupe, the Virgin of San Juan de los Lagos, Our Lady of Guanajuato, Señor de Villaseca, Santo Niño de Atocha, or other saints and virgins.[19] These are adorned with quartzes from the mines and candles provided by the Cooperative and tended by the captain; as Alvaro told me once, "The candles are for those little saints [*los santitos*], so they won't be in the dark."

It is interesting that, for the most part, I did not find evidence of malign spirits in the mines, such as the Tío described by Nash (1979) and others, or the "Familiar" (another devil figure said to haunt sugar plantations in the Argentinean Chaco (Gordillo 2002). Although one or two people described to me *brujos* (male spirits) who revealed themselves in flashes of light and who seem to be vaguely hostile, almost all description of the divine aspects of the underground were positive, even affectionate (and I did not get the sense that this was merely a propitiatory way of speaking). However, as with these other spirits, the saints and virgins venerated by miners "inform the *production* of places as meaningful localities" defined in contrasting terms (Gordillo 2002: 35; emphasis in the original). Saints and virgins, and the practices surrounding them, help to make the realms of patrimony I describe here.

By consecrating the interior of the mines to saints and virgins, and by placing altars to them at different points in the realm of *bajo tierra*, miners sacralize the geography of the mines, giving their daily journey into the mine a religious quality. The placement of altars in a sequential pattern underground makes the mine a landscape of sacred memory recalling not only the saints to whom the space is consecrated but also those former travelers along the route who have built the altars and placed candles and quartzes on them. The sacred journey through the mine becomes a palimpsest and a reminder of many journeys already taken and still to come, as well as a talisman against future accidents. Looking at the domain of *bajo tierra* as a sacred landscape, we can see the similarities to other scholarly inquiries into sites of memory, among others Maurice Halbwachs's explorations of collective memory (1940, 1950), Frances Yates's discussion of the rhetorical art of memory as embodied in an imaginary progression through a house or landscape punctuated by particular objects or sites (1966),[20] and, most recently, Ellen Schattschneider's discussion of the role of landscape in Japanese religious practice (2003). For instance, in the introduction to this latter work, *La Topographie Légendaire des Évangiles en Terre Sainte* (1940), Halbwachs describes the experiences of pilgrims in the Holy Land in the following way: "Perhaps they hope that their beliefs will be enlivened [*vivifiées*], that they will gain an intensity if what has been presented as a story finds itself face to face with the reality of the places that evoke [that story]" (1–2). The sacred places underground serve to enliven the presence of the mine's patron saints and virgins and the memory of the miners who passed through these same places before. They establish the mine itself as a place of memory.

Another common set of images of the mines is that of the mine as cemetery or burial ground (*panteón*). When workers speak of the mine as a cemetery, they mean it both literally and figuratively. The mine is a place of death, and it brings death to those who work in it. When people, and especially women from Cooperative families, lament accidents and mining illness, they often use the vivid image of the many men who have been literally buried in the mine by cave-ins. One former worker told me, "Mining empties the communities and fills the *panteón*."

Early in my fieldwork I sat with three miners (José, Hector, and Octavio) in Santa Rosa as they drank beer outside the small store across from my house. Their conversation highlights this sense of *bajo tierra* as a privileged and dangerous place, and also a place of death.

José: We miners are very happy [*alegres*; also "fun-loving"].
EF: Are you happy below [*abajo*] as well as above [*arriba*]?
Hector: Happier below than above.
Octavio: We're also very united. We have to be.
José: There's a saying—we know we are going down alive, but we never
   know if we'll come up again.
Hector: It could be that the mine is our tomb—you never know.

Miners recount many stories of premature burial and of the discovery of skeletons in long abandoned corners of the mine. This image of the mine as cemetery overlaps with the characterizations of the mine described above, as underground city and as sacred landscape, for a cemetery can be seen both as a buried city and a consecrated space.

The mine as cemetery also works as a site of memory. This was made very clear to me during a commemoration of the massacre of six miners from El Cubo on April 22, 1937. This massacre took place during the strike of the workers from Section 4 of the Miners' Union, who several years later formed the Santa Fe Cooperative.[21] I attended the sixtieth anniversary of this event, on April 22, 1997. The ceremony began with a mass in the central basilica, after which the congregation, including the municipal marching band (*banda de guerra del municipio*), miners from Las Torres and El Cubo, union functionaries, a group of young boys dressed up in miners' helmets, and the mayor and the PRI candidates for the upcoming municipal elections (to be held in July 1997), paraded to the Santa Paula Municipal Cemetery (*Panteón Municipal Santa Paula*) about 2 kilometers from the city center. This parade mirrors funerary custom, when after a burial mass the bodies are brought to the *panteón* with the congregation processing behind.

At the cemetery the various candidates and union leaders stood in front of the graves of the six men (they are marked by a monument that was put up by the Miners' Union in the 1970s) and gave speeches, much to the disgust of the listeners near me, who felt that the PRI was co-opting the event because of the elections. After several speeches that were received in semi-stony silence, the candidate for *diputado federal*, Francisco Arroyo Vieyra, began to speak. He spoke of the importance of remembering the miners who had died in the massacre and all those miners buried in the *panteón:*

> Those who don't remember history, who have no memory of it, are con-demned to repeat it. That is why we walk the streets of Guanajuato and participate in this funerary prayer (*oración funebre*). These comrade miners (*estos compañeros mineros*) gave riches to all of Mexico, and to the whole world. They have lungs of gold and silver (*tienen pulmones de oro y plata*). [Thanks to them] we now have companies that are much more conscious in the prevention of silicosis, and the unions are much readier to fight for miners' rights.

He then praised the union and mining companies for following the example of these miners buried in the *panteón* who fought and died for these very things. This speaker was much better received than his predecessors; one man next to me said, "This one we'll clap for, he's from Guanajuato, he knows [*eso sí sabe*]."

The speaker here used the overlapping motifs of memory, history, solidarity, urban place ("the streets of Guanajuato"), and burial to great effect. Further-more, the image "they have lungs of silver and gold" is particularly striking in the context of the characterization of the mine as cemetery. For it merges the miners' bodies and the ore in the listeners' imagination, so that not only are the earthly substances of the mines made up of miners' bodies, but their bodies are made up of those substances—gold and silver. I believe that this speaker was par-ticularly well received because he spoke in an idiom particularly evocative for Guanajuatenses, who think of the mines, the city, the *panteón*, and the bodies of miners/citizens as intimately related through material substance.[22] The sense that miners have that many of the dead buried in the mine may be their own fathers and grandfathers reinforces a sense of the mine as the source and repos-itory of patrilineal kinship.

The confluence of these associations recalls Fustel de Coulanges' (1864) characterization of domestic hearths as burial grounds and foci of the funda-mental ancient social unit, the *gens*. Fustel argues that the domestic worship of the ancestors, centered on the family hearth and tomb, and "always passed from male to male; [so] that a woman participated in it only through her father or her husband" (39), formed the basis of private property and political legitimacy. This characterization strongly resonates with the patrilineal model of Cooperative kinship, as it has with other political configurations, in the way in which it emphasizes the patrimonial possessions that are passed down along the patriline and the mine as the quintessential and earthy space of memory and sacrality associated with the social group (Verdery 1999).

Although men and women may use similar metaphors to describe the mine, they often give these metaphors markedly different valence. Many miners like working in the mine a great deal and when they are told that they can no longer work underground, they feel deprived of the chance to do the work they feel comfortable with and to be *bajo tierra*. Miners often told me "*es bonita la mina*" (the mine is beautiful/agreeable).[23]

One retired driller, who worked for twenty-three years in the Rayas mine and now works as a guard at the central plant, said:

> Working in the mine is *bonita*. The shift goes very quickly. You go into the mine at seven in the morning, and since it's very dark you don't know what time it is, and already it's time to leave. It's dangerous, sure, when you get hit by a rock here, or here, or here [gesturing to his head, heart, and leg], you never know when it might happen. But I was sad when I had to stop working in the mine, I thought, "Now what am I going to do?"

Jaime, Alvaro's nephew, who works in San Vicente, described the mine in similar terms:

> The mine is *bonita*, once you're used to it. So much so that there are some people who are sick and broken down and they don't want to leave the mine. . . . the bad thing is that through the years one gets damaged (*se casca uno*) and can't do the work so well.

Although men often talked about their love of the mine, they are also affected by the periodic deaths and severe accidents that take place there. The Cooperative mines are blessed with a location at the northern end of Veta Madre where the rock is quite hard and there are few cave-ins. Nevertheless, there were three fatal accidents during my twenty months of fieldwork and several other serious injuries (see chapter 6). One former miner (now one of the *malacateros*, who runs the car that transports workers and ore up and down the shaft, at Valenciana) described his feelings after an accident:

> I saw two deaths in the mine. I didn't see them at the moment of death, but right afterwards. You feel *un feo* (a bad, ugly feeling), you feel sadness

and also fear. Because every day you go down in the mine with these people, they're your *compañeros*. And one day they can die, so you afterwards you go down in the mine with a very nervous fear, but then you get used to it again.

Only men characterized the mine as *bonita*; women were far more likely to call it *fea* (ugly, dirty, dangerous; the opposite of *bonita*). One woman in Santa Rosa said to me, "It's a job for moles, not men." The divergence in male and female opinions of the mines begins very early in life. Among the children in my English class in Santa Rosa, the little boys often talked of how they loved to visit the mine on Sundays and how when they grew up they would work in the mine. They always showed great anticipation and bravado. The little girls, in contrast, called the mine *fea* and dangerous. One girl told me, "I hate it when my father goes down in the mine. It scares me [*me da miedo*]." Her female classmates nodded solemnly in agreement when she said this. On other occasions some boys stated that they wanted to work on the surface, perhaps echoing their parents' aspirations for them as professionals within the Cooperative or surface workers, but in a situation of group bravado, they all announced that they wanted to work in the mine.[24] From an early age both boys and girls understand the mine's association with male bravery, honor, and the potential for death.

Images of the mine as a dark, dirty, and dangerous place where other rules apply than those on the surface have both positive and negative valence. Even as these images can organize social labor in the interest of the more powerful, they also provide a space for counterhegemonic understandings of the mine, male labor, and the right use of patrimony. For instance, when women (and girls) characterize the mine as *fea*, they invert dominant Cooperative images of honorable dirt and sacred burial by invoking negative associations of pollution associated with dirt and with the dead.

Although the inhabitants of the mine are all male, and the mine as site of burial and memory emphasizes the patrilineal line, workers and their families often characterize the mine as a female space, and particularly as a woman or womb. The most obvious example of this is the term "Veta Madre" (Mother Vein or Mother Lode). T. A. Rickard (1907: 181) describes the "great lode of Guanajuato, called the *Veta Madre*, a term which in the guise of Mother Lode has also been applied to the main vein-system of California."[25]

The idea of the mine as female space goes back a long while; it is said that earlier women were not allowed to be down in the mine, because the vein would become jealous (*la veta se pondra celosa*) and withdraw its riches, or because the presence of women would cause accidents. This line of argument is also reported in other Mexican and Latin American contexts. In Pachuca, Hidalgo, women were only allowed down in the mines on Sundays (Cesar Vojdovich, personal communication). Janet Finn notes the "feminine mystique" of mines in Chile, described by one commentator as symbolizing "insecurity, capriciousness, betrayal" (quoted in Finn 1998: 127). June Nash reports that the engineer in charge of safety in the tin mines in Oruro, Bolivia, tried to prevent her from going down in the mines on the grounds that workers objected to the presence of women in the mines because, he said,

> "of suspicion that it would bring bad luck to the enterprise." However, all of the miners with whom I spoke wanted very much for me to enter the mines. . . . Whether they suspended belief in the adage about a woman's presence in the mines, or whether they reclassified me as a non-woman because of the more prevailing role of a foreign investigator, I do not know. (1979: 171–172)

Based on my own experience, I suspect a combination of factors were in play. Mexican woman did occasionally go down in the mines, and there was never any objection. This is not to say that when I went down in the mines, I received the same response as male visitors, such as my husband. Miners not used to seeing me in the mines always thought the sight was pretty hilarious, and not only because the clothes and equipment were all too big for me. Rather, it was seen as a humorous cross-dressing episode. I think the comedy came, at least in part, from the mixing of the categories of woman/miner.

At the same time Cooperative workers also coin new gendered characterizations for the mines. For example, one worker told me that when the Valenciana reopened operations in the mid-1960s, "the mine was just a girl" (*la mina era niña*). By this he meant that production was high and there were many avenues for exploitation. In contrast, production and grade of ore in the Valenciana have steadily declined over the past five years. His characterization both feminizes the mines and gives a sense that it is reaching the end of its productive/reproductive life. People often referred to the mines as "*acabadas*" (exhausted, worn out—often used to describe a person). In this formulation anxieties over the future are expressed in overlapping metaphors of the mine as young girl, bountiful mother, and exhausted womb. As we shall see, Cooperative workers and their families make an analogy between mineral production and sexual reproduction that posits the mine as a counterpart to human women.

Workers and their families have strongly gendered associations with the mine's exterior structure, interior contents, and inhabitants; that is, the exterior and interior of the mine are both particularly associated with the activities of gendered persons (especially men). They also exhibit qualities that appear distinctively male or female (Strathern 1988, Keane 1997). The enveloping framework of the mine and the quartz matrix that surround silver are seen as female, while the workers who enter the mine and the silver itself are male. By a synecdochic move similar to that deployed in the case of mine implements such as *charrascas* and the practice of whistling as communication, the mine stands in for the Cooperative as a whole, which is also imagined as female, while the vast majority of its members are male. For instance, the former head of the Cooperative referred often to "*Mama Cooperativa*" and current members echo this phrase to emphasize its maternal qualities and also to suggest the corruption of the former administrative council, implying that favored members suckle at the breast of the mother Cooperative. In describing the fallout between two Cooperative engineers during the political crisis in the fall of 1997, Martín said, "They used to be friends, but not anymore. They both chased the same woman, named 'Cooperativa.'"

These gendered associations of the mine and the Cooperative tap into powerfully held—and powerfully androcentric—notions of generativity, by assigning agency for the reproduction of patrimony to men who enter the passive female space of the mine. The mine comes to embody the asymmetric gender relations prevailing in the Cooperative and in the notion of patrimony. Men's acts of entering the mine to produce silver which will go out into the world and return in the form of houses and food for the sons of those men can be seen as an androcentric form of reproduction, in which male labor is seen as transformative and generative.

Such versions of sexual reproduction with respect to forms of production can be found in other ethnographic contexts. In Carol Delany's (1994) description of Turkish villagers' beliefs about agricultural production and procreation, women are seen as the passive bearers or conduits of male generative labor. And in Eugenia Herbert's (1993: 228) analysis of smelting, metallurgy, and gender in Sub-Saharan Africa, the actions of senior males upon gynecomorphic furnaces produces iron, the substance of fertility and transformation. In Herbert's words, "Female power is not denied; it is appropriated or assimilated because male power alone would be inadequate to the idiom of reproduction and regenerative power encapsulated in ironworking."

Closer still to our own case, June Nash's study of tin miners in Oruro, Bolivia, describes an equilibrium between the female force of the Pachamama, associated with subsistence agriculture, and the pre-Columbian order of things and the male power of Supay who rules the realm of the underground and mining. While these miners do not seem to make an explicit analogy between mining and sexual reproduction, they do "project . . . onto the natural world the image of the human" (Herbert 1993, 166) by ascribing to the realms of surface and underground gendered forms of power. However, the notion of mining as a conduit for male transformative power also provides the means for its own renegotiation.

Once it has emerged from the mine, silver continues on its journey to the processing plant at the Cooperative headquarters, where it is made into an ore-rich concentrate. It is then transported by truck to the Grupo México foundry at San Luis Potosí. At this point the foundry pays the Cooperative for the silver, gold, and copper in the concentrate and the silver passes out of Cooperative hands. The money is then used for capital investment, wages, loans and subsidies, and profit sharing. One of the most important destinations of the money that proceeds from the sale of silver is in the building of a Cooperative house and the maintenance of a Cooperative household. It is here that Cooperative patrimony translates into the inheritance of particular Cooperative families. Many Cooperative members and their families portray the space of the house where this takes place as a second realm of patrimony.

Houses as Realms of Patrimony

> They'll make him sweep the floors, and for a mining man that is an insult.
> —Cooperative miner, August 1997

Let us now turn to another realm in which patrimony is produced and reproduced—Cooperative houses. How do productive and reproductive practices—especially house building and housekeeping—produce the house, like the mine, as a gendered space? How are male and female labor incorporated and valorized in these processes, and how is difference—between men and women and between Cooperative members and outsiders—arranged within the house and its immediate surroundings? How do the houses that are built and kept by Cooperative men and women provide material models of sociality? Exploring these questions helps us to understand the arrangement of power and the construction of difference in the Cooperative, and the patrimonial idiom in which these arrangements are cast.

To have a clear sense of how power and difference are organized in Cooperative houses, we need to start by seeing how the houses themselves are built. In a survey conducted by the Social Work Department of the Cooperative, of 212 Cooperative families living in Guanajuato and in surrounding communities, 55 percent reported that they lived in houses made of brick, 22 percent in adobe houses, and 4 percent in houses made partly of brick and partly of adobe.[26] Families living in the city of Guanajuato tend to own, borrow, or rent houses that have already been constructed, often generations before. The denseness of these neighborhoods makes it difficult to build, and the municipal government requires strict adherence to the "historic" guidelines of certain neighborhoods, which also deters new construction. On the outskirts of town, people build houses first of cardboard and corrugated tin (*lámina*) and (if they can) successively replace the walls and roof with brick (*tabique*) and reinforced concrete (*loza*). Many characterize this evolution of houses as a part of the life cycle, an outward sign of maturity, familial responsibility, and upward mobility.[27] For instance, the accountant in charge of the ceramics workshop said to me:

> I live in a poor neighborhood (*barrio popular*) where there are many Co-operativistas, and it is nice to see how they grow over a few years. First they have their little house (*su casita*) with cardboard and tin, with no bathroom, and then little by little they make a nice house (*una casa bonita*) with brick and concrete. It usually takes about five years.

The unspoken subtext of this description of the growth of the family is that this outcome depends on the responsibility of the man, his ability to manipulate familial and sociopolitical networks within the Cooperative, and the right use of patrimony. In Santa Rosa and elsewhere in Guanajuato people often used houses to mark the right use of patrimony and to judge male heads of families (*padres de familia*). Indeed, Cooperative families in Santa Rosa, especially those who were in the Cooperative during the prosperous years of the 1970s and 1980s, see themselves as a kind of burgher class of Santa Rosa, more prosperous and more responsible than the woodcutters, charcoal makers, bricklayers, and migrant workers who are their neighbors. The knowledge of how to *aprovechar las circunstancias* (take advantage of the circumstances), to use patrimony well, results in a comfortable, handsome house that displays the family's prosperity and responsibility to the rest of the community.

In semi-rural communities, like Santa Rosa, houses begin as *adobe* and move toward brick and stone. This transition entails conceptions of class and urbanity. In conversations with Santa Rosa residents, people often praised adobe for its durability and that it is warm in the winter (*calientito*). However, many of these same people, especially those under forty years of age, would follow these remarks by saying that they were building a brick house or planned to do so when they could afford it. One worker told me, "Yes, adobe is warm, but brick makes the house look more or less good." One neighbor, the son and brother of a Cooperative worker, laughed with me about the new fashion of rich Guanajuatenses building their houses out of adobe.[28] He said, "I have lived in adobe all my life, and it has a lot of advantages, but it is for poor people [*para los po-bres*]. I won't go back to living in adobe."[29]

In Santa Rosa de Lima one sees houses at various stages of construction and dilapidation. Up and down the Camino Real and in the byways that lead off from it into the hills, there are cozy adobe cottages covered with flowers both growing wild and in flowerpots, as well as birds twittering in cages nailed to the walls facing the patio. Other adobe houses are falling down since they have not been lived in for years; perhaps their owners are waiting for higher silver prices to ask for a loan and begin rebuilding. Many houses have some rooms or walls made of *tabique* and some of adobe. On Sundays and summer afternoons— when the daylight lasts longer—men are working on houses, or on one of the small chapels and niches that dot the Camino Real.

In many cases the land has been in a worker's family for generations, and the adobe houses are very old. Most of the male Cooperative workers from Santa Rosa grew up in an adobe house on the same land where they are now living. Once they marry and begin to have children, they may build a house (*fincar*) in the same compound using Cooperative loans, and materials and the labor of their relatives by blood and marriage. As in other parts of Mexico people build houses slowly, over a period of months, even years. It takes time to make money or obtain loans for construction materials, and since men and their relatives, *compadres*, and friends provide the labor ("*entre cuates* [among friends]," as the saying goes) they often can only work on Saturday afternoons, Sundays, and holidays. It is common to see one or two walls of a house standing alone for many months until the family gets enough money, time, and labor to proceed.

Many of the men who work on these houses are also Cooperative members. In Santa Rosa and other communities, it is quite likely that a man's brothers, brothers-in-law (*cuñados*), and *compadres*, if they are still living in Santa Rosa, work for the Cooperative. The common experience of Cooperative members thus strengthens familial and ritual ties. On a practical level, it is easier to organize labor from those who share a regime of work discipline. Finally, the greater the number of Cooperative members working on a project, the more opportunities there are for manipulating Cooperative social ties in order to borrow trucks to transport materials or to use building tools and materials from the mines or plant.

The relatives and friends of the house builder are not paid in cash for their labor. Rather, they help because they know that they may soon wish or be able to build a house themselves, and that by giving labor they can hope to obtain labor in return. The house builder also usually provides food and beer, *mezcal*, or tequila for the workers.[30] Since most Guanajuatense men are accomplished builders, they rarely need to pay for any labor.[31] Nevertheless, building a brick and concrete house is a substantial financial undertaking even if one already owns the land. In 1997–98 my informants estimated that building a house of this sort costs between twenty thousand and thirty thousand pesos (two thousand and three thousand dollars) per room. In spite of this cost, nearly every family I spoke with hoped to build a "nice house" (*una casa bonita*).[32]

In Santa Rosa houses rarely open directly onto the street. Most have a gate leading to the central patio; the house may be the only one that faces this patio or it may be one of several arranged as a compound, often with an outhouse or kitchen or both for all the houses.[33] This gate may limit access to non-Catholics; many households affix a sign to the gate produced by the bishopric of León that reads, "This home is Catholic / We do not accept Protestant or other sects' evangelists" (*Este hogar es Católico/No se acepta evangelistas Protestantes o de otros sectos*).[34]

Generally speaking, men build houses; women keep them. Every morning the women of the house or compound sweep the patio, which may or may not be paved with stones or cement. If it has an earthen floor, they sprinkle water from a bowl to keep the dust down as they sweep up the trash that has blown in during the night. This makes the earth into a smooth burnished surface, at least until the dust returns in the heat of the day. Cats, dogs, and chickens have the run of this patio (with varying degrees of tolerance on the part of their owners), but larger animals such as goats or pigs are penned up.

Regardless of the material with which the house is built, almost all houses are kept spotlessly clean. Every day the wife and daughters of each house mop the floors, sweep the patio and the street in front of the house, wash the dishes, make or buy corn tortillas, prepare food and feed the men and children, wash bed linens and clothes, do the shopping (for any items not delivered by the Cooperative), and tend the animals. This daily labor makes the house *limpia* (clean) and *bonita*.

Women also arrange and care for the decorations of the rooms and outside patios. Together these adornments make the house into a decent Cooperative home. On the outside of the house they often place flowerpots or birdcages affixed to the outside walls facing the patio. On the walls inside (painted rich, cheerful shades of azure, teal, or rose) they hang family pictures, posters, and calendars from local business establishments. The walls are hung with plain white, flowered, or lacy curtains. There is usually a cross in the bedroom and a domestic altar in the living room (which, in smaller houses, may also serve as the bedroom). These altars combine personal and familial souvenirs (*recuerdos*) with the images of saints and virgins. Often they also include lace doilies, miniature dolls, animals or pieces of furniture, and natural or artificial flowers.[35] In Cooperative homes they invariably include arrangements of mineral specimens from the mines.[36] In a manner similar to the altars found in the mines, these altars establish sites of memory and sacrality in the heart of daily activity. In contrast to the altars in the mines, however, these altars incorporate more familial and "feminine" details (see Hirsch 2003) and are maintained by women rather than men. Their arrangement by women (for the most part) and the qualities they hold of delicacy, miniaturization, and interiority mark them as gendered female objects.

Susan Stewart (1993: 137–138) has written an account of the sense of scale in the production of nostalgia and longing that provides an interesting perspective on the altars and selections of souvenirs in Cooperative homes. She considers the miniature and the gigantic, the souvenir, scrapbook, and collection, as entwined in a dense web of signification related to questions of interiority/exteriority, gender, the state, and the body. The anthologies of objects found in these domestic altars "reduce the public, monumental, and the three-dimensional into the miniature, that which can be enveloped by the body [and the house], that which can be appropriated within the privatized view of the subject." In the case of the stones, they also reduce the realm of the mine into a size that can be enveloped by the realm of the house, interiorizing, domesticating, and feminizing the activities of production that generated the stones, which then stand for the mine in miniature.

In this way the altars, and the stones adorning them, act something like the offering trays described by Ellen Schattschneider (2003: 138) in her analysis of ritual in a Northern Japanese mountain shrine, in which the "trays are . . . exemplary, iconic models of the domain of the gods and other sacred sites. . . . In presenting daily offerings, the worshippers thus align themselves with the sacred shape of the mountain in its mysterious manifestations and transmutations."

This kind of housekeeping and these kinds of houses are common in Guanajuato and in the Bajío region in general.[37] Most rich and poor families in Guanajuato and its surroundings decorate their houses in these ways; the materials differ according to the prosperity of the household. For instance, middle-class homes in Guanajuato may have terra cotta pots affixed to balconies with intricate ironwork, whereas women in poorer households in Santa Rosa nail tin cans filled with flowers to adobe walls. However, in the case of the Cooperative, that the house is a site for the realization of Cooperative patrimony as family patrimony intensifies the meanings that accrue to it. What meanings are these? What kind of a space is produced through the male and female labor of house building and housekeeping?

House building and housekeeping by men and women make the house a space of cleanliness, pleasantness, civility, and respectability. These attributes provide a model of proper sociality. The house becomes a microcosm of and model for the city and civility, not only for Cooperative members and their families but also for many other Guanajuatenses and Mexicans. I saw many instances of this conceptualization in Guanajuato: in small signs posted at the doorway of private homes saying, "In this house, we sweep the street every day"; in a TV commercial for floor cleaner that adapted the mariachi song "México *lindo* y querido" (*Mexico—beautiful and beloved*) to "México *limpio* y querido" (*Mexico—clean and beloved*); and in posters from the municipal government saying "Sweep your street [*tu calle*; the length of street in front of your house]—do it for Guanajuato." These hortatory statements suggest equivalencies (both metaphoric and metonymic) between the house, the city, and the nation. They also seem to give the task of keeping a clean house (and thus a good city and good nation) to women.[38]

The suggestions for interior decorating and cleaning given to me by the children in my English class, who clearly saw that I could use some training as the lady of the house, also expressed these principles. The girls in my class took every opportunity to sweep in my house (Santa Rosa is very dusty) in what I took as a broad hint. On one occasion Kike, Alvaro's son, with his sisters watching approvingly, unloaded a crate of minerals from the mine and carefully arranged them next to a cross in my living room. "That's much better," he said, when he had finished, with a kind air that said, "If you don't know what you're supposed to do, I'd better show you." These children saw that I needed the training their mothers were giving them in keeping a home that expressed Guanajuatenses' aesthetics and ideals of respectability, religion, and sociality. They jumped at the chance to play this role, much as a child might play mother to a smaller sibling or doll.

The link between the house and community or city is the space in front of the house. This space is both domestic and private (*tu calle;* your street). In Santa Rosa the main street is cobblestone and dirt, and every morning between 7:00 and 9:00 A.M. women and girls sweep the length of the street in front of their home.[39] Often a mother or older daughter is sweeping accompanied by a little girl sweeping with a little broom, a sweet picture of the reproduction of gender through practice. So I began to sweep in front of our house. At first I just went out and began sweeping with a broom; I raised a huge cloud of dust and caused great amusement to the men sitting in front of the small store across the street, who began yelling "throw water [on the ground]!" (¡*Pongale agua!*). I then tried to be a bit more observant of my female neighbors and brought a pan of water out with me to sprinkle on the ground and keep the dust down.

Once I started to sweep, I became a part of the town in a new way; women and those men who already knew me would murmur hellos as they passed me while I was (still not very effectually) sweeping. Often women would ask amiably "¿ya?" (*already?*). This was a way of locating me in my daily tasks, since women usually sweep after feeding their husbands and children who are off to work and school; it is the first housekeeping task of the day.[40] Their remark also had a note of friendly complacency, for those who passed my house were usually on their way to or from the *tortillería*, having already finished the sweeping.

The qualities of the proper Cooperative house, then, include the following: being *limpia* and *bonita*, cheerfully and colorfully painted, and full of signs of familial affection and Catholic religiosity; demonstrating male responsibility and labor in its exterior while rich in "feminine" details in its interior; and being set off from the public street by the intermediate space of the patio while at the same time extending its domestic cleanliness into the street. This description shows how mine and house both share similarities and exhibit marked contrasts.[41]

In the analogy I have described between Cooperative mines imbued with male labor and Cooperative houses imbued with female labor, it is clear that there is also some imbalance. While Cooperative membership and mining are recognized as activities that have some similarities but many differences with other forms of male labor (even mining labor) in Guanajuato, the activities and surroundings of a Cooperative wife in Santa Rosa are largely the same as her non-Cooperative neighbors. However, that these activities and surroundings are made possible by the profits from silver extraction and are thus valued as Cooperative patrimony in another form gives them a peculiar quality, tying houses and female labor into the logic of patrimony within a Cooperative context. This logic of patrimony, furthermore, is seen as enabling and safeguarding an idealized version of Mexican female domesticity threatened by recent political and economic transformations. In other words, the right use of Cooperative patrimony allows people to be not only good Cooperative members but also good Mexican men and women.

Both mine and house are interior spaces built and arranged with Cooperative resources and maintained by the labor of Cooperative members and their families. Both spaces bring together sentiments of gender, memory, and sacrality in the specific sites of altars. Both include an architectural boundary between exterior and interior that is also a passage between social and symbolic states (Van Gennep [1914] 1960). Both combine a complex symbolism of interior/exterior and female/male. Both are strongly associated with the proper disposition of patrimonial possessions. And both provide models of sociality connected to that of the city and operating according to complex rules of membership, spatial organization, and comportment.

At the same time workers and their families use a series of conceptual oppositions to portray the relationship between mine and house. In the mine the exterior framework is constructed as female, while the contents and inhabitants are male. In the case of the house, the exterior is associated with male labor and the interior is understood as a female space under the care of women. Similarly, while cleanliness is the proper state of the house, dirtiness is appropriate to the mine. This contrast provokes some fascinating considerations. In the house, being *limpio* is a sign of a decent home and proper female work in its maintenance as a site for the reproduction of the family. In the mine, being *sucio* or *mugroso* (dirty) is a sign of the honor of the mine and proper male work in its maintenance as a site for the production of silver. In this way the spaces of mine and house provide alternative but complementary visions of sociality. The use of imagery of house and city to describe these spaces underscores these visions.

PATRIMONY AND MATRIMONY: WORK AND RESIDENCE

In questions of income and domestic economy, men and women also are understood to occupy distinct spaces. In houses inhabited by a Cooperative worker and his wife and children, the main household income is usually the wages, profit shares, and loans to the worker from the Cooperative. Some workers may also have a pension from Social Security for work-related injuries or illnesses (especially silicosis). In addition to this income, workers may have other jobs or sources of income. Miners and middlemen sell mineral specimens to tourists and collectors, while those in the various Cooperative workshops, such as the woodshop or automotive pool, can do outside jobs after hours, using the Cooperative workspace and tools. Other workers hire themselves out for construction jobs or work as tourist guides. The Cooperative's lenient absentee policy facilitates these practices.

The majority of the Cooperative workers whom I interviewed, as well as those interviewed by the Cooperative social work department, reported that their wives "dedicate themselves to the home" (*se dedican al hogar*). I accompanied the social workers on a number of interviews; when they asked men this question, the men almost always answered with pride and perhaps a touch of defensiveness. It seemed as if any other answer would suggest that they were improper men for not providing for their women, and perhaps also that their wives were improper women for going outside the home to work.[42]

But women who "dedicate themselves to the home" also can bring in income, by cooking for weddings and fiestas, doing washing or sewing, or selling second-run pottery from Dolores Hidalgo, freshly killed chicken *menudo* (tripe stew, a Sunday specialty and renowned hangover cure), cactus leaves (*nopales;* a tasty and popular vegetable not available in Santa Rosa stores), or Tupperware. People usually did not mention these income-producing activities in the Cooperative survey or in structured interviews but would bring them up in conversation or offer me a product or service when the occasion arose. These activities, which are based in the house, do not seem to interfere with the identification of a Cooperative wife as "dedicating herself to the home," although they may be a significant supplement to family finances.

There is a significant difference between "dedicating oneself to the home" while still producing income and working outside the home. The second wife of a Cooperative worker who was killed in a tailings dump accident in November 1996 complained to me that her stepchildren did not want her to work as a housemaid in Guanajuato.[43] "They think I am going to go wandering like a bad woman" (Piensan que voy a andar vagando como una mala mujer). But they did not mind her selling chicken and flour tortillas from her home in Santa Rosa. From this perspective, staying in one place and not "wandering like a bad woman" seems integral to the idea of a proper Cooperative wife.

A number of female members of Cooperative families and residents of Santa Rosa do work outside the home, traveling to Guanajuato on the bus along with men. It is worth noting, however, that in many cases these are unmarried daughters or sisters rather wives of Cooperative members. A sense persists among many townspeople—especially but not exclusively older people—that the man is supposed to bring in money from outside the home or at least that he is the one who is supposed to go outside the home to earn money.

The practices of production and reproduction, as conceived by many Cooperative workers and their families, link the spaces of mine and house and the location of men and women within those spaces. While the mine is the site of male sociality and productive activity, the house organizes reproductive activities and familial and sexual sociality (especially those forms of sociality associated with women). Income-producing activities by women are appropriate only if they take place in the home (when the woman cooks or sews in the home, or buys things to be sold out of her house) and are themselves appropriately feminine (cooking, sewing, or selling decorative or household items or food). This spatial division of labor organizes the complex way in which mine and house are bound together and distinguished. However, even as Cooperative workers and their families locate productive and reproductive activities in the distinct spaces of mine and house, they also link them through analogic practice.

This perspective is enacted in local residence patterns. In Guanajuato, as in many parts of Mexico, virilocal residence in extended kin compounds has prevailed until recently (Collier 1978, Hanks 1990, Hogar en México 1993, Nutini 1968). These compounds are often composed of several interconnected households, with the largest house occupied by the oldest married couple, surrounded by smaller houses with their married sons and unmarried or widowed daughters. When I asked a group of Cooperative members why it was more usual for a newly married couple to live with the parents of the man, they made the following responses: "It's the custom that we have here"; "Because of the man's authority"; "It's the man's obligation to have a house for the woman." When I asked Chano the same questions, he responded, smiling, "Don't you think that the man's parents will help him more than his in-laws will?" These statements indicate the degree to which virilocality (where men tend to stay in or near their natal homes with their wives and children, while women move to the homes of their husbands) is tied to ideas of male responsibilities as husband.

This arrangement represents one phase in the developmental cycle of the household. In some cases in Santa Rosa, young couples move away from these virilocal compounds after a few years; however, they often build a separate house next to or near the original house. Although Guanajuato lies almost outside the borders of Mesoamerica, the practice has affinities with what David Robichaux (1997: 149) has termed the "Mesoamerican stem family," characterized by "initial virilocal residence and culminat[ing] in male ultimogeniture [where the youngest son helps take care of his aging parents and ultimately inherits the house]."

Cooperative families who lived in this arrangement reported that they did not share domestic expenses, although the sons may support their widowed mother or their father if he is no longer working. As one pensioned Cooperative worker told me, "My boy maintains me [*mi chavo me mantiene*]. It's natural after so much time [when he maintained his son, presumably]." In this case, the *chavo* in question was the youngest son, conforming to the pattern of male ultimogeniture found elsewhere in Mesoamerica and its outskirts.

This configuration, while common, is not always preferred by its participants. Many people, especially women, told me that they would prefer to live away from their in-laws, and especially their mother-in-law (*suegra*). The difficulties of living with one's relatives, and, above all, the tensions between mothers-in-law and daughters-in-law living in the same house, remain the topic of many discussions and jokes. As one man said to me, "What we say in Mexico is: with relatives and the sun, the further away the better" (*con parientes y el sol, entre más lejos, mejor*).[44] The tension between *nueras* and *suegras* who live together has been widely reported in the literature on rural Mexico (Nutini 1968, Varley 2000).[45]

Virilocal residence can also tend to promote the idea of women as exchangeable goods among male trading partners (Lévi-Strauss 1969, Rubin 1974). And there is some ethnographic evidence within the Cooperative to support such a view. In the genealogies I took of Cooperative members, women were far more likely to move from one city, community, or neighborhood to another upon marriage. Some jokes also reflect the perceived negotiable character of women. When my friend Gabriel told a group of Cooperative members that he had an infant daughter, one grinned and said "¡*Cooperaste!*" (you chipped in, or anted up; that is, contributed a girl to the general pool of future available women). However, the complementarity of mine and house as spaces of production and reproduction also suggests other formulations of kinship and gender. In the introduction to their edited volume, *Gender and Kinship: Essays toward a Unified Analysis* (1978), Collier and Yanagisako propose a unification of the hitherto separate analytical domains of kinship and gender, and a focus on the social production of difference and inequality. By adopting these analytic premises they call into question the distinctions between "domestic/public" and "productive/reproductive" that have structured (and continue to structure) much social theory. Similarly Cooperative members and their families, even as they separate these domains, see them as existing within a unified "social whole" (35) of production/reproduction.

Recent influences such as migration can support virilocality (Hirsch 2003: 67–68). In Santa Rosa and the hamlets (*ranchitos*) nearby, it is not uncommon for a man to elope with his girlfriend and bring her to his mother's and father's house, and then leave shortly after for the United States to work. In cases where the wife has become pregnant, he may come back in time for the birth or shortly afterward, having earned money to begin to build the new family's own house and to pay for the baptism. In these conditions a young woman may be left for many months in the home of her new *suegra,* whom she may barely know.

Cooperative membership may support this domestic arrangement, since those who live with a Cooperative member can share in the benefits and subsidies that he (or sometimes she) receives. This organization of households around males reinforces an idea of patrimony as a gendered and familial category. When the men in these families/households belong to the Cooperative, the linked categories of family and Cooperative patrimony come to seem even more gendered and familial in character.

The incidence of virilocality and male ultimogeniture is not by any means universal in Santa Rosa. Rather, it seems to be a common preference that is often taken into account among other factors in determining residence and disposition of property. When I asked people in Santa Rosa, "Who inherits the house, in general?" they often responded first by saying, "it depends on the situation," and then adding, "the youngest [son] [*el más chico*], no?" This type of response indicates an awareness of a "residence rule" that is one among many considerations. In some cases, men see their role as fathers as extending beyond this basic obligation. For instance, Alvaro once told me that he planned to leave the house he lived in (which, in fact, belonged to his wife) to his son and to build a separate house for each of his daughters (see chapter 6).

The combination of virilocality and male ultimogeniture contributes to the classification of houses as patrimonial possessions to be handed down patrilineally. This mode of classification thus links houses to other forms of patrimony, such as membership in the Cooperative and the privileges that brings, and, at the level of the Cooperative, to silver and profits from silver. Hence all these forms of patrimony are linked: membership in the Cooperative gives one access to profits from silver (Cooperative patrimony), which can then be converted into houses (family patrimony).

PATRIMONY AND MATRIMONY: WOMEN AND MALE OBLIGATION

The language of patrimony incorporates notions of gender, kinship, and space that reproduce relations of power within the Cooperative. At the same time the implied complementarity of production and reproduction offers opportunities for women to use patrimony to their advantage. For instance, when women talk about the use of resources and the obligations of men and of the Cooperative, they often criticize both for not living up to their roles as men and fathers. They do so by accusing men and the Cooperative of disrupting the journey of patrimonial resources from mine to house.

For instance, in conversations with me and others, women often pointed to the habit of men getting paid on Saturday and not returning home until the next day, drinking away their entire weekly pay by Monday. Some men do this every week in Santa Rosa. The house where my husband and I lived during fieldwork was between the Cooperative bus stop and many of the workers' homes. Every Saturday some men would buy beer and sit near an old well opposite our house and get drunk from 2:00 P.M. until late at night. In criticizing these acts, women depicted them as squandering male potency and economic power outside the family, rather than reinvesting them in the family patrimony, by producing sons and providing them with a house, decent clothes, and an education.

As well as confronting their own husbands and other male relatives, women call the Cooperative to account for failing in its assumed responsibilities for Cooperative families. From one point of view, the Cooperative lays itself open to these accusations by actively promoting a paternalistic and familial image. When

I interviewed members of the Cooperative social work, provisions, and health and safety departments, they continually reiterated that the Cooperative existed primarily to help its members and their families. The Department of Social Work provides a case in point. This department most directly handles the distribution of family benefits, especially in the case of accidents, illness, and death. Furthermore, the social work department is a major site of interaction between the Cooperative as an institution and the families of Cooperative members. It handles school scholarships, textbook distribution, and subsidies for eyeglasses, kitchen appliances, and so on. The social workers also act as liaisons with Social Security and accompany any workers to the hospital in Guanajuato or León in the event of an accident. They organize Cooperative social events, such as the Christmas Posada and the Día del Niño (Day of the Child—April 30). Along with the workers who deliver subsidized groceries to the neighborhoods every week and the women who work in the Cooperative-owned supermarket, the social work department has the most contact with women in Cooperative families.

The head of the department is the wife of one of the engineers, who is also the head of the Oversight Committee and thus a *jefe*. She often criticized the behavior of both men and women connected to the Cooperative. She condemned Cooperative men for drinking and wasting money that should go to the home. She said:

> The miner is very difficult, very macho, he doesn't want his wife to leave the house to enjoy herself, he always goes alone to parties, drinking a lot. He often has other women and even other children. It makes him feel like a man to have more women and more children. This is a bad thing. Also, he often spends his whole week's wages on Saturday [payday].

But, at the same time, she criticized the women in the Cooperative for not participating in Cooperative events, not taking sufficient responsibility for their children and their house, and not welcoming her and other social workers when they went out on home visits or conducted surveys. While she never voiced this to women directly, she did talk to me separately about their difficulties in "making the wives [or "ladies"] understand" (*haciendo entender las señoras*).

This perspective has a history in the Cooperative. Traditionally the job of head social worker has been held by a woman associated with the social circle of the Cooperative elite, and the wives of Cooperative engineers and other *jefes* used to be very involved in "social programs" for the Cooperative workers. The former social worker, Señora Elöisa, had a "Mothers' Club" (*Club de Madres*) of two hundred to three hundred women, and a sewing and knitting group. Señora

Elöisa saw her role as educating the wives of workers to be "good wives" to their husbands and legalizing common law unions. In an interview with Aurora Jáuregui, the wife of the Cooperative's doctor during several decades and the author of a book chronicling the Cooperative's history, she said,

> I used to say to [the wives], "Take an interest in your husband, go find him on payday, go for the groceries, fix yourself up, take off your apron, make yourself pretty." . . . A couple of years ago Engineer Meave went to the [Cooperative] supermarket and he saw how the women formed lines with their shopping carts, all cleaned and well-dressed. They made such a picture! . . . There have been group weddings on a few occasions; if ten couples got married, each one would get a wedding gift from the Señora Terrazas [the wife of Engineer Terrazas, the head of the Cooperative before Meave]. . . . On August 2, 1972, we celebrated the 25th anniversary of Engineer Meave's arrival in the Cooperative with a group wedding. (1985: 81–83)[46]

This excerpt clearly demonstrates the paternalistic character of the social work department's activities. It also denotes the imposition of a certain ideal of male–female and household relations based on legalized matrimony, and stresses that the proper wife can control her husband's wild impulses. The idea of women's potential power to reform men lies behind statements such as "go find him on payday," and, later, "I've even had to go and get workers out of jail; that doesn't happen much anymore. The habit of wife-beating has also diminished a lot" (Jáuregui 1985: 83). Implicitly, because the Cooperative (through the Señora Elöisa) made Cooperative wives into "clean, well-dressed," properly married women, it indirectly improved their husbands' behavior. Again, we see the idea of the *limpia, bonita* wife who produces her house and herself as models of proper femininity and the right use of patrimony.

A conversation with Señora Martínez, the mother of my friend Gaby (the receptionist at the Cooperative), deepened my understanding of these policies. Señora Martínez came from a tiny village in the Sierra de Santa Rosa (about 35 kilometers from Guanajuato). She met her future husband once at a village fiesta when she was eighteen and then one day several months later he arrived leading a burro to take her away. "I had to go with him, or my brothers would have killed him. But it was so sad." Her husband worked for 29 years in the mines of the Cooperative and died at the age of 47, leaving her at 36 with ten children. She lived near the Cooperative beneficiation plant and sold *atole* [corn gruel] to the workers.

I was in the knitting group with other women, the Señora Elöisa, the social worker, she was the leader. She wanted me to marry a man from the welding shop—Don Ignacio, but he was so much older than me. She was very strict but I just kept saying no. She was angry at me for not marrying him, but I would never marry again, it is nothing but sadness (*pura tristeza*).

At the same time wives and widows often complained about the gap between the Cooperative's professed interest in the family and their actual practices. In many cases they asked me to intercede on their behalf, thinking I had some clout. Those women whose husbands had died from silicosis or in accidents felt their claim on the Cooperative particularly strongly.

The Cooperative's official policy is to give a biweekly provision of food to widows whose husbands died of silicosis or in accidents, and financial aid for the children of these workers until the age of eighteen. These payments are supposed to supplement the pitifully low Social Security benefits. However, the Cooperative often sidesteps these responsibilities. For instance, Señora Martínez told me that during the crisis in 1991–92 the Cooperative suspended its benefits for widows and orphans. It never resumed paying those people upon regaining solvency; it currently only helps those who were widowed and orphaned since 1994 (about twenty families). I also heard of several cases of fatal accidents in which the Cooperative did not pay benefits to the families because the worker was allegedly away in his work area or violated the safety codes.

The widows resented that the Cooperative shirked its responsibility toward those families whose head (*padre de familia*: "head of household," lit. "father of the family") had given his life to the mines. They claimed a right to support based on the fact that the Cooperative had taken away their men and thus had a responsibility to fill something of that role—to be, in effect, a husband/father to them in the economic sense. One widow said to me,

My husband died of *cascado* [the colloquial term for silicosis]. He couldn't do anything at the end; he was like a creature thrown out to die in the sun (*una criatura tirada al sol*). And now the Cooperative has abandoned me, too.

Here we see how these women use a moral idiom based on family and male responsibility to exert influence over the Cooperative. And, indeed, the Cooperative leadership recognizes this responsibility at least occasionally. For instance, on one occasion I was sitting in the office of one engineer when another, in charge of the San Ignacio mine, stopped by. A miner had recently been killed in San Ignacio and the engineer of that mine asked the other to arrange for someone to construct something for his grave: "So that he doesn't stay there forgotten (*perdido*; lit. "lost")—nothing fancy, just an arch or something with brick. Because Ramón Castillo (one of the Cooperative *jefes*) promised his wife, and we're not going to let her down."

Another instance demonstrates the analogy that Cooperative members (and other Mexicans) draw between male economic and sexual obligations. Paco is studying to be an accountant; through the influence of his wife, Lety, whose cousin is a *jefe* at the Cooperative, he has a place as a student/apprentice in the engineering department. Paco is twenty-seven and Lety is twenty; they have been married for about two years and do not yet have any children. In the spring of 1998 Paco had an affair with Carolina, a secretary at the Cooperative. During this time she wrote him two love letters, which, of course, Lety found one day hidden in a drawer. Lety confronted him with the evidence, and he confessed that he had kissed Carolina but did nothing more. She did not believe him and reported the incident to her family, but she did not leave him.

When she told me this story, Lety brought up the fact that she worked at Electra (a home appliance store) to help Paco meet expenses while he finishes school. She said to him, "If you are going to do that [have an affair], then take me out of work and buy me everything I want, because there are a lot of things I want." She also reported that her father said to Paco, "If you can't [implied: take care of, with the added meaning of sexual satisfaction] one, how are you going to take care of two" [*¿si no puedes con una, cómo vas a poder con dos?*]. Her father's insult to Paco condenses the connection between economic obligation and sexual potency into one utterance, "You can't," thus linking the failure to meet both economic and sexual obligations in their assessment of Paco's transgression.

In each of these examples of women's claims on men and on the Cooperative, we can see how they carve out a space for action through a moral idiom of gender, family, and patrimony. The idiom of patrimony provides the terms within which men can be called to account. When men drink up all the money they make or allow their wives to work outside the home, they are not only failing in their role as fathers; they are also squandering patrimonial possessions instead of using them to produce/reproduce future generations. Indeed, they are robbing those future generations of their use rights over patrimony and encroaching upon patrimony's putative inalienability. Because the idiom of patrimony permeates the social, economic, and political arenas of the Cooperative and draws heavily on ideas of gender and authority prevalent in Mexico, it would be difficult for women *not* to frame their claims in terms of this idiom.

The Practice of Analogy Making

The activities that go on in mine and house intersect deeply; mining becomes a gendered and sexualized activity and reproduction has many features akin to mining. We have seen how miners characterize *bajo tierra*, the mine, as a woman and/or womb. Linked to this metaphor is the sense that mining in the female space of the mine is a highly masculinized and sexual activity. The sexuality of these acts accrues honor to mine work.

The most prestigious and well-paid—above all the most manly (*más varonil*)—job in the mine is that of *perforista* (driller; lit. "perforator"). The manliness comes not only from the danger but also from the symbolic maleness of the activity of drilling. Miners' language about mine work is also at times highly eroticized, in counterpoint with the affectionate and familial language used toward the Cooperative. For instance, miners, and especially *perforistas,* speak about the passion and jealousy or fierce proprietary love (*celos*) that they have for the mine and mine work. The importance of local knowledge of the rock and vein necessary for mine work makes the act more intimate still. The job of *perforando* (drilling) and the act of "entering the mine" (*entrar la mina*) are the frequent subjects of the elaborate sexual word play known in Mexico as *albures*. In these images of mine work, the miner (male) is the sole protagonist in the sexual act of mining. The mine is the passive female upon which these acts are carried out.

However, other views of the mine give more power to the female role, so that it is the mine that gives forth or holds back silver. Men can do the right or wrong thing in mining, but ultimately it is the mine that produces/reproduces. For instance, the idea that if a woman goes down in the mine the vein will become jealous and withhold silver locates the power to produce in the female mine rather than the male miners. This is another configuration of the same analogic practice of mining and sexuality. It also suggests an alternate interpretation of the androcentric assumption of patrimony as produced and transmitted entirely through male effort. Mining and sexuality are intimately linked in the Cooperative, as are production and reproduction; however, these links are construed and wielded in different ways by different actors. Their plasticity makes them highly effective both for reproducing and posing challenges to long-standing relations of power.

In a sense, this analogic practice seems so unavoidable as to have little analytic value; in fact, for many months I avoided considering the connections between mining and reproduction because I worried that either I or my informants were unduly influenced by cliché characterizations of mining. What convinced me that the connection was neither superficial nor rhetorical was that Cooperative members not only saw mining as being like sex and birth; they also saw sex and birth as being like mining. For instance, when I returned to Guanajuato for a visit in November 1998, I learned that the girlfriend of Engineer Esteban (the director of production) had had a baby the previous week. He came out of the offices to greet me as I was standing with my friend Manuel. Manuel asked him "¿*cómo salió?*" (how did it come/turn out?—that is, was it a boy or a girl?). Esteban responded mock-ruefully, "*tepetate*" (non–ore-bearing rock, a girl). They both then explained to me that if his child had been a boy he would have said, mock-triumphantly, "¡*mineral!*" "(ore-bearing rock, a boy) and that this joke was the Cooperative modification of the response "*chocolate*" (the gift the father gives to friends when a girl is born) or "*puro*" (a cigar, the gift he gives when a boy is born).[47]

Parallel nostalgic statements concerning productivity and reproductivity further emphasize the connections between mining and childbearing. According to some men with whom I spoke, just as the mine no longer produces as it once did, so women of this generation do not have the strength to bear many children. And both men *and* women have told me that the need for restraint under current economic conditions accompanies this nostalgia. This need for restraint in reproduction is analogous to a need for restraint in production. In marked contrast to the other mining companies, the Cooperative consciously slows down production to preserve the source of jobs. In a similar way, many women have their tubes tied after the third child (they often describe this by saying, "they operated on me" [*se me operaron*]), and families are far smaller in Santa Rosa than they were in the past. A doctor who visited the mine of San Anton to give hepatitis B vaccines and test for diabetes, upon learning that one worker had eight children, told him, "I'm going to tell you frankly, you don't make a fortune [*no ganas un dineral*] to have such a big family." These statements show how the current economic crisis is understood by some as changes in the balance of vitality and restraint in male and female generative power.[48]

A decrease in family size can also be framed as a conscious choice for fewer children and wider spacing between children, as Jennifer Hirsch (2003: chap. 8) has described in her discussion of the growth of companionate marriage among transnational Mexicans. Although I did not directly investigate peoples' stated motivations for having fewer children, it is perhaps an indication of the strength of the analogy between mining and sexual reproduction (both of which are being curtailed) that smaller family size was often presented to me as a constraint or as evidence of decline rather than as a choice.[49]

Underlying these instances is an idea of the circular nature of production and reproduction within realms of patrimony. Mining (if done properly and well) produces silver (Cooperative patrimony) and, in doing so, turns national patrimony into the patrimony of the Cooperative membership. This Cooperative patrimony then converts into money when it is sold to the foundry. That money, in turn, converts into family patrimony which (if used properly and well) converts into a house, food, clothing, and education for the miners' children, especially sons. These sons then return to the mine to produce more Cooperative patrimony. In this way both the mine and the house encompass and are generated through proper production and reproduction, and survive to be handed down to the next generation.

Cooperative members conceive of the extraction of ore as a reproductive process; they think of the activities of production as potent and generative. Seeing things this way, they not only preserve and transmit patrimony but they also produce/reproduce it. Further, they conceive of a universe wherein mine and house exist together as part of a unified social whole based on the practices and movements of production/reproduction. Although this view has roots in decades of historical practice, it also takes on new significance at this particular political and economic conjuncture.

CONCLUSION: RESOURCES, REPRODUCTION, AND POWER

Through the production of the linked and distinct spaces of mine and house Cooperative members and their families conceive of mineral extraction as a process that is both productive and reproductive, analogous to sexual intercourse and birth. Thus the labor that takes place in the gendered, generative, and sexual space of *bajo tierra* is itself gendered, generative, and sexual. Within this conceptualization, the mines as female spaces/entities are impregnated by the sexually potent work of men and give birth to Cooperative patrimony. By gendering the mines and mining, they see themselves as reproducing the patrimony of the Cooperative (silver) even as that patrimony emerges from the Cooperative into the world.

These practices have several effects. First, they give production a moral valence, for only the right kinds of production reproduce the exhaustible resources of the Cooperative. Selfish or thoughtless production diverts or squanders the generative power of work and harms the social group organized around Cooperative patrimony. This notion of proper and improper forms of labor and their effects on Cooperative patrimony makes patrimony into a morally charged idiom.

Second, the reproductive notion of patrimony may also have the effect of resolving the conceptual problem of the inalienability of nonrenewable resources. In the introduction we observed that the concept of inalienability fits better with renewable resources than nonrenewable ones. In the case of the Co-operative, the only way that it can survive and that individual families can re-main within it is by extracting and selling silver. But silver is an exhaustible re-source, and the Cooperative mines are close to exhaustion. By imagining how these resources might be renewed, Cooperative members and their families may be able to mediate this contradiction through the notion of patrimony.[50]

Finally, the gendering of mine and house in an asymmetric complementar-ity embodies patrimony's androcentrism, by making men responsible for the sort of reproduction that counts (that of patrimonial possessions) and valorizing the patrilineal lines along which those possessions are transmitted.[131] Thus the distinct and complementary spaces of mine and house bring male and female labor together in an unequally valued hierarchy in the production/reproduc-tion of patrimonial possessions. This formulation helps to organize social labor by mobilizing concepts and cosmologies (Wolf 1998) concerning the right use of patrimony and the construction of moral spaces of mine and house. How-ever, it also provides tools for dissent, as when women describe the mine as *fea* or as a burial ground for the men it has devoured, or when miners appropriate the mine's space for political mobilization.

CHAPTER 6

Patrimony, Power, and Ideology

The Cooperative doesn't belong to them [the jefes]; it belongs to us and our children.
—Head of the Cooperative safety squad, September 1997

In chapter 5 I described mining and domestic practices in the Cooperative and the relationship of these activities to patrimony. Within this conceptualization, linked practices of production and reproduction in the gendered spaces of mine and household generate patrimonial possessions. Current generations receive them from their fathers and have a responsibility both to *produce* more patrimony (silver) and to *reproduce* new generations of Cooperative workers (sons and grandsons). This conception of patrimony lies beneath ideas of the proper or legitimate behavior of workers and *jefes* (bosses; chiefs), men and women, and fathers and sons; each of these has particular rights and obligations in relation to one another and to the patrimony of all. Such ideas form a moral language focused on the fulfillment of rights and obligations intimately associated with gender and kinship. I now turn to an analysis of the organization of local power relations and the deployment of patrimony as an ideology that both legitimates and challenges power. I examine both the ways that power and patrimony interact in the Santa Fe Cooperative and show how they articulate with relations of power and patrimony more broadly.

In this chapter I examine the ways an ideology of patrimony assigns distinctions between Cooperative members, and between Cooperative members and others. In doing so, I address a question that has occupied Mexican intellectuals and Mexicanist anthropologists, sociologists, and political scientists since the Cardenista period. These thinkers have tried to find ways to explain the remarkable stability of the state and political systems consolidated in the 1930s. In particular, how was the PRI able to establish pervasive control over the electoral system, state apparatus, labor unions, schools, peasant organizations, and prominent industrial sectors for more than seventy years? Their explanations for this have followed two main channels.

One common explanatory model depicts PRI power relations as organized into pyramids of reciprocal patron-client relationships (sometimes known as *camarillas*), in which clients offer their allegiance to patrons in return for access to power and resources (such as land, water, roads, etc.) and where every patron is also a client for those occupying the next level up on the pyramid (Camp 1985, Cornelius 1996, L. Lomnitz 1982, Smith 1979). As Peter Smith describes it:

> The central and defining characteristic of authoritarianism [in Mexico] is limited pluralism, a situation in which there is active competition for political power, but one in which access to the competition is sharply restricted. . . . the political process entails an unceasing competition between factional *camarillas*, groups bound by loyalty to an individual leader (or *gallo*, cock), who is expected to award patronage for their support. (1979: 50)

Larissa Lomnitz (1982) has provided one of the most effective interpretations of the role of vertical patron-client relations in the organization of power in Mexico, particularly urban Mexico. She points out that two cross-cutting types of allegiances and exchanges operate in urban Mexico, horizontal ties based on socioeconomic class and vertical ties based on reciprocal exchanges between patron and client. These horizontal and vertical relations together comprise the pyramid of Mexican political power.

Even as the PRI has lost the overwhelming hegemony that it held for several decades, the model of the pyramid has continued to be compelling for students of Mexican politics (see, for instance, Pansters 1997). Many of these discussions of the Mexican pyramid leave unexplained what has made these arrangements of power so compelling for so long. The focus on reciprocal patron-client relations goes a long way to explaining the success of the PRI (as anyone who has lived in rural Mexico during an election season can attest). However, it tends to reduce the question of motivation to purely utilitarian ends, in which the self-interest of each person provides the primary, if not the only, explanation for the maintenance of the system.

Other social scientists, writers, and *"pensadores"* (intellectuals-at-large; Lomnitz 1992) have proposed more culturalist explanations of the way power works in Mexico based on aspects of national character (*lo mexicano*) such as machismo, defensiveness, closure, attraction to death, and so on [Lomnitz 1992: 258]). These discussions (Paz 1961, Bonfil 1987, cf. Lomnitz 1992)[1] posit that aspects of Mexican national culture create a peculiar tendency toward personalistic, corporatist power relations based on patron-client ties. As Claudio Lomnitz has pointed out, this does not explain how and why power works in Mexico the way it does or has done but merely describes it in essentialist terms. However, as Lomnitz (1992: 13) says in reference to Octavio Paz, the most influential of the *pensadores,* "The sociologist can point to the fallacy of pseudo-history, but she or he cannot easily account for or shrug off Paz's description of 'The Mexican.'" Put otherwise, the deus ex machina of *lo mexicano,* for all its problems, does try to explain the emotionally and intellectually compelling nature of power relations as they stand in contemporary Mexico. By providing a fine-grained analysis of how power relations and ideology interact in the Santa Fe, I hope to propose an alternate explanation based on history and practice.

The use of idioms of gender, kinship and friendship by actors in the PRI and the postrevolutionary state it claims to represent is well established. For instance, Carlos Vélez-Ibáñez studies the growth and decline of popular organizing in Ciudad Netzahualcoyotl Izcalli, on the outskirts of Mexico City. Drawing on political and psychological anthropology, he distinguishes between the rich and satisfying ties between relatives, compadres, co-residents, and so forth, and the shallow and instrumental friendships between political patrons and clients. The pyramidal structure of Mexican politics, he argues, promotes a myth of equal access but in reality draws local-level leaders into these more superficial ties while further marginalizing already marginalized groups, such as the residents of Ciudad Netza. The outward form of these patron-client ties, however, mimics that of the deeper "primary" and "secondary" order connections.

Taking a more long-term view, Ana María Alonso (1995: 90–91) points out the gendered and kinship-inflected nature of enduring ideologies that legitimate power in Mexico. She says, "In Mexico the relationships between family and polity, patriarchal and patrimonial authority, have been configured iconically since colonial times. A construction of gender that entails and enforces patriarchal control of female generativity has long been seen as central to the reproduction of family, society, and state."[2] Alonso traces this iconic relation between patriarchal and patrimonial authority through the practices of work and warfare in Namiquipa, Chihuahua.

Other scholars have also pointed out the overlapping layers of gender, family, and authority in Mexico. For instance, Mintz and Wolf (1950) have sketched the practice of ritual co-parenthood (*compadrazgo*) in relation to two different forms of labor organization and structures of authority: haciendas and plantations. Lomnitz (1992) posits that what is called "corruption" in Mexican political culture persists because it is founded on central cultural values of loyalty and reciprocity among kin and friends. Critiquing other scholars' descriptions of clientelism as a form of loyalty, Roger Magazine (2004) shows how members of a soccer fan club interpret patron-client relations in terms of the idea of *el consentido,* the spoiled or favorite child.

Occupying the same semantic terrain as concepts of gender, kinship, and sexuality as they are debated in contemporary Mexico, the ideology of patrimony biologizes and therefore naturalizes prevailing relations of power that in turn provide the muscle for particular allocations of resources. At the same time, following William Roseberry (1994: 361) and others who take a Gramscian perspective on power and everyday life in contemporary Mexico (*cf.* Joseph and Nugent 1994), we can see patrimony as a "common language or way of talking about social relationships that sets out the central terms around which and in terms of which contestation and struggle can occur."[3]

This perspective shows how relatively powerless actors can sometimes use the idiom of patrimony to challenge those in power. This analysis of patrimony's vitality in the Santa Fe Cooperative also suggests why this idiom is powerful in other domains in Mexico where power is expressed as the power to distribute and use resources (as in *ejidos,* for instance).

Finally, my discussion of patrimony as a language of moral authority and as a process of value making in moral terms draws on the concept of "moral economy" described by E. P. Thompson (1971) and James Scott (1976) with respect to peasants. "Moral economy" refers to a system of values connected with particular forms of labor that make moral claims over resources (such as food or land) on behalf of peasants or other non-élites. These claims are often in contradiction to those that members of dominant classes may cast as purely "economic." As we will see in this chapter, the underground workers often make moral claims based on the danger and indispensability of their labor. Although the system of production and its attendant social relations differ from the peasants described by Scott and Thompson, Cooperative members, especially those who work underground, also draw on a moral code derived from and legitimated by particular forms of labor.

VECTORS OF POWER

In order to look at these questions more closely, we need to understand how relations of power are organized within the Santa Fe. We can identify several "vectors of power." These vectors both overlap and crosscut; one's relative position within them determines one's rights and obligations. First and most powerful is that of Cooperative councils and committees. The most recent version of the Mexican Law of Cooperatives states: "The direction, administration, and oversight of cooperative societies will be under the control of: 1. a general assembly [of all Cooperative members] 2. an administrative council 3. an oversight council (*consejo de vigilancia*). 4. committees established by law and/or designated by the general assembly" (*Periódico Oficial de la Nación*, August 3, 1994, 23). The administrative and oversight councils and the committees are elected by the general assembly. The administrative council, and especially its president, Jesus Castillo, decide what equipment and machinery to buy, when to give out profit shares, loans, and other benefits, punishments, security measures, and almost every other important business in the Cooperative. According to the Law of Cooperatives, the oversight council exists to provide a check on the administrative council, but in practice the members of this council are buddies (*cuates*) of Castillo and never contradict him. The councils are the governing bodies of the Cooperative. The Cooperative also has two committees, which exist to carry out the demands of the councils.

Each council has five members (a total of ten members).[4] Six of these are engineers and work in the central plant directing activities at all mines rather than as the head of only one mine; one is an accountant; and three are surface workers and members of long-standing Cooperative families. During the time of my fieldwork there were no mine workers on the councils. The council members are the most powerful agents in the Cooperative. However, within the councils, the president of the administrative council has ultimate authority, followed by the other five engineers. The Santa Fe Cooperative councils are elected for a period of five years and the committees for one year.

The council system is nominally separate from the organization of management and labor in the Cooperative, although the administrative council rules over even those people who are formally independent. In practice, however, people manipulate and display power in other ways and domains. The most exclusive signs of power are reserved for those who are both engineers in charge of departments at the central plant (superintendent of production, superintendent of mines, head of the engineering department, etc.) *and* members of the administrative or oversight council. These men receive (among other things) privileged access to information on production and finances, the title "*jefe*," the right to be addressed as *usted* (second person singular, formal) even by one's elders, the opportunity to find a girlfriend within the Cooperative (as well as a wife outside the Cooperative), and the exclusive use of a Cooperative pickup truck.

The *jefes'* position is most marked on Saturday, when miners come out of the mine early to receive their paycheck, and the *jefes* (especially the president of the administrative council) stay in their offices to receive supplicants and dispense orders. At two o'clock, the Cooperative closes and each *jefe* leaves in his truck accompanied by his girlfriend (*novia*) in the cab. Sometimes he may give a lift to some workers, who sit in the back of the pickup. Every few weeks the *jefes* meet at someone's house or *cabaña* (weekend bungalow) to eat and drink tequila (these *comidas* are examples, at the level of Cooperative leadership, of the "maleness" of activities on Saturday afternoon, as described in chapter 2).

Occasionally other people attend these meals, such as engineers or even captains of particular mines (especially Valenciana), heads of departments who are not engineers, or North American female anthropologists. The *jefes'* girlfriends, who are usually secretaries or assistant accountants, attend as well. These practices made Saturday an ideal time for studying Cooperative power relations. When I asked Martín early on in my fieldwork about social networks and the organization of power, he advised me,

> You just have to be a little observant. Go out into the courtyard of the plant
> at around 12:00 or 1:00 on Saturday, and watch who leaves with whom.
> That's the way to know what's really happening at the Cooperative.

The position of *jefe* is gendered and familial. The *jefe* should be a responsible and commanding father, as the title itself implies, for *jefe* can mean either boss or father.[5] He should manage the Cooperative patrimony wisely and justly, holding back enough so that the Cooperative can keep going but giving out enough so that individual members can turn it into the patrimony of their individual families (by building a house, for example). At the same time he should also be a real man or even a bit of a *cabrón*,[6] with the power and virility to keep a *novia* and get drunk with his friends on Saturday. One engineer told me (when we were discussing the Monica Lewinsky story), "We like our *jefes* to have lots of women. It means they have real power." A number of workers also expressed similar ideas. The *jefes'* actions on Saturday exemplify this dual role.

However, I do not wish to oversimplify ideologies and practices of machismo in Mexico, a tendency widespread in studies of Mexico and rightly critiqued by Matthew Gutmann (1996). Gutmann points out that those practices associated with machismo may also be accompanied by a strain of self-deprecating humor, the valorization of a nurturing father role and the accepted presence of women in the police force and similarly un-docile (*abnegada*) domains. I also found these elements to be present even among those who in many ways exemplified Mexican machismo. For instance, among a group of Cooperative members who also worked as volunteer firefighters, one woman, divorced with two children, also worked. She was treated as a friend by all her male companions, and included in work and social activities without any problem that I could see (as was I on the occasions I tagged along). Nor did I ever hear anyone question her fitness for the job because of her gender or for any other reason.[7] This example, one among many, demonstrates Gutmann's point that gender ideology in Mexico, like everywhere else, is complex, contradictory, and ever-changing and that attempts to characterize it in unitary fashion as machismo leave out a great deal.

So far, we have seen three vectors of political power in the Cooperative: position within or outside the councils; the holding of an engineering degree; and a position as "superintendent" of a department in the central plant with jurisdiction over all seven mines. Those who hold positions of power along all three vectors are *jefes*. But there are other forms of authority at work that people at times deploy against the *jefes*.

The *jefes*, perhaps for this reason, or perhaps in keeping with their paternal and responsible role, give respect to these other forms. They include age, time working in the Cooperative, and time working in the mines. These factors give a man deep local knowledge of the mines and the Cooperative, which can be more valuable than an engineering degree. One former miner told me on a number of occasions of the difference between *conocimiento* (knowledge) and *títulos* (degrees). He told me that when an engineer graduates from the School of Mines and comes to work in the Cooperative, a miner usually has to teach him about the mines from his own experience. If no one teaches him, he will be disoriented and get lost underground, will not know how to keep his balance and might hurt himself, and will become easily frustrated. In addition, he will not know how to "care for the vein" (*cuidar la veta*), and he could hurt the mine and the Cooperative by taking the mineral out too quickly or in the wrong way.

The local knowledge acquired in the mines is respected throughout the Cooperative, even by the *jefes*. Often people introduced themselves or others to me by saying, for example, "This is Pedro Quintero. He worked twenty-five years in the mines," or, "I am Jose Santiago Martínez López at your service. I know the Rayas mine like it was my own house/home." This experience gives the miners, especially those who have been working or who worked in the mine for many years, authority to speak on issues of production, and even to criticize the engineers. Older and former miners often challenge an engineer's knowledge and familiarity with the mine, saying, "That one doesn't know [anything]; he never goes down in the mine, or only for five minutes"; or "The people aren't going to trust an engineer who doesn't know the mine." Miners can wield a moral language of patrimony very effectively in certain circumstances, because of the honor of their work. Mine work produces patrimony, and so miners have authority to judge how that patrimony is administered. This authority can thus be seen as a kind of "moral economy" in Thompson's and Scott's terms.

Knowledge of the mines is also highly gendered. To question an engineer's knowledge of the mines is to question his masculinity, to suggest that perhaps he is too frightened or too weak to put in a hard day's work underground. The valor and strength needed for mine work and the knowledge of the mine also structure miners' sense of themselves in opposition to surface workers. Miners often say that they are the truly valorous (*valiente*) workers while surface workers are *huevones* (lazy bums) and that "it is the miners who feed the surface workers." Conversely, some surface workers told me that the miners were young and wild (*bravo* or *desmadroso*), whereas the surface workers were more likely to be industrious (*trabajador*), steady (*responsable*) family men. These comments were very few in comparison with the miners' criticisms of surface workers, however. The divisions between *bajo tierra* and *superficie* are fundamental to social organization in the Cooperative, and disputes invariably occur along these lines.

The division between *bajo tierra* and *superficie* reproduces alternative masculinities common among Mexicans. For instance, men may be described approvingly, disparagingly, or both, as *valiente, desmadroso* (literally, "unmothered"), *trabajador, responsable,* or *huevón* (literally, a condition in which one's balls [*huevos* or eggs] are so heavy that one is incapable of doing any work). These appellations are liberally used to characterize miners, surface workers, and *jefes* as groups and individuals. Thus the gendered nature of work and authority in the Cooperative articulates with more widespread notions of Mexican masculinity.[8]

The mine is also a space where solidarity is built among young men and among members of a part of the Cooperative workforce which sees itself as engaging in the most dangerous, necessary, and at the same time badly paid and disempowered (in general terms, *jodido* [screwed]) work in the Cooperative. The process of acquiring local knowledge such as identifying the silver in the veins, knowing the best way to work, and learning the geography and interior landscape in the mine, as well as the sense of potential danger, tend to build a strong sense of loyalty to one another and to an esoteric guild. Also the darkness, small passages, and out-of-the-way caverns make the mine a place where workers can talk about the Cooperative and the *jefes* more freely than on the surface. When I accompanied the industrial safety team on their inspection tours during the unrest of August–September 1997, Martín, who saw himself as agitating for change in the Cooperative, often spoke to workers about these matters while underground.

One's position along these diverse vectors of power (the councils and committees, the holding of degrees (*títulos*), time in the Cooperative, and local knowledge of the mines) determines rights and obligations in relation to other members and to patrimonial property. As we have shown, patrimony entails ideas of gender, family, and sexuality; for this reason, the bounds of legitimate behavior for each person are also understood as gendered, familial, and sexual.

Put another way, Cooperative members and their families see domains of political power, sexual conduct, family and household practices, and mining as analogous, because analogous ideas of rights and obligations concerning the production/reproduction, preservation, and transmission of patrimony govern each domain. Furthermore, the connections between these realms go both ways. Not only are power relations conceived of in gendered and familial terms; gender and family relations are also arranged along vectors of power. As in other parts of Mexico, relations of power are organized in terms of cross-cutting vertical and horizontal ties which are legitimated in terms of a gendered, familial ideology, that of patrimony.

In this chapter I examine how relations of power and their legitimating ideologies interact in the Santa Fe and show some of the ways in which they are connected to broader political, social, and economic processes in Mexico. I focus on three areas: provisioning, the creation of affective and economic obligation through debt, and relations of paternalism in the Cooperative; an attempted coup aimed at toppling the current *jefes,* which took place between August and October of 1997; and the claim made by about eighteen surviving founding partners (*socios fundadores*) of the Cooperative.

PROVISIONING, DEBT, AND PATRIMONY

The Santa Fe Cooperative functions simultaneously as a producers' and consumers' cooperative, a *sociedad de consumo* (society of consumers). Members share the profits from production of silver, gold, and copper (it acts as a producers' cooperative); they also pool their buying power in order to bring down the consumption costs of food, water, construction materials, medicine, and so on (it acts as a consumers' cooperative). To this end, the Cooperative extends a number of benefits to its members and their immediate families ("rightsholders"—*derechohabientes*).[9] These include subsidized groceries, construction materials, and water; medical care at the Cooperative clinic; subsidized medications; school textbooks; reduced fees to the Cooperative high school (Instituto Montes de Oca); and occasional deals on household appliances and other items. Payments for these services are deducted from the weekly paycheck.

In fulfilling the joint functions of a producers' and consumers' cooperative, the Santa Fe follows the original intentions of the postrevolutionary state, which attempted to promote self-determination in labor and production organization and in consumption and buying power. However, the Cooperative only began to develop its capacities as a society of consumers in the 1970s, when the exploitation of the rich Clavo de Rayas (and later, high silver prices) made for generous profits. Cooperative subsidies for food, construction materials, medicine, water, and education were implemented gradually in the 1970s and 1980s by Engineer Edgardo Meave Torrescano and his son Edgardo Meave Pérez, both mining engineers.

Cooperative *jefes* attempted from the beginning to use provisioning to bind workers to the Cooperative and to consolidate their own position as benevolent patriarchs. In August 1999 I interviewed a high-ranking member of the Meave administration, whom I will call Engineer Felix Ortega. His comments exemplify the attitudes of many Cooperative *jefes* concerning the proper role of the Cooperative toward members and their families. He told me that the Meaves instituted the Cooperative subsidies to spend some of the production surplus in years of plenty (especially in the 1980s) and to "improve the lives of the members." In a surprisingly direct manner, he stated:

> In those days a worker could work three days a week and earn enough to satisfy himself and his family, and then he would stay home the rest of the week. We started to have a big problem with absenteeism. So we offered lots of new things, irons, blenders, stoves, beds, refrigerators, we even had a vacation plan where workers could go to Acapulco. All this in addition to the provisions department, the hospital, the construction materials, all that. And we took the payments out of the weekly envelope. That way the worker had to come to work to pay his debt. Otherwise he would just stay home. (Interview #1 with Felix Ortega, August 9, 1999)

Ortega clearly states that the objective of the Cooperative's leaders in instituting the various subsidies was to compel workers through debt. To this logic, however, he added a mission to instill ideas of propriety, civility, and the right use of Cooperative resources, saying:

> The worker got his envelope (paycheck) and went directly to the cantina, and arrived at home with nothing (*sin un cinco*). [To deal with this problem] we created the provisions department; the wives could choose from a list: corn, beans, rice, soap, etc. We took it out of the workers' salary, that is very important.

He went on to say:

> [In the early 1980s] silver kept rising. We started to make a lot of money. We put in a supermarket, we offered home appliances, what we were trying to do was to elevate the quality of life. We knew that many workers

slept on straw pallets—if you have never slept in a bed you sleep fine on a pallet, but it's better to sleep in a bed. We tried to show that if they had a refrigerator, they could have a cold soda when they wanted, or a cold beer when they wanted. We showed them it was better to have a house with three or four rooms instead of just one room.[10] (Interview #1 with Felix Ortega, August 9, 1999)

Even when the Cooperative first began as a society of consumers, questions of consumption entailed ideas of proper homes and home life. Moreover, the Cooperative *jefes* took (and continue to take) a stance of benevolent paternalism toward their workers and their families enacted through provisioning and the encouragement of consumption.

This strategy of the Cooperative *jefes* at times penetrates into the most intimate domains of familial life. In describing the activities of the Cooperative social work department, another benefit instituted for workers during this time, Ortega said:

In a lot of the families, the children were having many problems because they lived in a house with only one room. We wanted them to build more rooms so that everyone would not be sleeping in the same room and the children would not see what the parents were doing at night. Sometimes there were even problems because the boys and girls in the family were sleeping in the same room. So we wanted them to build more rooms and to get a television, things like that. I mean, [smiling] I know that Mexican television is not that good, but it is better than doing "what shouldn't be" (*lo que no debe de ser*) (Interview #2 with Felix Ortega, August 16, 1999)

Ortega's remarks reveal an extreme (or perhaps only extremely explicit) version of attitudes exhibited by many Cooperative *jefes*. A number of *jefes* told me in a variety of ways that the members of the Cooperative are like children (*como niños*) and that it is the responsibility of the Cooperative (and the *jefes* as its representatives) to guide and care for them. This attitude legitimates the *jefes'* attempts to compel workers through provisioning and debt, and reinforces their position as leaders and caretakers of Cooperative patrimony.

The Cooperative can assert a good deal of control over how wages are spent, by deducting the (subsidized) cost of many of its benefits (such as food, construction materials, doctors' visits, medicine, payment of loans, etc.) from the weekly paycheck. By taking these deductions out of the paycheck, the Cooperative ensures that it will be paid back. As Ortega's comments suggest, this system has two other effects: it binds workers to the Cooperative, both in times of plenty (such as the 1980s) and during periods of crisis (such as the 1940s or the 1990s); and it controls workers' consumption of their wages in ways that the Cooperative *jefes* consider appropriate, thus reinforcing their stance as benevolent patriarchs.

Some *jefes* are concerned that these provisioning practices promote an image of the Cooperative as exploitative. That debts to the Cooperative were deducted from the paycheck, as discussed above, one engineer said to me half-indignantly, "I hope you're not going to be like a student from the School of Philosophy and History [at the University of Guanajuato] who compared the Cooperative to the system of 'the company store' (*tienda de raya*) in the Porfiriato. We help our workers, we don't make slaves out of them." Of course, the salient differences between the Cooperative's practices and systems of debt peonage (including company stores) are that the Cooperative charges less than outside sources and that workers are not forced to use these services. But the system does allow the Cooperative to bind its workers through financial obligation.[11] At the same time it taps into notions of benevolent paternalism and *compadrazgo* that in turn bind workers through affective obligation.

This system of obligation through debt has continued since the time of the Meaves. A worker interviewed by Yolia Tortolero Cervantes (1992: 47) stated in 1990:

> Here in the Cooperative the majority are in debt (*endrogados*) up to their necks. He who doesn't owe half a million owes more than a million (old *pesos*, equivalent to 500 and 1,000 new *pesos* respectively, or 50 and 100 dollars) and so on; so that your paycheck comes out to practically nothing from all the subtractions for what you owe.

The same was true during my fieldwork from 1996 to 1998, when workers showed me pay envelopes containing as little as seven pesos for the week after all the deductions.[12] In my study of the Valenciana mine I found that these workers continued to make significant use of the benefits provided by the Cooperative. From December 1996 to August 1997 workers at the Valenciana mine spent an average of 43 percent of their weekly earnings on loan payments to the Cooperative, groceries, construction materials, medicine, or other family benefits and took home 57 percent in cash.

These kinds of practices have a long history in the mines now controlled by the Cooperative. In an article published in Mexico, "la Formación de la Nación," Eric Wolf reports that "the Count . . . of the fabulous Valenciana mine . . . averred that the abolition of the laws prescribing special clothing for Indians would enrich the textile factories [of Querétaro] and that permitting them to wear Spanish clothing would augment their needs and in consequence would augment their need and desire to work" (AGN, Tributos, 44, file 6; quoted in Wolf 1953; translation mine).

Clearly debt, as it is organized in the Cooperative, promotes reliability of a form consistent with industrial capitalism. Once workers carry debt that must be paid off at regular intervals (every two weeks), they have added incentive to conform to the industrial work-discipline desired by the directors of the enterprise. Encouraging debt also allows the Cooperative to hold on to cash and reap its interest. Finally, this practice sets Cooperative leaders up as fathers, godfathers (*padrinos*), or ritual co-parents (*compadres*) of Cooperative members.[13] It thus attempts to bind workers to the Cooperative through ties of loyalty (affective obligation) as well as through debt (financial obligation). To show how this works, let me give an extended example.

One afternoon, in April 1998, my husband David and I visited Alvaro and his family. His nephew, Jaime, the shift head (*cabo*) at the San Vicente mine, was also there. Alvaro and Jaime share several close ties; in addition to being uncle and nephew, they are also brothers-in-law (their wives are sisters) and *compadres* (Alvaro is the godfather of Jaime's youngest daughter). They grew up together and now live in the same family compound, in addition to both working in the Cooperative. We sat until late in the night eating *carne asada* (steaks cooked on the grill) with rice, tortillas, and salsa, and drinking beer and tequila. Their children ran in and about the house, sometimes sitting down to watch *Sábado Gigante*, or sneaking M&Ms from the bag we had brought them. We talked about our families, the United States, baseball (both are avid players and fans, like many men in Guanajuato) and the Cooperative.

We also talked about a recent accident at the Valenciana. A few weeks before, a young *carrero*, Patricio, had broken his back when he and several others rode the car that brings ore between levels via an inclined shaft (*contratiro*). Alvaro told me that the young man had a new baby son (his first) and that he, Alvaro, had been the boy's godfather at his baptism in January, thus making Alvaro and Patricio *compadres*. He said in a tone of shock and pity:

> I had never been to my *compadre's* house before the accident, but I went to visit him afterwards, and the house is nothing but tin (*pura lámina*), walls and roof made of tin, and it was really hot. The house doesn't have anything, not even a chair, or anything to hang up the clothes, nothing. Castillo (the head of the Cooperative) wanted to visit him and we brought him and we didn't say anything, but he [Castillo] was standing there in the house, and you know, since he is very tall, his head almost touched the ceiling, and it was so hot. When we got out to the road he said, "tomorrow we'll send

him a fan." After that we said, "you know, *ingeniero*, why don't you also send him a table to put his medicines on, because they are all hanging on the wall in plastic bags, and some chairs so that people can visit him." And he said, "yes—we'll send them over right away." But he [Patricio] made decent money (*ganaba más o menos*) and who knows what happened to the money, if he drank it up (*que lo chupó*) or what. Imagine what it will be like for his son growing up there. You feel sorry (*a uno le da lástima*) [about] the accident, but you also feel sorry for the way they live there.

This incident and Alvaro's reaction to it bring together a number of elements central to our understanding of the Cooperative. First, we see once again how the house stands as the outward sign of male responsibility and familial respectability. Alvaro particularly mentions visitors' reactions to Patricio's poor, empty, and uncomfortable house, not only his own but also those of Engineer Castillo, the head of the Cooperative and a person who commands great respect and authority. In his appeal to Castillo on Patricio's behalf, Alvaro alludes to the importance of receiving outsiders in the house, asking for "some chairs, so that people can visit him."

Second, the statement shows how building a house and furnishing it comfortably is something a man does for his children by providing a pleasant place for them to live, a respectable place in the social world, and a share in the Cooperative patrimony, converted into family patrimony.[14] Alvaro's pity and censure comes from the fact that he cannot or does not like to "imagine what it will be like for his [Patricio's] son growing up there" but also because the money Patricio made in the Cooperative has disappeared and "who knows what happened to it."

Later the same evening Alvaro described his own house-building efforts and aspirations for his children, in this case his daughters.[15] In discussing the house he is building across the road from his current house, he said: "The house where we are living now belongs to my wife, and I want to have my own. Then once I finish that I will build another." He added with a wry smile, "My daughters are all going to have careers and they are all going to have houses, so that if their husbands are lazy drunks [*unos huevones borrachos*] they will have their own house." Alvaro sees the building of proper houses as an integral part of his duty as a father to protect his daughters from other men who may be less responsible than he and to pass on Cooperative and family patrimony. His disapproval of Patricio's house stems from his feeling that Patricio (his own *compadre*) is failing to fulfill this essential responsibility.

Another story emphasizes the importance of household furnishings in the proper disposition of patrimony and fulfillment of paternal obligations. One of the most successful mineral specimen merchants, known as "El Sol," who sells regularly to Dennis Beals, a mineral dealer who drives down from Colorado several times a year, began in the mid-1990s to become quite prosperous, as the minerals market in the United States boomed and fabulous specimens began emerging from the Rayas mine (see chapter 6). He lived in a narrow house on the Panoramic Highway with his wife and children. One of the first things he bought were two iron beds. He kept these stacked against the wall in his house, Dennis reported to me, for they were much too wide to put on the floor. It seems that having the beds, even though they could not be used, was a sign that El Sol was using his newfound prosperity in the proper way.

As shown in this case, complex transactions govern interactions between the Cooperative and individual familial and ritual kin groups. Alvaro's connection to Patricio comes from his position of authority over him in the Cooperative. He is Patricio's direct boss and the one who gives him orders daily. In January Patricio brought Alvaro into a ritual kin relationship with him and his family by asking him to be godfather to his son (and thus his own *compadre*). Both men and others around them took this new bond seriously; several people told me that the man hurt in the accident was Alvaro's *compadre*, and, in telling his story, Alvaro refers to Patricio as "my *compadre*." After the accident Castillo, the head of the Cooperative, asks to be taken to visit Patricio. Alvaro takes him, perhaps in his capacity both as captain of the Valenciana and Patricio's *compadre*. At the same time Castillo's visit and his promise of a fan for the house indicate his assumption of the Cooperative's responsibility toward the worker. Once Castillo expresses his intention to help Patricio and his family, Alvaro takes the opportunity to appeal for further help for Patricio and his family, in the form of a table and chairs. It is significant that all the help comes as household improvements and furniture.

Part of Alvaro's willingness to advocate for Patricio probably came from his sense of responsibility as Patricio's *compadre*. In this context, it made sense that he would ask for household items, since these directly build up the family patrimony and help his godchild. Alvaro, who is in a Cooperative/ritual kin relationship with Patricio, appeals to Castillo, who is both his own and Patricio's superior in the Cooperative, to act as a kind of *compadre* toward Patricio. At the same time the substance of his appeal, and Castillo's sense of what he can do, entails a conversion of Cooperative resources into family resources. These resources materialize in the house, which is now shameful and inadequate and which the literal and figurative *compadres* wish to improve.[16]

In August 1999 I returned to Guanajuato on a brief research trip. Part of my reason for coming was that I had heard that the Cooperative was entering a period of severe financial crisis, that they had stopped paying the tri-annual profit shares, and that there was some talk that they would not be able to pay wages. Upon my arrival it appeared that things were bad but somewhat more stable than they had been a few weeks before. A number of people had left the Cooperative, but most had stayed and were waiting to see whether the price of silver would rally and what would happen in December when the council elections came around.

One afternoon, as I was sitting in the offices of the Valenciana chatting with Alvaro, a little boy appeared at the door. Alvaro beckoned him over; this was Patricio's son (and Alvaro's godson), Juanito. I asked about Patricio and heard that he and his wife were selling trinkets and quartzes from a stand on the mine's patios. Soon after, Patricio made his way over. He walked with full-length leg braces and crutches, but told me that he was gradually getting feeling back in his legs and hoped to be able to walk unaided again. Meanwhile, his wife and he worked every day at the mine selling to tourists. He then turned to Alvaro and asked about a truckload of gravel that he was getting from the Cooperative. Alvaro called the Cooperative and checked to see when it would be ready and then told Patricio that they could go pick it up in a couple of days.

Later, I asked Alvaro how Patricio was doing and what was happening with his house. He told me, "The engineer [Castillo] is giving him a place to sell his things, and giving him materials to build his house for free. One has to help somehow (lit. "in something"; *uno tiene que ayudar en algo*)." Strictly speaking, Patricio is no longer part of the commonwealth of Cooperative members, but his former life in the Cooperative, the needless sadness of his accident, his ritual kin relationship with Alvaro, and his continued presence on the grounds of the Valenciana all keep him within the circle of Cooperative consumption. The provisions given by Castillo and Alvaro also show other members and their families that the Cooperative fulfills its obligations toward its workers much as a father or *compadre* would.

The story of Patricio's house falls into a larger category of charitable transactions known in the Cooperative as the practice of *alivianar*. This practice takes place in the context of overtime and incentive contracts. For instance, in the Valenciana not all workers leave work after the first shift. Every day several workers work extra hours underground until the late afternoon and evening. Since overtime is paid double, this work forms a significant part of earnings. As reported in chapter 2, from December 1996 to August 1997 Valenciana workers earned an average of 9.8 percent of their earnings from overtime. The captain and engineer completely control who works extra hours. The captain and engineer at the Valenciana describe this power as a way they can help (*alivianar;* a variant of "*aliviar*" [lit. "lighten," "alleviate"]) a worker at a time when he has particular needs (after the birth of a new baby and before the baptism, for example) or if he is not making enough from basic wages and incentives.[17]

The captain and engineer also exercise this discretion when calculating incentive pay. Every underground worker in the Cooperative has an incentive contract based on the number of meters he drills through, number of cars filled, and so forth. From December 1996 to August 1997 Valenciana workers earned an average of 19 percent of their earnings from incentive contracts.[18] On Wednesday mornings the captain and engineer come out of the mine early and "do the contracts." They confer about each worker, deciding first how much money he should receive in his contract and then computing the contract accordingly (i.e., recording the number of meters drilled or cars loaded that would result in the amount they have already decided upon). They then fill out the incentive contracts for each worker and send them to the payroll department at the central plant. This practice goes on in the other Cooperative mines as well. On one occasion an engineer explained to me how he used a surplus of production by one very skilled *perforista* to *alivianar* several others who were not making enough money.[19]

During my time at the Cooperative the television conglomerate Televisa filmed the *telenovela* (soap opera) *Angela* at the Rayas mine. I happened to be at Rayas when Emeterio, the mine captain, explained his job to the actor who was to play the mine's captain in the telenovela. The actor said to him, full of methodical enthusiasm, "You have to tell me what you do here, because I am going to play you." Emeterio explained his job and the basic organization of the Cooperative, its differences from a private mining enterprise, and so on. In listing his duties, he described the practice of *alivianar* in detail (leaving the actor, I think, somewhat mystified, although dutifully scribbling notes). Emeterio made a strong connection between the particularities of the Cooperative as an enterprise and his own attempts to *alivianar* deserving or needy workers.

Other mine captains share this view. The captain of the Valenciana mine told me that, as the youngest captain in the Cooperative, he feels a personal responsibility to help young men who want to *aprovechar* (take advantage of) the opportunity of moving up and help their children to *salir adelante* (get ahead), as he himself did. (He rose to his position at the Valenciana with very little formal education, since he had to leave school to work at the age of twelve.) He told me that the practice of *alivianar* helps some workers take advantage of working in the Cooperative.

Clearly this perspective portrays the practice of *alivianar* very positively. In contrast, miners sometimes complained to me that the captains used overtime and incentive contracts to suppress dissent, exact personal revenge, and favor (*consentir a*) some workers over others. Camilo, a worker in the Cata mine, complained that certain engineers and captains had their *cuates* whom they favored with fat incentive contracts. Jaime, who works in the central plant, told me that, during the labor unrest of August–October 1997, the superintendent of mines (Engineer Galvez; see below) cultivated favor in two mines through the manipulation of incentive contracts. And Crescencio, who worked in San Vicente but left the Cooperative and now works on two-month contracts in mines in Coahuila, said that once he had fallen out with (*salió mal con*) Galvez, he had to leave the Cooperative because he knew he would no longer be given overtime or incentive contracts. From this perspective the practice of *alivianar* provides a way for Cooperative *jefes* and those close to them to control the workforce while simultaneously legitimating their power through an ideology of benevolent paternalism and the right use of patrimony.

This darker perspective is consistent with that of some other analysts of Mexican politics. For instance, Susan Eckstein argues in her study of urban Mexico City neighborhoods in the 1960s and 1970s that,

> The structurally induced personalistic style of Mexican politics makes residents . . . feel dependent upon and indebted to the government for material benefits they receive, including the land and pavement for which they actually pay. These "gifts" were officially "given" to them at official rallies which often are attended by such high-ranking officials as the President of the country and the mayor of the city. . . . Moreover, in the very process of securing personal "favors" from the government the collective effectiveness of residents, paradoxically, was indirectly undermined. (1977: 93–94)

This process of undermining typifies PRI and governmental power relations and *also* many producers' cooperatives, which, as Sharryn Kasmir (1998) has pointed out, often divide the interests of workers by casting them in the role of owners. While acknowledging the effects of these strategies to induce a sense of indebtedness on the part of Cooperative members, I argue that these cannot be extricated from the deeply felt meanings entailed in them. To say that those with greater access to loci of power use the signs and practices of gender, kin, and affective obligation to their advantage is not to deny the force of these signs and practices but rather to underscore them.

A series of material and symbolic transactions organize relations between inferiors and superiors in the Cooperative and between ritual kin partners with unequal resources. Such transactions and the ideas of loyalty and obligation that go along with them make up the intimate politics of family and Cooperative.

That Cooperative resources are understood as patrimonial possessions, as we have seen, ties family and Cooperative even more tightly together.

The politics of obligation in the Santa Fe Cooperative and its role in men's conversion of silver into family patrimony shows some parallels with Patricia Spyer's work on pearl divers in the Aru Islands, Indonesia. In an article published in 1997, Spyer argues that Aruese pearl divers engage in complicated exchanges between Sino-Indonesian store and boat owners, on the one hand, and underwater "sea-wives," on the other. The sea-wives demand store-bought goods in exchange for the pearl oysters divers' extract from the sea, simultaneously deepening divers' indebtedness and creating an erotic and romantic bond parallel to, and also hostile to, the divers' families on land. In the case of Cooperative miners, as I have earlier described, the eroticized female space of the mine provides the substance by which men fulfill their familial obligations on the surface, while at the same time entrenching them more deeply in debt to the Cooperative itself. In something like an exchange, miners respond by attending to underground altars with mineral samples, images of saints and virgins, and candles provided by the Cooperative. Occasionally they also leave their lives and bodies in the mines as well. To be sure, the mine's femaleness is less individuated than the sea-wives. But, as in the case of Aruese divers, the process by which silver is converted into houses and furnishings, and the deepening of debt that goes along with this process, becomes a simultaneously commercial and conjugal act.[20]

The transformation of Cooperative patrimony into family patrimony (in this case, Patricio's house and its contents) reinforces a sense of social order in the Cooperative based on a kinship model, with the inflections of gender, emotion, and eroticism that go along with kinship. To the extent that this model of social order and the right use of patrimony are accepted, they can legitimate the power of the *jefes*. But when people dispute that power, they do so most effectively in the idiom of patrimony. In this way patrimony works to set the terms of debate over Cooperative resources.

MINERS' PATRIMONY AND THE LIMITS OF POWER

In the late summer and fall of 1997 the miners of the Cooperative began a movement to topple the administrative council, complaining that the *jefes* had overstepped their bounds and converted their legitimate authority into illegitimate abuses of power.

In chapter 3 I traced the formation of the Cooperative after two extended strikes against the Guanajuato Reduction and Mines company in 1935–36 and in 1938. The first strike came to an end after the "Hunger Caravan" (*Caravana* de Hambre) of February–April 1936, when hundreds of the Reduction Company workers marched to Mexico City and camped in front of the National Palace. The second strike ended when the company ceded its holdings to the workers and left the country. These workers formed the Santa Fe Cooperative in January 1939.

Thus the Santa Fe Cooperative was founded in conflict. In its inception it had many local and national supporters who sent numerous letters, telegrams, and newspaper articles. However, some observers supported consumption cooperatives but feared that the establishment of production cooperatives would lead to "worker elites" who controlled the means of production and used this control to secure election to the administrative councils that constituted cooperative leadership (Knight 1990).

In fact, the Cooperative has struggled throughout its sixty-year history with problems of consolidation of power, worker exploitation, and corruption. The administration of the previous director of the Cooperative, Edgardo Meave Torrescano, who was also Mayor of Guanajuato township in the late 1970s and early 1980s, provides the most egregious example. Meave was accused of using large sums of Cooperative money for his own and others' political campaigns, having illegal deals (cohechos) with the electric company (CFE) and the foundry in Torreón, and selling parts of the Cooperative to his own family under assumed names (prestanombres).

In 1990–92 the fall of the price of silver caused the CFE and other creditors to call in their debts, and the Cooperative entered into severe political and economic crisis. Workers were not paid for two weeks during the Christmas season, nor were they given payments from profit-sharing, the Christmas bonus, or from the Cooperative savings plan they had counted on for that year, since Christmas is a time of high expenses on gifts and festivals. Alvaro said to me, "Only imagine how sad, to come home with nothing for Christmas and the children asking for gifts and wanting to have some fun." The lack of money at this time also prevents families from performing their ritual duties for the Baby Jesus (Niño Dios) which include making a crêche and having a ceremony to "put the Baby Jesus to bed" (acostamiento) around December 24 and "wake him up" on February 2, the festival of the Virgin de la Candelaria (levantamiento).

The situation at the Cooperative did not erupt until the following July when Cooperative workers reenacted the Caravana de Hambre of 1936. In this case, however, they marched to the Governor's House instead of the National Palace. They asked the governor, Carlos Medina Placencia, to bail out the Cooperative. Governor Medina refused, saying that if the Cooperative could not survive on its own, "let it close" (que se cierre) (El Nacional, July 28, 1992). Medina, a member of the right wing PAN party, refused to help the Cooperative partly in order to attack the traditional PRI enclaves in the capital city (Guanajuato). Meave had consolidated his power as a *cacique* (local power broker) of Guanajuato within and through the PRI.

At this time two brothers, Jesus and Ramón Castillo, who worked as engineers in the Cooperative, fomented a movement against Meave and his son, who held the position of head of the administrative council. When the elections came up in September 1992, their efforts at organizing the workers, and especially those who worked in the mines, paid off, and the councils were swept clean of Meave's supporters. The new council, supported by the members, removed Meave from his position as director and offered him a job as head of the ceramics workshop. As one former worker told me, "That's like telling him he can work sweeping the floors." As expected, he resigned.[21] The new administrative council was elected to a two-year term in late 1992. The Castillo brothers headed it. Jesús, the younger and more charismatic brother, spearheaded the movement and took the post of President of the Administrative Council. He went down into the mines daily; his contact with miners and the fact that he often worked underground (*bajo tierra*) gained him respect and support among the miners. One miner said to me, "He [Castillo] does know [what he's doing]—he's always down in the mine." As stated above, support from the mines is crucial to maintenance of power in the Cooperative, even though, in 1992, those who worked *bajo tierra* comprised only a third of the workforce of approximately nine hundred members. Because the Cooperative's profits come almost entirely from mineral extraction, these workers hold an important strategic position. Also, as I stated in the previous section, in producing the patrimony of the Cooperative, miners accrue moral authority to criticize the stewardship of that patrimony.

With the support of the miners and the control over the administrative council, the Castillo brothers began work to pay off the enormous debts left by Meave and to restore confidence among the workforce. The state government of Guanajuato finally arranged a loan for the Cooperative to help it overcome the crisis, reversing its former position. Approximately two hundred people left the Cooperative during this crisis, and this reduction in the workforce also helped the Cooperative to cut down on costs. By 1994 the Cooperative had surpassed this latest upheaval in its rocky history and began admitting new members again. The membership reelected most of the two councils in 1994. At this time they also voted to alter the Cooperative by-laws to expand the council's term to five years.

Upon entry into the administrative council, the Castillo brothers portrayed themselves as cleaning up the Cooperative and taking care of the patrimony. On March 23, 1994, Luis Donaldo Colosio, the PRI candidate for president who had explicitly set out to battle corruption and promote political pluralism, was assassinated. Shortly afterward Jesus Castillo had two quotations from Colosio's last speech painted on walls outside the beneficiation plant and at the entrance to the old mine of Tepeyac just below the plaza of Valenciana. One slogan invoked "those who hunger and thirst for justice," clearly though implicitly including the Cooperative *jefes* in that group. Here we see how the *jefes,* operating from a locus of power that is both figurative and literal (the walls of the Cooperative plant and mine, located at key entrances to the city of Guanajuato), strategically set the terms of debate over their own authority. They did so by allying themselves with the martyred cause of Colosio and a national movement in favor of democratization and political accountability. In this way the new leaders sought to present themselves as a democratic alternative to the clientelist and corrupt politics of the past, and promised to usher in a regime of democracy and accountability. At the same time, as we shall see, they continued to take a stand of benevolent paternalism and to be criticized when they failed to live up to that role. The tension between a model of "modern" democratic authority and one of patriarchy based on patron–client ties runs through many debates in the Cooperative (as in other Mexican contexts).

During these years the Cooperative not only managed to cover its debts but also resumed the payment of dividends from production profits (albeit less than in previous years). From late 1994 to late 1996 the Cooperative paid one thousand new pesos (about ninety dollars, and two to three weeks salary for most Cooperative members) to each member three times a year: at the end of December, during Holy Week (*Semana Santa*), and in late August.[22] The Cooperative also donated lots for construction, provided subsidized groceries and building materials, and maintained a savings plan (*caja de ahorro*) which paid out at the end of the year.

However, although many supported the Castillos as saviors of the Cooperative, dissatisfactions continued. These were framed in terms more significant for Cooperative members than those posed by the *jefes*. Workers recast the *jefes* from political reformers to family patriarchs with the obligation to preserve and transmit patrimonial possessions. A broadside circulated clandestinely during 1994 was cut and pasted to look like a newspaper article and said: However, although many supported the Castillos as saviors of the Cooperative, dissatisfactions continued. A broadside circulated clandestinely during 1994 was cut and pasted to look like a newspaper article, and said:

> He [Castillo] is making 2,900 pesos a week while we are busting our asses (*nos jodemos*), let's see if he dares to deny it. He promised to post the list of salaries for every worker. Well let him post his own salary—we'll see if he

is man enough to do it (*a ver si es tan hombre*). We already know he isn't—he's probably impotent—he only has one daughter and to feel like a man he goes out with Gloria Medina [a nurse in the Cooperative clinic], but really he doesn't measure up [sexually] (*la verdad es que no marca*).

This letter ended with a bold exhortation: "COMRADE, LET'S UNITE FOR THE COOPERATIVE—IT IS THE PATRIMONY OF OUR SONS." The person who showed it to me thought that it was written by Meave's son in an attempt to discredit the new administration. However, even if this is true, the sentiment and language closely resembled statements I often heard during my time there. The sexual content of the jabs at Castillo is particularly striking, as is the reference to patrimony. This passage enacts the close connections between gender and sexuality, power and authority, and patrimony as they are conceived within the Cooperative.

Beginning in April 1997, with the death of a miner in the mine of San Ignacio and a particularly small payment of *utilidades* (about six hundred pesos [fifty dollars] as opposed to one thousand pesos [ninety dollars]), sentiment against the *jefes* began to build. Once again, it was the miners in particular who expressed dissatisfaction. One of the targets was the current superintendent of mines, Engineer Alfredo Galvez. Galvez was a young man from a wealthy Guanajuato family, with no familial connections to the Cooperative. He controlled the different mines through punishment and favoritism. To his enemies he assigned jobs in which they could not make enough money or which they found degrading. Or he sent them to the mine of San Ignacio some distance outside the city and also the most dangerous of the mines owing to the softness of the rock at that end of the Veta Madre.

Galvez managed and supported the Cooperative baseball team, which, in 1997, won the municipal championship (beating out their long-term rival El Cubo, in what was known locally as *El Clásico Minero*). Miners reported that he favored (*consentió a*) the baseball players among the workforce and diverted Cooperative funds to buy equipment and to pay players. In April 1997 it was reported in the local paper that the Cooperative (under Galvez's influence) had brought a pitcher from Tabasco by airplane and given him a job in the Cooperative in time for the championship in May. When I asked Cooperative members about this story, they merely replied, "No, he took the bus."

Galvez also maintained control in the mines by favoring (*consentiendo a*) some mines over others, especially Cata and Valenciana. Although he had no direct control over wages, which were uniform in all the mines, he could intervene to change miners' tasks (and thus the conditions of incentive contracts), their hours, or their areas of work. Since most miners depended heavily on the extra work they could make above their base pay through extra hours and incentive pay, Galvez effectively controlled these workers' livelihoods. Once a miner had fallen out with (*salió mal con*) Galvez, he often chose simply to leave the Cooperative and look for contract work in another mine.

Galvez personified one version of virility. Handsome and rather self-satisfied in appearance and carriage, he had at least two mistresses within the Cooperative as well as a wife. He often said with pride, "Women are my weakness" (*mi debilidad son las mujeres*). He was not on either of the councils and so was not considered part of the inner circle of *jefes,* but he often attended the Saturday *comidas* (lunches). However, he lacked the stance of just paternalism embodied by the true *jefes,* and many workers criticized him for this lack. For instance, his blatant arbitrariness in the mines incurred many miners' anger, for he did not even pretend to be just or even-handed. They also complained of his arrogance and insistence that his work was more worthy of respect than theirs. Indeed, he once said to me, "If you're doing a study of the Cooperative, then you're doing a study of me, because I am the first [*primero;* also, "most important"] miner of the Cooperative."

In addition, he openly disagreed with the "social goal" of the Cooperative, the preservation of jobs. In an interview with me, he insisted, "The Cooperative is just like any other company. We want to make a profit just like everybody else." When workers said to me, "The Cooperative is no different than a company," they meant it as a condemnation. The *jefes,* in contrast, always made sure to tell me, for example, "the goal of the Cooperative is completely different from that of the other mining companies. We have a social goal"; or "We [the *jefes*] are really the employees of the workers. We work for them, not the other way around." For Galvez, who earned a big salary and who—according to many—skimmed a lot of cream off the top, to say that the Cooperative existed for the profit of its leaders seemed presumptuous and arrogant. In short, Galvez refused to cast himself as the responsible steward of the Cooperative patrimony and even denied that that patrimony belonged to all the workers and not just to him and the other *jefes.* Cooperative members saw this behavior as a sign of Galvez's illegitimate rule. They called him the "Lord of the Heavens" (*el Señor de los Cielos*) after the famous narco trafficker Amado Carrillo, who had recently died while undergoing plastic surgery to change his appearance. This characterization reflected a growing sense among miners that his power was illegitimate and corrupt, and that he was assuming too much of it (*poniendose grande*).

At the same time resentment was brewing against the administrative council and especially Castillo, known as the Big Man (*El Viejote*) or Castillote (*-ote* is an augmentative suffix). In August 1997 the administrative council announced that there was a fund of 1.8 million pesos of profits. They stated that this fund was too small to distribute at that time and that they would wait till December so that they could give out more. Many Cooperative members, but especially many miners, became very angry at this. On August 18 the miners of San Vicente and Rayas (about 90 people on the day shifts at both mines) did not go down in the mine but rather came to the beneficiation plant where the central offices are and made two demands. First, they called for a special session of the general assembly to vote on whether to give out the money. Second, many miners informally stated that Galvez should step down. Castillo accepted the formal demand for an extraordinary assembly and set the date for September 11.

The next few weeks passed with tension and suppressed anger. On August 23 very few miners attended the birthday celebration of the director of the Cooperative, Engineer Vargas, an elderly and courtly gentleman respected by all. One engineer sympathetic to the miners (the only woman engineer in the Cooperative) told me, "If there is alcohol and rancor, there are bound to be problems. People said, no—better just to stay home." At the September meeting it was decided that 40 percent of the money would be given out in August and the rest saved until December. However, at this meeting Castillo also announced that he was going to resign and that there must be a future meeting to elect his successor. This act put a new spin on the crisis. Although the money remained important (for it had not yet been given out and, until it actually was, people remained angry and suspicious), Cooperative members' more diffuse discontent over how the Cooperative was run became channeled into the question of picking a successor. This first meeting initiated what amounted to an unofficial political campaign by several candidates.

The campaign was waged on the field of patrimony. Arguments for and against candidates were based on how each would preserve, or squander and steal, the patrimony of all members of the Cooperative. For instance, the quotation at the beginning of this chapter, "The Cooperative doesn't belong to them [the *jefes*]; it belongs to us and our children" was stated in some form by a number of people when criticizing the actions of the leadership. One plant worker, in telling me of the money that members of the administrative council reportedly siphoned off for their own use, said "They say, 'one peso for everyone, and thirty pesos for me, for my old age and the old age of my children and the old age of my grandchildren.' It's a fuckload of money (*un chingón de dinero*)." This statement criticizes council members for diverting Cooperative patrimony into their own families in an illegitimate manner; rather than being an inheritance for all members, it is only for the most powerful.

On the other hand, those who supported the administration's decision not to hand out the money, made statements along the lines of this woman who worked in the payroll department:

The problem is that [the miners] are very young, and the young don't see the future. They don't see that you have to think about the future of the children, to give something to the children, because the Cooperative is a large source of jobs for Guanajuato, and if it's not there, what will people do?

Ideas of appropriate gender and familial roles also helped to form the terms of the debate during this period. For instance, Galvez was one of the pretenders to chieftainship. He had some followers and was said to be "bribing" the miners with promises of more money. His supporters pointed to the masculine vigor he exhibited both in his sexual activities and in his decisiveness in the mines. In contrast, his detractors talked of his swaggering arrogance (imitating his walk became a favorite pastime). They also implied a connection between his "illicit" expressions of sexuality (a diverting of male potency for his own pleasure outside the family) and his use of Cooperative money to further his baseball team and to "campaign" for the post of Council President (a diverting of Cooperative patrimony for his own advancement).

Another candidate, Porfirio Montemayor, was the engineer in charge of the beneficiation process. Montemayor was perhaps the favorite of those who worked in the offices, and was rumored to be Castillo's choice. The people in the offices and some workshops said that he was cautious and "thought about the future," unlike those who worked underground, who were talked about as young, uneducated, and hotheaded. His supporters felt that he could be trusted to preserve the patrimony for the sons and grandsons to whom it really belonged. On the other hand, Porfirio was widely rumored to be homosexual (*joto*), and this quality was connected to a sense of his being effete, ineffectual, and marginal to the community of Cooperative members. "He doesn't have authority; he can't command" (*no tiene autoridad; no puede mandar*), people said.

Castillo wisely kept his mouth shut while all this was going on, playing the role of the impartial father who does not favor (*consiente a*) one son over another. He repeated until the day of the second meeting that he was going to step down, even though it was not clear whether according to the Cooperative by-laws he might be constrained to finish out his term if the members voted that they did not want him to resign. This uncertainty worked in his favor; several people told me that they were reluctant to say openly that they supported Galvez or Montemayor, for fear of repercussions if Castillo did stay in power.

Castillo also acted the part of the father of the Cooperative in other ways. Several weeks before the second meeting I met with him in the offices of the Valenciana mine early one morning. It was the first time I had been able to speak to him about the crisis, although he knew that I knew what was going on. I asked him what he thought about the whole thing, and he said the following:

I don't know—it's a difficult thing—I have just one daughter and she reads the papers and she feels bad because they say all these things about her father, and she asks me about revenge, but it's not about revenge. What I'm really thinking is that it's time for me to step down because after all the crisis before [1991–92] and now the problems are starting all over again, even though it's different this time. I could pay out the money right now, but the Cooperative would go into bankruptcy. It wouldn't be responsible to do that. The people don't take into account all the things the Cooperative gives them—scholarships, food, loans. What I want is for the generations in the Cooperative to continue and for the children to have professional careers, but inside the Cooperative—like [here he listed the names of Cooperative engineers and accountants whose fathers and grandfathers were miners in the Cooperative]. That doesn't happen in the other mining companies. I am proud that I was able to experience it.

This excerpt shows how Castillo positions himself in a fatherly role, and how he views the Cooperative as a family whose mission is to help its children get ahead (*salir adelante*) by caring for and passing on the family patrimony. I think he believes what he said to me that day, but his discourse also had a strategic purpose; he most likely hoped that in my peripatetic rounds of the mines, workshops, and offices, I might repeat what he had said to others in the Cooperative. He masterfully invoked paternalism in a variety of ways. The mention of his own daughter, the suggestion that "it's time for me to step down," the emphasis on "responsibility," and, finally, the description of the Cooperative as ongoing generations progressing through time all underscore his role as the wise and responsible father, whose children may not understand what he does now but will thank him later.

Castillo's careful handling of the crisis paid off. Several days before the second meeting, he announced that he would stay on if the people voted for him to do so. On September 30 the members voted for him to finish his term, crushing the aspirations of Galvez, Montemayor, and several others. Things quieted down, and most workers and engineers had managed the crisis carefully enough so as not to have incurred Castillo's anger.

Only Galvez suffered severe consequences. The *jefes*, in violation of the Cooperative Law, did not include on the agenda a time for items proposed by members of the general assembly. Nevertheless, after the vote, someone in the assembly called out that Galvez be removed from his post and given authority over only one mine instead of all seven. People shouted "make him do cleanup" (*a la limpia;* using a crowbar to push rocks through the chutes underground , a low-paid and demeaning job). The leader of the meeting was a captain at the

Rayas mine and an enemy of Galvez. He put the proposal that Galvez be demoted on the floor.

Approximately two hundred of the three hundred people present at the assembly raised their hands in support of the proposal. At this moment Galvez entered the assembly with several friends;[23] they heard the name "Alfredo Galvez" and assumed that Castillo had stepped down and that his successor was being elected. Galvez and his friends all raised their hands, voting for Galvez's downfall. Two days later he resigned from the Cooperative.

In this crisis Castillo used a moral language of benevolent though firm paternity to consolidate his slipping base of power. The miners called on their own moral economy, based on their role in producing and safeguarding a shared patrimony, to oust Galvez and to receive at least some of the money to which they were entitled. Only Galvez did not use the idiom of gender, authority, and patrimony to his advantage. Raised in a bourgeois home and arriving only recently in the Cooperative, he had often voiced his opposition to the stated goals of the enterprise. He acted like a virile, cosmopolitan man-about-town. But within the local idiom of gender and authority he was judged a spoiled and presumptuous brother, a *consentido* who did not live up to his father's trust to care for and carry on the family patrimony.

Questions of Inheritance: The Case of the *Socios Fundadores*

Most people in the Cooperative see it as an entity whose intergenerational character links the past, present, and future. But many of these people disagree over who are the rightful heirs to the patrimonial possessions passed along these generations. This lack of consensus over the proper lines of inheritance causes severe conflicts within the Cooperative. For instance, earlier in this chapter I referred to the fact that the former director, Meave, sold Cooperative properties to himself through *prestanombres*. People were angriest over this theft not so much because of present financial loss but rather because it diverted the inheritance of their sons and grandsons from its rightful path.

Another dispute over inheritance caused even more controversy. It involved the founding partners (*socios fundadores*; that is, the surviving workers from 1938, when the Guanajuato Reduction and Mines Company turned over its holdings to the workforce). To my knowledge, eighteen of these workers are still living.[24] They hold certificates attesting to their share in what became the Cooperative.

In the mid-1980s, and at different points up to the present, some of these men and their descendants have claimed that, because the holdings of "La Reduction Company" (as it is generally called) were given directly to them and they have certificates to prove it, the Cooperative is the patrimony not of the current members and *jefes* but of their own sons and grandsons. Their claim is probably not legally sustainable, since they were all bought out when they left the Cooperative, but it carries a heavy moral weight. It goes to the heart of the Cooperative's moral precepts based on the disposition of patrimonial possessions to their proper heirs.

As Don Basilio (a former master ironworker in the Cooperative and a *socio fundador*) and several others tell the story, several people began to formulate a case against the Cooperative in the mid-1980s (a time of high silver prices and prosperity in the Cooperative). These people included a *compadre* of Don Basilio, Don Gustavo Lara, his daughter Susana, and Mariela, the daughter of another *socio fundador* who had already died. Don Basilio went with the Señora Mariela to Mexico City to consult with the head of the *Sindicato Nacional de Mineros, Metalúrgicos y Similares de la Republica Mexicana* (National Union of Miners, Metallurgists, and Similars of the Mexican Republic). They hoped to form a separate section of the union to demand their rights from the Cooperative. As Doña Mariela put it (according to Don Basilio), "It's not right that you are the founders and they are going to throw you out without giving you anything . . . and there are widows and there are orphans and I think that we [in this case Don Basilio as a *fundador* and herself as an "orphan"] have rights" (interview, March 20, 1997). At the time that they went to Mexico City (ca. 1985), they represented approximately fifty people, but the union president told them that that was not enough to form a local section of the union. He encouraged them to press their case, however, saying, "That Cooperative is working with a mask, now it is only a cooperative in name."

Don Basilio said that his *compadre* invited so many widows, children, and grandchildren to join the movement that they had to rent a room to have their meetings, because they did not fit inside his house. They formed an administrative council that mirrored the Cooperative structure. However, when Don Gustavo began charging twenty-five pesos a week to pay the costs of the meeting room and other expenses, the movement began to break up. As Don Basilio put it, "I saw that my little *compadre* was getting above himself (*poniendose grande*) and I came away."

In the early 1990s Don Gustavo and Doña Mariela each reinitiated the same claim, this time separately. Both branches of the movement attracted criticism. The doctor of the Cooperative was quoted in an article published in December 1991 as saying that a movement was brewing to destabilize the Cooperative. He denounced the claim of the *socios fundadores* and their children as illegitimate, saying:

A *señora* by the name of [Mariela], who lives in Alhóndiga Street has been able to incite ill will among many of the "ex-cooperativistas" . . . many of those who did work here and might have been considered as *fundadores* have died, and this señora is claiming supposed rights for them. . . . Their descendants, who have not given one hour of work to the Cooperative, nor one peso, now that the Cooperative has entered into crisis, simply want to share the spoils as if it were a cake. (*El Nacional*, December 15, 1991)

In spite of attacks like these, the claim of the *socios fundadores* struck a nerve. The *socios fundadores* and their families pointed out the contradictions between the Cooperative's image of just patriarchy and its actions (much as women use this same tactic to criticize men and the Cooperative). Timing also helped their cause. At the time of the council elections in 1994 and afterwards the new *jefes* had to appear morally legitimate in contrast to the former administration.

The extreme secrecy and evasion on the part of the Cooperative regarding the *socios fundadores* proves the strength of their claim on the Cooperative. The case of the *socios fundadores* was perhaps the most sensitive topic I encountered in fieldwork, more sensitive than wages, accidents, and infractions of the Mining Safety Code. The delicacy of the issue arises from the fact that the *socios fundadores* posed a serious threat to the *jefes'* moral legitimacy, because they presented themselves as the true fathers of the Cooperative and demanded a share in the patrimony on those grounds. The threat of an alternate Cooperative genealogy with the *socios fundadores* as progenitors forced the *jefes* to address their demands.

In April 1996 the Cooperative responded by sending a letter to the daughter of Don Gustavo, Susana Lara, in response to a letter she had sent to them.[25] The letter, signed by Engineer Vargas, the director of the Cooperative, did not acknowledge any of the claimants' rights over the Cooperative and scrupulously referred to them as "ex-*socios fundadores*" (underscoring the fact that they had left the Cooperative). But it did state that the Cooperative would give 290 pesos a month and subsidized prescription drugs to seventeen surviving *socios fundadores*, those who had been involved with the movement. The Cooperative did not give any payments to the children of *socios fundadores*.

At this time the social work department carried out a "socioeconomic study" of the *socios fundadores*.[26] They visited each of the men in their homes and surveyed them on income, medical history, family members, and living conditions in order to determine their "needs." They conducted this study before I arrived in the Cooperative, so I was not able to observe its reception on the part of the *socios fundadores*. However, I did accompany the social workers on several occasions when they carried out similar studies of the current workforce. These encounters were often fraught with tension. The interviewers wanted to record high incomes and standards of living to counter any potential requests for help.

Conversely the families tended to underreport income in the hope of getting more resources. They saw the surveys as a tool for the Cooperative to avoid what they considered its moral obligations. I suspect that the interviews of the *socios fundadores* had a similar dynamic. The monthly payments began to arrive in the fall of 1996. They were delivered in person by the social workers, ostensibly so that they could combine the payments with home visits. The social workers often put off these visits, and thus the payments, for several months at a time. They spoke of the visits as a tedious obligation and usually referred to the *socios fundadores* with the belittling term "*viejitos*" (little old men). In these ways the social work department, acting in the name of the Cooperative, subtly humiliated the *socios fundadores* by treating them as charity cases rather than as legitimate shareholders in the Cooperative patrimony.

This strategy on the part of the Cooperative was very clever. By refusing to recognize the claim of the *socios fundadores* but giving them money to alleviate their economic need, the *jefes* preserved an appearance of benevolent patriarchy. At the same time they made them the responsibility of the social work department, emphasizing the good works of the Cooperative while at the same time recasting the *socios fundadores* as pitiable creatures. The social work department focuses mostly on women, children, and ill or injured workers. By putting the *socios fundadores* under their jurisdiction, the *jefes* attempted to deny them a role as fathers and grandfathers of the Cooperative. The *socios fundadores* to whom I spoke understood these coded messages perfectly. They scoffed at the payment (about thirty dollars a month), calling it "*una limosna*" (alms), a word that emphasizes both how little money it was and the condescending way that it was given out. The daughter of one *socio fundador* summed up the general feeling: "The attitude of the Cooperative towards my father and the rest is very disrespectful. Especially since, really, you could say that the Cooperative belongs to them [that is, to her father and the other *socios fundadores*, and therefore to her own family]."

However, the *socios fundadores* were able to achieve some small gains by using the moral language of patrimony to their own advantage. While they may have conceded their war with the Cooperative, they continue to engage in small skirmishes, and sometimes they come out ahead. When I last spoke with Susana Lara in November 1998, she said, "Even though the *jefes* don't acknowledge the basic question of our rights, I am going to ask them about giving us a Christmas bonus. We'll see."

The *socios fundadores* and their supporters base their claims on the principles of patrimony. Some use the word directly. One afternoon as I sat in the social work department, an old gentleman came to leave a note for the social worker. In the note he gave his name, followed by "*Socio fundador.* This is my patrimony." In my talks with Susana Lara, she also spoke of the patrimonial rights of the *socios fundadores.* The basis of these patrimonial rights is their status as "founding fathers" and their place at the center of Cooperative cosmogony. The *Caravana de Hambre* of 1936 and the strikes that preceded and followed it stand as the foundational moments of the Cooperative. The *socios fundadores* are both the protagonists and the immediate heirs of this legendary struggle. All six of the *socios fundadores* I interviewed recounted the story of the *Caravana*; in most cases it was their only visit to Mexico City, or even outside the Bajío, in their lives.[27] Some described the events of that time with great drama, others more laconically. In all cases they clearly felt that their participation in these great events entitled them to moral authority and a share in the Cooperative patrimony.

The contest between the *socios fundadores* and the *jefes* came down to the question of defining a legitimate Cooperative genealogy. Each side strove to define its own genealogy as the true one, and the other as an illegitimate offshoot. Ultimately the *jefes'* version prevailed; they were able to establish themselves as the legitimate fathers of the Cooperative and stewards of its patrimony. But, in doing so, they had to fulfill the obligations prescribed by the principles of patrimony. They did this by giving financial and medical help to the *socios fundadores.* In this way they tacitly recognized and responded to the claims of those who went before, even as they publicly excluded them from the Cooperative genealogy.

In this chapter and the one preceding it we have seen how often competing languages of patrimony have in common their attempts to establish and maintain understandings of proper ways to enact gender and kinship, and to use these to organize power and resources in advantageous ways. One strength of this formulation of patrimony as language is that it allows us to bracket the ultimately insoluble question of intention. We can examine the effects of languages of patrimony that take place when people use them, whether they "mean to" or not.

In chapters 7 and 8 I examine the material substances on which these languages of patrimony are based, especially that most important substance for Guanajuato and the Cooperative: silver. I look at silver as patrimony in the context of other substances that are *not* seen as patrimony, although they *are* seen as resources. Such resources, in particular the mineral specimens and miners extract from the mine in the process of blasting for silver, do not damage the collective in their depletion, and yet their existence allows for the consideration of silver as patrimony—and arguably have allowed the Cooperative to survive in difficult times. By analyzing these substances in tandem, I also hope to contribute to the burgeoning literature on the anthropology of value from the perspective of the idiom of patrimony as a local version of inalienability.

CHAPTER 7

Veins of Value, Rocks of Renown

An Anthropology of Mined Substances

When the crisis happened in the Cooperative [in 1991–92], that's when I started to sell achichicles. *I bailed myself out that way [así me saqué].*
—Valenciana worker, February 1998

I like this stone. It reminds me of a mountain range covered with snow.
—Cooperative wife in Santa Rosa, December 1996

As the Cooperative's most important product, silver condenses many of the meanings and practices associated with patrimony; it thus forms a major focus of my study. In this chapter I look at how silver is valued along with other mined substances that are not considered patrimonial by Cooperative members. This perspective allows me to focus attention on the practice and consequences of assigning different kinds of value to objects at different moments rather than beginning with already established categories such as "commodity," "gift," or "inalienable possession," as other theorists of value have done.

Two different mined substances produced in the Cooperative mines, silver and mineral samples (known locally as *achichicles*)[1] originate side by side but emerge into widely dispersed networks of exchange and systems of power and meaning. How do the differences in the ways these substances are assigned value and sent into or withheld from circulation complicate anthropological notions of value, place, and substance? How do the organization of power within the Santa Fe Cooperative, and the broader context of neoliberal ascendance, the crisis of legitimation of the PRI, and the deindustrialization of Guanajuato affect the politics of value enacted through these objects? What can these relations of power in one place tell us about how patrimony as a form of value works elsewhere in Mexico?

In the case of silver, I emphasize the ways in which silver, which seems to operate exclusively as a commodity for market exchange, is also characterized as inalienable. For mineral specimens, I show that what appears to circulate primarily as a gift and to derive its value from its "giftlike" ability to establish a connection between giver and recipient (what we might call the *hau* of mineral specimens [Mauss 1990 (1950), Sahlins 1972]) not only circulates as a commodity but also helps the Cooperative to survive by providing an alternate source of income for members and their families. However, the more apparent the hau of a mineral specimen, the greater its value as a commodity. Taken as a whole, an anthropology of mined substances in the Cooperative can enrich our understanding of how people assign multiple forms of value simultaneously. It can also show the range of ways that Cooperative members assign value, within which some—and some of the most important—of these assignments use a language of patrimony.

INALIENABLE COMMODITIES: SILVER

As mentioned earlier, the Cooperative holds the concessions to six of the oldest mines in the district: San Ignacio, El Sirio, Valenciana, Cata, Rayas, and San Vicente. It produces and refines approximately eight hundred metric tons per day. The extraction work is done by drilling and blasting with emulsion explosives. Miners then load the blasted rock into mining cars and transport them to the surface. Other Cooperative workers bring the mineral to the processing plant by dump trucks (from El Sirio, San Ignacio, Valenciana, and Cata) or by a small tram of seven cars that trundles through the hills from Rayas and San Vicente. There the plant workers crush the ore and make it into a concentrate.

After the beneficiation process, the Cooperative transports the mineral concentrate to a smelting plant in San Luis Potosí, one of only two precious metal smelting plants in Mexico. The smelting plant pays the Cooperative for silver, gold, and copper according to the New York daily price per Troy ounce. Most of this payment is for the silver; this is by far the Cooperative's main source of income. Thus, perhaps, the most important factor affecting the Cooperative is the price of silver on the world market.

In processing and selling silver (and gold and copper), Cooperative workers focus all their efforts on removing the ore from its original matrix, divesting it of its unique properties, regulating its quality, and converting it into a product that can be smelted down with other products from other mines. The more easily and efficiently the Cooperative does these things, the more successful it will be. Engineers in charge of production, planning, and beneficiation often spoke to me about ways in which they tried to make this process as regular and consistent as possible. The superintendent of mines once said to me, "There is a saying in mining, 'the [beneficiation] mill is not like a corn mill [*molino de nixta-mal*].'" When I looked at him quizzically he explained that it is easy to grind different kinds and different qualities of corn together or sequentially, but if you try to do the same thing with ore, you lose all consistency and predictability and therefore all cost-effectiveness.

Similarly, once the ore has been made into a concentrate, its exchange value depends on its being smelted into an undifferentiated product [ingots of copper with small amounts of gold and silver] and fetching a price set in New York per Troy ounce. Furthermore, the one feature of the Cooperative concentrate that gives it an advantage over other suppliers to the foundry is its high content of iron, which is used as a *founding agent*. In other words, its crucial distinctive characteristic is one that makes it more useful in the smelting process, that is, the process of erasing the distinctions between different lots of ore concentrate. Thus the sequence of mining, assay, beneficiation, transport, and sale of Cooperative ore is bent on suppressing its distinctive character; the success of the Cooperative depends on its ability to accomplish this consistently and constantly.

The exchange of silver ore encapsulates the global in the local. First, silver mining is highly regulated by nation-states. This is why studies of mining so often have used the industry as a way of studying the state (Brading 1971, Bernstein 1965, Sariego et al. 1988). Historically the Mexican state and the Spanish state before it derived huge revenues from silver mining, and from these particular mines. The state, in the name of the nation, claims silver from the very start as national patrimony.

Since silver is the Cooperative's main source of income, the most important factor affecting the Cooperative is the price of silver on the world market. As the superintendent of mines told me. "The price of silver decides whether we live or die." The price of silver oscillated between $4.16 and $7.26 per ounce during the most extended period of my fieldwork (November 1996 to June 1998). The lowest trough began in April 1997, when the monthly average fell below $4.73 per ounce and then to $4.33 per ounce in July 1997. This downturn lasted until November 1997 when the price finally climbed to a monthly average of $5.05 per ounce, and remained high through August 1998 (a monthly average of $5.12 per ounce). When the price of silver dips, the Cooperative becomes unstable. The major political crisis of the past decade, when the administrative council was ousted by a coup, took place after the first downturn in the price in silver in real terms, in 1990–91. During my fieldwork another period of political unrest started, when the administrative council attempted to postpone profit sharing in August 1997, in the middle of a later trough in silver prices. This instability righted itself (at least temporarily) after November 1997, when silver began to rise again. Given the perennial fluctuations in the price of silver, the Cooperative's strategy, like that of all mining enterprises, is to try to keep the cost of production down by suppressing silver's distinctive characteristic in favor of an easily meldable concentrate.

But alongside this mode of value production based on the erasure of distinction, we find another form, based on the gendered and moral relations of production. Here it is the specific local knowledge of the mines and the qualities of silver that are valued. I have described the masculine honor and moral authority of mine work at several points. This honor and authority depend not only on the amount of time spent working underground but also on the worker's spatial location in the extraction process. The closer one is to the sites of drilling in the mine, the greater one's honor. The place where the drill bites into the rock is thus a site of danger and prestige, for the life of the Cooperative and the livelihood of its members emanate from that point.

The social unit most involved with Cooperative silver extraction consists of the *perforista* and his assistant (*ayudante*). This asymmetrical relationship derives from older forms of apprenticeship that used to be dominant in the industrial sector in Guanajuato. The two workers are bound together by the difficulty and danger of their job, by their physical proximity to the source of silver, and by their interdependence in filling productivity incentives. Since both are paid on the same basis (per meters drilled), it is in the interest of both to work together.

As one former *perforista* described the *perforista*-assistant dyad to historian Ada Marina Lara:

> Let's imagine you're working with me and we see that we work well together, we don't fight and we do everything that has to be done as partners between us, we are [as] two and let's do this (*semos dos y hay que hacer esto*).[2] That is the law of the miner. . . . the two together, since we're both working together . . . we are [as] two (*semos dos*) . . . the *perforista* and the assistant, we're both in the same danger, in the same place.[3]

This statement reveals the importance of place and danger in establishing the elemental moral community of two men, the *perforista* and his assistant. The phrase "we are [as] two" (*semos dos*) repeated several times in the full interview, aptly expresses this relationship which is not based on unity in the sense of merging but on an asymmetrical and interdependent community. As we saw in chapter 5, this community of Cooperative men at times poses an alternative form of patrimony to family patrimony; women often accuse men of choosing the former over the latter.

Furthermore, the "law of the miner" invoked by this worker is that of solidarity and egalitarianism born of work, danger, and proximity to the site of

"perforation." The law extends outward to govern all relations between underground workers. Just as the *perforista* and his assistant form a bounded community that excludes all other underground workers, so underground workers
form a community limited to those who inhabit the "men's house" of the mine.
This community also bases itself on the "law of the miner." As the captain of the
San Ignacio mine put it, "Underground we are united, because we have to take
care of each other. We are companions [*somos compañeros*]."

Proximity to the source of silver also entails intimate familiarity with its substance. Membership in the moral community of the underground depends on
knowledge of and familiarity with the mine. The ability to recognize silver in
the rock forms part of this local knowledge that establishes the moral and honorable community of Cooperative miners. This ability distinguishes miners'
knowledge from engineers' book learning and diplomas (*títulos*).[4] Every time I
went down in the mines, I was given a lesson in how to identify the Veta Madre.
Cooperative workers, and miners especially, clearly saw the ability to recognize
silver in the mines as a fundamental part of my preparation as a (putative) authority on mining in the Santa Fe.

The recognition of silver forms part of an old tradition of *buscones* and *lupios* in Guanajuato. *Buscones* are underground prospectors who may work on

FIGURE 7.1 Pointing out the Veta Madre. *Photo by Stephen Ferry*

their own account or for a company. Up until the 1930s *buscones* were a major portion of the mining class in Guanajuato. For instance, the Guanajuato Reduction and Mines Company (the former [U.S.] owners of the mines now held by the Cooperative) used its own workforce but also bought ore from *buscones* for reduction (beneficiation) (AGN fondo Presidentes, Lázaro Cárdenas, exp 532/49).[5] *Lupios* are workers who steal ore from the mines and take it to local buyers who conduct their business from their homes in different parts of Guanajuato. According to the local newspapers and reports from engineers both in the Cooperative and in El Cubo, the Industrial Safety Team, and miners in Rayas and Valenciana, there are still many *lupios* around. Unfortunately, but not surprisingly, no one ever told me that they themselves were *lupios* at this time (although some told me that *other* people were *lupios*, and a few older miners recounted their younger exploits stealing and selling ore). Clearly the categories of *buscón* and *lupio* overlap depending on who is speaking.

The occupation of *buscón/lupio* depends on visual recognition of the silver in its natural state (*en lo natural*), especially when the activity is prohibited and therefore surreptitious. "Not much use risking yourself if all you bring out is *tepetate* [rock with no ore]," as Chano told me. He went on to say what many miners pointed out, that true silver is not shiny. "The black that is opaque, not shiny, that is the natural silver," he instructed me.

> When I first began in the Cooperative [in the 1960s], I knew some people who were taking out rocks secretly and taking them to a guy in Barrio Nuevo [a neighborhood near the Cooperative's central plant]. So I started grabbing very shiny rocks (*piedras muy brillantes*) and taking them to sell. But he just laughed at me. Then a friend showed me how to know (*conocer*) the silver.

The recognition of silver in its underground context depends on an intimate knowledge of the substance of the silver; for this reason, the knowledge of silver as it appears underground is necessary for membership in the moral community of miners. It enhances a man's moral authority and claim over the patrimonial possessions of the mines. It is part of the *pasión* (erotic passion) and *cariño* (affection) that miners have for the mines and their contents. In this way, the substance of silver forms part of an intensely masculine constitution of Cooperative selfhood and sociality.[6] These gendered and morally inflected associations contribute to an understanding of silver as the fundamental basis of Cooperative patrimony. While in some ways these associations are obscured once silver is sold (in accordance with Marx's fetishism of commodities), they are not entirely forgotten, neither by Cooperative members nor other Guanajuatenses. This becomes evident in the ways that silver is exchanged.

Even as silver is sent on its way to be melted down with other silver in un-differentiated blocks, it carries a memory of the substance and place it leaves behind, and anticipates a return to Guanajuato in the form of other substances. This scheme of value is akin to Nancy Munn's (1977, 1986) concept of "fame" as a form of value production. Munn analyzes "the fame of Gawa" as "the expansion of intersubjective spacetime"—in itself a value-producing act. Similarly silver produces the fame of Guanajuato in its emergence from the mines into the world market.

When silver first returns in the form of money, it seems to exist only as exchange value on the world market. But in the minds of many, money made from the sale of silver anticipates reconversion into what we might call "place-making" substances. There is a real shame in diverting silver money from its path back into Cooperative patrimony—stealing or wasting it—for then it never turns back into substance. Rather, it breaks the circle of emergence and return and "goes [off] into the air" (*se va en el aire*) like smoke. This is the basis of the principles of patrimony that form the subject of this book. What substances does money derived from the sale of silver turn into when it returns to Guanajuato? Or, perhaps, what substances should it turn into? There are three categories of worthy substances: children (especially sons); respectable houses in the regional *abajeño* style; and public and sacred architecture. Each resubstantiates the silver that has been extracted and exchanged. The cycle within which silver moves out into the world and then returns expands the "fame of Guanajuato."

The fine Cooperative homes built with high silver prices in the early 1980s is a case in point, as are the magnificent churches and public plazas built in the eighteenth century with mining riches. It is not the fact that these edifices were built with silver money that establishes silver's inalienable qualities but rather the high degree of awareness on the part of Cooperative members and others of their origin as silver. As one wife of a Cooperative miner said to me of the houses in Santa Rosa de Lima:

> Those who were in the Cooperatives in the 1980s, the ones who knew how to take advantage (*aprovechar*) of the circumstances, you can see it in their houses. You know those nice stone houses (*bonitas casas de piedra*) on the Camino Real [Santa Rosa's only road] going up the hill. Those are the families that didn't drink up all the money.

In her statement, this woman links the money produced by silver, the right use of that money, and the "nice stone houses" of Santa Rosa. All three of these phases are understood as Cooperative and familial patrimony by Cooperative members. While from one perspective it is clear to all Cooperative and Guanajuatense observers that houses and silver and money are not "the same thing," by using an idiom of patrimony to control how Cooperative silver, wages and profits, and houses are produced, circulated, and consumed, Cooperative members and their families assert silver's inalienability. I am not arguing that silver works uniquely in this way (although I believe that the uses of patrimony in the Cooperative make the case particularly clear). These qualities and the process by which they are assigned and negotiated appear in many, but by no means all, situations of commodity exchange. But when they do, they are often ignored.

In this book I have attempted to describe the range of overlapping forces that have contributed to the development of a language (or languages) of patrimony in the Santa Fe and in contemporary Mexico more generally. These include the application—and appropriation—of colonial notions of patrimony and *mayorazgo* (entailed estates) in the New World, the establishment of land and subsoil resources as national patrimony in Article 27 of the Constitution of 1917, the organization of cooperative members as shareholders in collective, nonrenewable resources, and the inclusion of Guanajuato in UNESCO's list of *Ciudades de Patrimonio Mundial*. These different factors have contributed to the development of a national idiom that places high value on the preservation of certain resources and their transmission to future generations. Indeed, the integrity of the nation, the Cooperative, and other collectives is seen as depending on the proper stewardship of patrimonial possessions. People often disagree over who the proper guardians of these resources are and who are the legitimate members and heirs to the collective that they define, but they tend to use the idiom of patrimony to make their claims and dispute those of others.

The question then becomes, how do Cooperative members resolve the contradiction of using a language of patrimony to describe a form of wealth that must be continually extracted and sold. A number of scholars of exchange have addressed similar questions. Annette Weiner (1988, 1992) has described this as the "paradox of keeping-while-giving." She has proposed the category of inalienable possessions, those things that even as they are exchanged must be returned in kind in order to maintain the collective (Godelier 1999). She uses this to explain the principle of reciprocity as described by Marcel Mauss and to propose a cross-cultural category of "inalienable possessions." While her analysis may tend to overly reify the categories she wishes to establish, her consciousness of the interplay between departure and return for some kinds of possessions is extremely suggestive for the Cooperative case.

In her discussion of the production and exchange of Gawan canoes, Nancy Munn also invokes the idea of inalienable objects that return to their owners in another form. She states that "the canoe as an object of exchange *never comes back*. . . . Nevertheless, the canoe's *irreversible journey as an exchange value* does not alienate it from its producers: *all* its conversions return to the owning clan" (1977: 45; emphasis in the original). Similarly silver itself never comes back to Guanajuato but is converted to other forms that do return and, in their return, make the city of Guanajuato and the Santa Fe Cooperative.

Richard Parmentier, in analyzing Palauan money (*udoud*) from a Peircian perspective, remarks on the "paradox of movement and stasis" that pertains to important pieces of money.[7] He states that "movement and stasis actually imply each other: to generate its exchange value *udoud* must travel, yet to accomplish its maximal work it must be kept long enough in contiguity with some social unit to become identified with it" (2002: 65). This tension between holding onto valuables to increase their identification with a social unit and letting them circulate freely is analogous in some respects to the movements and stasis of Guanajuatense silver.

The Cooperative, because of its particular treatment of silver as patrimony, is seen by many as enriching Guanajuato through silver extraction. In contrast, other mining companies in the area are said to deplete Guanajuato through silver extraction. Cooperative members and observers often say that these other companies extract silver as fast as possible and then leave, taking their profits with them and giving no thought to what happens to the city and workers who remain behind. At times this criticism takes literal, embodied form; Martín described to me at length how Peñoles, the largest private company in Guanajuato and one of the two largest in Mexico, with substantial investment from Canada and South Africa, had altered the physical landscape to the northeast of the city, blasting out some of the most beautiful rock formations surrounding Guanajuato. He said, "That road (from Peregrina to Monte de San Nicolás to the east of the city) was so beautiful [*bonito con ganas*] before Peñoles started to work [also "fuck things up"] in the hills [*chingar en el cerro*]." In contrast, he and others said that the Cooperative has not altered Guanajuato, and the silver it extracts returns to nourish Cooperative children and build Cooperative houses.

This comparison recalls more general discussions about Spanish and North American miners. Although local historians and chroniclers acknowledge the brutality of the Spanish mine owners, they often point to the traces they left in the churches and plazas of the city, in contrast to North American mining companies of the early twentieth century, who took everything away. The uproar surrounding the melting down of the San Juan de Rayas bell, described in chapter 1, provides a case in point. The practice of removing all forms of value from Guanajuato is seen as particularly reprehensible because it prevents silver's appropriate return and the reassertion of its inalienability. In this way, local actors use the Cooperative and the deployment of a patrimonial idiom to critique or provide an alternative to "capitalism" as exemplified by North Americans and noncooperative mining enterprises. But it is only in this ideological sense that inalienability and exchangeability are opposed. In a practical sense, they must be combined in order for the Cooperative to survive.

It is not only Cooperative members who see silver in this way. Several other instances show how Guanajuatenses anticipate silver's return to Guanajuato. First, the illustration shown in Figure 7.2 appeared without explanation in an advertising supplement handed out on street corners in January 1998 in Guanajuato. It depicts the installations of the Rayas mine, with the caption: "From the dark depths we emerged / The light creates forms that disperse / from Guanajuato to the world." The words emphasize the movement out from Guanajuato and the connection between Guanajuato and the world created by that movement. The picture shows both the origin and the final destination of the "forms" created by the movement from the darkness of the mines to the light of the sun. The Rayas mine is several things at once: the source of these forms (silver); the place that was built with silver money; and the attraction for tourists coming to see the origin of Guanajuato's fame. The interplay between the words and picture encapsulates the emergence and return of silver. In this emergence and return, silver expands the fame of Guanajuato; this fame is in itself a form of value.

Many places in Guanajuato represent the return of silver visually or materially or both, and the expanded fame of Guanajuato. One instance is the Temple to the Virgin of Guadalupe, where the interior woodwork, ironwork, and altarpiece are entirely painted silver. Another is the crown of the city's patron saint, Santa Fe de Guanajuato, which is made of silver. When this crown was stolen in the 1980s, the Cooperative donated a replacement, also made of silver. A recent book on eighteenth-century baroque architecture in Guanajuato emphasizes this connection in its title: *From Silver, Fantasies* (*De La Plata, Fantasías* [Serrano Espinoza and Cornejo Muñoz 1998]). These instances represent silver's anticipated return to—and constitution of—Guanajuato, and complicate the notion of silver as "pure commodity." This manner of reconstituting silver, albeit in different forms, is one way of resolving the tensions between silver's inalienability and its commodification, for even though silver as a finished product is freely exchanged on the market, it must still return to its place of origin in some form. Silver, at first a part of Cooperative patrimony, also becomes the patrimony of Guanajuato. The idiom of patrimony as a category of property to be passed down to future Cooperative members (and Guanajuatenses) allows local actors to resolve the "paradox of keeping-while-giving," and to assert the inalienability of silver even as they extract it for commodity exchange.

FIGURE 7.2 Advertising flyer handed out on the street of Guanajuato, 1997. *Unknown origin*

The Hau of Mineral Specimens

Mineral specimens are not considered to be Cooperative patrimony. Cooperative members may value them, and may in some cases lament the prospect of their depletion, but such depletion in no way threatens the survival of the collectivity through time. Nor is there any particular shame in squandering the stones or money made from them. Nevertheless, extracting and exchanging mineral specimens is an extremely important activity in the Cooperative, especially among workers in the Valenciana and Rayas mines. As will become apparent, the right to extract mineral specimens is one reason why many stay in the Cooperative, and may allow the Cooperative to continue to operate with very low labor costs—even in local terms. In this sense, although mineral specimens are not seen as patrimonial substances, the ways that they are valued allow silver to be valued as patrimony. An anthropology of mined substances in the Cooperative that includes mineral specimens enables us to see the context of production and value within which languages of patrimony are made possible. It also shows that we cannot think about how people assign qualities of inalienability without also understanding how they assign other forms of value simultaneously or sequentially.

When Alexander von Humboldt visited the Veta Madre at the turn of the nineteenth century, he wrote of the mineral samples to be found there:

> The mineral substances which constitute the mass of the vein of Guanaxuato, are common quartz, amethyst, carbonate of lime, pearlspar, splintery hornstone, sulfurated silver, ramular native silver, prismatic black silver, deep red silver, native gold, argentiferous galena, brown blenide, spar iron, and pyrites of copper and iron. . . . Those mineralogists who are interested in the study of regular forms, [sic] find a great variety of crystals in Guanaxuato. (1911, 2:191)

Later in the nineteenth century Guanajuato participated in several international mineral competitions, winning first prize in an international competition in Saint Louis and a commendation from Paris. Beginning at this time and through at least the mid-twentieth century, Mexico in general and Guanajuato in particular occupied a significant role in the development of museum mineralogical collections. For instance, A. C. Burrage established a sizable collection of Guanajuato specimens around 1910; he donated them to the Harvard University Mineralogical Museum (part of the Peabody Collections) in 1940. In Guanajuato, Ponciano Aguilar, the director of the University of Guanajuato School of Mines, developed an extensive collection of minerals from Guanajuato and other parts of Mexico.[8] That collection now forms the bulk of the School of Mines Museum of Mineralogy.

More recently a geologist named Miguel Romero Sánchez developed an enormous collection of Mexican minerals (approximately seventy-five hundred specimens) which were housed in his own museum in Tehuacán, Puebla, and donated to the University of Arizona upon his death in 1997 (*Mineralogical Record,* March–April 1985, 16:129–136; *Rocks and Minerals,* January–February 1999, 16–19). Among these were many examples from Guanajuato. This dona-tion, and the efforts of a collector in the Guanajuato area, spurred new interest in Mexican minerals in general and Guanajuato in particular. In February 1999 there was a special exhibition on the Guanajuato mining district at the Forty-third Tucson Gem and Mineral Show (personal interviews with Christopher Tredwell, August 1999; Peter Megaw, October 1999; and Carl Francis, August 2000.) This international interest in Guanajuato dovetails with local cycles of exchange, wherein mineral specimens are seen as gifts and commodities.

The extraction of mineral specimens occurs alongside, and because of, the extraction of silver. When the drillers blast to remove the ore-bearing rock, they also dislodge the matrix through which the Veta Madre runs. You can see this matrix in the wall of the mine, in patches of crystallization and glints of white, gold, and purple. After blasting, there are many chunks of quartz, pyrite, calcite, and other stones all around, and portions of the mine's walls are loosened and can be worked out with a crowbar. In fact, the *perforistas* (and other miners) are supposed to knock out all loose rocks from the walls of the mine (*amacizar* [so-lidify]) in order to prevent falling rocks and cave-ins.[9] In the process they dis-lodge more semiprecious stones. One *perforista* told me, "After we blast, getting the mineral specimens is easy, like picking pears." Other miners also collect stones from old drilling areas or from the walls of the mine, but the older areas do not have as many good stones left, and making new holes to extract stones takes time and energy (and is not allowed by the Cooperative, since the miner is then taking time from his work activities). As the head of the Valenciana mine said to me, "If you see a worker who has some nice crystals that aren't broken and he isn't a driller or sampler, then you know he's been leaving his work area. Because the stones only come out that pretty in parts where there has been drilling recently."

This means that *perforistas* and their helpers most often extract mineral spec-imens, because their work area is at the point where drilling is done. Also, there is a code among miners that *perforistas* and their assistants have first rights to the mineral specimens in their area; others may only take stones from areas that are not being worked at that moment. The organization of rights to mineral spec-imens, then, reproduces the spatial configuration of honor and authority in the mine. At times, however, there may be exceptions to this code; for example, *perforistas* in the Valenciana allowed the sampler (*muestrero*) to take out stones from their areas on the grounds that he was raising his grandchildren as his own children since his daughter's husband had run away.

The Cooperative is the only mining company in Guanajuato that allows miners to extract mineral specimens for their own uses (although miners from other companies certainly extract minerals, the informal right to do so is much weaker in the case of these companies). Most Cooperative *jefes* blink at the extraction of mineral specimens, seeing the mineral specimen trade as the province of the miners. The head of the Valenciana explained, "It's not really allowed, but I have never stopped anyone from doing it. It's the least we can let them do, considering how low the pay is." This is another instance of the moral economy related to underground work described in the previous chapter.

This tacit permission means that mineral specimens have become an important source of income for many Cooperative members. The engineer of the Valenciana estimated that about 90 percent of the Valenciana's workers were involved in the trade in some way, and my observations roughly confirmed this estimate. Workers can make up to three times their weekly wage selling mineral specimens, and a few have become quite prosperous.

The fact that, under most circumstances, Cooperative engineers allow miners to take out mineral specimens does not mean that mineral specimen extraction is free from the workings of power in the Cooperative. At times it has become an arena for political struggle between *jefes* and miners. A recent issue of the collector's trade journal, *Rocks and Minerals,* includes an article by a European collector who spent a great deal of time at the Valenciana, leaving just before my arrival. His description exemplifies the different vectors of authority described in the previous chapter and how these affect the mineral specimens trade:

> Most of the mines in Guanajuato, including the Rayas, belong to the miners' cooperative which, although it makes a decent profit, runs the operation in a very gentlemanly manner: As long as shift quotas are met, management turns a blind eye to miners who take time off work to dig out specimens for people like me. (The only change in this policy was when the geologist and the captain of the mine owed me money for genuine Estwing geologist picks. They searched all miners coming off shift, confiscated all specimens, and sold them to me until the debt was paid! It wasn't my idea, but it made buying really easy and cheap. I felt uneasy at first, worried about losing faithful suppliers, but the miners' attitude was very reasonable: "Buy everything, for Gawd's sake, so we can get back to nor-

mal!" (*Rocks and Minerals,* March/April 1999, "Tales from Mexico, Pt. 2," 106)

This excerpt shows very well how authority works in the Cooperative: the *jefes* allow a certain space of authority and agency for miners, reserving the right to intervene in that space and use it to their own advantage. At the same time miners tolerate these interventions, realizing that it is the condition for continuing to extract stones. The account goes on to illustrate the limits of this uneasy truce. The collector tells how Alfredo Galvez, the former superintendent of mines whom we know from chapter 6,

> was number three in management with a mission in life to get the Cooperative into a businesslike mentality (i.e. cut out specimen collecting and, if possible, me too). [Alfredo spent] his working hours stamping around mine faces and sending workers home for several days without pay if they had specimens. (106)

This fits in perfectly with Galvez's general disrespect of legitimate miners' authority; as we saw, he ultimately paid for this attitude. This account also shows how the right to collect mineral specimens is seen as an integral aspect of cooperativism in the Santa Fe. This was the main reason people gave when I asked why the Cooperative let people take out mineral samples when the private mining companies did not.

With mineral specimens, as with silver, members deploy multiple notions of value simultaneously. The most immediately obvious of these is the way that Guanajuatenses use mineral specimens as gifts. I first noticed the circulation of mineral specimens as gifts because everyone kept giving them to me. Every time I visited the mine or a miner's house I came away laden. Soon I had crates of mineral specimens lining the wall of my living room. Not that I am complaining, but the prevalence of mineral specimens as a "visiting gift" struck me. Once I began to ask around, several other things about the circulation of mineral specimens as gifts became clear. First, they are almost always given by men to women with whom they have neither a familial nor a romantic connection.

For instance, on the occasions when my husband accompanied me to the Valenciana, my friends there would give him hunks of rock containing silver, joking about how he should sell it for a good price. When my parents visited me in Guanajuato, my friends only gave mineral specimens to my mother (somewhat to my father's chagrin). The only instance I heard of a man receiving a mineral specimen as a gift was when the priest visited a miner's home and was told to choose the prettiest stone on display in the house. This seems like the exception that proves the rule, for while the priest is not seen as a woman, nor is he exactly seen as a man.

Aside from giving mineral specimens to visitors to the house or mine, Cooperative miners often give them to women whom they encounter at work or other non-domestic contexts. All the secretaries, nurses, and social workers at the Cooperative had small displays of mineral specimens that had been brought to them by miners coming to arrange loans, doctor's appointments, and so on. They also give stones to women outside the Cooperative; one miner stated, "Whenever I have to go to the civil registry or a doctor's office or somewhere like that, I bring along a mineral specimen to give to the secretary. It smoothes the way." These examples and the fact that people often give stones to women they do not know very well show that the gift of a mineral specimen is a kind of courtesy gift, extremely useful for consolidating social relations outside one's household. In some ways it is akin to the gifts of food women give to other women who visit the house.

That the miner did not buy the stone but rather took it from the mine himself lends a particular character to the gift. The miner's act of extracting the stone and giving it away embodies the connection between the mine, the stone, the miner, and the receiver. Miners often made comments to me in the act of giving that enhanced this connection. They usually told me not only which mine the stone came from but also precisely which level in the mine, remarking, for example, that "nobody will believe that this rock came from 425 meters below the surface of the earth."

After my first six months of fieldwork I prepared to return to the United States for a visit with my family. The night before I left, one of my neighbors, Eugenio, came to bring me a present to take to my mother in Boston. Eugenio is a *carrero* (a worker who fills and empties cars of ore) in the Cata mine; his gift was a cardboard box full of calcite, white quartz, and amethyst. To the box he had affixed a card: Level 375/ Cata Mine / Guanajuato, Mexico. The specificity with which he located the mineral specimens not only in their original matrix but nested in the mine, the city, and the nation underscored both the importance of place of origin and the connection of that place to larger spaces.

The emphasis on the specific location of the mineral specimens encompassed by larger and larger spaces and their implied trajectory to my mother's place, outside all those spaces, enhanced the value of the gift, because it represented a connection between where the stones had come from and where my mother was waiting. The value again produces "the fame of Guanajuato" but this time on a more intimate plane. It is as if the stone has what Marcel Mauss (1990 [1950]: 13), borrowing from the Maori, called the *hau*—the spirit of the giver embodied in the gift that connects the giver and recipient. The hau of mineral specimens, as expressed through the specificity with which miners emphasized the exact source of the stones and the exact path of its journey to the recipient, increases the object's value as a gift.

We find similar processes at work when we look at how people use mineral specimens as religious offerings. The use of mineral specimens as religious offerings and for adornment of religious altars is a local variation of a broader cultural practice. As in other parts of Mexico and in Mexican American communities in the United States, most private homes in Guanajuato have small altars tended by the residents. The altars have small images or statues of one or several saints or virgins, candles, vases with artificial or fresh flowers, family pictures, and *recuerdos* from family occasions such as weddings or *quince años* celebrations, placed on top of lace doilies crocheted by the wife or another female resident. Other altars are also placed in workplaces and public spaces such as markets and bus stations. These tend to have fewer familial details and to be specifically focused on the worship of one particular figure, such as the Virgin of Guadalupe or the patron saint of the particular trade—carpentry, mining, market vending, and so on. Again, this custom is common in Mexico and indeed in many other parts of Latin America.

In Guanajuato these altars are often also adorned with mineral specimens in addition to the other items described above. Cooperative miners especially use mineral specimens (usually the largest and most striking or unusual-looking) both to beautify their household altars and to give a gift to the virgin or saint being venerated.[10] Some altars are built into a recession in the wall and lined with mineral specimens.[11] Altars in the mines and central plant are also filled with choice minerals, and the Temple of Señor de Villaseca in Cata, next to the Cooperative central plant, has an entire chapel lined with stones extracted by Cooperative miners and given to the saint during his festival in early May.[12]

Whereas miners would spontaneously offer me stones that were on display on a shelf or table in their house, they never gave me stones that were placed near a religious image or altar. On one occasion I visited the house of Hilario, a miner from Cata; I visited in May, and he showed me a box of mineral specimens he stores all year for the Christmas season, when he brings out the Baby Jesus and places Him in a crèche (*nacimiento*) with the stones. "I can't give you one of these," he said apologetically, "These are for the Baby Jesus." An offering to a saint or the deity cannot become a gift to another person, nor can it be sold as a commodity; one local merchant told me, "As long as I can remember, miners have been using the stones in altars, and those stones—they won't sell them for anything."

People had a number of different explanations for the use of mineral specimens as religious offerings or adornments. In some cases the stone is seen as a

FIGURE 7.3 Underground altar with minerals. *Photo by Stephen Ferry*

gift to the deity. When Hilario said that he could not offer me stones meant for the Baby Jesus, it was as if to do so would be like taking a gift meant for one person and giving it to another. Similarly people talked of all the adornments on altars as *regalitos* (little presents) or *obsequios* (gifts, also used in secular contexts), to make the little saint (or virgin) happy (*darle alegría al santito/a la virgencita*). This affectionate and familiar language directed toward religious figures is very common in Guanajuato.

Cooperative members and their families also speak more solemnly about the use of mineral specimens on religious altars. In response to my questions about why mineral specimens were good to put on altars, people had several responses: to give respect to the saint/virgin (*darle respeto al santo/virgen*); to give thanks for a safe return from underground, and to pray for future safe journeys; and, in the case of household altars, to show that a miner and his family live in that house.[13] These are the same reasons miners gave for the altars down in the mines, described in chapter 4, and for the practice of pilgrimage (*peregrinación*) to visit the Virgin of San Juan de los Lagos on February 2, the Cristo de la Montaña ("Christ of the Mountain," on the Cerro de Cubilete, 25 kilometers outside Guanajuato), or the Virgin of Guadalupe. This suggests that the household altars, like the mine altars, establish a sacred landscape and site of memory within quotidian space. As one Cooperative worker told me, "The altar is there for the day when the miner dies, so that we will remember that a miner lived in that house with his family."

FIGURE 7.4 Altar to the Virgen de Dolores with minerals, Engineering
Department, Santa Fe Cooperative

Here again, the hau of mineral specimens serves as a connection between the mine and the house that can transcend the death of the miner.

Mineral specimens also form part of a thriving minerals market in Guanajuato and beyond. Interestingly, however, it is the giftlike qualities of mineral specimens, especially their ability to establish a connection between the mine and other places, that enhances their value as commodities. In contrast to the centralization and regulation of silver extraction, the mineral specimen economy is diffuse and unregulated. The networks within which mineral specimens circulate vary dramatically, operating according to a whole range of social relations, pricing factors, and modes of payment, including credit and barter. As far as I was able to determine, a petty merchant named Santos Macías (Santitos) was the first to sell mineral samples to the public in Guanajuato, beginning in the late 1930s (around the time that tourism to Guanajuato began in a serious way). I spoke to Santitos's son, who continues his father's business of sewing machine repair, bookselling, and the mineral specimen trade. He told me that his father learned about minerals from a geology professor at the School of Mines, first had a stall in the Plaza San Roque, and then ran his business out of his house in the Calle Alonso.[14] Today there are dozens of mineral merchants in Guanajuato as well as a number of outside buyers and collectors.

Miners usually sell either directly to collectors from outside Guanajuato or, more often, to one of the *malacateros* who run the car that takes workers and ore up and down the shaft. The *malacatero* has an advantage in selling because he is usually on the surface and therefore is available for buyers. At the Valenciana mine there are three *malacateros,* each covering one eight-hour shift, which they rotate every week. This means that one week out of every three a *malacatero* will be working a day shift, and the other two weeks he will be off during the day; thus he can meet buyers on the surface at any time.[15] All three of the *malacateros* worked in the mineral specimens business, and all three had stalls set up on the grounds of the Valenciana mine. The most successful of the three told me that he made at least twice what he made in his salary through selling mineral specimens, and that having access to mineral specimens and the right to have a stall inside the mine walls were the only reasons he continued to work for the Cooperative.

The miner usually sells mineral specimens to the *malacatero* or other retailer almost as is—simply rinsing off the excess dirt with water. The merchant who buys from the miner for resale then cleans the stones more thoroughly by soaking them in acid for one to two days. This acid removes the rust and other stains from the stones. It costs twenty-five pesos a liter in the hardware store. The acid is the only extra investment for mineral specimen merchants (beyond paying for the stones) who are Cooperative members or relatives, as Cooperative members and their families do not have to pay for a stall adjacent to the mine of Valen-

FIGURE 7.5 Mineral merchant, Valenciana mine

ciana (or Rayas, located on the panoramic highway that wreathes the city). These merchants usually cultivate their suppliers over time in a variety of ways, by advancing money or giving miners' sodas, *tortas* (sandwiches), and trinkets bought from other itinerant salesmen. Miners rate different merchants based on how much and how promptly they pay for stones and how generous they are with advances, saying for example, "'I always sell to El Sol because he gives me a good price, and sometimes he'll give me twenty pesos 'for a soda.'"[16]

Membership in the Cooperative and in long-standing "Cooperative families" gives merchants an advantage in the mineral specimen trade. First, Cooperative membership allows workers to set up stalls at key locations around the mines without paying a daily fee.[17] Furthermore, as with other activities, such as house construction, workers use family and ritual connections to obtain materials and transport and to establish networks of exchange.

Many of the buyers located closest to the mines are also members of the Cooperative. For instance, Pepe, one of the Valenciana's *malacateros,* has a store facing the entrance to the Valenciana mine as well as a stall within the grounds tended by his son. According to Pepe, he built the store with the proceeds from mineral specimens. He sells almost entirely to tourists, focusing on small inexpensive stones sold individually rather than selling groups (*lotes*) of stones for a single price or focusing on especially rare samples.

In contrast, Feliciano, who works in Rayas and lives in a borrowed house on the Panoramic Highway to one side of the mine, sells some stones to tourists but also has regular clients from outside Guanajuato, both collectors and itinerant merchants and jewelers. He also has a large group of Cooperative suppliers, because he is the primary buyer for Rayas, San Vicente, and Cata, as well as some suppliers from Sirena and Peregrina.[18]

A third Cooperative member, Isidro, stores his stones in his locker at the Valenciana[19] and also in a small shed behind the mine's offices. He is less willing than other buyers to sit on his wares until the tourist season; instead, he chooses to make a steady profit. If he waited till July he might be able to sell his samples for more money when demand is higher, and when more people come from outside Guanajuato. But he has less storage space than do Pepe and Feliciano, and more contacts with collectors and New Age buyers, who come irregularly to buy exclusively from him. For this reason he is less attuned to the tourist season than the other two merchants.[20]

Cooperative merchants also sell to stores or vendors in the center of town who then sell to tourists or collectors for a higher price. These buyers also use varying strategies in their buying, storing, and selling. For instance, Gloria Escobar runs a small stall on weekends in the Arcos de Humboldt in the center of town (next to the Presidencia Municipal). She sells loose minerals and small ceramic mining cars (*carritos*) filled with minerals and labeled "Recuerdo de Guanajuato" (*Souvenir of Guanajuato*). The stones cost two to five pesos each and the *carritos* five and eight pesos. Her family makes the ceramic cars in their house, and every week one of the *malacateros* from the Valenciana visits their house to trade them stones for *carritos*. Gloria makes a good profit on the weekends, for several reasons: *carritos* are inexpensive and easy to make; she does not pay for her place in the Arcos (the Municipal Secretary of Tourism is trying to promote the Arcos as a weekend craft market);[21] and she tends the stall herself. She reported that she makes between three hundred and four hundred pesos per weekend (the equivalent of a week's salary for a bricklayer or woodcutter). Gloria is one of an increasing number of women involved in the mineral specimen business as an intermediary. Many of these women (but not Gloria) are wives or relatives of Cooperative members.

Jean-Michel, a French collector, comes to the Valenciana mine several times a year to buy from Isidro. Jean-Michel buys in Santa Eulalia (Chihuahua), Zacatecas, and Guanajuato, and sells in France, Germany, and Chile. He looks specifically for rare samples, especially those where several minerals have developed together, and specimens of valencianite and guanajuatite, both of which are particular to the Guanajuato district. He told me that the more locally specific a mineral sample is seen to be, the more money it will fetch. Jean-Michel has to pick his stones very carefully for two reasons: he sells to a more discriminating market of collectors who are prepared to pay more for choicer samples; and he has to pay customs based on the weight of the stones he brings in to France and Germany. I asked him whether he would consider using the Internet to sell stones, as a few of his colleagues are beginning to do, but he said that the joy of his life was traveling from mine to mine to choose stones.

Chris Tredwell, a British auto executive working in the nearby city of Irapuato, used local contacts and a generous dose of zeal and determination to teach himself the principles of mineral collecting; in 1998 he sold his collection of minerals from the Guanajuato mining district to Harvard University and the University of Arizona for twenty-two thousand dollars.[22] Tredwell, the dealer in Tucson with whom he worked (Peter Megaw) and the director of Harvard's Mineralogical Museum (Dr. Carl Francis) all told me that the value of his collection derived from its extensive documentation; it was possible to trace the stones to their origin in particular mines and even to specific levels within the mines.

In these brief vignettes, several points become clear. To succeed in the mineral specimens business, one needs to cultivate personal contacts, to use the prevailing systems of credit and barter to effect, and to understand the market. Above all, one needs to understand that the price a stone can fetch is directly related to the degree to which a connection to the mines can be established and made apparent. This is true whether the stone is treated as commodity or gift; that is, the hau of the stone, expressed in its physical appearance and identifiable trajectory, must be visible to enhance its value (as a commodity, this value is expressed as *price*; as a gift or offering, it is expressed in the meaning of the gift as a connection between the mine, the giver, and the human or divine recipient). In marked contrast to silver, which must lose its distinctive qualities to achieve optimal exchange value but which compels a return and resubstantialization in other forms, the value of mineral specimens depends on their distinctiveness.

The hau of mineral specimens seems to be a visually apparent quality, and miners and others often use visual metaphors when they describe it.[23] For instance, one miner who often sells to Feliciano told me:

> Sometimes you don't know how much to pay for the mineral specimen or how much to charge. It really depends on who looks at it. Sometimes there is a value (*valor*) inside the stone, and you can only see it if you believe. That has happened to me when I am buying. The miner tells me a price, and it seems like a lot, but then I look, and I can see the value inside the stone. The problem, though, is that the person I sell to, the merchant or the tourist, maybe they won't see this value. And then I lose out.

In this statement, the miner describes value as located within the stone but visible from the outside, at least to some observers. This value can be expressed in external terms as price, but its accurate appraisal depends on the perceptiveness of the viewer. And perhaps this miner is also implying that merchants and tourists, because of their lack of connection to the mines, often lack this perceptiveness. Furthermore, even though he is talking about how mineral specimens are bought and sold, he links their price to a more subtle form of value, visible only to some, those who can properly appreciate it (much like a gift).

Another instance shows how Cooperative members value mineral specimens in ways that take account of shifting perspective, location, and connection to the mines. One afternoon I visited my friend Alicia, the widow of a Cooperative truck driver, who joined the Cooperative after her husband's death. She works selling tickets at the tourist entrance to the Valenciana at the Bocamina San Cayetano. We sat in the cool shade of the mine's entrance drinking Cokes and watching the vendors hawk their stones. I asked Alicia what made people buy the stones, and she speculated:

> A miner might give me some stones and they have value (*tienen valor*) because he took them out of the mine with his own hands. Myself, because I am from Guanajuato, I would never pay for one, because here they are

all over the place (*dondequiera*). But if you come from outside they do have value (*sí tienen valor*).

Here Alicia seems to be identifying two different phases of exchange, mineral specimen as commodity and mineral specimen as gift; in doing so she makes a sharp distinction between herself as native Guanajuatense and Cooperative member, and outsiders. Buying mineral specimens was all right for outsiders but she would not do it. For her, mineral specimens derive value from the place they came from and the miner who extracted them and gave them to her. However, whether they are sold or given away, the minerals make a connection between their source and somewhere else (either the position Alicia occupies as Cooperative member but not miner or the position of a visitor to Guanajuato).[24]

The hau of mineral specimens also comes into play for buyers and collectors outside Guanajuato. In an interview in August 2000, Carl Francis, the director of Harvard's Mineralogical Museum, discussed the importance of developing a mineral collection around regional and local specialties. Although he described his strategy for buying minerals to build up strong collections that focused on particular places, including Guanajuato, as "contrarian," I suspect that the reproduction of a place through minerals is one of the motivations for collecting. Francis pointed out that different kinds of buyers value different things in mineral samples. Scientific collections, for instance, are understandably interested in detailed documentation in order to place the samples geologically. Some buyers look for a pretty souvenir to remind them of a place or simply to look nice on a shelf or table. Many jewelers in places like Ann Arbor, Sedona, and Laguna Beach use minerals to help display their wares. And, as Francis said, "Mineral dealers are really trying to interest the very rich.[25] These people look for beauty, rarity, and uniqueness. It's a tangible form of value."

These are just some of the motivations and criteria for valuing mineral specimens. However, all these different ways of valuing minerals draw on a sense of place, and in many cases the value of the stone increases if the connection to a particular location can be clearly established.[26] Even when the stone is sold as a commodity, which it often is—and sometimes for a great deal of money—its qualities of tangibility (it is, after all, a chunk of Guanajuato), uniqueness, and the visible connection to the mines give it a "giftlike" quality. In fact, the stronger this quality, the higher the stone's exchange value.

THE HYBRIDITY OF VALUE

During the course of this century the city of Guanajuato has moved from an economy entirely dependent on mining and its ancillary activities to one that combines mining, tourism, state and university administration, and artisanal production (especially ceramics). The price of silver falls while the value of the mines as "human patrimony" (and magnets for tourists) increases. These days Guanajuato competes with other "silver cities" such as Zacatecas (both cities—and a number of others in Mexico—are included on UNESCO's list of Ciudades de Patrimonio Mundial) over the authenticity and grandeur of its mining past and the distinctiveness of its mines, plazas, and churches. It is not surprising that mineral specimens, a commodity that gains its value from its distinctiveness and the degree to which it looks like the place it came from, sell so well.

At the same time it is a mistake to interpret the rise of mineral specimens and the importance of distinctiveness of place as an exclusively new phenomenon. The history of commodities is replete with objects that appeal to consumers by means of their distinctiveness and their traceability to particular places or people: examples that spring to mind include fine art markets,[27] the traffic in religious relics, and the sale of Hank Aaron's bat, Elvis Presley's guitar, Princess Diana's dresses, and other charged objects (cf. Graeber 2001:212). Fernando Ortiz (1998) gave a fascinating account of what he saw as the quintessential "Cuban counterpoint" between tobacco and sugar. His account emphasizes the ways in which Cuban sugar travels profligately the world over, indistinguishable from any other sugar, whereas tobacco remembers and continually announces its origins. Harking back to Ortiz we might speak of a "Cooperative counterpoint" composed of silver and mineral specimens. Like the Cuban counterpoint described by Ortiz, this counterpoint between silver and mineral specimens can tell us a great deal about how Cooperative members use competing and overlapping languages of value at this particular historical moment.

In his analysis of Palauan money, introduced above, Parmentier (2002) uses the tension between motion and stasis for certain types of money to counter Annette Weiner's (1988, 1992) assertion of the cross-cultural utility of a category of inalienable possessions. His observation rightly points to the complexities that Weiner's model glosses over. I would suggest, however, that the problem lies in the "categoriness" of Weiner's formulation and not its emphasis on inalienability.[28] Like many scholars of exchange, in attempting to elucidate the concept of "inalienable possession," Weiner tends to reify it, to treat it as an already constructed category; the same kind of thing happens with the categories of "gift" and "commodity." The next step is often to look through the ethnographic record in search of the kinds of things that fit into these categories, a step that obscures how different ways of valuing compete and interleave.

An anthropology of mined substances in the Santa Fe Cooperative allows us to see the arena within which people are able to and profit from characterizing some kinds of things as patrimony. Mineral specimens are not treated as patrimonial possessions by Cooperative members or other Guanajuatenses; nevertheless, their existence and the right to extract and sell them allows Cooperative members to survive and to continue to treat silver as patrimony. Furthermore, the hau of mineral specimens promotes a vision of Guanajuato built from the mines that can be sent abroad and maintain a connection even as it travels. Silver expands the fame of Guanajuato by returning in other forms, while mineral specimens expand the fame of Guanajuato by carrying with them a visible and documentable connection to the mines. Both are essential to Cooperative survival and both depend on the ability of Cooperative members, their families, and other Guanajuatenses to assign multiple or hybrid forms of value.

Throughout this book we have seen Cooperative members and their families, as well as others in Guanajuato, struggling with a fundamental paradox: how to use wealth to maintain and reproduce the collective, while at the same time making a living off that wealth. Cooperative members try to resolve this contradiction in a number of ways. As we saw in chapter 4, they do so by imagining the generative aspects of mining and the mine and house as analogous generative spaces. As discussed in chapter 6, they do so by making proper stewardship of patrimony a marker for proper masculinity and leadership. In this chapter we have seen that these conceptual, ideological strategies are underwritten by the parallel existence of other forms of wealth, upon which the proper maintenance of collectivity does *not* depend. Mineral specimens are an example of this other form of wealth. However, as with patrimonial wealth, multiple modes of assigning value condition their profitability and their meaning for those within and outside Guanajuato.

The multiple uses and associated meanings of mineral specimens and silver, while in some ways peculiar to Guanajuato and the Santa Fe, also highlight fundamental political and economic transformations at the national level and provide an example of the strategies by which Mexicans in general strive to weather these transformations. The question I posed at the beginning of this book—How do you use forms of inalienable wealth to maintain and reproduce the collectivity and at the same time make a living from that wealth?—is a vital one for people living under a wide variety of circumstances in contemporary Mexico, and also takes a prominent place in debates over political, economic, social, and cultural matters. Like the members of the Santa Fe Cooperative, many Mexicans engaging in these debates use an idiom of inalienable value to maintain and contest the boundaries of competing national and subnational collectivities. The following chapter traces the connections and disjunctions of value and collectivity within the broader Mexican context.

CHAPTER 8

Mexican Languages of Patrimony

Land, Subsoil, "Culture"

The Cooperative, the state [of Guanajuato], the nation—they're all the same.
—Cooperative geologist, October 1997

Having examined the uses of patrimony by members of the Santa Fe Cooperative, their families, and other Guanajuatenses in some depth, we are now in a position to see how these uses play into and partake of broader national-level conversations and practices. The dense webs of meaning entailed in practices of mining, reproduction, and resource allocation help to explain patrimony's force in the Santa Fe and suggest sources for its vitality in other Mexican domains. Insights gained from the examination of these practices can be used to suggest how patrimony works elsewhere in Mexico, where the practice of characterizing possessions as inalienable property has been extremely vigorous. This allows us to see how debates over land, petroleum, and the privatization of archaeological sites—to name several salient examples—are all organized according to the same highly charged, vigorously contested idiom within which the loss of these patrimonial possessions poses a direct threat to Mexico and *mexicanidad*.

These debates concern the ways that value should be assigned and the consequences of those assignments for the maintenance and negotiation of collectivity. In this chapter I look at how *patrimonio* became a dominant idiom for debating questions of value and collectivity in contemporary Mexico. We will see some very similar processes to those we saw in the Santa Fe itself. This is not surprising, since the Santa Fe has always been embedded in the same kinds of relations of power that have characterized Mexican political and economic formations more broadly. We can see the Santa Fe as a local terminus of national processes precisely because it participates in the same webs of power and ideology that we find on the national level. Having examined the local meanings and instantiations of patrimony in Guanajuato and the Santa Fe, I now move to an analysis of the uses of this idiom in other Mexican contexts.

Languages of patrimony that classify resources as the inalienable property of the nation have been enormously influential in Mexico (Lomnitz 2001: chap. 2). Mexican national patrimony includes (but is not limited to) the following: collectively organized land organized under the *ejido* program, the system of collectively organized land tenure instituted following the revolution; subsoil resources including mineral and petrochemical resources; and cultural properties, that is, objects of artistic, historical, or cultural importance to the nation. Each of these uses has its own particular history; out of these histories has come a multivalent idiom of patrimony. The idiom of patrimony helps to organize competing claims over power and resources, and allows those well *and* ill situated in relation to loci of power to mobilize social labor in the name of patrimony's right use and disposition.

In the introduction to this book I described the ways that Mexican jurists and architects of the Constitution of 1917 legitimated the category of national patrimony by reference to the transfer of "juridical personality" from the Spanish king to the Mexican nation. They argued that this event created the conditions by which patrimony has come to be used as a strategy for making claims over resources and for arguing over the legitimacy of particular collectivities. Throughout the nineteenth century, debates between Liberals and Conservatives, indigenous people and *mestizos*, northerners and southerners (to name just a few significant distinctions) centered on questions of how the nation should be defined through its possessions and their proper dispositions. These questions naturally entailed others about the nature of Mexican belonging, its sovereignty in an international context, and its relation with a collection of attributes that Mexicans and others thought of as "modernity" (Brading 1991, Hale 1968, Lomnitz 2001).

For instance, Molina Enríquez (1909: introduction) argued that since many indigenous groups within the national territory had not yet developed a concept of private property, they needed to be protected by the state from exploitation. Molina felt that the disruption of the state's juridical role as steward of national patrimony was the primary obstacle that prevented Mexico "from becoming a true *patria*." For this reason, according to Molina, the colonial category of royal patrimony protected indigenous communities by providing them with a classification of property consistent with their evolutionary development. In saying this, Molina deployed a notion of the patria as more than simply the nation-state or national territory and population but rather as an organic political body held together by ties analogous to kinship ties (171). His view of the *patria*, modified from Creole nationalist borrowings from the French concept of *patrie* (Brading 1991), includes indigenous people within the national collective.

This view would be picked up and expanded by the revolutionaries of the early and mid-twentieth century (cf. Gamio 1960 [1916]) so that the mestizo would become valorized as a national subject; as Claudio Lomnitz puts it:

> From the point of view of nationality, the Mexican Revolution was a watershed at least as important as the Júarez reforms. . . . [it exhibited] two features: the revaluation of the *mestizo* as quintessentially national [cf. Vasconcelos 1920] and the redefinition of the inalienable goods of the nation. (2001: 52)

In the fall of 1916, after Venustiano Carranza had defeated Francisco Villa and taken power under the banner of "Constitutionalism," a delegation was formed to draft a new national constitution. Although Carranza's victory represented the defeat of more radical peasant and worker factions among the revolutionaries, most of whom were not interested in abolishing private property or capitalist relations, a few more radical members of the constitutional delegation did have some influence. The 155 delegates met in Querétaro, Mexico, during November and December 1916 and January 1917. They set out to provide a juridical basis for surmounting the kinds of problems delineated by Molina Enríquez. One of the most important goals of this constitutional delegation, in their own view, was the transformation of property relations to promote social equality, access to land, and national integration.

These debates were by no means resolved by the Mexican Revolution, but they were turned in new directions. One of the major indicators of this was a resurgence of the notion of national patrimony as an important (not to say) vital category of property, one that safeguarded the continuation of the Mexican nation through time. This is particularly evident in 1916–17, when the architects of the new Constitution appropriated the notion of national patrimony and used it to legitimate the state and its version of Mexico and its proper members and belongings.

Some years later, when Lázaro Cárdenas entered the presidency in 1934, his Six-Year Plan, by emphasizing nationalization of the subsoil, worker self-determination as enacted in producers' cooperatives, and land reform, brought questions of national patrimony onto center stage. By foregrounding these aspects of the Constitution of 1917, especially Articles 5 and 27, Cárdenas defined the goals of the postrevolutionary state in terms of the remaking of property relations, and linked national health and sovereignty to the inalienability of the subsoil, workers' rights, and communal land (Cárdenas 1986 [1934]).[1] It was in this context that languages of patrimony acquired particular efficacy in mobilizing labor in support of the postrevolutionary state and the PRI.

In this chapter I examine how this process has worked in the domains of land tenure, subsoil resources, and cultural properties. These instances demonstrate the interplay between prevailing political and economic conditions and the ways in which people press their claims by framing them in terms of inalienable possessions and the collective defined through those possessions.

LAND TENURE

Perhaps the most important site in which patrimony operates in Mexico is that of land tenure, especially in indigenous communities. The integration of indigenous peoples into the larger polity has been crucial to Mexican nation-state formation since the time of Independence. Because property relations, particularly with regard to land, are constitutive aspects of Mexican citizenship and national belonging, landed property has become the terrain over which questions of indigenous integration and differentiation have been fought. And landed property, in turn, has often been described by means of an idiom of patrimony. My discussion here does not claim to capture the immense complexity of the topic in Mexican history, which has been studied in great detail by many scholars (among others, see Baitenmann 1998, A. Bartra 1985, R. Bartra 1993, de Janvry, Gordillo, and Sadoulet 1997, G. de la Peña 1988, Gledhill 1991, and Warman 1980). Rather, I hope to suggest the potency of patrimonial idioms in the domain of land tenure and to show their constitutive role in the formation and contestation of the Mexican nation and other collectivities.

Under colonial rule, indigenous communities, or *pueblos*, were treated as separate and self-contained polities that retained control over their lands for the use of the community as a whole or for particular family groups. These pueblos, while subordinate to Spanish authorities, had their own juridical status in Spanish law (Gibson, 1984: 388–393, Kourí 2002: 77–80). The Spanish colonial state acted as a guardian over the indigenous *pueblos* embedded within colonial territory. This paternalistic stance along with the isolation of many lands from urban and Spanish centers, allowed some indigenous groups to retain their land throughout the colonial period.

In some parts of central and southern Mexico, where there had been sedentary populations prior to the arrival of the Spanish, indigenous communities were able to hold on to land by invoking the principle of *primitivo patrimonio*, that is, by showing that they had controlled a particular piece of land in pre-Conquest times.[2] The principle of primitivo patrimonio was largely replaced by the end of the seventeenth century by *"composiciones de tierras,"* or land surveys. However, its existence demonstrates that classifying property as inalienable and intrinsic to a particular group was a forceful strategy from the beginning of the colonial period (Florescano 1976, MacLachlan and Rodríguez 1980, Taylor 1972). Though *primitivo patrimonio* ceased to be the legal basis for claims to land, its logic continues to be effective in some contexts even today.

Once Mexico gained independence from Spain in 1821, debates over the place of indigenous groups within the new republic and the role of land tenure in defining that place began to shift. Mexican Liberals pushed for laws that divested land from indigenous pueblos and from the church. The Ley Lerdo of 1856 and the Constitution of 1857 represent culminating moments of this trend. Behind it was an understanding of citizenship and national belonging based on individualized private property (Hale 1968: 218–219) and an "attempt to rid the definition of *nation* of any links with race" (Lomnitz 2001: 51).[3] Such arguments were supported by those Mexican intellectuals and politicians, including President Benito Juárez (himself of indigenous descent) and José María Luis Mora, who argued that, in order to "modernize" the country, it was necessary to break down the juridical and political distinctions between indigenous people and others. Others, like the congressional deputy Rodríguez Puebla (Lomnitz 2001: 48–49), disputed these arguments, insisting on the importance of maintaining the rights of indigenous communities over communal land. Such contentions often rested on the principle of *primitivo patrimonio* or on the argument made by Molina Enríquez that indigenous peoples had not reached the level of development appropriate to individualized property arrangements.

These arguments were crystallized in the debates surrounding the passage of Article 27 of the Mexican Constitution of 1917, which established the category of national patrimony for the postrevolutionary period, including collectively owned and managed lands known as *ejidos*. Article 27 established the juridical apparatus for returning land to communities that had been divested during the Liberal period. In fact, however, relatively little land was actually distributed until the presidency of Lázaro Cárdenas began in 1934. The Cárdenas government distributed more than twice as much lands as all the former administrations since 1915, the year that marked the beginning of formal land reform (Cornelius 1996: 17). From 1934 to 1940 (the Cárdenas six-year term), the government gave out nearly 6 million acres of land to 771,640 families organized in 11,347 *ejidos* (Aguilar Camín and Meyer 1993: 143). As he had done with industrial workers such as those in the railroad and petroleum industry, Cárdenas publicly supported the petitions of landless peasants against large landholders in places like the Laguna region in northern Mexico (Knight 1990).[4]

Land parcels distributed as part of this program were designated as *ejidos* and governed by local *comisariados ejidales* where male members of the *ejido* (*ejidatarios*) voted on the management of the *ejido*. *Ejidatarios* are not allowed to rent or sell land, since the rights granted to them by the state as managers of national patrimony are use rights and not rights of alienation or transmission.

The process by which land was classified as national patrimony and distributed to peasant communities was not by any means egalitarian in all its aspects. Rather, it helped to organize relations of power in ways that benefited some and not others. Furthermore, the ideology of patrimony as applied to the *ejidos* helped to underwrite these relations of power. For instance, because the state controlled national patrimony, the ideology of patrimony as applied to land supported the system of clientelism and *camarillas*, described in chapter 6.[5] Gaining access to resources meant convincing powerful state agents or those in contact with them of a legitimate claim over patrimony. Reciprocal exchanges of favors or support helped to maintain a sense of a collective defined in terms of patrimonial possessions. In addition, *ejidatarios* as a whole were represented at the national level by the Confederación Nacional de Campesinos (National Peasant Confederation), an organization that did not recognize the claims of landless peasants or holders of non-*ejido* land (González Navarro 1981). Thus a connection to national patrimony also allowed for better political and economic representation at the national level.

Several scholars have shown the degree to which women were excluded from holding *ejidos* in their own names and from participating in the meetings of the *comisariado ejidal* (Baitenmann 1998, Stephen 1998, Deere 2001). It was assumed that the male "*padres de familia*" would represent the entire family at these meetings and that woman would participate in the *ejido* program through their male relations (especially fathers, husbands, and sons). As the etymology of the word implies, the language of patrimony supports this androcentrism, since classifying objects as patrimony presupposes the existence of a patrilineal kin group existing through time. Male representatives of the patrilineage defined through patrimonial possessions have an obligation to pass these possessions down to their (male) descendants. Women tend to have legitimate claims over these resources primarily through their connection to men.[6] In this way, also, languages of patrimony as applied to *ejido* land have helped to maintain particular configurations of power.

This brief picture of the interaction of patrimonial ideology with regard to *ejido* land and postrevolutionary relations of state and local power has focused on the period of time when these relations of power were at their high water mark.[7] This hegemonic configuration continued with surprising vitality, at least on the face of it, over the next three decades, and began to decline in the 1970s. Factors contributing to its downfall include a crisis in agrarian production; the loss of legitimacy of the federal government after the student movement of 1968 (and the army's massacre of students in the Plaza de Tlatelolco in Mexico City on October 2, 1968); the fall of oil prices and the debt crisis of the 1980s.

As part of these national and global shifts, there has been a trend in Mexico—as elsewhere—toward neoliberal practices and policies. In Mexican neoliberalism, to use Gilly's language, we see a reassertion of private interests over public domain and, in particular, a shift from the national state to individuals and nongovernmental groups as the managers of economic activity and property relations. For this reason, it is not surprising that, in the era of Mexican neoliberalism, the idea of national or collective patrimony or both has often shifted to one of individual and familial patrimony. These versions of patrimony have always been a part of its uses; the history of languages of patrimony must be seen in terms of a debate over public and private interests. Within this debate, successful users of patrimonial languages are those who can define the distinction between public and private in ways advantageous to themselves. It is not surprising, then, that in an era of neoliberalism those aspects of patrimony that emphasize individual and familial responsibility are at the forefront. These days, groups and agents pushing for privatization, free trade, and the separation of government and economic activity use the practice of classifying land as patrimonial in ways they might not have, say, in the 1930s or 1970s.

In January 1992 the Mexican Congress passed a series of changes to Article 27. These reforms mostly affected *ejidos*. The modified Article 27 calls an end to land distribution, leaving thousands of petitions unanswered. It also establishes a system of registration of land parcels within *ejidos*, allows *ejidatarios* to rent their parcels, and creates the possibility of the *ejido* assembly voting (by a three-quarters majority) to privatize the entire *ejido*, so that individual shareholders would have "plenary domain" (*dominio pleno*) over their parcel of the *ejido* land. The changes to Article 27 call into question the category of national patrimony in one domain, that of *ejidos*, by creating the possibility of separating these lands from national patrimony once and for all.[8]

These modifications received a good deal of criticism from many sides, most vociferously by the left-leaning PRD party and the Ejército Zapatista de Liberación Nacional (EZLN) in Chiapas. In general, opponents to the changes decried their privatizing intent and feared that they would open the door to land consolidation and foreign intervention. They described the *ejido* program and the entire apparatus of national patrimony as a last bastion of Mexican nationalism and an alternative to neoliberalism (Collier 1994, Associated Press, November 29, 1991, *SourceMex: Economic News & Analysis on Mexico,* April 27, 1994).

In responding to these charges, many proponents of the changes emphasized the continuity between the revolutionary program and their own efforts. They

often stated or implied that the original intentions of Article 27 would be sat-
isfied better under a reformed law than under the law currently in effect. For
instance, in the "Initiative to Reform Article 27," presented to congress on November 7, 1991, President Carlos Salinas de Gortari asserted that "the objectives
of this initiative are to broaden justice and liberty, just as with the agrarian struggles that have gone before" (Diario de los Debates Constituyentes, November
7, 1991: 198; translation mine).

In this original proposal Salinas strongly defended the "spirit" of Article 27,
which "establishes the original property of the nation and submits the organization of ownership and use to the public interest" (ibid.: 197). Here he uses
classic postrevolutionary rhetoric to make his case. He then goes on to assert
that this principle can only be upheld through the "democratic decision-
making and the free initiative of those men and women who work the land [en
el campo]" (202). Here he moves back toward the language of neoliberalism, democratization, and modernization, while at the same time linking these qualities to past revolutionary goals.

Attempts to change the most symbolically important piece of Mexican legislation of the last 140 years were fraught with pitfalls. The language of patrimony, with its ability to refer to multiple collectivities at once, provided the
terms within which these questions of property and sovereignty were debated,
so that both sides invoked patrimony and its proper claimants and dispositions
to make their arguments. For instance, Arturo Warman, the director of the
newly instituted state agrarian authority, the Procuraduría Agraria (and a
prominent social anthropologist in his own right [Warman 1980]), argued in the
national newspaper La Jornada that

> the concept of the new law protects rights, especially those of the major-
> ity, but recognizes the obvious, what history has shown, the capacity and
> citizenship of the peasants (campesinos) who are responsible for their own
> decisions. It rejects [the idea of] guardianship, paternalism, and other con-
> cepts that transfer and submit the will of the peasants to the requests of
> corporate and bureaucratic groups. (1994: 15)

Warman goes on to say, "[the modification of Article 27] restricts the power of
authorities and bureaucracies and strengthens that of society. . . . Democracy
within the ejidos is clearly related to the goal of a plural democratic culture towards which all Mexicans are pushing and aspiring" (17).

The alteration of Article 27 and the surrounding debate show that the
process of changing property relations in Mexico is highly contested and
charged for many Mexicans. Within this debate the concept of patrimony plays

a large role. For instance, Warman uses the concept, somewhat defensively, saying, "'Privatization' is not happening. The ejido will remain, in better condition
and with more alternatives. At least [it will remain] as long as the ejidatarios
want it to. The land is their conquest and *patrimony*, they manage it with seri-
ousness and responsibility" (16; emphasis added).

Here patrimony is used to refer to an individualized domain of inheritable
property, rather than that of national patrimony.[9] Although Warman disavows
"privatization," he locates his defense of the modifications of Article 27 within
a shift toward individualized and nongovernmental property relations consistent
with broader trends toward neoliberalism. In this context, his use of patrimony
to describe individual responsibility and management of property rather than
collective claims marks a broader ideological shift. The invocation of patrimony
in some instances signals and seeks to legitimate this shift, just as in others it is
used by those who critique it (for example, the EZLN and other opponents to
the changes to Article 27).

SUBSOIL

Debates over proprietorship of the subsoil demonstrate how important these
resources have been for Mexico. Since soon after the arrival of the Spanish with
the discovery of the mines of Zacatecas and on through to the petroleum boom
of the 1970s, subsoil resources have been essential to Mexico's economy and intimately tied to colonial and national identity. Subsoil resources were classified
as royal patrimony in the colonial period, most explicitly in the 1783 Real Or-
denanzas de Aranjuéz. These ordinances established the system of mining concessions so that mine owners could exploit the veins and sell their product
without separating the subsoil itself from "la propiedad del Real Patrimonio"
(M. de la Peña 1920: 14).[10] In the words of the nineteenth-century liberal states-
man José María Luis Mora:

> the principle of the Spanish legislation concerning mines was that those
> who worked them did not have a true right of ownership, but only
> usufruct rights, with the property remaining exclusively in the hands of
> the Crown. (Quoted in Silva Herzog 1963: 21)

As in the case of other forms of royal patrimony, this designation was carried over into the national period, with the nation as the heir to the Spanish
king at Independence. The Mining Law of 1884 made an exception in the case
of combustible minerals and hydrocarbons (Bernstein 1964: 18–19), but this was

reversed first in the Mining Law of 1910 (82) and even more emphatically in the Constitution of 1917 (M. de la Peña 1920: 15–16). The language of Article 27 of the Constitution makes it clear that the status of the subsoil as national patrimony descended from the patrimonial rights of the Spanish kings was now transferred to the nation. Establishing this category of national patrimony and making it (at least in theory) the juridical basis of all forms of property in Mexico form an integral part of the nationalist stance of the revolutionaries and of the state that grew out of the revolution.

Thus the state's nationalist project converted the subsoil (along the former profitability of silver and the increasing profitability of petroleum) into a source of heated debate. Article 27 provided the juridical underpinnings for these conflicts. It established the "direct dominion" by the nation of "all minerals or substances which in veins, layers, masses, or beds constitute deposits whose nature is different from the components of the land, such as minerals from which metals and metalloids used in industry are extracted; . . . solid mineral fuels; petroleum and all solid, liquid, or gaseous hydrocarbons" (Niemeyer 1974: 257). By emphasizing the nation's *direct* control over these holdings, Article 27 made the subsoil into a focus of nationalism and arguments against foreign interests and investment. This in part was because of the long history of foreign ownership and investment in mining, which had reached a new apogee in places like Guanajuato by the first decade of the twentieth century (Bernstein 1964, Meyer Cosío 1999, Sariego et al. 1988). It also suggests that the architects of Article 27 expected industrial and petroleum mining to have a prominent place in the national economy. The article focuses particularly on the mining of metalliferous deposits for industrial uses and makes pointed mention of petroleum (which had not appeared in the previous mining law of 1910) (Bernstein 1964: 83).

Lázaro Cárdenas was elected president of Mexico in 1934 and achieved the first politically stable administration of the postrevolutionary period. His party, the Partido Nacional de la Revolución (National Party of the Revolution [PNR]), officially established in 1929, later renamed itself the Partido Revolucionario Institucional (Institutional Revolutionary Party [PRI]) and maintained presidential power for over seventy years until the election of Vicente Fox in 2000. Cárdenas is often credited with consolidating revolutionary aspirations into a state economic apparatus.[11] In particular, the Cardenista state focused on the establishment of labor unions (tied to the PNR), the creation of a national peasant organization, land reform, and the nationalization of significant sectors of the economy (Knight 1992).

One of these was the petroleum industry, which Cárdenas expropriated from foreign hands, including Royal Dutch Shell and Standard Oil of New Jersey, in 1938. This act caused great consternation on the part of U.S. businesses and the

Roosevelt administration, which responded in part by suspending Treasury Department purchases of Mexican silver. Perhaps luckily for Mexico, the entry of the United States into World War II soon distracted U.S. attention away from Mexico (Gilly 1994, Raat and Beezley 1986, Silva Herzog 1963). By expropriating petroleum resources from foreign control, the Mexican federal government asserted its right, defined in Article 27, to act as a collective individual (Dumont 1970, Handler 1988) and, as such, the legitimate owner of subsoil resources. Having expropriated the foreign oil companies, it nationalized the industry under the state-owned company PEMEX (Petróleos Mexicanos), described by Alan Knight as "that embodiment of revolutionary—especially *cardenista*—nationalism" (Knight 1992: xv). Of course, the right of the state to take hold of resources in the name of national patrimony became more complicated in situations where the targets of expropriation were also Mexican citizens and thus putatively owners of national patrimony. Cases such as these came up particularly with land expropriations as part of the *ejido* program. Such conflicts make the contradictions inherent in owning national patrimony more visible.

Metalliferous mining also became the focus of nationalist, antiforeign sentiment and policies. Bernstein states that, after Cárdenas's inauguration in 1935, he

disavowed any intention of closing Mexico to foreign investors; however, he emphasized that those investing in Mexican natural resources should be prepared to establish their homes in Mexico and to reinvest their profits there. . . . In addition, he announced that the schools were to train Mexican schoolchildren to think in terms of seeking their fortunes in the minerals of the subsoil "that also belongs to them and which it is their duty to bring out to the light of day." (1964: 182)

The connection expressed here between a shared ownership over subsoil resources and a shared obligated to exploit those resources taps directly into those concepts and sentiments associated with patrimony in the Mexican context. The emphasis that the profits from Mexican minerals should remain in Mexico also picks up on the notion of wealth that remains in place (inalienable wealth) as having a positive moral valence. Like the silver in the San Juan de Rayas chapel bell, the wealth of Mexico's mines should stay put to enrich and embellish Mexico.

The national mining union (founded in 1934), its locals, and other mining organizations echoed this nationalist sentiment in relation to the subsoil. A wave of strikes in the mining industry focused on the need to Mexicanize the industry and to ensure that the profits from silver and other subsoil resources stayed within the country (Aguila 1997, Bernstein 1964, Knight 1990).

These processes reveal themselves very clearly in the case of Guanajuato. As one of the longest established mining centers in Mexico, with few economic alternatives and heavily damaged from both the revolution and the earlier War of Independence, Guanajuato became a focal point of labor unrest related to mining. For instance, in an open letter to President Cárdenas, published in the newspaper *El Noticioso* in Guanajuato on July 8, 1934, the Sindicato de Mineros Guanajuatenses (Guanajuatan Miners' Syndicate, a body that would soon be folded into the national miners' union) requested a solution to a conflict concerning the treatment of *buscones* (underground prospectors, or "high-graders," so-called because they only extract high-grade ore) by foreign mining companies. For many decades *buscones* had been extracting ore, often (though not always) from abandoned mines, and selling it to local processing plants (*haciendas de beneficio*). In the 1930s U.S. mining companies operating in Guanajuato sought to reduce this practice by paying buscones less for the ore and, at times, by branding and prosecuting them as ore thieves (*lupios*). The open letter, entitled "Proletarian Lament," framed this conflict in nationalist terms:

> In spite of the years that have passed since the revolution took over the government, we the Mexican miners continue to be beasts of burden and continue producing as we used to, with the difference that before we could enjoy our silver and gold as our own, but with the arrival to our country of these greedy insatiables everything was lost. . . . If it is necessary to take land away from the large landholder (*latifundista*) for the benefit of the majority, the same should be done to those who seize mining resources, who are the worst exploiters of human labor (*El Noticioso*, "Lamento Proletario," July 8, 1934).

By framing their appeal in terms of the goals of the revolution, the loss of gold and silver from the country, and the avarice and general bad behavior of foreigners (especially those from the United States), the writers of this letter hoped to combine the workers' cause with the idea that the Mexican subsoil should belong to Mexicans. These actors use the legal designation of national patrimony to buttress Mexican sovereignty and self-determination; in doing so, they attempt to define the national collective and to police its boundaries.

The various presidential administrations since 1982 have attempted to privatize different sectors of the government and to open Mexico up to free trade. One of the most intractable economic sectors from the perspective of these administrations has been that of the oil and gas industry represented by PEMEX. In an article describing the political constraints on oil and gas policy since 1982, George Philip (1999: 38) points out that presidents Miguel de la Madrid

(1982–1988) and Carlos Salinas (1988–1994), both of whom dramatically restructured the Mexican state-economy relationship, "regarded PEMEX with extreme caution." As Philip points out, the association of the 1938 oil expropriation with the goals of revolutionary economic nationalism (cast explicitly in the idiom of national patrimony), as well as a particularly strong labor union, made oil and gas one of the most difficult sectors to "open up."

Since his election as president in July 2000 Vicente Fox has attempted to open both the petroleum and electricity industries to foreign investment. In the case of petroleum, the government established "Multi-Service Contracts" for petrochemicals that would be open to foreign oil companies, thus setting up an ancillary fund for private investment while at the same time insisting that there was no plan in place to privatize PEMEX. These efforts have been met with considerable resistance on the part of politicians from the PRI, activists, and labor unions ("PEMEX Celebrates 65th Anniversary with Eye on Private Capital," EFE News Service, March 18, 2003). In these debates, once again, the themes of national sovereignty and the appropriate boundaries of the collectivity are framed in the language of national patrimony. In a radio address in July 2002, Fox declared that "Petróleos Mexicanos (PEMEX) will not be privatized because it is not only the patrimony of all Mexicans, but also a symbol of national unity and identity. But there is a challenge to transform the [petroleum] industry into an instrument for development and modernization, [and thus] convert it into a blessing for Mexico" ("Se privatiza petroquímica, Pemex no: Fox," *Unomásuno*, July 21, 2002). Here Fox sounds much like Warman in his justification of the reforms to Article 27. While holding on to a language of patrimony, he seeks to bend that language to more "modern" national goals, in this case those of "development" and "modernization." This is precisely the juxtaposition we find in nineteenth-century debates over land tenure and other resources.

"Culture"

Actors also use the notion of patrimony to classify Mexican cultural properties, that is, "historical" or "cultural" artifacts of a nation or other polity (García Canclini 1995, Greenfield 1989, Handler 1988, 1991, *Le Debat* 1994, UNESCO 1996). As Richard Handler (1988) has pointed out in the case of Quebec, such "properties" constitute the nation as a property-owning "collective individual." Designating cultural properties as national patrimony—that is, as the inherited possessions of the national lineage—helps to establish the nation as existing through time as well as in space, and underlies ideologies that exhort the safeguarding of its national cultural patrimony as a way to ensure the nation's continuity.

The term *patrimoine* was first used in relation to national cultural properties after the French Revolution (Taboury 1999) as an integral step toward the formation of the renewed French nation while at the same maintaining a claim over the French past. The use of a language of patrimony to classify the material traces of the pre-Columbian past has worked in a similar fashion in Mexico (Florescano 1997, García Canclini 1992, Knight 1990, Morales-Moreno 1994, Lomnitz 2001, Paz 1972).

In the case of Mexico, the class of property known as "national patrimony" has particular juridical force, owing to the establishment of the colonies as royal patrimony and the appropriation of this concept by the drafters of the Constitution of 1917. This may have made it easier to institutionalize laws concerning cultural properties as national patrimony. In any case, Mexico is one of the countries with the most extensive legislation concerning cultural properties *and* the strongest connection between the material traces of the past and the nation. The connection between different types of patrimonial possessions, including land, the subsoil, and cultural properties, can be seen as part of the same ideological trajectory. As Enrique Florescano states:

> The Ministry of National Patrimony, of Education, of Agriculture and Hydraulic Resources and recently of Environment and Ecology; the various decrees of nationalization and expropriation; the foundation of companies such as Petróleos Mexicanos and the Electricity and Energy Company [another para-statal enterprise set up on the basis of Article 27] are examples of that nationalist and revolutionary current that transformed the country and gave to it an institutional apparatus dedicated to the protection of Mexicans' patrimony. (1997: 17)

This statement demonstrates the degree to which these quite different entities—including oil, electricity, cultural properties, biodiversity (Hayden 2003), and so on—were classified as national patrimony and thus became subject to analogous legal, political and social processes. To see how this happens in the domain of cultural properties, I shall focus on one powerful institution: the National Institute of Anthropology and History (INAH).

In 1939 the state institutionalized national cultural property through the INAH, which focused especially on archaeological and ethnological monuments and sites (Ley Federal sobre Monumentos y Zonas 1972, Olivé Negrete and Urteaga Castro-Pozo 1988). The establishment of the INAH formed part of a general trend of the institutionalization and bureaucratization of Mexican nationalism during the Cárdenas administration. In the words of Alex Saragoza (2001: 98), "Preceded by various loosely tied agencies, offices, bureaus and commissions, INAH constituted a capstone to the evolution of an organizational structure for the government-sanctioned presentation of Mexican history and culture."

The INAH is a national organization that controls a web of regional and local centers (including one in Guanajuato). It administers museums, archaeological sites, and archives; sponsors conferences; and maintains a presence in churches of historical or artistic "value." The INAH also conducts research on the cultural properties under its jurisdiction and has produced a *Catalogue of Immovable Goods of the Mexican Republic* (1976), which serves as a reference point for many scholars, architects, and others. It also supervises all building projects within "zones of monuments" (Guanajuato became such a zone in 1982).

According to a lawyer working in the INAH regional center in Guanajuato, whom I interviewed in May 1998, the importance and role of the INAH has changed since its inception. In 1939, when the INAH began, it was "related to the ideology of Lázaro Cárdenas." He went on to say, "The patrimony used to be managed by the army, it was a question of guarding the borders [*cuidar las fronteras*]." For example, one of the main concerns of the INAH has been that of *saqueo* (looting) of Mexican artifacts and other cultural properties outside Mexico.[12] The emphasis on *saqueo* exemplifies INAH's stance of defensive nationalism, typically of mid-century versions of postrevolutionary nationalism. As in debates over land and the subsoil, the practice of "cuidar las fronteras" is enabled through the strategic use of a language of inalienability.

The INAH maintained dominance over cultural properties since its formation in the 1930s; however, that dominance may be on the wane. In recent years the presence of UNESCO has altered local and national languages of patrimony, and now the INAH tends to "provide local logistical support for UNESCO" (as one INAH lawyer put it). As we saw in chapter 3, when cultural properties are described as patrimony these days, they are often described as "world" or "human" rather than "national" patrimony.

One sign of the INAH's decreasing power was the introduction of a bill to congress in April 1999 that would dissolve the INAH and encourage nongovernmental organizations (NGOs) and private individuals to assume responsibility for objects and sites that are now regarded as the cultural patrimony of the nation (Jiménez González 1999). Although the bill did not pass, that it could be considered shows how uses of patrimony are changing in the era of free trade and economic restructuring.

Another example from Guanajuato also shows how the INAH responds to attempts to privatize (and profit from) cultural properties. In 2002, as mentioned earlier, the Santa Fe Cooperative was forced to sell the installations of the Guadalupe mine to a local businessman, who planned to turn it into a luxury hotel. To do so, he needed clearance from the INAH to renovate the installations. In July 2003 I spoke with another lawyer at the INAH regional center in Guanajuato, who took a pragmatic, accomodationist stance toward the affair. After speaking of the importance of caring for *patrimonio historico* and the kinds of changes that were and were not acceptable in renovating a mine into a hotel, he ended by saying: "But we also need to be realistic. We don't want to become a ghost town [*pueblo fantasma*] either." This phrase has particular resonance in Guanajuato, which is indeed surrounded by a number of *pueblos fantasmas*, former mining centers that lost their populations when the mines closed. By raising the specter of the ghost town, as it were, the lawyer points to the real threat to Guanajuato's economy caused by the decline of mining and to the real opportunities offered by luxury "heritage tourism."

The existence of this kind of accommodation does not imply that all those who use a language of patrimony to describe cultural patrimony agree with one another. In fact, groups with opposing interests and goals often use a language of patrimony against one another. Patrimony's multiple referents and its ability to signal multiple collectivities simultaneously make this possible. For instance, Quetzil Castañeda describes how ambulatory merchants from Pisté, a town next to the great Yucatec Maya site Chichén Itzá, made a series of "invasions" into the INAH-controlled archaeological site throughout the 1980s to sell crafts and other objects to tourists. INAH workers and their families protested on the basis that the site was controlled by the central government as national cultural patrimony, but it was also true that they sought to control prime selling spots near the site. In contrast, the Pisté merchants claimed their right to sell on the grounds of the site based on their long-standing proximity (a kind of *primitivo patrimonio*) and on the fact that the site was partly within the boundaries of *ejido* land over which they had communal land rights (another form of national patrimony to which the community of Pisté had privileged access). In 1987 a "traditional" handicrafts market was established as part of a mostly successful strategy to remove the "invaders" (Castañeda 1996: 2001). This case aptly shows how the seemingly self-evident category of patrimony reveals a multitude of possible uses in the service of multiple collectivities. In the diverse ways that patrimony is wielded, there is always an invocation of proper and improper uses of resources as indications of proper and improper forms of belonging.

CONCLUSION: PERMUTATIONS OF PATRIMONY

Let us recall for a moment the two stories told at the beginning of this book: the melting down of the chapel bell in the 1930s by the "greedy Yankees"; and the *cronista*'s statement in 1991 concerning Guanajuato's obligation to the world to preserve its own cultural patrimony. In the first case it is asserted that "the nation is the victim"; in the second, that Guanajuato's patrimony is "not ours alone" but belongs to the whole world. The distance traveled between these two uses of patrimonial language delineates a major shift in Mexican nationalism and in the use of patrimony to define and maintain collectivities.

An example from Cori Hayden's work on bioprospecting in Mexico (2003) exemplifies the shift in patrimonial languages that we have traced in Guanajuato throughout this book and located more broadly in Mexico in the previous chapter. Hayden (2003: 43) points out that the scientists engaged in collecting plant specimens (which, as tied to indigenous knowledge, have been designated as national patrimony since the presidency of Echeverría in the 1970s) for research into possible pharmaceutical uses often prefer to use the so-called public domain as a zone safe from the benefit-sharing claims of "local communities" (see also Soto Laveaga 2003). Hayden states that,

> This safety zone is, it would seem, variously and well-populated [including] microbes on government protected lands and medicinal plants sold in urban markets, weeds on the sides of roads and knowledge published in anthropologists' articles, Petri dishes in private university laboratories and vines in private back yards. . . . What allows researchers to identify this assortment of sites, some of which are indeed private property, as effectively public? Their denomination as such takes shape as against what they are not; it's not the private that is other here, but the *ejidal*, the communal and the indigenous—and a host of national[ist] specificities and histories that give those categories their shape. (2003: 45–46)

What is fascinating here for our purposes is that these opposed categories—the public from which researchers can draw specimens with less fear of challenge and the nationalist spaces of the *ejido* and the "indigenous community"—are both referred to as patrimony. It is the language of patrimony that has shifted to accommodate new versions of collectivities, and new ways of making a profit.

As a part of this process, the term "patrimony" has vastly expanded its domain of reference. In Mexico, as elsewhere in the world, there has been a proliferation of the kinds of things that can be classified as patrimony (Florescano 1997, Hartog 1997, Tovar y de Teresa 1997). For instance, an edited book published in 1993 in Mexico entitled *Patrimonio Cultural de Mexico* included chapters on intellectual, ecological, paleontological, archaeological, architectural, artisanal, cinematic, and photographic patrimony (Florescano 1993). The 1997 reissue of this volume retained these chapters and added musical, archival, bibliophilic, linguistic, and cartographic patrimony (Florescano 1997). This continuous expansion of the category indicates both the degree to which an idiom of power ties into other sociocultural processes in Mexico and other places, and to the efficacy of laws pertaining to patrimony. To successfully claim that an object is patrimony is to gain access to certain rights and protections for that object and for those who belong to the collectivity defined through its legitimate ownership. In Mexico that collectivity has often (though not always, and perhaps less in recent years) been defined as the nation.

I have described a series of parallel shifts in the ways that an idiom of patrimony has been used in Mexico. As the postrevolutionary state has lost legitimacy, patrimony has increasingly been invoked either in the context of individual or familial property, sub- or supra-national collectivities (such as indigenous groups, or "world patrimony"). It is not that other kinds of collectives were not significant in the lives of Mexicans in the past but that, until recently, the central state had a monopoly over the idiom of patrimony as a tool for making claims over resources and making those claims stick. That is no longer the case.

It is possible to interpret these shifts as the disappearance of the idiom of patrimony, perhaps in a progressive or nostalgic teleology of "modernity" in the form of market capitalism and free trade. However, I see changes in the ways that an idiom of patrimony is deployed as the latest permutations of ongoing debates that have been constitutive of Mexico since the arrival of the Spanish on the Coast of Veracruz. In contrast to many scholars and many of my informants, I do not see these idioms as moribund or (necessarily) destined to fade away. In my analysis of commodity production and allocation of resources in the Santa Fe, I have demonstrated how they coexist and intermingle with other languages of value more oriented toward market exchange. In this chapter I have endeavored to show their vitality in contemporary Mexican discussions over the proper organization of land, subsoil resources, and cultural properties. In the next and final chapter I suggest some implications of this study for the examination of contemporary global property relations.

CHAPTER 9

Conclusion

Not Whose Alone?

Generations come and go, but the Cooperative continues—only if the price of silver goes down, the Cooperative will fail.
—Cooperative member working in the silver workshop, April 1997

Along with its working mines and mills, the Santa Fe Cooperative also received a large amount of nonworking mining properties and land when the Guanajuato Reduction and Mines Company ceded its holdings to the workers in 1938. One of these holdings was the magnificent ruin of the mine of Guadalupe, located above the Valenciana mine in the northern part of Guanajuato. The Guadalupe is located in an area where poor dwellings inhabited by miners and those who sell minerals and trinkets share the hillside with luxury villas, including the estate of Juan Carlos Romero Hicks, who was rector of the University of Guanajuato in the 1990s and who has gone on to take Vicente Fox's place as governor of Guanajuato State. The Guadalupe mine was difficult to visit in the 1990s, since the dirt roads were not good and semiferal dogs lived in the underbrush surrounding the mine.

The mine itself was inhabited by a family of Cooperative members who guarded the premises in exchange for the right to live there. As one Cooperative wife told me "There were some members who didn't have a home, so they asked the engineers to lend them the Guadalupe mine and they did, so now they're living there." Inside the grandiose gates of the mine, this family kept a modest home, hanging their laundry on the ramparts and keeping goats and chickens among the old chimneys.

Although the Cooperative could not afford to restore the Guadalupe mine, it did prize it as an imposing and beautiful structure; the 1997 calendar printed by the Cooperative featured a photo of the Guadalupe along with a "Workers' Prayer" pleading for the protection of God and the Virgin Mary "in the mine [and] in the workshop." On this calendar, the Guadalupe appears as an example

FIGURE 9.1 Guadalupe mine, 1998

of Cooperative patrimony inhabited and shared by devout and industrious workers.

In the spring of 2002, in the face of impending bankruptcy, the president of the administrative council sold off a number of the unused holdings of the Cooperative, including the mines of Tepeyac and Guadalupe (see chapter 4). He faced strong criticism for this act from the general membership, who questioned his motives and the transparency of the transaction. A number of members also expressed deep sadness at losing the holdings. When I asked about the Guadalupe, one engineer and grandson of a socio fundador said to me, "I haven't been to see it. It makes me too sad to think of what we might have done with it and weren't able to."

He was referring to the massive renovations done by the purchasers of the mine: two prosperous local businessmen, who planned to convert it into a luxury hotel.[1] When I visited Guanajuato in July 2003 I walked up from the Valenciana along the newly smooth (though still dirt) road to see the renovations in process. A huge jewel-green lawn stretched before me, topped by elaborate stone terracing echoing the colors of the Guadalupe's walls and made rosy with geraniums. It was, as my friends in the Valenciana had remarked, a massive and

FIGURE 9.2 Guadalupe mine, 2003

expensive renovation and one that would require continuous investments of labor and water to maintain.

I wanted to go inside the mine and see what had been done so far to the interior, but, as I had been warned, I was unable to gain access. A hand-lettered sign stopped me, declaring in no uncertain terms: "PRIVATE PROPERTY. ANY PERSON SURPRISED HERE WILL BE CONSIGNED TO THE AUTHORITIES." This sign, and the site it guarded, exemplify the changes going on in Guanajuato and in the Santa Fe. It was never easy to approach the Guadalupe mine, but one could get there through personal ties to the Cooperative or to the family living in the mine, along with a certain amount of physical courage or a vehicle with four-wheel drive. The site was never public, but its routes of access were negotiable on an informal level. Now the mine has been beautified, "restored" to a new glory (for in its heyday it surely never looked as sleek as it does now) and privatized in a newly definitive way. Formerly enmeshed in a series of hotly debated claims of loyalty and obligation, the mine is on its way to being positioned squarely in the realm of commercialized private property, open to those who have paid for it as developers and to those who might pay as hotel guests. No longer Cooperative patrimony, it is becoming recognized as "*patrimonio histórico*" (at least it is the intention of the developers that it be recognized as such, since its status as a former mine is its main attraction) and therefore ideally the possession of all humanity. At the same time the broadening of the collectivity laying claim to this particular piece of patrimony makes it newly available for exclusionary practices and profit-making ventures.

How can we understand the implications of this shift without resorting solely to soft-focus visions of past communalism or breathless celebrations of the arrival of "modern," efficient businesses in Guanajuato? As I have argued throughout this book, one way to avoid these twin pitfalls is to look at the political and economic changes before us in light of changing conversations over the nature of value, its proper channels of exchange, and the nature of the collectivities defined through such exchange.

Within Guanajuato and Mexico these conversations are largely phrased in the idiom of patrimony. As we have seen, the plasticity of this idiom allows actors in the Cooperative, Guanajuato, and Mexico to articulate a whole range of positions on the proper relation between value and collectivity. By studying the politics of patrimony, then, we are able to see the ways that Mexicans in a whole variety of circumstances face up to and negotiate the changes they encounter.

This process has parallels in other ethnographic domains both within and outside Mexico. For instance, drawing from a different though in some ways analogous set of data, Cori Hayden has argued that bioprospecting in 1990s Mexico calls into being the subjectivities, "communities," and "publics" among which its practitioners seek to effect transactions of plant specimens, knowledge, benefits, and so on. This is, of course, not unique to bioprospecting, nor is it a particularly new phenomenon. However, bioprospecting joins a set of relatively recent practices based on such things as intellectual property rights, "local" or "indigenous" knowledge, and benefit sharing that seem characteristic of neoliberal versions of this tendency. In other words, the subjectivities, publics, and communities called into being within bioprospecting make possible certain

> ideologies and practices . . . designed to facilitate or enforce the intensification and expansion of capitalist markets and trade . . . [and that] promote privatization and "free" trade not just as ends in themselves but as privileged modes of governance for addressing social, economic and environmental problems. (Hayden 2003: 48)

Bioprospecting in Mexico and elsewhere is one of the domains wherein new instantiations of an idiom of patrimony have emerged. However, although bioprospecting, as it is currently defined, is a relatively recent phenomenon, the debates it engenders over the relationship between the market and governance—itself a particular version of the relationship between value and collectivity—have occupied the center of public debate in Mexico since the early colonial period and have become even more intense since the Revolution of 1910.[2] By tracing these debates in their various ethnographic instantiations, we can see how power, value, and collectivity are articulated in postrevolutionary and neoliberal Mexico. We can also see how, in the context of the early 2000s, the overweening dominance of neoliberalism is beginning to be questioned.

Patrimony has several features that make it particularly rich and successful as an idiom of neoliberal property relations: malleability with regard to the collectivity defined through its deployment; powerful kin and gender-based meanings entailed within it; and an emphasis on the separation of use rights and rights of alienation (making it possible to generate a profit from an inalienable resource). These features also make it available as a language for critiquing neoliberal efforts.

In a collection of essays entitled *Property, Substance and Effect: Anthropological Essays on Persons and Things* (1999), Marilyn Strathern has issued a series of meditations on the nature of property relations in contemporary global contexts, drawing on her Melanesian fieldwork in comparison with new debates in genetics, reproductive technologies, intellectual property, and so on (see also Boyle

1996, Pannell 1994, Verdery 2003). Strathern remarks that "new relations are coming into being all the time, through the invention of objects of knowledge and utility, as well as new contests over existing resources, and in their wake new negotiations over rights" (139) and asserts the need for a new analytical vocabulary to accommodate these changing phenomena. These essays also provide fruitful suggestions for the analysis of patrimonial idioms.

Strathern uses the notion of "hybrid" persons, things, and relations to analyze contemporary Melanesian and Euro-American property relations. For instance, drawing on ethnographic accounts of Melanesian property concepts, she points out that, "on the one hand, the person is a clan or lineage member, tied to his (and it is his rather than her) ancestors and descendants alike; on the other hand, the person is individuated through his own actions and claims" (Strathern 1999: 125). This concept has, in Strathern's vision, both analogies and contrasts with Euro-American concepts of personhood as revealed in debates over genetics, new reproductive technologies, and so on.[3]

The idiom of patrimony as examined in this book implies a similarly hybrid (male) person. The hybrid character of patrimonial resources, which entail both use rights and rights of alienation that may be differently allocated, can thus be seen as a precipitate of the hybrid character of personhood. In turn—as we saw especially in chapter 7—hybrid persons and resources are made thinkable within a context of hybrid forms of value (and vice versa).

In her recent book, *The Vanishing Hectare* (2003), Katherine Verdery locates the transformation of property relations in postsocialist Transylvania in the context of "a global economic reorganization" wherein, along with many other shifts, "governments withdrew support from activities in which they had held financial stakes, turning those over to private interests" (5). Although the Santa Fe Cooperative was never a state-owned enterprise, it owes its survival to support from the state from the 1940s through the 1980s as part of a general governmental stance in favor of mining enterprises in general and cooperatives in particular.

Verdery argues that privatization should be analyzed not solely as a shift of relatively stable things from one domain of ownership to another but also as the symptom of a much more complex and highly politicized process of renegotiation of values. Land in the village of Vlaicu is not only changing hands and coming under types of ownership but is also being revalued (and more recently *de-valued*) in both the economic and social sense. Verdery thus analyzes the global phenomenon of privatization as a question of value-making and remaking, using value in its fullest anthropological sense as "meaningfulness in context." She points out that "this understanding makes values a part of what we often mean by *culture*, seen as not just mental models but also practices" (21). By taking this perspective to land privatization in Transylvania, Verdery is able to place it in a much broader comparative context, one that elucidates the nature of value making as a political process.

My own investigation of property relations in the Santa Fe Cooperative, ending with a moment of "privatization" exemplified by the Guadalupe mine described above, similarly engages the micropolitics of value creation and negotiation. To do so, I argue, allows us to transcend simplistic and often ethnocentric dichotomies of "public/private," "capitalist/non- [or pre-] capitalist," "alienable/inalienable," and so on.

It has often been asserted or implied by scholars that inalienability as a form of value is inherently (or situationally) opposed to market exchange. And, indeed, maintaining this opposition is a powerful political strategy for those using languages of inalienability. However, by examining the ways that Santa Fe Cooperative members, scientific bioprospectors, tourist developers, genetic researchers, intellectual property lawyers, and indigenous rights advocates (to name a few salient groups) invoke inalienable forms of wealth at the heart of commodity production or other highly commercialized ventures, we see a different picture. The effective manipulation of multiple and hybrid languages of value depends both on the seeming opposition of inalienable and alienable forms, and on the actual possibilities for their juxtaposition and combination.

As of this writing the Santa Fe Cooperative continues to operate, but it may well be forced to close in the near future. It is terribly unclear what will happen to its members, their families, and the working class of Guanajuato as a whole.

HISTORICAL SILVER PRICES FROM 1975 TO 2002

Comex Spot Settlement (U.S. dollars per ounce)

Year	High	Low	Average	Year	High	Low	Average
2002	5.11	4.22	4.60	1988	7.83	6.00	6.53
2001	4.81	4.03	4.36	1987	9.66	5.38	7.02
2000	5.55	4.56	4.97	1986	6.29	4.85	5.47
1999	5.76	4.87	5.22	1985	6.84	5.53	6.15
1998	7.26	4.61	5.53	1984	10.06	6.30	8.16
1997	6.31	4.16	4.87	1983	14.72	8.40	11.43
1996	5.82	4.68	5.18	1982	11.21	4.98	7.93
1995	6.10	4.38	5.19	1981	16.29	7.99	10.50
1994	5.78	4.57	5.28	1980	48.70	10.80	20.66
1993	5.44	3.52	4.30	1979	34.45	5.92	11.11
1992	4.32	3.64	3.93	1978	6.32	4.81	5.41
1991	4.55	3.51	4.04	1977	4.98	4.29	4.62
1990	5.33	3.94	4.82	1976	5.14	3.83	4.35
1989	6.19	5.03	5.49	1975	5.25	3.92	4.42

Source: The Silver Institute, 2003.

Aspects of Mineral Production in the Santa Fe Cooperative

THE PRODUCTION PROCESS

Flotation

The mineral is brought to the refining plant (about half a mile away from the Valenciana) by dump trucks (from El Sirio, San Ignacio, Valenciana, and Cata) or by a small train of seven cars that trundles through the hills from Rayas and San Vicente. It is taken to a point at the very top of the refining plant. The next section describes the primary activity of the central plant: refining ore from all the mines into a mineral concentrate through the flotation process. This concentrate is then ready to be transported to the smelting plant. The data for this discussion come from interviews with Engineer Armando Aguilar.

Before the ore can be smelted it must be refined into a concentrate. This process makes it cost-efficient to transport the ore and prepares it for smelting at the smelting plant in San Luis Potosí. The Cooperative has used the flotation process of refining (also called "beneficiation") since 1948 (*El Nacional*, July 3, 1948). This process consists of six stages: (1) Grinding/Sieving; (2) Milling; (3) Flotation with reactives; (4) Thickening; (5) Filtering/Drying; and (6) Tailings deposit.

1. *Grinding/Sifting.* Approximately 700 to 800 metric tons of rock are delivered to the plant for refining daily. The mineral to be refined for the day (always during the first and third shifts (11:00 P.M. to 12:00 A.M. and 2:00 P.M. to 3:00 P.M. to take advantage of lower electricity costs) is placed in one of two large chutes (*tolvas*) with capacities of 1,000 and 500 metric tons of rock measuring less than 15 inches in size. The chutes lead to a series of vibrating sieves and cone crushers that progressively break up the rock into pieces of less than .5 inch. At this point the mineral is dumped into three chutes that lead to three separate mills. At the bottom of this chute a worker guides the mineral into the mills, making sure that the entrance does not jam up. This man is the "grinding peon" (*peón quebradorista*); it is one of the jobs in the Cooperative with the lowest status and is usually given to a young worker without family connections in the Cooperative.

It is comparable to the job of "cleanup" (*limpia*) in the mines. It is also a particularly unhealthy job, for the newly ground mineral brings with it a lot of dust and silica particles.

2. *Milling*. The mills (*molinos*) are long cylinders (29 feet, 8 inches, in length and 54 inches in diameter) that slowly revolve with the mineral inside. Mill workers periodically fill them with iron balls (4 inches in diameter) and water from the mine that churn the minerals in the rock into a thick soup as the mills turn. The Cooperative produces 8 metric tons of these ironballs for the mills per month by melting down scrap metal. This only provides about one-quarter of the milling balls needed each month (30 metric tons per month). The mine workers do this to cut costs and to promote self-sufficiency; however, they do not have the capacity to produce more than this amount, so they buy the difference from outside. This process separates the gold and silver from its matrix of quartz. The resulting mixture is fed by conveyor belt, with the supervision of several workers, into the flotation troughs.

3. *Flotation with reactives*. Several workers then add a mixture of chemical reactive agents to this stone soup. The flotation process is so called because the reactives added cause the metal within it to float to the surface of the mixture where they can be skimmed off and thickened into a concentrate. The flotation troughs are long and narrow multicelled rectangles. The mineral, now in the form of a thick and strong-smelling foamy substance, passes slowly from one end to the other. At the end of these troughs, the precipitate of this reaction (tailings/*colas*) are pumped out of the mixture, leaving the final concentrate.

4. *Thickening*. Workers then transport the concentrate by *scooptram* to the "thickening tank" where more of the water is taken out and the concentrate assumes its final form. When Engineer Aguilar took me on a tour of this process, he paused at this point to say, definitively, "this is our product, what we sell in San Luis Potosí."

5. *Drying*. This concentrate still contains a lot of water from the mills, so it is sent to a filter where it is filtered and then dried until it has a cake-like texture, and is in fact referred to as "the cake" (*la torta*). Finally, workers load the final product to the eighteen-wheeler trucks (*trailers*) that will take it to San Luis Potosí.

6. *Tailings deposit*. The cumulative tailings from each stage are collected and taken by truck to the tailings dumps. The Cooperative has nine tailings dumps in the vicinity of Guanajuato, of which two are still active. These dumps form a significant danger to the city of Guanajuato, especially during the rainy season, when they are more likely to burst. Recently a tailings dump operated by Peñoles for the tailing of the Las Torres refining plant burst and threatened to engulf the small village of El Cedro, southeast of Guanajuato City. When I first arrived in Guanajuato, tailings dump 9 overflowed a drainage tunnel, drowning one worker and flooding the Cata River (*El Nacional*, November 30, 1996, and December 1, 1996).

The Cooperative leadership stresses the positive and even communitarian aspects of tailings dumps. Engineer Armando Aguilar, the head of the refining mill, delivered a paper to the National Conference on Tailings Dumps hosted by the Guanajuato School of Mines on December 10, 1997, in which he described the circumstances of the accident in November 1996 but also pointed out the social uses of former tailings dumps as the sites for sports fields donated to the state of Guanajuato (Centro Deportivo Juan José Torres Landa) or operated by the Cooperative (Cancha Deportiva Ing. Alfredo Terrazas V.), workers' housing (Presa de Durán, Cerro del Cuarto), and a nursery school. Another engineer described a project of growing onions in the soil of the tailings dumps, saying that "the onions grew even better in the tailings soil (*lama*) than in regular soil." (One hesitates to speculate how much better). The entire beneficiation process takes two hours and employs approximately forty-five to fifty workers in three shifts (fifteen to eighteen workers per shift).

Sampling and Assay

This section describes the processes of sampling and assay of the daily production in order to plan further production. The data were collected through interviews with Engineer Arturo Colmenero, the head of the sampling and assay departments.

Sampling (*muestreo*) and assay (*ensaye*) are linked processes that determine the grade of silver, gold, and copper (the minerals sold to the smelting plant) in the production for each shift of each mine. The Cooperative assays the mineral after it is prepared for the flotation process, and the concentrate just before it is loaded into trucks for transport. They also assay the precipitate of the refining at several points, to determine how much silver, gold, and copper is being lost.

These tests serve several functions. They allow the engineers and production department to plan future work. They form the basis of predictions for monthly and yearly profits. And, finally, they provide the information on mineral content that will then be compared to that of the smelting plant's assay laboratory. The assay department sends daily reports on mineral grades to each individual mine, and to the superintendent of mines, the superintendent of production, and the president of the administrative council.

Sampling is the preparatory stage for assay analysis. The sampling department pulverizes, weighs, and catalogues each of the samples, and prepares a daily report on samples from the mines, refining mills, concentrate, and tailings. After being prepared in this way, each sample is placed in a carefully labeled envelope indicating point of origin, shift when it was extracted, and weight. The samples are then passed on to the assay laboratory on the other side of the refining plant. There a smaller sample of 20 grams is placed in a small ceramic cup (*crisol*) with a mixture of reactive agents. The samples are then placed in two ovens (one after the other) set, respectively, at 850 and 900 degrees Celsius for thirty to thirty-five minutes each. The extreme heat makes the minerals other than silver and gold melt first and become trapped at the bottom of the cup. The silver and gold form a small nugget at the top of the cup; once the sample has cooled, the silver/gold mixture can be separated from the rest. This is the so-called "dry method" (*via seca*) for determining the grades of silver and gold.

The "wet method" (*via húmeda*) involves mixing the concentrate with nitrous oxide and other compounds to separate out the minerals through a chemical reaction. This method is slower and costlier, but it allows the assayer to calculate the grades for all the minerals being tested at the smelting plant: silver, gold, copper, lead, zinc, arsenic, and antimony. Accordingly the assay department only uses the "*via húmeda*" to assay the concentrate, which is going directly to the smelting plant. The entire process of sampling and assaying takes four-and-a-half to five hours. The assay department analyzes about 150 samples per day. Once the grades of gold and silver have been determined for each mine, the actual ore production is calculated by multiplying the amount of ore in one metric ton by the number of metric tons produced.

Transporting and Selling the Concentrate

The Cooperative sent the following quantities of concentrate in the first quarter of 1998: 425 metric tons in January; 345 in February; 355 in March. It sends between two and four truckloads of concentrate to the smelting plant per week. The concentrate is sent in two Cooperative-owned eighteen-wheeler trucks with the name of the Cooperative painted on the side. On the back is painted the phrase "En México primero conozca Guanajuato" ("In Mexico, visit/know Guanajuato first"), making the trucks ambassadors of regional pride. I was unable to find out who had painted this cheery exhortation; everyone said it had always been there. The trucks carry twenty to twenty-five metric tons of concentrate; the trucks are so heavy that it takes them eleven hours to get to the city of San Luis Potosí, a trip that can be done in a car in four-and-a-half hours. When the trucks climb the hill leaving Guanajuato toward the Sierra de Santa Rosa, they must crawl at 5 to 10 kilometers per hour.

The trucks leave on Monday afternoon and Thursday afternoon at about 4:00 P.M., and arrive at the smelting plant on the outskirts of San Luis Potosí early the following morning. The two drivers (*traileros*), José Luis and Marcos, portly gentlemen in their fifties, sleep in the cab for several hours until the plant opens at 8:00 A.M. and the Cooperative's representative arrives. The Cooperative has hired an independent representative to supervise the weighing and sale of the concentrate, Mr. Ariel González. On April 20–22, 1998, I traveled to San Luis Potosí and accompanied Mr. González as he supervised the delivery of the Cooperative concentrate to the plant. I also interviewed the director of this plant and was given a formal tour to watch the smelting process.

The San Luis plant is currently only operating at 50 percent capacity; this is a recent and potentially serious development for the plant and for the Cooperative. The plant was built in 1897 by the American Smelting and Refining Company (ASARCO—a vast North American mining conglomerate under the control of the Guggenheim family). It is currently owned by Grupo México. At that time, it was situated well outside the city of San Luis Potosí. According to one of the plant engineers, ASARCO conducted meteorological studies before construction to determine where the fumes from the plant would least affect the population of the city. However, San Luis Potosí has grown considerably over the past century. And the recent arrival of transnational corporations such as Nissan and the migration of middle-class Mexico City residents to the *ciudades medianas* (mid-sized cities) of central Mexico have caused something of a population boom in San Luis Potosí, especially among the middle class. Many of these new residents live in a posh neighborhood adjacent to the plant. They have begun to complain bitterly about the air pollution that hangs in an ominous purple cloud above and around the smelting plant, especially during the dry season. For this reason, since the spring of 1997, the smelting plant has been forced to refuse 50 percent of its vendors' supply and lay off 75 percent of its workforce. The Cooperative is the smallest vendor to the San Luis plant, which now accepts approximately seven truckloads of concentrate daily. It is also the only producer that has not had to curtail its deliveries. As noted in chapter 7, this is partly owing to the high content of iron in the Cooperative concentrate; iron is used in the smelting process as a founding agent. During this tour, although we had arrived too late after the weighing to see the molten metal poured into molds, we did see the final product of the smelting plants—ingots 1 meter square and weighing just over 1 metric ton. These blocks contain 96–97 percent copper and 3–4 percent gold and silver. Eighty-five percent of the plant's production is for export, destined for Amarillo, Texas, where it is subjected to another smelting process that separates the gold, silver, and copper. Fifteen percent is sold nationally.

The Grupo México plant continually asserts its power over mineral producers. Because it reserves the right to turn away producers, it can control the exchange without much fear of reprisal. For example, there are often discrepancies between the assay report of the producers and those of the plant—nearly always in the plant's favor. There used to be government inspections of the smelting plants, but they were discontinued after 1994, when the Secretary of Energy, Mines, and Parastatal Industry was subsumed into the position of Secretary for the Promotion of Industry and Trade [SECOFI]. The Cooperative paces how much it sends based on the current need for capital and the price of silver.

As we can see, the control of the market by the smelting plant is a significant external factor in the Cooperative's success. Up to now, the Cooperative has enjoyed a certain amount of favor, but if the plant's attitude or needs change, or if it is forced to close, the consequences for the Cooperative would be extremely serious. For this reason, the goodwill of the plant and its directors is of vital importance.

PRODUCTION DATA: VALENCIANA, JUNE 1997 TO MAY 1998

In precious metal mining, consistency and predictability are of the utmost importance. Consistency in the amount of production and grade of ore (*ley*: the amount of ore [in this case silver] in a metric ton of rock) makes the refining process cost-efficient and allows the producer to pace sales to current market prices. Thus the Cooperative sets an optimal grade for silver and gold for all production. During the period of my fieldwork, the optimal grades for silver and gold were 100 grams of silver per metric ton and .85 grams of gold per metric ton. Table A-II.1 shows the real production and grades at the Valenciana for each month from June 1997 to May 1998.

JOB CATEGORIES IN COOPERATIVE MINES

This description of job categories is based on observation data collected at the Valenciana between December 1996 and June 1998. The same categories exist in all Cooperative mines, however, and I have included information from other mines where it dif-

TABLE A-II.1 REAL PRODUCTION AND GRADES AT THE VALENCIANA, JUNE
1997 TO MAY 1998

	Gold Production (kg)	Gold Grade (gm/metric ton)	Silver Production (kg)	Silver Grade (gm/metric ton)
June 1997	3.10	1.31	259.08	109.48
July 1997	2.52	1.03	287.13	118.72
August 1997	4.85	1.86	703.69	212.70
September 1997	1.85	.69	274.07	79.42
October 1997	2.06	.75	271.96	98.33
November 1997	2.01	.80	238.35	95.26
December 1997	2.02	.85	189.37	79.23
January 1998	2.04	.77	197.05	74.57
February 1998	1.71	.87	187.33	95.45
March 1998	1.38	.58	141.04	59.44
April 1998	1.50	.66	162.89	71.61
May 1998	1.40	.52	169.46	62.78

fers from the Valenciana. The workforce of the Valenciana includes the following positions (the number in parentheses refers to the number of workers of this category employed in December 1996). For the purposes of this discussion, I have only included
those workers who are classified as part of the Valenciana workforce. Truck drivers, repairmen from the central plant, and salespeople at the Cooperative store at the entrance
to the mine are also Cooperative members but are not part of the Valenciana per se. As
plant workers they are on the other side of a crucial political divide within the Cooperative, and so should be considered separately.

Underground (*Bajo Tierra*)

Ingeniero, encargado de la mina **(engineer)** (1). In the case of the Valenciana, the
engineer in charge was a geologist rather than a mining engineer, as was
true for all the other production mines. The San Anton mining project was
also directed by a geologist.

Capitán de la mina **(captain)** (1). The captain was responsible for assigning
daily jobs at the beginning of the shift (*pueble*), accompanying the engineer,
and organizing the labor. His was the highest nonprofessional (*que no tiene
carrera*) position within the mine. At Rayas, the largest mine, there were three
captains. Cata, Sirio, and San Ignacio had two, but at the Valenciana there
was only one.

Cabo de mina **(shift head)** (1). The shift head is just below the position of captain. He is responsible for directing the work in particular areas each day, and
is not assigned to a special area but works generally with the personnel. The

cabo keeps track of how many cars of ore have been extracted during each shift, and also directs the work underground in the absence of the captain. Rayas had up to six *cabos*; at the Valenciana there was only one working during my fieldwork.

Perforistas **(drillers)** (4). These workers are the most directly involved in extraction. The *perforistas* drill holes in the rock to place explosives (emulsion explosives and fertilizer; dynamite is no longer used for safety and health reasons) and then detonate their charges at the end of the shift every day. They often drill twelve to twenty holes per shift. Like all the mine workers, they receive incentive payments for the amount of work they do, in addition to their regular wage. In their case, work is measured by the number of meters of rock they blast through. They also have most direct access to minerals, which are often an important source of income (see chapter 7).

Ayudantes de perforistas **(drillers' assistants)** (4). These workers help the *perforistas* drill, and prepare and place explosives. They earn approximately the same as *carreros*, who are described below, but they are in line for the more lucrative drilling positions. As one *ayudante* told me, "One day the *maestro* [master—in this case the *perforista*] wasn't there, and the *cabo* said, 'Felipe, you go ahead, and at first it was hard but I liked it, and then the next time they gave me my own *maquina* (drill).'"

Paleros (4). These workers are posted at the *tolvas* (chutes) at different points underground where the ore is moved from level to level. They are responsible for emptying the chute with poles (*palos*) into mining cars which are then loaded onto the *malacate* (the car that carries personnel and ore up and down the mineshaft).

Carreros (5). The *carreros* fill the mining cars with ore and then push them along metal rails to the *tolvas* and the *despacho* (point of dispatch). They are paid incentives based on the number of cars they fill (each car holds 1 metric ton of rock).

Despachador (1). This worker is stationed at the *despacho* (in the Valenciana this was on level 365 and guides the cars onto the *malacate*.

Peones (5). These are the lowest paid workers and are responsible for filling cars, cleaning up the debris in the tunnels (*la limpia*) and chutes that lead from level to level, and other necessary tasks.

Muestrero **(sampler)** (1). The *muestrero*, also known as *correcaminos* (roadrunners) takes samples (*muestras*) from all the places where drilling is being done (*rebajes, huecos*) to send for testing at the central plant. The results of these samples are used in planning future exploitation.

Explorador **(explorer)** (1). Some explorers in the Cooperative traveled from mine to mine in order to find new reserves through diamond drilling (the extraction of cross-sections of rock to locate veins of mineral). In the Valenciana the explorer was considered part of the mine's workforce. The sections extracted through diamond drilling were catalogued and examined by the engineer and captain, and then sent for assaying at the central plant.

Surface (*Superficie*)

Malacatero (3). The *malacatero* sits in a cabin off to one side of the shaft and runs the pulleys that take the *calesa* (the metal car that transports personnel, equipment, and mineral) from level to level. The entire system of pulleys, cables, motor, and *calesa* is called the *malacate*. A system of bells informs the *malacatero* where to send the car.

Cajoneros (2). These workers are in a wooden shed (*cajón*) on top of the headframe, approximately 30 meters above the ground. The *malacate* takes the mining cars up to this shed, and the *cajoneros* take them off the *calesa* and over to the top of the chute at the other end of the shed. The chute is emptied into the truck which then carries the ore to the central plant. The chute holds the same amount as the trucks, approximately 10 *toneladas* (metric tons = 1,000 km) of ore. The dump truck usually makes ten trips to the Valenciana daily to transport approximately 100 metric tons.

Bomberos (6). The *bomberos* operate and watch the *bombas* (water pumps) which pump water continuously out of the Valenciana to keep it from flooding. The *bomberos* work in pairs over the three shifts. Underground water is one of the most intransigent problems at the Valenciana, which flooded during both the War of Independence (1810–22) and the Revolution of 1910.[1] Once political unrest forced work stoppage, the water quickly took over the mine.

Conprensorista (1). The *conprensorista* works the air compression machine that runs the drills underground. The air compressor at the Valenciana was an Ingersoll Rand model made in New York in 1906. The workers at the Valenciana took it as a source of pride that they had maintained this machine in good working order for so long. The *conprensorista* at the Valenciana was a former miner who had lost an eye in an accident and so no longer worked underground. He was known as *El Pirata* (The Pirate).

Reparadores **(repairmen)** (2). These two workers do general repairs on machinery and equipment at the Valenciana. Occasionally they are helped by workers from the department of mines of the central plant. A student worker (*practicante*), whose father is a Cooperative member, also accompanies the *reparadores*.[2] These *reparadores* are generally more respected than their equivalents from the central plant, possibly because they spend most of their time working underground fixing equipment, ladders, and so on.

Lampistero (1). The *lampistero* is responsible for maintaining the lanterns used while underground. The battery of the lantern hangs from the miner's wide leather belt and is recharged when the lantern us not in use. The lantern itself is clipped onto the front of the helmet. At the Valenciana, the *lampistero* also maintained the explosives and cutting fuses (*mechas*) for the *perforistas*, and emptied the chutes full of ore into the dump truck from the plant (he is paid per truckload for this task). When the current captain at the Valenciana was first given his position, the *reparador* performed this last task. However, this worker refused to take orders from the new captain, saying that he was too young and had only finished primary school. For this reason, the captain gave the job of emptying the chutes to the *lampistero,* who had shown him more respect.

Rayador (1). The *rayador* is in charge of all administrative tasks in the mine office, and especially keeping track of and calculating wages and incentive contracts (*la raya/la liquidación*). The *rayador* at the Valenciana was a former *perforista* whose lung damage had forced him to be moved to the surface (*echado pa' fuera;* lit., "thrown outside").

Jardineros (gardeners) (4). Miners who could no longer work underground because of age, injury, or lung damage maintained the grounds of the mines and central plant, using the water pumped from the mine to care for the bougainvillea and geraniums climbing up the old Spanish walls, and also kept the chapel to Cristo de los Mineros in good order. The Valenciana mine is particularly well tended because it is open to tourists.

EARNINGS, OVERTIME, AND DEDUCTIONS IN THE VALENCIANA MINE

Table A-II.2 shows workers' earnings, overtime, and deductions per week from December 18, 1996, to August 13, 1997. Deductions included social security payments and a variety of voluntary and other Cooperative deductions for the savings plan, repayment of loans, groceries and construction materials, contributions to the Christmas *posada,* Viernes de Dolores, and other celebrations, and so on.[3]

TABLE A-II.2

Average Earnings (pesos)	Average Overtime (hours)	Average Overtime Pay (pesos)	Average Incentive Pay (pesos)	Average Deductions (pesos)	Average Take-Home Pay (pesos)
379.49	3.63	37.14	72.01	163.41	223.41

1. Introduction

1. *Cronistas* are appointed in many Latin American cities by the town council (*ayuntamiento*); they are typically local historians who may or may not have a university degree (Rionda has a *licenciatura* [a degree that falls between a BA and an MA] from the University of Guanajuato). Cronistas are responsible for representing the perspective of local history at public municipal events. The cronista role both embodies and acknowledges the importance of "the past in the present" in Latin American civic ritual.

2. By this, Rionda means that Guanajuato's patrimony belongs to the world as a whole (not only to the nation).

3. Chapter 6 addresses these questions more fully.

4. Taussig's notion of the Oruro miners as incompletely assimilated into capitalist production is also somewhat surprising, since mines in this region have been in large-scale operation for global markets since the sixteenth century, making Bolivian miners one of the oldest proletarian classes in the world.

5. We might also call this, in a linguistic rather than physical mode, the power to set the terms of the debate in particular settings, much like Bourdieu's *doxa* (1977).

6. Although patrimonial possessions are sometimes incorporeal, I believe that they are still appropriately described as "objects." As Handler (1988) has pointed out, to use a language of property entails a process of "objectification."

7. At this point Mauss adds, in a note, "Perhaps, also, for sale."

8. Nicholas Thomas (1991) points out that the word "inalienable" was not used by Mauss but rather "immovable." However, I do not think that this poses much of a problem; "immovable" comes from the Latin designation "*res mancipi*" (chained things) which has also been translated as "inalienable."

9. But see Miller (2001) for a recent argument, based on ethnography in North London, that it is commodities rather than gifts that show characteristics of inalienability.

2. SANTA FE COOPERATIVE

1. Data on production come from the Cooperative's production department and from the secretary of the Valenciana mine. I was unable to obtain independent corroboration of these figures.

2. Some of the workers in the construction company and some tourist guides at the Bocamina San Cayetano, as well as one or two of the engineers, are not members. There are also some student workers (*practicantes*), usually the sons of members who are working toward professional degrees as mining engineers or accountants. These workers and those who have spent less than six months in the Cooperative make up the 10 percent of nonmembers.

3. In general, the division between cooperative power and technical expertise has often caused serious conflict in Mexican producers' cooperatives, and the Santa Fe is no exception.

4. Many Mexican companies have similar profit-sharing plans. Under Mexican law, companies are required to distribute 10 percent of their profits among the workforce.

5. This section describes all the Cooperative mines in detail, except for Valenciana, which is covered in the following section.

6. The fatalities in San Ignacio happened on April 5, 1997, and December 16, 1997. The third fatality happened on November 28, 1996, when one of the Cooperative tailings dumps on the outskirts of Guanajuato burst, drowning a worker from Santa Rosa.

7. The process of concentrating ore and removing impurities is known as milling or beneficiation.

8. In 1948 it switched to the flotation process, which is somewhat less efficient (in the sense that it recovers a lower percentage of ore) but considerably cheaper ("Nuevo sistema de flotación es todo un éxito," *Estado de Guanajuato,* July 3, 1948).

9. Data gathered from field notes and Cooperative personnel records.

10. Appendix II describes this process.

11. I am indebted to Licenciada Ada Marina Lara Valdez, who allowed me to use interviews she conducted with Valenciana workers for the Oral History Laboratory of the Centro de Investigaciones Humanísticas of the University of Guanajuato.

12. The towns in the Sierra de Santa Rosa have a perennial water shortage, and the municipality only releases water through the pipes for fifteen minutes every other day (at 6:00 P.M.). Every other evening women fill barrels and buckets, but this does not provide enough water for the family for two days. A reservoir project on the outskirts of Santa Rosa has been stalled for several years for political reasons.

13. The 2000 census of the Instituto Nacional de Estadística, Geografía e Información (INEGI) yielded similar results, with 916 people living in 181 households. I have used the 1996 data here because my data on cooperative workers in Santa Rosa are also from 1996.

14. I found no data on how many of those over fifteen are male. Such data would give us a more accurate account of the concentration of Cooperative workers in Santa Rosa.

15. The INEGI census counts "individual households" (*viviendas particulares)*, which typically house a nuclear family unit. In Santa Rosa, as in other parts of Mexico, several "individual households" are often grouped together in family compounds around a cen-

tral patio. Several Cooperative members often live in these compounds, but normally only one man of working age lives in each "individual household."

According to the Cooperative's personnel records, the only community or neighborhood that rivals Santa Rosa in its concentration of workers is Mellado, in the city of Guanajuato. I chose to live in Santa Rosa rather than Mellado because I wanted to study underground workers, and Santa Rosa has more miners and fewer surface workers and engineers than does Mellado.

16. In this book I define a "Cooperative family" as a nuclear or extended family living in the same or adjacent household that fills two criteria: at least one male member is currently a member of the Cooperative; at least two male members of preceding generations previously worked in the Cooperative.

17. For my interview sample I also drew on Cooperative members living in the adjacent community of Puerto de Santa Rosa, where 15 Cooperative members live in a total population of 211 people.

18. It is not uncommon in the villages in the municipio of Guanajuato for two brothers to marry two sisters.

19. When my brother, a photojournalist, came to take pictures at the Valenciana, he told Alvaro, Clotildo, and Chano about some of his experiences taking photos in dangerous situations. Chano listened for a while and then said to him, "OK, let's think about this. What, in your opinion, is the nature of fear?" A lively discussion then ensued on mental and physical fear and courage.

20. Earlier generations of women would have had to make their own tortillas, but now there is a tortillería in Santa Rosa that most women use (Pilcher 1998).

21. This is a local instance of a common Latin American distinction between the civilized, domesticated, and often female "*casa*" and the wild, impure and often male "*calle*" (Hirsch 2002).

22. In other parts of Mexico these parties are called *quinceañeras,* but in Guanajuato I only heard this word used to refer to the girl and not the event.

23. While Guanajuatenses do not recognize a figure corresponding to the Tío or Devil described by June Nash (1979), for Oruro, Bolivia, or the Familiar described by Gastón Gordillo (2002) the cycle of commendation and propitiation does have certain comparable characteristics to these South American beliefs.

3. Labor, History, and Historical Consciousness

1. During the time of my fieldwork the Cooperative also held the concession to a small mine in the town of San Anton de las Minas, in the municipality of Dolores Hidalgo. This mine has some potential for gold and has not been exploited since the late nineteenth century. However, the Cooperative does not have the capital to invest in exploration, ore extraction, or transport from an isolated location back to the beneficiation plant in Guanajuato.

2. Historians differ over the extent of Cárdenas's hostility toward foreign investment, and its intensity could certainly be overemphasized. However, the Six-Year Plan did pose this as one of its primary objectives, and contemporary statements by Cárde-

nas bear this out. For instance, to an audience of miners in 1935, he declared: "Mexico will not reach prosperity by serving the attractive siren of foreign capital" (quoted in Meyer 1968: 200–201 n. 10; translation mine).

3. "*Son puros borrachos*" ("they're a bunch of drunks"), for instance.

4. Since the data for forestry cooperatives are not included in this sector, and since the petroleum industry was consolidated into one state-owned company in 1938, we can surmise that this category includes those cooperatives engaged in working mines and quarries; of these, mining cooperatives probably formed the majority.

5. Data for this section come from visits to the mines and offices of the two companies, interviews, company literature, and three secondary sources: Arvizu Flores 1997, Consejo de Recursos Minerales 1992, and Ortíz 2003.

6. Recall that the Santa Fe Cooperative reports mineral grades of approximately 1 gram of gold and 100–125 grams of silver per metric ton. These are clearly lower than the grades reported at El Cubo and Peñoles; however, my greater access to the Cooperative may have resulted in more accurate figures. I have noticed that public reports of Cooperative yields and grades are higher than the numbers reflected in the daily reports of the beneficiation plant. The same may be true of the other companies.

7. These benefits include smooth relations with the Secretaries of Labor and Health, the ability to arrange land purchases and use city resources, and possibly the avoidance of fines for violation of environmental or safety codes.

8. The Camino Real did not pass through the town of Santa Rosa de Lima, but some silver was transported through there. Perhaps in commemoration of its use for this purpose, the town's only road, which appears to date from the colonial period, is also called the Camino Real.

9. When the *partido* was discontinued in the 1770s (in the Rayas mine) and in the 1790s (in the Valenciana mine), riots and severe labor shortages ensued, forcing the mine owners to use press-gang labor (Brading 1971: 289, Tutino 1986: 96).

10. John Tutino (1986: chap. 2), focusing on the popular rather than the elite motivations for insurrection, has argued that the effects of increasing dependency, instability, and drought on rural producers in the Bajío, rising costs and competition in the textile industry based in Querétaro, and unemployment and the removal of the *partido* for Guanajuato's miners cumulatively predisposed the region's poor and working classes toward revolt.

11. If silver is present in the structures of their city, Guanajuatenses also know that, in order for these structures to be built in the first place, silver had to be taken from the mines and sold on the world market. In this sense, it is the departure of silver that made Guanajuato; the built environment of the city embodies the absence of silver.

4. RECENT CHALLENGES AND RESPONSES

1. Mexicans (like other Hispanophones) typically use two surnames: the father's surname followed by the mother's surname. This is why Meave and his son have the same first surname and different second surnames.

2. I say "relatively," because clearly mining companies are more rooted in place than, say, textile or electronics companies

3. This information was kindly supplied by Engineer Hector M. Aguilar Rendón of the Santa Fe Cooperative.

4. These foundries are encountering serious opposition from the government and environmental groups. In Torreón, Peñoles, the plant's owner has been ordered to conduct a massive cleanup of the neighborhoods surrounding the plant, and the San Luis Potosí plant has had to curtail its production by 50 percent.

5. It appears that the low wages paid by the Cooperative were typical of mining cooperatives in the past (back when there were mining cooperatives besides the Santa Fe). Rojas Coria (1952: 411–412) reports that, according to a study conducted by the Confederación Nacional Cooperativa in 1948, the salaries of employees in private mining companies in Guanajuato were 170 percent greater than the advances paid to Cooperative members. Similar or worse imbalances were found for the states of Michoacán, Hidalgo, Nuevo León, Coahuila, Durango, and Querétaro.

6. In 1997 the Cooperative built a second in-house foundry that makes the iron balls used in the beneficiation process.

7. However, some wives engage in income-producing activities centered in the house (such as cooking or making clothes), and others (especially if they are under forty) leave the home to go to work.

8. Of the several satellite industries run by the Cooperative (ceramics, silversmithy, tourism, and construction), only tourism and construction make profits, and these are quite modest even by Cooperative standards (see the introduction). Ceramics and silversmithy consistently lose money, and the supermarket, provisions department, and hospital exist mainly for use by the Cooperative workforce as part of the consumption cooperative functions of the enterprise.

9. Historically silver prices have been volatile even in comparison with gold. For this reason, silver is called "the restless metal" (Jastram 1981).

10. As Handler (1988) has pointed out, "cultural property" tends to objectify its referents as things even when those include practices, meanings, and so on. Simon Harrison (2000) has identified an analogous tendency in pre- and postcolonial Melanesia, in which cultural practices become reified as prestige goods. UNESCO's definition of "cultural heritage" provides a clear example of this objectifying logic.

11. The notion of "collective individual" is cognate with that of "corporate group" or "corporation," defined in the *Oxford English Dictionary* as "a body corporate legally authorized to act as a single individual; an artificial person created by royal charter, prescription, or act of the legislature, and having authority to preserve certain rights in perpetual succession."

12. El Diario del Bajío, October 14, 1941, "Guanajuato—Un lugar turístico [Guanajuato—a tourist site]"; November 14, 1941, "Buenos hotéles se levantarán en Guanajuato [Good hotels will be constructed in Guanajuato]."

13. UNESCO, like all organs of the United Nations, uses French, English, and Spanish in all its activities. While "heritage" does not mean the same thing as "patrimony" in

other contexts, in UNESCO's dialect in triplicate, which is used by increasing numbers of institutions related to cultural property, the terms "heritage," "*patrimonio*," and "*patrimoine*" are interchangeable. I use the word "patrimony" in English because it preserves some of the richness of the concept as it is used in Mexico and in the Cooperative. But the reader should remember that UNESCO documents referring to "heritage" translate the term as "*patrimonio*."

14. I am grateful to Eric Van Young for this formulation.

15. The monthly distribution of ticket sales suggest that most visitors are Mexican nationals, for the periods of highest use—March, July, and August 1997 and April 1998—are relatively low in terms of foreign tourism to Guanajuato but correspond to Holy Week (which fell in March 1997 and in April 1998) and Mexican school vacations, when many middle-class families travel within the country.

16. With a delicate combination of graciousness and hubris, Mrs. Holbrook concludes her letter to the president of Mexico by saying, "Being from the state of Kentucky, we particularly enjoyed your magnificent and commodious Hipódromo de las Américas [in Mexico City]. We should like to have you visit a Kentucky Derby with us someday" (AGN, fondo Presidentes: 135.2/630, letter from Anna Jane Holbrook to President Miguel Alemán, August 12, 1949).

17. Not everyone in the Cooperative favors tourism promotion. Even in the midst of Guanajuato's fever over cultural patrimony, some Cooperative members criticize any attempt of the Cooperative to capitalize on projects not directly related to ore extraction. The new administrative council, elected in December 1999, campaigned on the platform of increased capitalization of the mines to the exclusion of other projects. It remains to be seen what will happen to Cooperative tourism in this new climate.

18. My attempts to contact IHC after 2000 were unsuccessful.

19. The word *gente* can be used to refer to a single person as well as to a group, in a manner similar to the English phrase "he/she is good people."

20. This is not the first time this has occurred. In the Santa Fe, underground workers have often led rebellions at moments of economic crisis.

21. It was often difficult to obtain reliable numbers about internal finances. The lack of transparency in accounting has often been a source of tension between Cooperative members and leaders.

22. The mines exploited by Peñoles have since been bought by MexGold, a company based in Nova Scotia.

5. REALMS OF PATRIMONY

1. Pierre Bourdieu (1977: 115) noted, "The Kabyle woman setting up her loom is not performing an act of cosmogony; she is simply setting up her loom to weave cloth intended to serve a technical function. It so happens that . . . the symbolic equipment available to her for thinking her own activity . . . constantly refers her back to the logic of ploughing."

2. I take the phrase "realms of patrimony" from the colonial title of the town of Guanajuato: Real de Minas Santa Fe de Guanajuato (Realm of Mines Santa Fe of Guanajuato).

3. My description of the extraction process at the Valenciana derives from participant observation, mine visits, structured interviews, and production and wage data from June 1997 to June 1998.

4. Since Daylight Savings Time has only been in use for the past several years in Mexico, the change in schedule is recent. Miners used to begin the day shift at 6:00 A.M. year-round.

5. In general, I use the word "community" in a literal sense to refer to the smallest jurisdictional designation in Mexico: *comunidad*. Each *comunidad* has a delegate to the *municipio*. The designation is commonly used and understood in Guanajuato.

6. That the Spanish kings never wore crowns casts doubt on this interpretation.

7. Just before I left, my friend Manuel ceremoniously presented me with a *charrasca*, saying, "This makes you part of the Cooperative."

8. I have never heard of a Cooperative worker being dismissed for absenteeism. The standard punishment was exclusion from work for a set number of days or weeks, decided by the captain.

9. At Cata the workers walk down a short staircase before entering the shaft; at Rayas they enter the tunnel and walk for twenty meters, then descend the shaft. In San Vicente, the entrance is an adit. Workers can also enter Rayas through San Vicente, since they are relatively close together. The four mines in Guanajuato City (Valenciana, Cata, Rayas, and San Vicente) are connected underground.

10. Some people told me that when the mine is very hot, miners strip to their underwear, but I never saw this. The other mining companies require long sleeves and pants at all times, for safety reasons.

11. I know this because a *perforista* in Rayas let me use the drill and then amused himself by waving affably at me, walking away, and leaving me there.

12. Visitors from outside the Cooperative, such as inspectors from the secretary of labor or of health, local historians, and PRI supporters of the president of administration's bid for the city council, are guided by Martín and Jorge Luis, the industrial safety team.

Getting permission to go down in the mines was not always easy for me. From March to July 1997 I often accompanied Martín and Jorge Luis on their rounds of the mines to check safety conditions, and tagged along when outside visitors came. In July 1997, after I was taken to a particularly dangerous part of Cata, the captain of the mine (an enemy of the industrial safety deptartment and a friend of Alfredo Galvez, the superintendent of mines) reported Martín and Jorge Luis to the *jefe*, and I was denied access for several months. Eventually I was able to resume my trips down in the mine, although I had to arrange each trip separately and was no longer allowed to go down on a daily basis.

13. Guanajuatenses typically eat four meals a day: a small breakfast (*desayuno*) consisting of bread and coffee or atole and tamales; a lunch (*lonche*) at around eleven in the

morning, usually tacos or rice, beans, and eggs; a big meal (*comida*) anywhere from 2:00 to 5:00 in the afternoon; and a small supper (*cena*) at 9:00 or 10:00 in the evening, which, like breakfast, is usually bread or tamales and a warm drink. The first or last meal is sometimes skipped.

14. The Cooperative does not have a workers' union (since the members are *dueños* [owners] rather than *obreros* [workers]) and in some ways is less answerable to outside authorities such as the secretary of labor (although it must still report to these agencies). For obvious reasons, I would have found it very hard to get specific proof of these assertions, although workers talked to me about these things on many occasions. At the same time some workers seemed to take the rougher conditions in the Cooperative as a point of honor and masculinity.

15. T. A. Rickard (1907: 204 n. 26) reports on the practice of whistling underground during his visit in 1905. He noticed it particularly in contrast to the Cornish belief that it is unlucky to whistle underground.

16. The expression *la mina* can refer to a specific mine or to the underground world of mine work in general. When I asked a worker who had gone to Coahuila to work in a mine of contract whether it was different than the Cooperative mines he had worked in before, he responded, "The mine is the mine. It's always the same" (*La mina es la mina.. Es siempre igual*).

17. Nobody seemed to know to which saint El Sirio (whose name means "the candle") was dedicated.

18. The sacred onomastics of *bajo tierra* dates from the Spanish colonial period and is a feature in mines in other parts of Guanajuato as well. When I went down in mines owned by El Cubo and Peñoles I asked about the existence of sacred names and found that they did exist in these mines as well. However, I observed that in those mines the sacred names were rarely used. Instead, the engineers and workers tended to use a more mundane industrial terminology—a combination of numerals and cardinal directions "Contratiro 6 South" or "Level 14 NW."

19. The practice of putting altars in the mines is common all over Mexico. Mines in different parts of the country have altars to different figures, depending on local popularity (Engineer Eduardo García, personal communication; Engineer José A. Montoya, personal communication).

20. Yates describes a consciously constructed mnemonic device. The Cooperative's underground altars do not act in this deliberate way. Nevertheless, some instructive parallels exist between the two cases.

21. Although this was a formative event in the history of the Cooperative, its commemoration has fallen under the jurisdiction of the union, and the Cooperative does not usually attend.

22. This relation of mutual substantiality of Guanajuatense bodies and minerals occurs in another, rather humorous (so to speak) context in Guanajuato. One of the city's main tourist attractions is its Mummy Museum (*Museo de las Momias*), which was started in the 1960s, after the city dug up a number of bodies from the municipal *panteón* because the families of these deceased had fallen behind in the grave duties. Reportedly the offi-

cials of the cemetery stacked the bodies outside the *panteón* in the hopes of shaming the relatives into paying up. However, they noticed that many of the bodies, even some that had been buried since the turn of the century had not decomposed but rather had mummified. Analysis showed that this was owing to the high mineral content of the soil in Guanajuato. So naturally they put the mummified bodies into a museum and gave the proceeds to the state welfare organization. The Mummy Museum displays these corpses in glass cases, some with cheerful labels saying, for example, "The smallest mummy in the world!!" Photos of fin de siècle bourgeois Guanajuato families adorn the walls. The museum is exceedingly popular and has inspired a story by Ray Bradbury illustrated by photographs of the mummies (Bradbury 1978) and a Mexican cult movie titled *Santos vs. the Mummies of Guanajuato*. Santos is a famous wrestling (*lucha libre*) star of the 1970s.

23. This was the case even though miners knew that the mine was a low-paid and dangerous job. Many men who described the mine as *bonita* and mining as *varonil* (manly) told me at other moments that they wanted their sons to work on the surface or to study to become professionals (*tener una carrera*). Workers and leaders often pointed out with pride that many of the Cooperative engineers and accountants were the sons of Cooperative miners.

24. One little boy, the son of Jaime, the *cabo* at San Vicente, told me, "When I grow up I don't want to work in the mine. I want to work in a building, because there you make lots of money [*hartos billetes*]"

25. It is possible that the term Mother Lode originated in English as a translation of "Veta Madre"; the *Oxford English Dictionary* gives 1830 as the earliest instance of the term "Mother Lode," shortly after the Valenciana brought worldwide renown to Guanajuato. In 1804 Humboldt described the Guanajuato system as the "principal vein" and translates it in parentheses as "(*veta madre*)" (1811: 135); this is a form he tends to use to denote local terminology. While not conclusive, these things lend weight to the idea that the gendered characterization of the mines is a significant local phenomenon.

26. Twelve percent of the respondents did not answer the survey questions concerning housing materials. No reason was given on the surveys for these missing data. Also, I suspect that this survey tended to overreport respondents living in "better" brick houses, since these houses tend also to be more accessible from the city or the center of outlying communities. I accompanied the social workers on several trips to gather data and noted that it was generally the poorer houses that were left out of the survey.

27. For a similar case, in some respects, see Holston 1992.

28. I think that this trend is owing, in part, to the spread of the "Santa Fe style" especially by U.S. retirees to places such as San Miguel de Allende.

29. His house is one of those whose adobe walls are slowly being replaced by brick.

30. *Mezcal* in Santa Rosa is a locally (and illegally) distilled drink from the maguey plant, sometimes sweetened with orange or quince (*membrillo*). The town is well known for its "*mezcal de la sierra*" which is sold in the town's one restaurant and out of Doña Carolina's home.

In other parts of Mexico (especially those areas with higher indigenous populations) this practice is called *mano vuelta* (Emiko Saldívar, personal communication).

31. Guanajuatenses' skill at masonry is known as far away as Ciudad Juárez (Sarah Hill, personal communication). This may be partly why so many migrants to the United States from Guanajuato work in construction industries.

32. The desire for a house is typical among many Mexicans, especially those living in rural and semi-rural areas. Jennifer Hirsch (2003: 67) notes the Mexican proverb with respect to women's desire for a house: "La que se casa quiere casa" [She who marries wants a house].

33. This arrangement bears some similarity to the Caribbean house-yard complex described by Mintz (1989: chap. 9) and others.

34. In Guanajuato today most threatening outsiders are seen as either Protestant or narcotic traffickers or both; Eric Wolf (1998: 13) reports that these signs used to include admonitions to Communists as well.

35. These objects and their arrangement are part of broader cultural practices. In her comparative study of Mexican women from the Bajío region on the border of Jalisco and Michoacán with their sisters and friends in Atlanta, Jennifer Hirsch (1998) conducts a careful examination of household objects, including many of the objects described above. She notes that the same kinds of objects often appear in houses in Mexico and Atlanta, but their particular meanings may shift. She also points out the female valence of many of these household objects, especially the lace clothes and *recuerdos*.

36. Chapter 6 describes in detail the use of *achichicles* in domestic altars.

37. Apparently the use of flowerpots (*macetas*) in *abajeño* architectural design goes back for some time. Luis González (1988: 82) describes the characteristic housing style in eighteenth-century Bajío towns as including "corridors with narrow columns and flowerpots, flowerpots, flowerpots [*macetas, macetas, macetas*]."

38. Burke (1996) has given a fascinating account of cleanliness, commodification, and ideas of "civilization" in Zimbabwe. See also George Orwell's discussion of cleanliness and class in *The Road to Wigan Pier* (1937). These ideas of cleanliness, gender, and sociality bear some resemblance to notions held by Cooperative members and their families.

39. Men typically only sweep the street in front of stores.

40. Cooperative wives get up with or before their husbands for the day shift in order to prepare their lunch.

41. As in the Kabyle case analyzed by Bourdieu (1977: 127), the activities of mine and house are "the product at once of the *diacritical intent* (separation) which orders by opposing, and the *synthetic intent* (union) which create *passages* between the contraries."

42. Some Cooperative wives and many daughters do work outside the home, often as teachers or secretaries. These women tend to be younger or unmarried or widowed.

43. The worker married her after his first wife died. I know of no cases of divorce in Santa Rosa and very few in the Cooperative.

44. These kinds of jokes or remarks are often told by the same people who cite "close families" as a major difference between Mexicans and people from the United States.

45. The ambivalence over virilocality and neolocality is hardly new. Indeed, the question of neolocality as opposed to virilocality has long entailed ideas of modernity as opposed to backwardness or traditionalism or both in Mexico. For instance, Ann Var-

ley examines judicial definitions of "the marital home" in Mexican Supreme Court rulings over divorce cases (Varley 2000). Following Alonso (1995), Varley (2000: 247) argues that judicial rulings "reinscribed" new understandings of the modern family that depended on neolocal residence. She states that, "in rural Mexico, young couples have traditionally spent several years living with the man's parents before forming a separate household. In urban areas the tendency is now weaker but still significant." At the same time she also points out that, as early as the 1950s, this practice was seen by the Mexican state and some others as antimodern and that the practice has always been a source of tension and ambivalence, especially between daughters-in-law (*nueras*) and mothers-in-law (*suegras*) (247; see also Nutini, Carrasco, and Taggart 1976, Nutini 1968, and Robichaux 1997).

46. Klubock (1998) and Finn (1998) note similar strategies by which mining companies seek to control domesticity and femininity in Chile. Anthropologists and historians working in Chile and in the Zambian copper belt have noted similar strategies by which mining companies seek to control domesticity and femininity (Ferguson 1999, Finn 1998, Klubock 1998).

47. These jokes turn on the sexual connotations of chocolate and cigars, and the Cooperative version also imbues *mineral* with a sexual meaning (*semen*). These jokes about the sex of a baby are always accompanied by much laughter. Gutmann (1996, chap. 3) has noted the prevalence of jokes about sexuality and exchange made when a baby is born in Mexico City.

48. It should be noted that in both cases female generative power in mining and in childbirth is brought to fruition or controlled through male potency and restraint. The expression "*se me operaron*" aptly expresses women's passive role even in their own reproductive capacities.

14. This is not something that most Cooperative members or observers are necessarily conscious of but may be an effect of the generative ideas and practices described in this chapter.

15. While patrilineality is a central aspect in the ideology of patrimony, it is tempered by the fact that, by Mexican civil law, women do not give up their property upon entering marriage and continue to control that property in the event of widowhood or divorce (Arrom 1985; Dore 2000).

6. PATRIMONY, POWER, AND IDEOLOGY

1. For a recent example of this tendency in the popular press, see Kaplan 1999.

2. Alonso takes the term "patrimonial" from Max Weber's typology of patriarchal authority; as discussed in the introduction, the patrimonial arrangements of colonial Spanish America certainly helped to reinforce conditions under which an idiom of patrimony is potent today. Furthermore, one could argue that the postrevolutionary state, with its pyramidal system of patron-client relations, is a form of patrimonial authority.

3. Roseberry's statement comes from his contribution to the influential volume *Everyday Forms of State Formation: Revolution and the Negotiation of Rule in Modern Mexico* (1994), which brought the theoretical contributions of James Scott (1985) on everyday

forms of resistance, anthropological interpretations of the Gramscian concept of hegemony, and the work of Philip Corrigan and Derek Sayer (1985) on state formation as a cultural project toward the study of power and popular culture in postrevolutionary Mexico.

4. Thanks to Carlos Ruíz for explaining to me the complexities of Cooperative organization.

5. See Alonso's (1995: 83) discussion of the meanings of *jefe* in Namiquipa, Chihuahua.

6. The word *cabrón* can be either positive or negative depending on the context and speaker. If said by a man—often in the company of men (especially his peers in age or station)—it usually is meant as a compliment, something along the lines of "a badass." It also has a nationalist connotation; for instance, Clotildo once presented to me with great tongue-in-cheek ceremony a license plate that read "¡VIVA MEXICO CABRONES!" Said by a woman, it is often a criticism, meaning "bastard" or "motherfucker." Women use it especially to criticize men for going out and getting drunk and "sleeping around" without taking care of their family responsibilities.

7. This young woman, Eloïsa Pérez Bolde, has since died in the line of duty. QEPD.

8. For discussions of masculinity in Mexico, see Alonso 1995, Gutmann 1996, Limón 1994, Magazine, forthcoming.

9. The notion of *derechohabientes*, common in Mexico, takes on a special force in the context of patrimony in the Santa Fe. To be a *derechohabiente* is to have a claim on patrimonial possession by virtue of a kinship relation to a Cooperative worker. In many cases the category refers to women who claim patrimony through male workers.

10. The acquisition of, irons, blenders, radios, TVs, and so forth, began after World War II in Guanajuato among the upper classes and spread to the working class over the next several decades (Krantz 1978, Tortolero Cervantes 1992).

11. Recent revisionist work on debt peonage in central Mexico emphasizes its advantages for workers in a context of labor shortage (Tutino 1986, Van Young 1983).

12. Even though the Cooperative only instituted its provisioning activities in the last thirty years, some evidence suggests that its very foundation as a cooperative is connected to the need to keep workers in the mines. The mines of the Santa Fe Cooperative were thought to be nearly exhausted at the time of the Cooperative's foundation. And, in fact, most mining cooperatives formed in the 1930s and 1940s controlled older and relatively low-yield or problematic mines in central Mexico rather than the newer and more profitable mines of northern Mexico (Sariego et al. 1988, Aguila 1997).

13. The terms *padrino* and *compadre* refer to the same cultural practice from different perspectives. The *padrino-ahijado* (godfather-godchild) relationship refers to the connection between the ritual sponsor and the child; the *compadre* relationship is that between the *padrinos* and the parents. At times both *jefes* and members describe Cooperative members as children, and at other times as less powerful and poorer *compadres* (Mintz and Wolf 1950).

14. Finn (1998) found a somewhat different pattern in the copper mines of Chiquicamata, Chile. She states that women are expected to be the stewards of men's consumption (199). While I heard some remarks about women's inability to manage re-

sources and keep a good house (see chapter 5), in general the responsibility for consumption rested with men. I argue that this difference is connected to the prevalence of the idiom of patrimony in the Cooperative and its efficacy in calling men to account.

15. Alvaro has three daughters and one son.

16. It should be noted that Patricio's accident occurred when he was in the *caja*, a car that is only supposed to carry ore, not personnel. For this reason the Cooperative had, and knew that it had, no legal responsibility toward him beyond his Social Security payments.

17. This practice is understood to be based not on merit but on need.

18. This is the main difference between miners and surface workers at the central plant, the latter generally not having incentive contracts and therefore making significantly less money. When plant workers complain about this difference, miners often retort that those on the surface also do less work and face less danger.

19. Unfortunately I do not know whether the skilled *perforista* knew what was going on or what he thought about it.

20. For another case of supernatural exchange in underground mining, see Breckenridge 1995.

21. Meave died of a heart attack in November 1996, one week after I had arrived in Guanajuato, and one day after I learned of his existence. At the time of his death he was still locked in legal combat with the Cooperative over the large sums of money that they claimed he had stolen from them. I did attend his funeral mass in the Basilica of Nuestra Señora Santa Fe de Guanajuato, which was attended by several hundred of Guanajuato's elite. The priest of Guanajuato's basilica gave the eulogy.

22. Mining, like some other export industries, actually benefited from the peso devaluation at the end of 1994, since the products of the mines are sold for U.S. dollars, while labor and costs are largely paid for with pesos.

23. In fact, he had arrived late and had been standing outside talking to me. I had not been given permission to go to the meeting and was outside cadging information.

24. There are surely others whom I was unable to find.

25. I was never able to locate Doña Mariela, so I could not find out how the Cooperative responded to her demands. I am quite certain that they did not result in payments other than the ones arranged through Don Gustavo and Susana.

26. The socioeconomic survey yielded the following results: (1) all the surviving members were surface workers; (2) all lived in Guanajuato City rather than in rural communities; (3) most were natives of Guanajuato and lived in older working-class neighborhoods of the city (Mazagua, Carrizo, Panteón, etc.); (4) all owned their own homes; and (5) all but two had sons or other relatives currently or formerly working in the Cooperative.

7. ANTHROPOLOGY OF MINED SUBSTANCES

1. The word *achichicle* is not in common usage in Mexico or in Guanajuato but is used by miners, merchants, engineers, and others associated with mining. It is also used in the same way in other Mexican mining centers. Santamaría (1959: 27) defines *achichi-*

cle as "(from the Azteca *atl*, water, and *chichipictli*, drop) noun, Type of stalactite or stalagmite that forms in mines, secreting water drop by drop." Dennis Beals, one of the foremost dealers in Mexican minerals, reports that this term is only used in Guanajuato and that it refers to the more common types of mineral specimens (the rarer silver minerals are called *changuitos*).

2. "Semos" is a vernacular form of "somos," first-person plural, present indicative form, of the verb "ser" (*to be*).

3. Interviewed by Licenciada Ada Marina Lara Valdez, Oral History Laboratory, Centro de Investigaciones Humanísticas of the University of Guanajuato.

4. Engineers can also acquire this deep knowledge of the mines expressed in the ability to grade ore by sight; when they do, they are respected as miners as well as engineers; that is, local knowledge is the main criterion for entrance into the guild of miners, and engineers can join if they have that knowledge.

5. Once the Cooperative was founded in the late 1930s, it quickly encountered conflict with buscones who continued to work the mines they had worked in the time of the "Reduction Company." The Cooperative appealed to the federal government for aid in ejecting these underground prospectors. In response, and as a gesture of support for the newly founded Cooperative, the government sent troops to guard the mine from these "lupios" (AGN fondo Presidentes Lazaro Cárdenas, exp 432.1/93, Bernstein 1965: 208–209).

6. The selves and socialities produced by Cooperative members are by no means harmonious; rather, workers and their families continually struggle over how to define them, who are their proper members, and who is upholding or betraying their rights and obligations. However, they do agree to a remarkable extent on the criteria for membership, one of which is the recognition of silver underground.

7. In this article Parmentier examines both Saussurean (systemic) and Peircian (transactional) aspects of Palauan money.

8. Ponciano Aguilar is immortalized in the name of a mineral found in Guanajuato: aguilarite.

9. The industrial safety department spent a great deal of time trying to get miners to amacizar; miners often resisted doing so since the Cooperative does not pay an incentive contract for this activity, and also because it would indicate, perhaps, an unmanly concern for safety. The conflict over getting people to amacizar recalls Zola's *Germinal* (1993 [1885]) where workers refused to put in timbers for support because the company lowered the amount they paid per timber.

10. I found that Cooperative households were more likely to have mineral specimens on display than the households where men worked in the other mining companies. When I visited the houses of miners from El Cubo and Peñoles, after some time of chatting, these hosts would bring out the stones they had hidden, as a gesture of hospitality. I presume that this difference is because the Cooperative tacitly permits the extraction of these stones and the other companies do not.

11. Since nearly all miners build their own houses, they are able to place the niche (*nicho*) wherever they wish.

12. Recently the University of Guanajuato has started a Patronato del Templo de Villaseca (Trust for the Templo de Villaseca) to preserve both the mineral specimen chapel and a collection of retablos (small paintings or other images denoting thanks to the Señor de Villaseca for the performance of a miracle or other favor). The director of the Cooperative and the head of the engineering department are both members of this group, and the Cooperative often lends workers to help with restoration and other tasks in the church. Recently this group, attempting to halt the theft of mineral specimens from the chapel, posted signs saying "CARE FOR YOUR PATRIMONY, DON'T REMOVE THESE STONES."

13. I had to be careful about how and to whom to ask this question. Whereas, in other parts of Latin America, people have assumed that, as an interested observer of local custom, I must be a CIA agent, in Guanajuato they assumed I must be a Protestant missionary. Household and workplace altars are seen as a pillar of local Catholic practice and therefore a target of missionaries. For this reason, I only asked about altars once I knew a person fairly well.

14. He himself rents a prime spot under a shade tree to one side of the Mercado Hidalgo. He first got this location in the 1970s with the help of a friend who worked in the city government (presidencia municipal). He says, however, that ever since the bus station was moved out of town (ca. 1994), business has never been as good as it was before.

15. Another important buyer at the Valenciana was the *reparador* (repairman), who also spent a lot of time on the surface.

16. A soda only costs two to three pesos; this expression indicates a small amount of money that is not expected to be paid back. It is often what police or others say, or are reported to have said, when asking for a bribe.

17. The fee for a permit from the municipio is one peso per day, and the locations are not as good as the Cooperative locations, right against the mine walls or inside the grounds of the Valenciana.

18. These are Peñoles mines that are known for the beauty and rarity of the mineral specimens. Since these miners are forbidden to extract mineral specimens, samples from Peñoles mines are more in demand and fetch a higher price.

19. He is the *reparador* for the Valenciana.

20. Isidro told me that selling mineral specimens is only one of several strategies he uses to make money. For example, he often works ten to fifteen extra hours per week doing repairs in the Valenciana. He told me with great, and greatly justified, pride that these various efforts have allowed him to raise six children and give each a professional education.

21. She may well have had some personal connection with the Presidencia Municipal that secured her one of these coveted places.

22. Of this amount, seven thousand dollars was for one particular fine and valuable specimen.

23. Thanks to Alaina Lemon for suggesting this point.

24. In discussing the souvenir in general, Susan Stewart (1993) draws on some of the themes I mention here, such as the attempt to encapsulate and transport a miniature ver-

sion of a place. That mineral samples are literally pieces of Guanajuato makes this even more marked.

25. The "very rich" refers to those who would pay five, ten, or twenty thousand dollars for a single specimen.

26. An interesting example of this is the emergence of a market for old labels for mineral samples (Mineralogical Record, September–October 1977, 407–408).

27. In describing a particularly fine specimen, Carl Francis said "It's a real Rembrandt of a piece."

28. We find an analogous example of the tension Parmentier describes at the heart of U.S. capitalism in the image of the impregnable fortress of Fort Knox, where bars of gold must remain motionless and protected in order for U.S. dollars to circulate confidently. While this image implies a gold standard to which the dollar is no longer pegged, it continues to have cultural power for most Americans.

8. Mexican Languages of Patrimony

1. In the case of the Santa Fe Cooperative, jobs can also be seen as a class of patrimonial possessions.

2. Taylor (1972) has argued that indigenous elites in Oaxaca were able to appropriate the Spanish notion of *mayorazgo* to receive protection for their "traditional" lands on the grounds that they, like *mayorazgos,* were inalienable. Something of the same process seems to be happening with *patrimonio primitivo,* so that the concept may be more usefully understood as an indigenous use of a Spanish concept rather than an indigenous holdover of colonial times.

3. Mallon (1994) documents how the term "liberalism" in nineteenth-century Mexico referred to and concealed many different local understandings of the role of indigenous communities or the peasantry or both in the emerging nation.

4. The forestry sector provides another fascinating domain of national patrimony because well over half the Mexican forests are on *ejido* land (Bray et al. 2003), forest cooperatives are numerous, and forests have been a recent focus of community activism based on principles of ecological sustainability in uneasy tension with nationalist and neoliberal ideologies (Boyer 2004, Doane 2004, Wexler and Bray 1996.)

5. Guillermo de la Peña (1981: 77), writing about land reform in the Morelos highlands (Emiliano Zapata's home region), emphasizes the degree to which peasants mistrusted state agents and questioned their right to manage national patrimony (see also Warman 1980). Ana María Alonso and Daniel Nugent (1994) tell how one Chihuahuan *municipio* challenged the assumptions and actions of the national state in the establishment of an ejido. In contrast, Lynn Stephen (1998: 49) reports on the positive image of state agrarian officials in the popular histories of three *ejidos* in Oaxaca.

6. As we saw in chapter 5, women are sometimes able to use this androcentric ideology to their own benefit, such as when they call men to account for failing to care for patrimony in the proper way.

7. Recent scholarship (cf. Becker 1994, Vaughn 1982) points out the degree to which these negotiations were not simply the imposition of either a benevolent or Machiavel-

lian state but rather the complex forging of hegemony between state and popular agents (including peasants and women).

8. Particular ejidos have responded to these modifications in widely differing ways. As Stephen (1998) has pointed out, even those who have voted to accept individual titles to *ejido* parcels have not always thereby accepted the neoliberal economic principles of the Mexican state.

9. In Mexico, as in other places where a Romance language is dominant, patrimony can also indicate the holdings of an individual or a family group. These include items such as a house, a car, or a plot of land.

10. The alternative to this system is practiced in England and the United States, where the owner of the surface land also owns the subsoil beneath. The juridical designation of the subsoil as royal domain dates from Imperial Rome (M. de la Peña 1920).

11. Recent revisionist scholarship emphasizes local resistance to Cardenismo, the incompleteness of state power, and the extent to which Cardenismo can be seen in terms of continuity rather than change (Becker 1995, Rubin 1997).

12. At the same time that state agents such as those in the INAH took a stand against *saqueo*, such practices have always gone on sub rosa. It seems clear that some within the INAH have been complicit in selling artifacts to foreigners.

9. Conclusion

1. There are a number of successful hotels in Mexico located in renovated and converted colonial sites, such as haciendas, convents, and so on. The Ex-Convento San Pablo in Oaxaca is a famous example.

2. Molly Doane addresses similar issues in the context of a nongovernmental organization concerned with forests in the Isthmus of Oaxaca and opposition to Vicente Fox's Plan Puebla-Panamá (PPP) (Doane 2004).

3. Daniel Miller delineates the connection between ownership, inalienability, and personhood in this context, saying: "The vanguard of discussion has become a concern with topics such as the new reproduction technologies or organ transplants, where the core principles of the inalienable as a property of personhood come under threat" (Miller 2001: 93–94).

Appendix II

1. The problem of underground water was not particular to the Valenciana. Brading (1971: 134) quotes the Mexican commentator on the mining industry, Francisco Javier de Gamboa, as saying, "Water is the greatest obstacle in mining. Strike the mine's lode, and water springs forth like blood from the veins of a body."

2. The Cooperative employs approximately thirty *practicantes* who are family members of Cooperativistas and are completing their education. These students are often later accepted as permanent members of the Cooperative.

3. During this time the exchange was at approximately nine pesos to the dollar, meaning that workers made an average of twenty-five dollars per week.

Aguila, Marcos T. 1997. "The Great Depression and the Origins of *Cardenismo* in Mexico. The Case of the Mining Sector and Its Workers, 1927–1940." Ph.D. dissertation, University of Texas at Austin.

Aguilar Camín, Hector, and Lorenzo Meyer. 1993. *In the Shadow of the Mexican Revolution: Contemporary Mexican History, 1910 –1989.* Austin: University of Texas Press.

Aguilar Rivera, José Antonio. 1996. *Liberalism in Mexico.* Mexico City: Centro de Investigación y Docencia Económicas.

Alonso, Ana María. 1995 *Thread of Blood: Colonialism, Revolution, and Gender on Mexico's Northern Frontier.* Tucson: University of Arizona Press.

Andrieux, Jean-Yves. 1998. *Patrimoine et Société.* Rennes: Presses Universitaires de Rennes, collection "Art et Société."

Antuñez Echegaray, Francisco. 1964. *Monografía Histórica y Tecnológica del Distrito Minero de Guanajuato.* Mexico City: Consejo de Recursos no-Renovables.

Appadurai, Arjun. 1986. "Introduction: Commodities and the Politics of Value." In idem, *The Social Life of Things: Commodities in Cultural Perspective.* New York: Cambridge University Press.

Arrom, Silvia M. 1985. "Changes in Mexican Family Law in the Nineteenth Century: The Civil Codes of 1870 and 1884." *Journal of Family History* 10:305–317.

Arvizú Flores, Erik. 1997. "La Minería como Estructuradora del Espacio Social y Económico del Municipio de Guanajuato, 1980–1996." Tésis de Licenciatura en Geografía, Universidad Nacional Autónoma de México.

Baitenmann, Helga. 1998. "The Article 27 Reforms and the Promise of Local Democratization in Central Veracruz." In *The Transformation of Rural Mexico: Reforming the Ejido Sector,* ed. Wayne Cornelius and David Myrhe. La Jolla : Center for U.S.-Mexican Studies, University of California, San Diego.

Bakewell, Peter J. 1971. *Silver Mining and Society in Colonial Mexico: Zacatecas, 1546–1700.* Cambridge: Cambridge University Press.

———. 1984. *Miners of the Red Mountain: Indian Labor in Potosí, 1545–1650.* Albuquerque: University of New Mexico Press.

Ballard, Chris, and Glenn Banks. 2003. "Resource Wars: The Anthropology of Mining." *Annual Review of Anthropology* 32:287–313.

Bartra, Armando. 1985. *Los Herederos de Zapata: Movimientos Campesinos Posrevolucionarios en México, 1920–1980*. Mexico City: Ediciones Era.

Bartra, Roger. 1989. "Changes in Political Culture: The Crisis of Nationalism." In *Mexico's Alternative Political Futures*, ed. Wayne Cornelius, Judith Gentleman, and Peter H. Smith. Monograph Series #30. San Diego: University of California Press.

———. 1993. *Agrarian Structure and Political Power in Mexico*. Baltimore, Md.: The Johns Hopkins University Press.

Becker, Marjorie. 1995. *Setting the Virgin on Fire: Lázaro Cárdenas, Michoacán Peasants, and the Redemption of the Mexican Revolution*. Berkeley: University of California Press.

Bernstein, Marvin D. 1965. *The Mexican Mining Industry: A Study of the Interaction of Politics, Economics, and Technology*. Albany: State University of New York Press.

Birchall, Johnston. 1994. *Co-op: The People's Business*. Manchester, U.K.: Manchester University Press.

Blanco, Mónica, Alma Parra, and Ethelia Ruiz Medrano. 2000. *Breve Historia de Guanajuato*. Mexico City: Fondo de Cultura Económica.

Bonfil Batalla, Guillermo. 1987. *México Profundo. Una Civilización Negada*. Mexico City: Secretaria de Educación Pública, CIESAS.

Bourdieu, Pierre. 1977. *Outline of a Theory of Practice*. Cambridge: Cambridge University Press.

Boyer, Christopher. 2004. "Modernizing El Monte: Scientific Forestry in Mexico, 1880–1957." Paper delivered at the 2004 Latin American Studies Association Meetings, Las Vegas, Nevada.

Boyle, James. 1996. *Shamans, Software, and Spleens: Law and the Construction of the Information Society*. Cambridge, Mass.: Harvard University Press.

Bradbury, Ray. 1978. *The Mummies of Guanajuato*. Photography by Archie Lieberman. New York: Abrams.

Brading, David. 1971. *Miners and Merchants in Bourbon Mexico, 1763–1810*. Cambridge: Cambridge University Press.

———. 1991. *The First America: The Spanish Monarchy, Creole Patriots, and the Liberal State, 1492–1867*. Cambridge: Cambridge University Press.

Bray, David, Leticia Merino-Pérez, Patricia Negreros-Castillo, Gerardo Segura-Warnholz, Juan Manuel Torres-Rio, and Henricus F. M. Vester. 2003. "Mexico's Community-Managed Forests: A Global Model for Sustainable Landscapes." *Conservation Biology* 17 (3): 672–677.

Breckenridge, Keith. 1995. "'Money with Dignity:' Migrants, Minelords and the Cultural Politics of the South African Gold Standard Crisis, 1900–1950." *Journal of African History* 36 (2): 271–304.

Brown, John, and Alan Knight, eds. 1990. *The Mexican Petroleum Industry in the Twentieth Century*. Austin: University of Texas Press.

Buchanan, Sylvester. 1964. "Beneficio de los Minerales de Oro y Plata de Guanajuato." *Minería y Metalurgia* 29:27–29.

Burke, Timothy. 1996. "Lifebuoy Men, Lux Women: Commodification, Consumption, and Cleanliness in Modern Zimbabwe." Durham, N.C.: Duke University Press.

Burawoy, Michael. 1972. "Another Look at the Mineworker." *African Social Research* 14: 239–287.

Cano Jáuregui, Joaquín. 1986. *Visión del Cooperativismo en México*. Mexico City: Secretaría del Trabajo y Previsión Social, Secretaría "B", Unidad Coordinadora de Políticas, Estudios y Estadísticas del Trabajo, Subcoordinación de Programas Institucionales y Documentación.

Cárdenas, Lázaro. 1986 [1934]. "Plan Sexenal de 1934." In *La Gira del General Lázaro Cárdenas*. Partido Revolucionario Institucional (PRI).

Carr, Barry, and Steve Ellner, eds. 1993. *The Latin American Left: From the Fall of Allende to Perestroika*. Boulder, Colo.: Westview.

Carsten, Janet, ed. 2000. *Cultures of Relatedness*. Cambridge: Cambridge University Press.

Castañeda, Quetzil. 1996. *In the Museum of Maya Culture: Touring Chichén Itzá*. Minneapolis: University of Minnesota Press.

———. 2001. "The Aura of Ruins." In *Fragments of a Golden Age: The Politics of Culture in Mexico since 1940*, ed. Gilbert Joseph, Anne Rubinstein, and Eric Zolov. Durham, N.C.: Duke University Press.

Chávez Orozco, Luis, ed. 1960. *Conflicto de Trabajo con los Mineros de Real del Monte, Año de 1766*. Mexico: Biblioteca del Instituto Nacional de Estudios Históricos de la Revolución Mexicana.

Clancy, Michael J. 1999. "Tourism and Development: Evidence from Mexico." *Annals of Tourism Research* 26 (1): 1–20.

Clavero, Bartolomé. 1974. *Mayorazgo: Propiedad Feudal en Castilla, 1369–1836*. Madrid: Siglo Veintiuno Editores.

Cole, Jeffrey. 1985. *The Potosí Mita, 1573–1700: Compulsory Indian Labor in the Andes*. Stanford: Stanford University Press.

Collier, George. 1978. "The Determinants of Highland Maya Kinship." *Journal of Family History* 3 (4): 439–453.

———. 1994 *¡Basta! Land and the Zapatista Rebellion in Chiapas*. Oakland: Institute for Food and Development Policy.

Collier, Jane, and Sylvia Yanagisako, eds. 1987. *Gender and Kinship: Essays toward a Unified Analysis*. Stanford: Stanford University Press.

Consejo de Recursos Minerales. 1992. *Geological-Mining Monograph of the State of Guanajuato*. Mexico City: Consejo de Recursos Minerales.

Cooper, J. P. 1976. "Patterns of Inheritance and Settlement by Great Landowners from the Fifteenth to the Eighteenth Centuries." In *Family and Inheritance: Rural Society in Western Europe, 1200–1800*, ed. Jack Goody, Joan Thirsk, and E. P. Thompson. Cambridge: Cambridge University Press.

Cornelius, Wayne, Judith Gentleman, and Peter H. Smith, eds. *Mexico's Alternative Political Futures*. Monograph Series #30. La Jolla: Center for U.S.-Mexican Studies, University of California at San Diego.

Coronil, Fernando. 1996. "Beyond Occidentalism: Toward Nonimperial Geohistorical Categories." *Cultural Anthropology* 11 (1): 51–87.

Corrigan, Philip, and Derek Sayer. 1985. *The Great Arch: English State Formation as Cultural Revolution*. Oxford: Blackwell.

Le Debat. 1994. Vol. 78. Special Issue. *Mémoire, Commemoration, Patrimoine.*

Da Matta, Roberto. 1991. *Carnivals, Rogues, and Heroes: An Interpretation of the Brazilian Dilemma.* Notre Dame: University of Notre Dame Press.

Deere, Carmen Diana. 2001. "Institutional Reform of Agriculture under Neoliberalism: The Impact of Women's and Indigenous Movements." *Latin American Research Review* 36 (2).

De Janvry, Alain, Gustavo Gordillo, and Elisabeth Sadoulet. 1997. *Mexico's Second Agrarian Reform: Household and Community Responses, 1990–1994.* La Jolla: Center for U.S.-Mexican Studies, University of California, San Diego.

Delaney, Carol. 1991. *The Seed and the Soil: Gender and Cosmology in Turkish Village Society.* Berkeley: University of California Press.

De la Peña, Guillermo. 1981. *Legacy of Promises: Agriculture, Politics, and Ritual in the Morelos Highlands of Mexico.* Austin: University of Texas Press.

De la Peña, Manuel. 1924. "Prolegómenos de la Historia Jurídica de la Propiedad en México." *Boletín del Petroleo* 17:5–124.

Deutsch, Sarah. 1987. *No Separate Refuge: Culture, Class, and Gender on an Anglo-Hispanic Frontier in the American Southwest, 1880–1940.* Oxford: Oxford University Press.

Diario de los Debates del Congreso Constituyente 1916–1917. 1960. Vols. 1–2. Mexico City: Gobierno Federal de los Estados Unidos Mexicanos.

Doane, Molly. 2004. "The Resilience of Nationalism in a Global Era: Megaprojects in Mexico's South." In *Social Movements: an Anthropological Reader,* ed. June Nash. Oxford: Blackwell.

Dore, Elizabeth. 2000. "One Step Forward, Two Steps Back: Gender and the State in the Long Nineteenth Century." In *Hidden Histories of Gender and the State in Latin America,* ed. Elizabeth Dore and Maxine Molyneux, 3–32. Durham, N.C.: Duke University Press.

Eckstein, Susan. 1977. *The Poverty of Revolution: The State and the Urban Poor in Mexico.* Princeton, N.J.: Princeton University Press.

Edwards, J. Arwel, and Joan Carles Llurdés. 1996. "Mines and Quarries: Industrial Heritage Tourism." *Annals of Tourism Research* 23 (2): 341–363.

Edwards, Jeannette, and Marilyn Strathern. 2000. "Including Our Own." In *Cultures of Relatedness,* ed. Janet Carsten. Cambridge: Cambridge University Press.

Eliade, Mircea. 1962. *The Forge and the Crucible.* London: Rider.

Epstein, A. L. 1958. *Politics in an Urban African Community.* Manchester: Manchester University Press on behalf of the Rhodes-Livingstone Institute.

——. 1981. *Urbanization and Kinship: The Domestic Domain on the Copperbelt of Zambia, 1950–1956.* New York: Academic.

Espinosa, Crispín. 1917–1920. *Efemérides Guanajuatenses.* 3 vols. Guanajuato: Imprenta de "El Comercio."

Evans-Pritchard, E. E. 1940. *The Nuer : A Description of the Modes of Livelihood and Political Institutions of a Nilotic People.* Oxford: Clarendon.

Fabian, Johannes. 1983. *Time and the Other: How Anthropology Makes Its Object.* New York: Columbia University Press.

Ferguson, James. 1985. "The Bovine Mystique: Power, Property and Livestock in Rural Lesotho." *Man* (n.s.) 20:647–674.

Ferry, Elizabeth Emma. 2002. "Inalienable Commodities: The Production and Circulation of Silver and Patrimony in a Mexican Mining Cooperative." *Cultural Anthropology* 17 (3): 331–358.

———. N.d. "Memories of Wealth, Memory as Wealth: A Changing Economic Landscape in Mexico." Unpublished manuscript.

Ferry, Stephen. 1999. *I Am Rich Potosí: The Mountain That Eats Men*. New York: Monacelli.

Finn, Janet. 1998. *Tracing the Veins: Of Copper, Culture, and Community from Butte to Chuquicamata*. Berkeley: University of California Press.

Fisher, John. 1975. "Silver Production in the Viceroyalty of Peru, 1776–1824." *Hispanic American Historical Review* 55 (1): 25–43.

Florescano, Enrique, comp. 1993. *El Patrimonio Cultural de México*. Mexico City: Consejo Nacional para la Cultura y las Artes: Fondo de Cultura Económica.

———. 1997. *El Patrimonio Nacional de México*. Mexico City: Consejo Nacional para la Cultura y las Artes: Fondo de Cultura Económica.

Fox, Genevieve May. 1920. *An Idea That Grew from a Little Cooperative Store to a Worldwide Movement*. New York: Young Women's Christian Association.

Fustel de Coulanges, Numa Denis. 1980 [1864]. *The Ancient City: a Study on the Religion, Laws, and Institutions of Greece and Rome*. Baltimore, Md.: The Johns Hopkins University Press.

Gamio, Manuel. 1960 [1916]. *Forjando Patria*. Mexico City: Editorial Porrua.

García Canclini, Nestor. 1995. *Hybrid Cultures: Strategies for Entering and Leaving Modernity*. Minneapolis: University of Minnesota Press.

———. 1997. "El Patrimonio Cultural de México y La Construcción Imaginaria de lo Nacional." In *El Patrimonio Nacional de México*, comp. Enrique Florescano, 57–86. Mexico City: Consejo Nacional para la Cultura y las Artes: Fondo de Cultura Económica.

Garner, Richard L. 1980. "Silver Production and Entrepreneurial Structure in 18th-Century Mexico." *Jahrbuch für Geschichte von Staat, Wirtschaft und Gesellschaft Lateinamerikas* 17:157–185.

Gilly, Adolfo. 1994. *El Cardenismo: Una Utopía Mexicana*. Mexico City: Cal y Arena.

Godelier, Maurice. 1999. *The Enigma of the Gift*. Chicago: University of Chicago Press.

Godoy, Ricardo. 1985. "Mining: Anthropological Perspectives." *Annual Review of Anthropology* 14: 199–217.

González Navarro, Moisés. 1985. *La Confederacion Nacional Campesina en la Reforma Agraria Mexicana*. Mexico City: Sociedad Cooperativa Publicaciones Mexicanas.

González y González, Luis. 1988. "El Bajío, Cuna y Cocina de la Independencia." In *La Querencia*. Mexico City: Editorial Hexágono.

Goody, Jack, Joan Thirsk, and E. P. Thompson, eds. 1976. *Family and Inheritance: Rural Society in Western Europe, 1200–1800*. Cambridge: Cambridge University Press.

Gordillo, Gastón. 2002. "The Breath of the Devils: Memories and Places of an Experience of Terror." *American Ethnologist* 29 (1): 33–57.

Graeber, David. 2001. *Toward an Anthropological Theory of Value: the False Coin of our Dreams*. New York: Palgrave.

Greaves, Thomas, and William Culver, eds. 1985. *Miners and Mining in the Americas*. Manchester: Manchester University Press.

Greenfield, Jeanette. 1989. *The Return of Cultural Treasures*. Cambridge: Cambridge University Press.

Gregory, C.A. 1982. *Gifts and Commodities*. New York: Academic.

Guevara Sanginés, María. 2001. *Guanajuato diverso: Sabores y sinsabores de su ser mestizo (siglos xvi a xvii)*. Guanajuato: Instituto Estatal de la Cultura de Guanajuato.

Gutmann, Matthew C. 1996. *The Meanings of Macho: Being a Man in Mexico City*. Berkeley: University of California Press.

Guy, Jeff, and Motlatsi Thabane. 1988. "Technology, Ethnicity, and Ideology: Basotho Miners and Shaft-Sinking in the South African Gold Mines." *Journal of Southern African Studies* 14 (2).

Hacker, Sally. 1989. *Pleasure, Power, and Technology: Some Tales of Gender, Engineering, and the Cooperative Workplace*. Boston: Unwin and Hyman

Halbwachs, Maurice. 1940. *La Topographie Légendaire Évangiles en Terre Sainte; Étude de Mémoire Collective*. Paris: Presses Universitaires de France.

——. 1950. *La Mémoire Collective*. Paris: Presses Universitaires de France.

Hale, Charles. 1968. *Mexican Liberalism in the Age of Mora, 1821–1853*. New Haven, Conn.: Yale University Press.

Handler, Richard. 1988. *Nationalism and the Politics of Culture in Quebec*. Madison: University of Wisconsin Press.

——. 1991. "Who Owns the Past? History, Cultural Property, and the Logic of Possessive Individualism." In *The Politics of Culture*, ed. Brett Williams. Washington, D.C.: Smithsonian Institution Press.

Hanks, William. 1990. *Referential Practice: Language and Lived Space among the Maya*. Chicago: University of Chicago Press.

Hann, C. M. ed. 1998. *Property Relations: Rethinking the Anthropological Tradition*. Cambridge: Cambridge University Press.

Hardesty, Donals. 1998. "Power and the Industrial Mining Community in the American West." In *Social Approaches to an Industrial Past: The Anthropology and Archaeology of Mining,* ed. A. Bernard Knapp, Vincent Pigott, and Eugenia Herbert. London: Routledge.

Harris, Olivia. 1988. "The Earth and the State: The Sources and Meanings of Money in Northern Potosí, Bolivia." In *Money and the Morality of Exchange*, ed. Jonathan Parry and Maurice Bloch. Cambridge: Cambridge University Press.

Harrison, Simon. 2000. "From Prestige Goods to Legacies: Property and the Objectification of Culture in Melanesia." *Comparative Studies in Society and History* 42 (3): 662–679.

Hartog, François. 1998. "Patrimoine et Histoire: Les Temps du Patrimoine." In *Patrimoine et Société*, ed. Jean-Yves Andrieux, 3–17. Rennes: Presses Universitaires de Rennes, collection "Art et Société."

Harvey, David. 1989. *The Condition of Postmodernity: An Enquiry into the Origins of Cultural Change*. Oxford: Blackwell.

Hayden, Cori. 2003. *When Nature Goes Public: The Making and Unmaking of Bioprospecting in Mexico City*. Princeton, N.J.: Princeton University Press.

Herbert, Eugenia. 1993. *Iron, Gender and Power: Rituals of Transformation in African Societies*. Bloomington: Indiana University Press.

Hernández Chávez, Alicia. 1979. *La Mecánica Cardenista*. Mexico City: Colegio de México.

Hewitt de Alcántara, Cynthia. 1984. *Anthropological Perspectives on Rural Mexico*. London: Routledge and Kegan Paul.

Heyman, Josiah McC. 1995. "In the Shadow of the Smokestacks: Labor and Environmental Conflict in a Company-Dominated Town." In *Articulating Hidden Histories: Exploring the Influence of Eric R. Wolf*, ed. Jane Schneider and Rayna Rapp. Berkeley: University of California Press.

Hirsch, Jennifer S. 2003. *A Courtship After Marriage: Sexuality and Love in Mexican Transnational Families*. Berkeley: University of California Press.

Hoberman, Louisa Schell. 1991. *Mexico's Merchant Elite, 1590–1660: Silver, State, and Society*. Durham, N.C.: Duke University Press.

Holston, James. 1991. "Autoconstruction in Working Class Brazil." *Cultural Anthropology* 6 (4): 447–465.

Hogar en México. 1993. Mexico City: Instituto Nacional de Estadística, Geografía e Información (INEGI).

Howard, M. C. 1991. *Mining, Politics and Development in the South Pacific*. Boulder, Colo.: Westview.

Humboldt, Alexander [von]. 1811. *Political Essay on the Kingdom of New Spain*. Translated by John Black. London: Longman, Hurst, Rees, Orme, and Brown.

Industrial Heritage Consultancy (IHC). 1999. "Guanajuato's Mining Heritage." Unpublished report delivered to the Guanajuato State Secretary of Economic Development.

Instituto Nacional de Antropología e Historia. 1976. *Catalogo de Bienes Inmuebles de la República Mexicana [Guanajuato]*. Mexico City: Instituto Nacional de Antropología e Historia.

Instituto Nacional de Estadística, Geografía e Información [INEGI]. 1993. *Cuaderno Estadístico Municipal: Guanajuato, GTO*. Aguascalientes, Mexico: INEGI.

Instituto Nacional de Estudios Históricos de la Revolución Mexicana. 1986. *La Constitución de 1917: Visión Periodística [antología]*. Mexico City: Instituto Nacional de Estudios Históricos de la Revolución Mexicana.

Jackson, Robert H., ed. 1996. *Liberals, the Church, and Indian Peasants: Corporate Lands and the Challenge of Reform in Nineteenth-Century Spanish America*. Austin: University of Texas Press.

Jardel, Enrique J., and Bruce F. Benz. 1997. "El Conocimiento Tradicional del Manejo de los Recursos Naturales y la Diversidad Biológica." In *El Patrimonio Nacional de México*, comp. Enrique Florescano, 193–248. Mexico City: Consejo Nacional para la Cultura y las Artes: Fondo de Cultura Económica.

Jastram, Roy. 1981. *Silver, the Restless Metal*. New York: Wiley.

Jáuregui, Aurora. 1985. *Evolución de la Cooperativa Minera Santa Fe de Guanajuato y la Gestión del Ing. Alfredo Terrazas Vega (1947–1972)*. Guanajuato: University of Guanajuato Press.

——. 1996. *Mineral de la Luz*. Guanajuato: Instituto de la Cultura del Estado de Guanajuato.

Jeudy, Henri-Pierre, ed. 1990. *Patrimoine en Folie*. Paris: Ministére de la Culture et de la Communication. Maison de Sciences de l'Homme, collection "Ethnologie de la France" 5.

Jiménez Moreno, Wigberto. 1988. *La Colonización y Evangelización de Guanajuato en el siglo XVI. Arqueología e Historia Guanajuatense*. León: Colegio del Bajío.

Jiménez González, Rodolfo. 1999. "La Lucha por el Patrimonio Cultural de la Nación." *Macro-Economía*, August 15, 1999.

Johnson, Susan Lee. 2000. *Roaring Camp: the Social World of the California Gold Rush*. New York: Norton.

Joseph, Gilbert, and Daniel Nugent, eds. 1994. *Everyday Forms of State Formation: Revolution and the Negotiation of Rule in Modern Mexico*. Durham, N.C.: Duke University Press.

Kasmir, Sharryn. 1996. *The Myth of Mondragón: Cooperatives, Politics and Working-Class Life in a Basque Town*. Albany: State University of New York Press

Keane, Webb. 1997. *Signs of Recognition: Powers and Hazards of Representation in an Indonesian Society*. Berkeley: University of California Press.

Kingsolver, Barbara. 1989. *Holding the Line: Women in the Great Arizona Mine Strike of 1983*. Ithaca, N.Y.: ILR Press.

Kirchhoff, Paul. 1966 [1943]. "Mesoamerica: Its Geographic Limits, Ethnic Composition, and Cultural Characteristics." In *Heritage of Conquest*, ed. Sol Tax. New York: Cooper Square

Kirsch, Stuart. 2002. "Anthropology and Advocacy: A Case Study of the Campaign against the Ok Tedi Mine." *Critique of Anthropology* 22:175–200.

Klubock, Thomas Miller. 1998. *Contested Communities: Class, Gender, and Politics in Chile's El Teniente Copper Mine, 1904–1951*. Durham, N.C.: Duke University Press.

Knapp, A. Bernard, Vincent Pigott, and Eugenia Herbert. *Social Approaches to an Industrial Past: The Anthropology and Archaeology of Mining*. London: Routledge.

Knight, Alan. 1990. "Mexico 1930–46." In *Cambridge History of Latin America*, ed. Leslie Bethell, Vol. 7. Cambridge: Cambridge University Press.

——. 1992. "The Politics of the Expropriation." In *The Mexican Petroleum Industry in the Twentieth Century*, ed. Jonathan C. Brown and Alan Knight. Austin: University of Texas Press.

Kourí, Emilio. 2002. "Interpreting the Expropriation of Indian Pueblo Lands in Porfirian Mexico: The Unexamined Legacies of Andrés Molina Enríquez." *Hispanic American Historical Review* 82 (1): 69–117.

Krantz, Lasse. 1978. *Minería y Marginalidad. Ensayo Socioeconómico sobre el Desarrollo Minero en Guanajuato*. Guanajuato, México: Escuela de Ingeniería de Minas y Metalurgia de Guanajuato.

Ladd, Doris. 1988. *The Making of a Strike: Mexican Silver Workers' Struggles in Real del Monte, 1766–1775*. Lincoln: University of Nebraska Press.

Lawrence, Susan. 1998. "Gender and Community Structure on Australian Colonial Goldfields." In *Social Approaches to an Industrial Past: The Anthropology and Archaeology of Mining*, ed. A. Bernard Knapp, Vincent Pigott, and Eugenia Herbert. London: Routledge.

Lévi-Strauss, Claude. 1969. *The Elementary Structures of Kinship*. Boston: Beacon.

Ley Federal sobre Monumentos y Zonas. 1972. Mexico City: Instituto Nacional de Antropología e Historia.

Limón, José. 1994. "Carne, Carnales and the Carnivalesque: Bakhtinian Order, Disorder, and Narrative Discourses." In *Dancing with the Devil: Society and Cultural Politics on the Mexican-American Border*. Madison: University of Wisconsin Press.

Lomnitz, Larissa. 1982. "Horizontal and Vertical Relations and the Social Structure of Urban Mexico." *Latin American Research Review* 17 (2): 51–74.

Lomnitz Adler, Claudio. 1992. *Exits from the Labyrinth: Culture and Ideology in the Mexican National Space*. Berkeley: University of California Press.

——. 2001. *Deep Mexico, Silent Mexico: Toward an Anthropology of Nationalism*. Minneapolis: University of Minnesota Press.

Lowie, Robert. 1928. "Incorporeal Property in Primitive Society." *Yale Law Journal* 37:551–563.

MacLachlan, Colin, and Jaime Rodríguez. 1990. *The Forging of the Cosmic Race: A Reinterpretation of Colonial Mexico*. Berkeley: University of California Press.

MacMillan, G. 1995. *At the End of the Rainbow? Gold, Land and People in the Brazilian Amazon*. New York: Columbia University Press.

MacPherson, C. B. 1962. *The Political Theory of Possessive Individualism: Hobbes to Locke*. Oxford: Clarendon.

Magazine, Roger. 2004a. "'You Can Buy a Player's Legs, but Not His Heart': A Critique of Clientelism and Modernity among Soccer Fans in Mexico City." *Journal of Latin American Anthropology* 9 (1):8–33.

——. 2004b. "Both Husbands and Banda (Gang) Members: Conceptualizing Marital Conflict and Instability among Young Rural Migrants in Mexico City." *Men and Masculinities* 7 (3): 1–22.

Maine, Sir Henry Sumner. 1963 [1861]. *Ancient Law; Its Connection with the Early History of Society and Its Relation to Modern Ideas*. Boston: Beacon.

Malinowski, Bronislaw. 1950 [1922]. *Argonauts of Western Pacific: An Account of Native Enterprise and Adventure in the Archipelagoes of Melanesian New Guinea*. New York: Dutton.

——. 1965. *Coral Gardens and Their Magic*. London: Allen and Unwin.

Manning, H. Paul. 2002. "English Money and Welsh Rocks: Divisions of Language and Divisions of Labor in Nineteenth-Century Welsh Slate Quarries." *Comparative Studies in Society and History* 44 (3): 481–510.

Marmolejo, Padre Lucio. 1988 [1886]. *Efemérides Guanajuatenses*. Guanajuato: Estado de Guanajuato.

Martin, Percy F. 1905. *Mexico's Treasure House: Guanajuato*. New York: Cheltenham.

Marx, Karl. 1976. *Capital, A Critique of Political Economy*. Vol. 1. New York: Vintage.

Mauss, Marcel. 1990 [1950]. *The Gift: The Form and Reason for Exchange in Archaic Societies*. New York: Norton.

Mayer, Philip, with contributions by Iona Mayer. 1962. *Townsmen or Tribesmen: Conservatism and the Process of Urbanization in a South African City*. Capetown: Oxford University on behalf of the Institute of Social and Economic Research, Rhodes University.

Messenger, Phyllis Mauch, ed. 1989. *The Ethics of Collecting Cultural Property: Whose Culture? Whose Property?* Albuquerque: University of New Mexico Press.

Meyer Cosío, Francisco Javier. 1995. *Población y Minería en Guanajuato, 1893–1898*. Guanajuato: Estado de Guanajuato.

———. 1999. *La Minería en Guanajuato: Denuncios, Minas, y Empresas (1898–1913)*. Zamora, Michoacán: El Colegio de Michoacán/Universidad de Guanajuato.

Meyer, Jean. 1976. *The Cristero Rebellion: The Mexican People between Church and State, 1926–1929*. Cambridge: Cambridge University Press.

Meyer, Lorenzo. 1972. *México y los Estados Unidos en el Conflicto Petrolero (1917–1942)*. Mexico City: El Colegio de México.

Miller, Daniel. 2001. "Alienable Gifts and Inalienable Commodities. In *The Empire of Things*, ed. Fred Myers. Santa Fe: School of American Research Press.

Mintz, Sidney. 1989. *Caribbean Transformations*. New York: Columbia University Press.

Mintz, Sidney W., and Eric R. Wolf. 1950. "An Analysis of Ritual Co-Parenthood (*Compadrazgo*)." *Southwestern Journal of Anthropology* 6 (4): 341–364.

Molina Enríquez, Andrés. 1909. *Los Grandes Problemas Nacionales*. Mexico City: Imprenta de A. Carranza e Hijos.

Monroy, Pedro. 1888. *Las Minas de Guanajuato: Memoria Histórico-Descriptiva de este Distrito Minero*. Mexico City: Secretaría de Fomento.

Moodie, T. Dunbar, with Vivian Ndatshe. 1994. *Going for Gold: Men, Mines, and Migration*. Berkeley: University of California Press.

Morales-Moreno, Luis Gerardo. 1994. *Orígenes de la Museología Mexicana: Fuentes para el Estudio Histórico del Museo Nacional, 1780–1840*. Mexico City: Universidad Iberoamericana, Departamento de Historia.

Munn, Nancy. 1977. "The Spatiotemporal Transformations of Gawan Canoes." *Societé des Océanistes* 33 (54–55): 39–53.

———. 1986. *The Fame of Gawa: A Symbolic Study of Value Transformation in a Massim [Papua New Guinea] Society*. Cambridge: Cambridge University Press.

Nadasdy, Paul. 2003. *Hunters and Bureaucrats: Power, Knowledge and Aboriginal-State Relations in the Southwest Yukon*. Vancouver: UBC Press.

Nash, June. 1979. *We Eat the Mines and the Mines Eat Us: Dependency and Exploitation in Bolivian Tin Mines*. New York: Columbia University Press.

Nash, June, and Nicholas Hopkins. 1976. "Anthropological Approaches to the Study of Cooperatives, Collectives and Self-Management." In *Popular Participation in Social Change: Cooperatives, Collectives and Nationalized Industry*, ed. June Nash, Jorge Dandler, and Nicholas Hopkins. The Hague: Mouton Press.

Niemeyer, E. Victor. 1974. *Revolution at Querétaro: the Mexican Constitutional Convention of 1916–1917*. Austin: University of Texas Press for the Institute of Latin American Studies.

Nora, Pierre. 1989. "Between Memory and History: Les Lieux de Mémoire." *Representations* 26:7–25.

Nugent, Daniel. 1993. *Spent Cartridges of Revolution: An Anthropological History of Namiquipa*. Chicago: University of Chicago Press.

Nutini, Hugo. 1968. *San Bernardino Contla: Marriage and Family Structure in a Tlaxcalan Municipio*. Pittsburgh: University of Pittsburgh Press.

Olivé Negrete, Julio Cesar, and Augusto Urteaga Castro-Pozo. 1988. *INAH, Una Historia*. Mexico City: Colección Divulgación, Instituto Nacional de Antropología e Historia.

Orozco, Wistano Luis. 1895. *Legislación y Jurisprudencia sobre Terrenos Baldíos*. Mexico City: Imprenta de El Tiempo.

Ortiz, Fernando. 1995 [1940]. *Cuban Counterpoint: Tobacco and Sugar*. Durham, N.C.: Duke University Press.

Orwell, George. 1937. *The Road to Wigan Pier*. Left Book Club ed. London: V. Gollancz.

Palavicini, Felix. 1915. *Un Nuevo Congreso Constituyente*. Veracruz: Imprenta de la Señoria de I.P. y B.A.

Palerm, Angel. 1980. *El Primer Sistema Económica Mundial. In Antropología y Marxismo*. Mexico City: Editorial Nueva Imagen.

Pannell, Sandra. 1994. "Mabo and Museums: The Indigenous [Re]Appropriation of Indigenous Things." *Oceania* 65: 18–39.

Pansters, Wil, ed. 1997. *Citizens of the Pyramid: Essays on Mexican Political Culture*. Amsterdam: Thela.

Parmentier, Richard J. 2002. "Money Walks, People Talk: Systemic and Transactional Dimensions of Palauan Exchange." *L'Homme* 162 (special issue: *Questions de Monnaie*).

Partido Revolucionario Institucional (PRI). 1986 [1934]. *La Gira del General Lázaro Cárdenas*. Mexico City: Partido Revolucionario Institucional.

Paz, Octavio. 1961. *The Labyrinth of Solitude: Life and Thought in Mexico*. New York: Grove.

——. 1972. *The Other Mexico: Critique of the Pyramid*. New York: Grove.

Pilcher, Jeffrey. 1998. *¡Que Vivan los Tamales!: Food and the Making of Mexican Identity*. Albuquerque: University of New Mexico Press.

Piot, Charles. 1991. "Of Persons and Things: Some Reflections on African Spheres of Exchange." *Man* 26 (3): 405–424.

Polanyi, Karl. 1944. *The Great Transformation*. New York: Rinehart.

Powell, Philip. 1952. *Soldiers, Indians and Silver*. Berkeley: University of California Press.

Pratt, Mary Louise. 1992. *Imperial Eyes: Travel Writing and Transculturation*. New York: Routledge.

Raat, W. Dirk, and William H. Beezley, eds. 1986. *Twentieth-Century Mexico*. Lincoln: University of Nebraska Press.

Rabinow, Paul. 1977. *Reflections on Fieldwork in Morocco*. Berkeley: University of California Press.

Randall, Robert W. 1972. *Real del Monte: A British Mining Venture in Mexico*. Austin: University of Texas Press for the Institute of Latin American Studies.

Rankine, Margaret E. 1992. "The Mexican Mining Industry in the Nineteenth Century with Special Reference to Guanajuato." *Bulletin of Latin American Research* 11 (1): 29–48.

Rickard, T. A. 1907. *Journeys of Observation*. San Francisco: Dewey.

Rionda, Isauro. 1993. *Capítulos de Historia Colonial Guanajuatense*. Guanajuato: Universidad de Guanajuato.

Rionda, Luis Miguel. 1994. "Una Visión Antropológica del Altar de Dolores en Guanajuato." *El Nacional,* March 24, 1994, 7.

Rionda, Luis Miguel. 1997. *Primer Acercamiento a una Historia Política Contemporánea de Guanajuato, Siglo XX*. Cuadernos de CICSUG #10. Guanajuato: Universidad de Guanajuato.

Rivera, Abraham. 1992. *La Huelga Minera en Guanajuato en 1936*. Tésis de Licenciatura, Escuela de Filosofía, Historia, y Letras, Universidad de Guanajuato.

Robichaux, David Luke. 1997. "Residence Rules and Ultimogeniture in Tlaxcala and Mesoamerica." *Ethnology* 36 (2): 149–171.

Robinson, Katherine M. 1986. *Stepchildren of Progress: The Political Economy of Development in an Indonesian Mining Town*. Albany: State University of New York Press.

Rojas Coria, Rosendo. 1952. *Tratado de Cooperativismo Mexicano*. Mexico City: Fondo de Cultura Económica.

Roseberry, William. 1994. "Hegemony and the Language of Contention." In *Everyday Forms of State Formation: Revolution and the Negotiation of Rule in Modern Mexico*, ed. Gilbert Joseph and Daniel Nugent. Durham, N.C.: Duke University Press.

Rouaix, Pastor. 1959. *Génesis de los Artículos 27 y 123 de la Constitución Política de 1917*. Mexico City: Biblioteca del Instituto Nacional de Estudios Históricos de la Revolución Mexicana.

Rubin, Gayle. 1975. "The Traffic in Women: Notes on the "Political Economy" of Sex. In *Toward an Anthropology of Women*, ed. Rayna R. Reiter. New York: Monthly Review Press.

Rubin, Jeffrey. *Decentering the Regime: Ethnicity, Radicalism, and Democracy in Juchitán, Mexico City*. Durham, N.C.: Duke University Press.

Rus, Jan. 1994. "The ' ComunidadRevolucionaria Institucional': The Subversion of Native Government in Highland Chiapas, 1936–1968." In *Everyday Forms of State Formation: Revolution and the Negotiation of Rule in Modern Mexico,* ed. Gilbert Joseph and Daniel Nugent. Durham, N.C.: Duke University Press.

Russell-Wood, A.J.R. 1984. "Colonial Brazil: The Gold Cycle, c. 1690–1750." In *The Cambridge History of Latin America,* ed. Leslie Bethell. Vol. 2. Cambridge: Cambridge University Press.

Sabean, David Warren. 1988. *Kinship in Neckarhausen, 1700–1870*. Cambridge: Cambridge University Press.

Sahlins, Marshall. 1972. *Stone Age Economics*. Chicago: Aldine-Atherton.

Salt of the Earth [film]. 1954. Directed by Herbert Biberman.

Santamaría, Francisco Javier. 1959. *Diccionario de Mejicanismos*. Mexico City: Ediciones Porrua.

Saragoza, Alex. 2001. "The Selling of Mexico: Tourism and the State, 1929–1952." In *Fragments of a Golden Age: The Politics of Culture in Mexico since 1940*, ed. Gilbert Joseph, Anne Rubinstein, and Eric Zolov. Durham, N.C.: Duke University Press.

Sariego, Juan Luis, et al. 1988. *El Estado y la Minería Mexicana*. Mexico City: Fondo de Cultura Económica.

——. 1994. *La Lucha de los Mineros de Chihuahua por el Contrato Unico*. Ciudad Juárez: Universidad Autónoma de Ciudad Juárez.

Schattschneider, Ellen. 2003. *Immortal Wishes: Labor and Transcendance on a Japanese Mountain*. Durham, N.C.: Duke University Press.

Scott, James. 1976. *The Moral Economy of the Peasant: Rebellion and Subsistence in Southeast Asia*. New Haven, Conn.: Yale University Press.

Scott, James. 1985. *Weapons of the Weak: Everyday Forms of Peasant Resistance*. New Haven, Conn.: Yale University Press.

Serrano Espinoza, Luis Antonio, and Juan Carlos Cornejo Muñoz. 1998. *De la Plata, Fantasías: La Arquitectura del Siglo XVIII en la Ciudad de Guanajuato*. Guanajuato: INAH/Universidad de Guanajuato

Shaffer, Jack. 1999. *Historical Dictionary of the Cooperative Movement*. Lanham, Md.: Scarecrow, 1999.

Sheridan, Thomas E.. 1998. "Silver Shackles and Copper Collars: Race, Class and Labor in the Arizona Mining Industry from the 18th Century until World War II." In *Social Approaches to an Industrial Past: The Anthropology and Archaeology of Mining*, ed. A. Bernard Knapp, Vincent Pigott, and Eugenia Herbert. London: Routledge.

Silva Herzog, Jesus. 1963. *La Expropriación del Petroleo en México*. Mexico City: Cuadernos Americanos.

Silver Institute. 1998. World Silver Report. Washington, D.C.: Silver Institute.

Simmel, Georg. 1990. *The Philosophy of Money*. New York: Routledge.

Simmons, Alexy. 1998. "Bedroom Politics: Ladies of the Night and Men of the Day." In *Social Approaches to an Industrial Past: The Anthropology and Archaeology of Mining,* ed. A. Bernard Knapp, Vincent Pigott, and Eugenia Herbert. London: Routledge.

Smith, Bill, and Carol Smith. 1999. "Tales from Mexico, Part II." *Rocks and Minerals* 74 (2): 103–109.

Soto Laveaga, Gabriela. 2003. "Steroid Hormones and Social Relations in Oaxaca." In *The Social Relations of Mexican Commodities,* ed. Casey Walsh et al. La Jolla: Center for U.S.-Mexican Studies Press.

Spyer, Patricia. 1997. "The Eroticism of Debt: Pearl Divers, Traders, and Sea Wives in the Aru Islands, Eastern Indonesia." *American Ethnologist* 24 (3): 515–538.

Stephen, Lynn. 1998. "Between NAFTA and Zapata: Responses to Restructuring the Commons in Chiapas and Oaxaca, Mexico." In *Privatizing Nature: Political Struggles for the Global Commons*, ed. Michael Goldman. New Brunswick, N.J.: Rutgers University Press.

Stern, Steve J. 1995. *The Secret History of Gender: Women, Men, and Power in Late Colonial Mexico City*. Chapel Hill: University of North Carolina Press.

Stewart, Susan. 1993. *On Longing: Narratives of the Miniature, the Gigantic, the Souvenir, the Collection*. Durham, N.C.: Duke University Press.

Stone, Lawrence. 1977. *The Family, Sex, and Marriage in England, 1500–1800*. New York: Harper and Row.

Strathern, Marilyn. 1988. *The Gender of the Gift: Problems with Women and Problems with Society in Melanesia*. Berkeley: University of California Press.

——. 1999. *Property, Substance and Effect: Anthropological Essays on Persons and Things*. London: Athlone.

Taboury, Sylvain. 1999. *Le Patrimoine en Mouvement: La Maison de Banlieue d'Athis-Mons, Centre d'Interpretation sur L'Environment Urbain et le Patrimoine de Banlieue*. Université Bourgogne, D.E.S.S. Action Artistique, Politiques Culturelles e Muséologie.

Tandeter, Enrique. 1993. *Coercion and Market: Silver Mining in Colonial Potosí, 1692–1826*. Albuquerque: University of New Mexico Press.

Taussig, Michael. 1980. *The Devil and Commodity Fetishism in South America*. Chapel Hill: University of North Carolina Press.

Taylor, William B. 1972. *Landlord and Peasant in Colonial Oaxaca*. Stanford: Stanford University Press.

Thomas, Nicholas. 1991. *Entangled Objects: Exchange, Material Culture, and Colonialism in the Pacific*. Cambridge, Mass.: Harvard University Press.

Thompson, E. P. 1971. "The Moral Economy of the English Crowd in the Eighteenth Century." *Past and Present* 50 (1): 76–138.

Thornley, Jenny. 1981. *Workers' Cooperatives: Jobs and Dreams*. London: Heinemann Educational Books.

Tortolero Cervantes, Yolia. 1992. *Vida Cotidiana de Mineros Guanajuatenses, Siglo XX*. Tésis de Licenciatura, Escuela de Filosofía, Historia, y Letras, Universidad de Guanajuato.

Tovar y de Teresa, Rafael. 1997. "Hacia una Nueva Política Cultural." In *El Patrimonio Nacional de México*, comp. Enrique Florescano, 87–110. Mexico City: Consejo Nacional para la Cultura y las Artes: Fondo de Cultura Económica.

Trollope, Anthony. 2002. *The Way We Live Now*. New York: Penguin.

Tutino, John. 1986. *From Insurrection to Revolution in Mexico: Social Bases of Agrarian Violence 1750–1940*. Princeton, N.J.: Princeton University Press

UNESCO. 1972. Convention concerning the Protection of the World Cultural and Natural Heritage.

Van Gennep, Arnold. 1960 [1914]. *The Rites of Passage*. Chicago: University of Chicago Press.

Van Onselen, Charles. 1976. *Chibaro: African Mine Labour in Southern Rhodesia, 1900–1933*. London: Pluto.

Vargas Cetina, Gabriela. 2000. "Cooperativas y Globalización: el Movimiento Cooperativo Internacional Localizado." In *Globalización: Una Cuestión Antropológica. Carmen Bueno Castellanos, coordinadora*. Mexico City: CIESAS, Porrúa.

Varley, Anne. 2000. "Women and the Home in Mexican Family Law." In *Hidden Histories of Gender and the State in Latin America*, ed. Elizabeth Dore and Maxine Molyneux, 238–261. Durham, N.C.: Duke University Press.

Vélez-Ibañez, Carlos. 1983. *Rituals of Marginality: Politics, Process, and Culture Change in Urban Central Mexico, 1969–1974.* Berkeley: University of California Press.

Verdery, Katherine M. 1999. *The Political Lives of Dead Bodies: Reburial and Postsocialist Change,* Harriman Lectures. New York: Columbia University Press.

———. 2003. *The Vanishing Hectare: Property and Value in Postsocialist Transylvania.* Ithaca, N.Y.: Cornell University Press.

Villalba, Margarita. 1999. *Valenciana: Expansión y Crisis en el Siglo XVIII.* Tésis de Maestría, Universidad Nacional Autónoma de México.

Ward, Henry G. 1828. *Mexico in 1827.* London: Henry Colburn.

Warman, Arturo. 1980. *"We Come to Object": The Peasants of Morelos and the National State.* Baltimore, Md.: The Johns Hopkins University Press.

———. 1994. *La Reforma al Artículo 27 Consitucional.* Mexico City: Procuraduría Agraria. Originally published in *La Jornada,* April 8, 1994.

Weber, Max. 1978. *Economy and Society: An Outline of Interpretive Sociology.* Edited by Guenther Roth and Claus Wittich. Berkeley: University of California Press.

Weiner, Annette B. 1988. "Inalienable Wealth." *American Ethnologist* 12:52–65.

———. 1992. *Inalienable Possessions: The Paradox of Keeping-while-Giving.* Berkeley: University of California Press.

Wexler, Matthew, and David Bray. 1996. "Reforming Forests: From Community Forests to Corporate Forestry in Mexico." In *Reforming Mexico's Agrarian Reform,* ed. Laura Randall. Armonk, N.Y.: M.E. Sharpe.

Williams, Brett, ed. 1991. *The Politics of Culture.* Washington, D.C.: Smithsonian Institution Press.

Williams, Jeffrey. 1995. *Manipulation on Trial: Economic Analysis and the Hunt Silver Case.* Cambridge: Cambridge University Press.

Wilson, Godfrey. 1941–1942. *An Essay on the Economics of Detribalization in Northern Rhodesia.* Livinstone, Northern Rhodesia: Rhodes Livingstone Institute Papers.

Wilson, Godfrey, and Monica Wilson. 1965. *The Analysis of Social Change, Based on Observations in Central Africa.* Cambridge: University Press.

Wolf, Eric R. 1953. "La Formación de la Nación." *Ciencias Sociales* 4:50–62, 98-111, 146–171.

———. 1955. *The Mexican Bajío in the Eighteenth Century: An Analysis of Cultural Integration.* New Orleans: Tulane University Middle American Research Institute.

———. 1956. "Aspects of Group Relations in a Complex Society: Mexico." *American Anthropologist* 58:1065–1078.

———. 1990. "Distinguished Lecture: Facing Power—Old Insights, New Questions." *American Anthropologist* 92:586–596.

———. 1998. *Envisioning Power: Ideologies of Dominance and Crisis.* Berkeley: University of California Press.

Yates, Frances. 1966. *The Art of Memory.* Chicago: University of Chicago Press.

Zola, Emile. 1993 [1885]. *Germinal.* Oxford: Oxford University Press.

Zulawski, Ann. 1987. "Wages, Ore-Sharing, and Peasant Agriculture: Labour in Oruro's Silver Mines, 1607–1720." *Hispanic American Historical Review* 67 (3): 405–430.

male obligation, 151–54; and mineral specimens, 188–91; as patrimony, 67, 118, 119–26, 144, 157, 178–79, 248
Humboldt, Alexander, 31, 32, 74, 183
Hunt brothers, 76, 78
Inalienability, 3, 4, 12–16, 134, 198, 180, 181, 183; cooperative resources as inalienable, 70, 134, 171, 172, 197–99, 201, 223, 235, 251; and nonrenewable resources, 137–38; see also Inalienable possessions; Patrimony
Inalienable possessions, 10, 13, 15, 2, 78, 179, 197–99
Inalienable Possessions, 15
Incentive contract, 154–56, 161–62, 175; see also Wages
Instituto Nacional de Antropología e Historia (INAH), 96, 212–14, 251
Instituto Nacional de Estadística, Geografía e Información (INEGI), 34, 256

Jefes, 24, 46, 70, 98, 103, 131, 134, 139, 146, 156, 157, 165, 168, 169, 170, 175, 184, 241, 246; as "fathers" of the Cooperative, 143–45, 148–50; and knowledge of the mine, 109, 145; and masculinity, 143–44; and mineral specimens, 185–86; conflict between socios fundadores and, 160–70
Jobs, 65, 79, 96, 108, 126, 135; as patrimony, 24–25, 80–82, 88, 99, 136; at Valenciana mine, 230–33

Knight, Alan, 59, 209

Lévi-Strauss, Claude, 15, 128
Lewinsky, Monica, 144
Limón, José, 43
Limpieza, 108, 122, 124–26, 132; see also Cleanliness
Lo mexicano, 140, 141; see also Mexicanidad
Lomnitz, Claudio, 141, 200, 201, 203, 212
Lomnitz, Larissa, 140
Lung disease, 38, 40; see also Silicosis

Lupios, 107, 176–77, 210, 248; see also Buscones

Machismo, 140, 144–45; see also Masculinity
Magazine, Roger, 141–42
Maine, Sir Henry, 1, 14
Malacatero, 115, 191, 193, 232
Malinowski, Bronislaw, 15
Marx, Karl, 177
Masculinity: and housebuilding, 120–22; and mining, 8, 12; 44, 46, 116–18, 144, 145, 146, 162, 165, 175, 177, 245; see also Androcentrism; Femininity; Patriarchal authority; Machismo
Mauss, Marcel, 15, 173, 179, 235
Meave Torrescano, Edgardo, 76, 148, 161; defeat of, 77, 159; and ties to PRI, 77, 110, 150, 158–59, 166, 247
Merchants, 57, of mineral specimens, 153, 191–94, 195
Mestizo, 5, 58, 71, 72, 73, 200, 201
Mexican Revolution, 27, 58, 59, 201, 205, 208, 209, 210, 211, 221, 232; see also Revolution of 1910
Mexicanidad, 199; see also Lo mexicano; Nationalism
Migration, 7, 68, 96, 129
Mine, 1, 4, 9, 20, 100–9; as cemetery, 113–15; as female space, 116–18; as sacred space, 110–13; as space for political mobilization, 109, 146; as underground city, 109–10
Mineral specimens, 20, 107, 122, 126, 153, 157, 170, 172, 183–96, 249–50; see also Achichicles; Stone samples
Miners' pilgrimage, 50–54
Mining law, 207–8
Mintz, Sidney, 141
Molina Enríquez, Andrés, 200
Money (as anthropological concept), 178–81
Monte de San Nicolás, 23, 33, 65, 102, 180
Moral economy, 142, 145, 166, 185